KING LEAR

Major Literary Characters

CHELSEA HOUSE PUBLISHERS

Major Literary Characters

DAVID COPPERFIELD
Charles Dickens, *David Copperfield*

ROBINSON CRUSOE
Daniel Defoe, *Robinson Crusoe*

DON JUAN
Molière, *Don Juan*
Lord Byron, *Don Juan*

HUCK FINN
Mark Twain, *The Adventures of Tom Sawyer, Adventures of Huckleberry Finn*

CLARISSA HARLOWE
Samuel Richardson, *Clarissa*

HEATHCLIFF
Emily Brontë, *Wuthering Heights*

ANNA KARENINA
Leo Tolstoy, *Anna Karenina*

MR. PICKWICK
Charles Dickens, *The Pickwick Papers*

HESTER PRYNNE
Nathaniel Hawthorne, *The Scarlet Letter*

BECKY SHARP
William Makepeace Thackeray, *Vanity Fair*

LAMBERT STRETHER
Henry James, *The Ambassadors*

EUSTACIA VYE
Thomas Hardy, *The Return of the Native*

TWENTIETH CENTURY

ÁNTONIA
Willa Cather, *My Ántonia*

BRETT ASHLEY
Ernest Hemingway, *The Sun Also Rises*

HANS CASTORP
Thomas Mann, *The Magic Mountain*

HOLDEN CAULFIELD
J. D. Salinger, *The Catcher in the Rye*

CADDY COMPSON
William Faulkner, *The Sound and the Fury*

JANIE CRAWFORD
Zora Neale Hurston, *Their Eyes Were Watching God*

CLARISSA DALLOWAY
Virginia Woolf, *Mrs. Dalloway*

DILSEY
William Faulkner, *The Sound and the Fury*

GATSBY
F. Scott Fitzgerald, *The Great Gatsby*

HERZOG
Saul Bellow, *Herzog*

JOAN OF ARC
William Shakespeare, *Henry VI*
George Bernard Shaw, *Saint Joan*

LOLITA
Vladimir Nabokov, *Lolita*

WILLY LOMAN
Arthur Miller, *Death of a Salesman*

MARLOW
Joseph Conrad, *Lord Jim, Heart of Darkness, Youth, Chance*

PORTNOY
Philip Roth, *Portnoy's Complaint*

BIGGER THOMAS
Richard Wright, *Native Son*

CHELSEA HOUSE PUBLISHERS

Major Literary Characters

KING LEAR

Edited and with an introduction by
HAROLD BLOOM

CHELSEA HOUSE PUBLISHERS
New York ◊ Philadelphia

Jacket illustration: Sir Laurence Olivier as King Lear in the Granada
Television production of *King Lear* (April 3, 1983) (Granada
Television). *Inset:* Title page of the first quarto edition of *King Lear*
(London: Printed for Nathaniel Butter, 1608 (by permission of the
Folger Shakespeare Library).

Chelsea House Publishers

Editor-in-Chief   Remmel T. Nunn
Managing Editor   Karyn Gullen Browne
Picture Editor   Adrian G. Allen
Art Director   Maria Epes
Manufacturing Director   Gerald Levine

Major Literary Characters

Senior Editor   S. T. Joshi
Associate Editor   Richard Fumosa
Designer   Maria Epes

Staff for KING LEAR

Picture Researcher   Ellen Barrett
Assistant Art Director   Noreen Romano
Production Manager   Joseph Romano
Production Coordinator   Marie Claire Cebrián

Printed and bound in the United States of America

First Printing

1   3   5   7   9   8   6   4   2

Library of Congress Cataloging-in-Publication Data

King Lear / edited and with an introduction by Harold Bloom.
        p.   cm.—(Major literary characters)
        Includes bibliographical references and index.
        ISBN 0-7910-0922-X.—ISBN 0-7910-0977-7 (pbk.)
    1. Shakespeare, William, 1564–1616. King Lear.   2. Lear, King
(Legendary character) in literature.   I. Bloom, Harold.   II. Series.
        PR2819.K487   1992
        822.3'3—dc20
        91-17129
        CIP

CONTENTS

THE ANALYSIS OF CHARACTER

Harold Bloom

"Character," according to our dictionaries, still has as a primary meaning a graphic symbol, such as a letter of the alphabet. This meaning reflects the word's apparent origin in the ancient Greek *charactēr*, a sharp stylus. *Charactēr* also meant the mark of the stylus' incisions. Recent fashions in literary criticism have reduced "character" in literature to a matter of marks upon a page. But our word "character" also has a very different meaning, matching that of the ancient Greek *ēthos*, "habitual way of life." Shall we say then that literary character is an imitation of human character, or is it just a grouping of marks? The issue is between a critic like Dr. Samuel Johnson, for whom words were as much like people as like things, and a critic like the late Roland Barthes, who told us that "the fact can only exist linguistically, as a term of discourse." Who is closer to our experience of reading literature, Johnson or Barthes? What difference does it make, if we side with one critic rather than the other?

Barthes is famous, like Foucault and other recent French theorists, for having added to Nietzsche's proclamation of the death of God a subsidiary demise, that of the literary author. If there are no authors, then there are no fictional personages, presumably because literature does not refer to a world outside language. Words indeed necessarily refer to other words in the first place, but the impact of words ultimately is drawn from a universe of fact. Stories, poems, and plays are recognizable as such because they are human utterances within traditions of utterances, and traditions, by achieving authority, become a kind of fact, or at least the sense of a fact. Our sense that literary characters, within the context of a fictive cosmos, indeed are fictional personages is also a kind of fact. The meaning and value of every character in a successful work of literary representation depend upon our ideas of persons in the factual reality of our lives.

Literary character is always an invention, and inventions generally are indebted to prior inventions. Shakespeare is the inventor of literary character as we know it; he reformed the universal human expectations for the verbal imitation of personality, and the reformation appears now to be permanent and uncannily inevitable. Remarkable as the Bible and Homer are at representing personages, their characters are relatively unchanging. They age within their stories, but their habitual modes of being do not develop. Jacob and Achilles unfold before us, but without metamorphoses. Lear and Macbeth, Hamlet and Othello severely modify themselves not only by their actions, but by their utterances, and most of all through *overhearing themselves,* whether they speak to themselves or to others. Pondering what they themselves have said, they will to change, and actually do change, sometimes extravagantly yet always persuasively. Or else they suffer change, without willing it, but in reaction not so much to their language as to their relation to that language.

I do not think it useful to say that Shakespeare successfully imitated elements in our characters. Rather, it could be argued that he compelled aspects of character to appear that previously were concealed, or not available to representation. This is not to say that Shakespeare is God, but to remind us that language is not God either. The mimesis of character in Shakespeare's dramas now seems to us normative, and indeed became the accepted mode almost immediately, as Ben Jonson shrewdly and somewhat grudgingly implied. And yet, Shakespearean representation has surprisingly little in common with the imitation of reality in Jonson or in Christopher Marlowe. The origins of Shakespeare's originality in the portrayal of men and women are to be found in the *Canterbury Tales* of Geoffrey Chaucer, insofar as they can be located anywhere before Shakespeare himself. Chaucer's savage and superb Pardoner overhears his own tale-telling, as well as his mocking rehearsal of his own spiel, and through this overhearing he is emboldened to forget himself, and enthusiastically urges all his fellow-pilgrims to come forward to be fleeced by him. His self-awareness, and apocalyptically rancid sense of spiritual fall, are preludes to the even grander abysses of the perverted will in Iago and in Edmund. What might be called the character trait of a negative charisma may be Chaucer's invention, but came to its perfection in Shakespearean mimesis.

The analysis of character is as much Shakespeare's invention as the representation of character is, since Iago and Edmund are adepts at analyzing both themselves and their victims. Hamlet, whose overwhelming charisma has many negative components, is certainly the most comprehensive of all literary characters, and so necessarily prophesies the labyrinthine complexities of the will in Iago and Edmund. Charisma, according to Max Weber, its first codifier, is primarily a natural endowment, and implies a primordial and idiosyncratic power over nature, and so finally over death. Hamlet's uncanniness is at its most suggestive in the scene of his long dying, where the audience, through the mediation of Horatio, itself is compelled to meditate upon suicide, if only because outliving the prince of Denmark scarcely seems an option.

Shakespearean representation has usurped not only our sense of literary character, but our sense of ourselves as characters, with Hamlet playing the part of the largest of these usurpations. Insofar as we have an idea of human disinterestedness, we tend to derive it from the Hamlet of Act V, whose quietism has about it a ghostly authority. Oscar Wilde, in his profound and profoundly witty dialogue, "The Decay of Lying," expressed a permanent insight when he insisted that art shaped every era, far more than any age formed art. Life imitates art, we imitate Shakespeare, because without Shakespeare we would perish for lack of images. Wilde's grandest audacity demystifies Shakespearean mimesis with a Shakespearean vivaciousness: "This unfortunate aphorism about art holding the mirror up to Nature is deliberately said by Hamlet in order to convince the bystanders of his absolute insanity in all art-matters." Of *Hamlet*'s influence upon the ages Wilde remarked that: "The world has grown sad because a puppet was once melancholy." "Puppet" is Wilde's own deconstruction, a brilliant reminder that Shakespeare's artistry of illusion has so mastered reality as to have changed reality, evidently forever.

The analysis of character, as a critical pursuit, seems to me as much a Shakespearean invention as literary character was, since much of what we know about how to analyze character necessarily follows Shakespearean procedures. His hero-villains, from Richard III through Iago, Edmund, and Macbeth, are shrewd and endless questers into their own self-motivations. If we could bear to see Hamlet, in his unwearied negations, as another hero-villain, then we would judge him the supreme analyst of the darker recalcitrances in the selfhood. Freud followed the pre-Socratic Empedocles, in arguing that character is fate, a frightening doctrine that maintains the fear that there are no accidents, that overdetermination rules us all of our lives. Hamlet assumes the same, yet adds to this argument the terrible passivity he manifests in Act V. Throughout Shakespeare's tragedies, the most interesting personages seem doom-eager, reminding us again that a Shakespearean reading of Freud would be more illuminating than a Freudian exegesis of Shakespeare. We learn more when we discover Hamlet in the Freudian Death Drive, than when we read *Beyond the Pleasure Principle* into *Hamlet*.

In Shakespearean comedy, character achieves its true literary apotheosis, which is the representation of the inner freedom that can be created by great wit alone. Rosalind and Falstaff, perhaps alone among Shakespeare's personages, match Hamlet in wit, though hardly in the metaphysics of consciousness. Whether in the comic or the modern mode, Shakespeare has set the standard of measurement in the balance between character and passion.

In Shakespeare the self is more dramatized than theatricalized, which is why a Shakespearean reading of Freud works out so well. Character-formation after the passing of the Oedipal stage takes the place of fetishistic fragmentings of the self. Critics who now call literary character into question, and who proclaim also the death of the author, invariably also regard all notions, literary and human, of a stable character as being mere reductions of deeper pre-Oedipal desires. It becomes clear that the fortunes of literary character rise and fall with the prestige of normative conceptions of the ego. Shakespeare's Iago, who wars against being, may be the first deconstructionist of the self, with his proclamation of "I am not what I am." This constitutes the necessary prologue to any view that would regard a fixed ego as a virtual abnormality. But deconstructions of the self are no more modern than Modernism is. Like literary modernism, the decentered ego came out of the Hellenistic culture of ancient Alexandria. The Gnostic heretics believed that the psyche, like the body, was a fallen entity, mechanically fashioned by the Demiurge or false creator. They held however that each of us possessed also a spark or pneuma, which was a fragment of the original Abyss or true, alien God. The soul or psyche within every one of us was thus at war with the self or pneuma, and only that sparklike self could be saved.

Shakespeare, following after Chaucer in this respect, was the first and remains still the greatest master of representing character both as a stable soul and a wavering self. There is a substance that endures in Shakespeare's figures, and there is also a quicksilver rendition of the unsettling sparks. Racine and Tolstoy, Balzac and Dickens, follow in Shakespeare's wake by giving us some sense of pre-Oedipal sparks or drives, and considerably more sense of post-Oedipal character and personality, stabilizations or sublimations of the fetish-seeking drives. Critics like Leo Bersani and René Girard argue eloquently against our taking this mimesis as the only proper work of literature. I would suggest that strong fictions of the self, from the Bible through Samuel Beckett, necessarily participate in both modes, the sublimation of desire, and the persistence of a primordial desire. The mystery of Hamlet or of Lear is intimately invested in the tangled mixture of the two modes of representation.

Psychic mobility is proposed by Bersani as the ideal to which deconstructions of the literary self may yet guide us. The ideal has its pathos, but the realities of literary representation seem to me very different, perhaps destructively so. When a novelist like D. H. Lawrence sought to reduce his characters to Eros and the Death Drive, he still had to persuade us of his authority at mimesis by lavishing upon the figures of *The Rainbow* and *Women in Love* all of the vivid stigmata of normative personality. Birkin and Ursula may represent antithetical and uncanny drives, but they develop and change as characters pondering their own pronouncements and reactions to self and others. The cost of a non-Shakespearean representation is enormous. Pynchon, in *The Crying of Lot 49* and *Gravity's Rainbow*, evades the burden of the normative by resorting to something like Christopher Marlowe's art of caricature in *The Jew of Malta*. Marlowe's Barabas is a marvelous rhetorician, yet he is a cartoon alongside the troublingly equivocal Shylock. Pynchon's personages are deliberate cartoons also, as flat as comic strips. Marlowe's achievement, and Pynchon's, are beyond dispute, yet they are like the prelude and the postlude to Shakespearean reality. They do not wish to engage with our hunger for the empirical world and so they enter the problematic cosmos of literary fantasy.

No writer, not even Shakespeare or Proust, alters the available stock that we agree to call reality, but Shakespeare, more than any other, does show us how much of reality we could encounter if only we retained adequate desire. The strong literary representation of character is already an analysis of character, and is part of the healing work of a literary culture, which implicitly seeks to cure violence through a normative mimesis of ego, *as if it were stable,* whether in actuality it is or is not. I do not believe that this is a social quest taken on by literary culture, but rather that we confront here the aesthetic essence of what makes a culture *literary,* rather than metaphysical or ethical or religious. A culture becomes literary when its conceptual modes have failed it, which means when religion, philosophy, and science have begun to lose their authority. If they cannot heal violence, then literature attempts to do so, which may be only a turning inside out of the critical arguments of Girard and Bersani.

I conclude by offering a particular instance or special case as a paradigm for the healing enterprise that is at once the representation and the analysis of literary character. Let us call it the aesthetics of being outraged, or rather of successfully representing the state of being outraged. W. C. Fields was one modern master of such representation, and Nathanael West was another, as was Faulkner before him. Here also the greatest master remains Shakespeare, whose Macbeth, himself a bloody outrage, yet retains our imaginative sympathy precisely because he grows increasingly outraged as he experiences the equivocation of the fiend that lies like truth. The double-natured promises and the prophecies of the weird sisters finally induce in Macbeth an apocalyptic version of the stage actor's anxiety at missing cues, the horror of a phantasmagoric stage fright of missing one's time, of always reacting too late. Macbeth, a veritable monster of solipsistic inwardness but no intellectual, counters his dilemma by fresh murders, that prolong him in time yet provoke him only to a perpetually freshened sense of being outraged, as all his expectations become still worse confounded. We are moved by Macbeth, however estrangedly, because his terrible inwardness is a paradigm for our own solipsism, but also because none of us can resist a strong and successful representation of the human in a state of being outraged.

The ultimate outrage is the necessity of dying, an outrage concealed in a multitude of masks, including the tyrannical ambitions of Macbeth. I suspect that our outrage at being outraged is the most difficult of all our affects for us to represent to ourselves, which is why we are so inclined to imaginative sympathy for a character who strongly conveys that affect to us. The Shrike of West's *Miss Lonelyhearts* or Faulkner's Joe Christmas of *Light in August* are crucial modern instances, but such figures can be located in many other works, since the ability to represent this extreme emotion is one of the tests that strong writers are driven to set for themselves.

However a reader seeks to reduce literary character to a question of marks on a page, she will come at last to the impasse constituted by the thought of death, her death, and before that to all the stations of being outraged that memorialize her own drive towards death. In reading, she quests for evidences that are strong representations, whether of her desire or her despair. Such questings constitute the necessary basis for the analysis of literary character, an enterprise that always will survive every vagary of critical fashion.

EDITOR'S NOTE

This book gathers together a representative selection of the best criticism devoted to Shakespeare's King Lear, one of the greatest of all characters in dramatic literature. Each of the two sections—Critical Extracts and Critical Essays—is arranged chronologically, following the order of publication. I am grateful to S. T. Joshi for his skilled assistance in the editing of this volume.

My introduction analyzes Lear by juxtaposing him with the Fool and Edmund, figures so antithetical to the tragic hero as to illuminate him by a kind of negation. A rich montage of critical extracts follows, beginning with Nahum Tate's dedication to his 1681 revision of the play, in which everyone ends happy ever after. Among the selections are such crucial accounts of Lear as those by Dr. Johnson, Lamb, Hazlitt, Coleridge, Tolstoy, and Freud. The modern critical tradition then is exemplified by G. Wilson Knight, William R. Elton, Howard Felperin, and the French poet Yves Bonnefoy, among many others.

Full-scale critical essays begin with the central portraits sketched by A. C. Bradley and Harold C. Goddard, two major critics who believed in the reality of literary character. Barbara Everett is in their tradition by refusing to Christianize the tragedy of Lear, while William Rosen also studies the complex moral ambivalences of Lear's nature.

Russell A. Fraser and the late Rosalie L. Colie help define Lear's greatness, the grandeur of his language and of his capacity for change. Leslie Smith returns us to Edward Bond's modern version of Lear, previously described in critical excerpts by Bond himself and by Benedict Nightingale.

In Michael Goldman's essay the focus is upon the histrionic elements in Lear's complex character, while Arthur Kirsch defends Lear's emotional stature against some currently fashionable critics who resent all sublimity and all greatness. This book concludes with a shrewd account by David Farley-Hills of how Shakespeare's Lear partly results from challenges to Shakespeare's art by rival dramatists under the highly intellectualized King James I, a learned scholar in matters of theology and kingship, and certainly the leading figure in the audience that first confronted Lear and his tragedy.

INTRODUCTION

I

Lear is so grand a literary character that he tends to defy direct description; nearly everything worth saying about him needs to be balanced by an antithetical statement. Like my mentor, the late and much-lamented Northrop Frye, I tend to find Lear's precursor in the Yahweh of the J Writer, as mediated for Shakespeare by the Geneva Bible. As Frye remarked, that Yahweh "is not a theological god at all but an intensely human character as violent and unpredictable as King Lear." Lear's sudden furies indeed are as startling as Yahweh's, and like Yahweh, Lear remains somehow incommensurate with us. Beyond the scale of everyone else in his drama, Lear is as much a fallen, mortal god as he is a king. And unlike the J Writer's Yahweh, Lear is loved as well as feared by everyone in the play who is at all morally admirable: Cordelia, Kent, Gloucester, Edgar, Albany. Those who hate the king are monsters of the deep: Goneril, Regan, Cornwall. That leaves Lear's Fool, who loves the king, yet also manifests an uncanny ambivalence towards his master. The Fool, at once Lear's fourth child and his tormentor, is one of the two great reflectors of the king in the play. The other is Edmund, who never speaks to Lear or is spoken to by him, but who illuminates Lear by being his total antithesis, as nihilistically devoid of authentic, strong emotions as Lear is engulfed by them. I propose in this Introduction a twofold experiment, to analyze the Fool and Edmund in themselves, and then to consider Lear in their dark aura as well as in his own sublimity. The Fool I see as a displaced spirit, and even after having abdicated Lear cannot be that, since he remains massively in what always must be his place. Edmund, so dangerously attractive to Goneril and Regan, and to something in ourselves as well, is loved by the fatal sisters precisely because he incarnates every quality alien to their father, whom they at once loathe and dread.

II

Why call Lear's Fool a displaced spirit, since his sublimely bitter wit catches up so much of the wisdom to be learned from Lear's tragedy? Do we ever sense that the Fool has wandered in from some other play, as it were? Love, Dr. Johnson remarks, is the wisdom of fools, and the folly of the wise. He presumably was not thinking of Lear and the Fool, but as with Lear and Cordelia, the bond and torment of that relationship certainly is authentic and mutual love. William R. Elton shrewdly says of the Fool that "his Machiavellian realism [is] defeated by his own foolish sympathy," his love for Lear. As Coleridge noted, the Fool joins himself to the pathos or suffering of the drama; he does not stand apart in a jester's role. Yet Shakespeare excludes the Fool from the tragedy of Lear and Cordelia; the Fool simply drops out of the play, notoriously without explanation. I take it that he wanders off to another drama, which Shakespeare unfortunately did not choose to write, except perhaps for certain moments in *Timon of Athens*.

Elton also observes that the Fool is "at once more than a character and less," which seems to me just right. Shylock, Barnardine (despite his brevity), Malvolio, Caliban: these all are grand characters, but the Fool's dramatic function, like Horatio's, is partly to be a surrogate for the audience, mediating Lear's sublimity for us even as Horatio mediates the sublime aspects of Hamlet. The Fool and Horatio are floating presences, rather than proper characters in themselves. Horatio's only affect, besides his love for Hamlet, is his capacity for wonder, while the Fool's love for Lear is accompanied by a capacity for terror, on Lear's behalf as on his own. Perhaps it is fitting that the Fool's last sentence (Act II, Scene vi, line 84) is the hugely enigmatic "And I'll go to bed at noon" in response to Lear's pathetic: "So, so. We'll go to supper i'th' morning." Like Falstaff, the Fool has little to do with the time of day; the wisdom of his folly indeed is timeless. As with nearly everything uttered by Falstaff, each outburst of the Fool seems endless to our meditation, yet Falstaff enlightens us; a great teacher, he makes us wittier and more vital, or at least more aware of the pathos of an heroic vitality. The Fool drives us a little mad, even as perversely he punishes Lear by helping Lear along to madness. To instruct in Folly, even in the Erasmian sense, is to practice a dark profession, since one is teaching unreason as the pragmatic alternative to knavery. Folly is a kind of Renaissance version of Freud's Death Drive, beyond the pleasure principle. Blake's Proverb of Hell, that if the Fool would persist in his folly, he would become wise, is perfectly exemplified by Lear's Fool, except that this Fool is uncannier even than that. Lear lovingly regards him as a child, and he is or seems to be a preternaturally wise child, but a child who cannot grow up, almost as though he were more sprite than human. He does not enter the play until its fourth scene, and before his entrance we are told that he has been pining away for Cordelia, with whom Lear famously confuses him at the tragedy's close: "And my poor fool is hanged." Unlike Cordelia, who more than Edgar is the play's idealized, natural Christian in a pre-Christian cosmos, the Fool exacts a kind of exasperated vengeance upon Lear, who both courts, and winces at, the Fool's truthtelling. In one rather subtle way, the relationship between Lear and his Fool parallels the problematic relationship between Falstaff and Hal, since both Lear and Falstaff are in the position of loving fathers somewhat bewildered by the ambivalence shown towards them by their adopted "sons," the Fool and the future Henry V.

Criticism has tended to underestimate the Fool's responsibility for the actual onset and intense nature of Lear's madness. Hal knows that he will reject Falstaff; the Fool knows that he cannot reject Lear, but he also cannot accept a Lear who has unkinged himself, who indeed has abdicated fatherhood. To teach Lear wisdom so belatedly is one thing; to madden the bewildered old monarch is quite another. On some level of purposiveness, however repressed, the Fool does labor to destroy Lear's sanity. Hal labors, quite consciously, to destroy Falstaff's insouciance, which is why the prince so desperately needs to convince himself, and Falstaff, that Falstaff is a coward. He has convinced some moralizing scholars, but not any audience or readership of any wit or vitality whatsoever. The Fool belongs to another world, where "fool" means at once "beloved one," "mad person," "child," and "victim." Lear's Fool is all of those, but something much stranger also.

When the newly crowned Henry V brutally rejects Falstaff, he rather nastily observes: "How ill white hairs become a fool and jester!" We wince (unless we are moralizing scholars) both at the reduction of Falstaff's role as Hal's educator to the status of "fool and jester," and also because that unkind line fuses Lear and Lear's Fool together, and for an instant the crushed Falstaff embodies such a fusion. Desperately wistful in his broken-heartedness, Falstaff falls out of comic supremacy into a pathos tragic enough to accommodate Lear's Fool, if not quite Lear. It is as though, in that terrible moment, he leaves the company of the heroic wits—of Rosalind and Hamlet—and joins Shylock and Lear's Fool, Barnardine and Malvolio, and even Caliban, as a displaced spirit. Suddenly the great and vital wit finds himself in the wrong play, soon enough to be *Henry V*, where all he can do is waste away into a pathetic death. Lear's Fool vanishes from Lear's tragedy because its terrible climax would be inappropriate for him. Dr. Johnson could not bear the vision of Lear carrying the dead Cordelia in his arms. How much more unbearable it would have been, had Lear carried the dead Fool in his arms! Mercutio dies, and a joyous if obscene exuberance departs from *Romeo and Juliet*. Lear's Fool vanishes, but the displaced wisdom of his folly lingers in the king's final return to a sublime madness. We do not resent or even wonder at the Fool's tormenting of Lear, but the torment itself is wisdom, however bitter. Yet a wisdom that is madness returns us to the uncanny, to a sublime that is beyond our capacity to apprehend.

We cannot love Lear's Fool, but then we are not Lear. Feste, that marvelous contrast to Malvolio, is the best of Shakespearean fools, because he is so superbly humanized, unlike the rancid Touchstone, who is human-all-too-human. Lear's Fool stands apart; he does not quite seem a representation of a merely human being. He is a spirit who has wandered in from some other realm, only to be enthralled by the patriarchal, flawed greatness of Lear. Perhaps Lear's Fool, more even than Shakespeare's other displaced spirits, incarnates what Nietzsche thought was the motive for all metaphor, and so for all high literature: the desire to be elsewhere, the desire to be different.

III

One need not be a Goneril or a Regan to find Edmund dangerously attractive, in ways that perpetually surprise the unwary reader or playgoer. With authentic learning, William R. Elton makes the suggestion that Edmund is a Shakespearean anticipation of the seventeenth-century Don Juan tradition, which culminates in Molière's great play (1665). Elton also notes the crucial difference between Edmund and Iago, which is that Edmund paradoxically sees himself as overdetermined by his bastardy even as he fiercely affirms his freedom, whereas Iago is totally free. Consider how odd we would find it, had Shakespeare decided to present Iago as a bastard, or indeed given us any information at all about Iago's father. But Edmund's status as natural son is crucial, though even here Shakespeare confounds his age's expectations. Elton cites a Renaissance proverb that bastards by chance are good, but by nature bad. Faulconbridge the Bastard, magnificent hero of *The Life and Death of King John,* is good not by chance, but because he is very nearly the reincarnation of his father, Richard Lionheart, whereas the dreadful Don John, in *Much Ado About Nothing,* has a natural badness clearly founded upon his illegitimacy. Edmund astonishingly combines aspects of the personalities of Faulconbridge and of Don John, though he is even more attractive than Faulconbridge, and far more vicious than Don John of Aragon.

Though Edmund, unlike Iago, cannot reinvent himself wholly, he takes great pride in assuming responsibility for his own amorality, his pure opportunism. Don John in *Much Ado* says: "I cannot hide what I am," while Faulconbridge the Bastard affirms: "And I am I, how'er I was begot." Faulconbridge's "And I am I" plays against Iago's "I am not what I am." Edmund cheerfully proclaims: "I should have been that I am, had the maidenl'est star in the firmament twinkled on my bastardizing." The great "I am" remains a positive pronouncement in Edmund, and yet he is as grand a negation, in some other ways, as even Iago is. But because of that one positive stance towards his own being, Edmund will change at the very end, whereas Iago's final act of freedom will be to pledge an absolute muteness as he is led away to death by torture. Everything, according to Iago, lies in the will, and in his case everything does.

In Act V, scene iii, Edmund enters with Lear and Cordelia as his prisoners. It is only the second time he shares the stage with Lear and it will be the last. We might expect that he would speak to Lear (or to Cordelia), but he avoids doing so, referring to them only in the third person, in his commands. Shakespeare, in this vast, indeed cosmological tragedy, gives us the highly deliberate puzzle that the two crucial figures, the tragic hero Lear, and the brilliant villain Edmund, never speak a single word to one another. Clearly Edmund, in Act V, scene iii, does not wish to speak to Lear, because he is actively plotting the murder of Cordelia, and perhaps of Lear as well. Yet all the intricacies of the double plot do not in themselves explain away this remarkable gap in the play, and I wonder why Shakespeare avoided the confrontation. You can say he had no need of it, but this drama tells us to reason not the need. Shakespeare is our Scripture, replacing Scripture itself, and one should learn to read him the way the Kabbalists read the Bible, interpreting every absence as being significant. What can it tell us about Edmund, and also about Lear, that Shakespeare found nothing for them to say to one another?

These days, paternal love and filial love are not exactly in critical fashion, and most younger Shakespeareans do not seem to love Lear (or Shakespeare, for that matter). And yet it is difficult to find another Shakespearean protagonist as deeply loved by other figures in his or her play as Lear is loved by Kent, Cordelia, Gloucester, and the Fool, and by Edgar and Albany as well. Goneril, Regan, Cornwall, Edmund, and the wretched Oswald do not love the King, but they are all monsters, except for the subtly amoral Edmund. Lear may seem as violent, irascible, and unpredictable as the Biblical J Writer's Yahweh, upon whom he is based, but clearly he has been a loving father to his people, unlike the original Yahweh. Edmund, for all his sophisticated and charismatic charm, inspires no one's love, except for the deadly and parallel voracious passions of Goneril and Regan, those monsters of the deep. And Edmund does not love them, or anyone else, or even himself. Perhaps Lear and Edmund cannot speak to one another because Lear is bewildered by the thwarting of his excess of love for Cordelia, and by the hatred for him of Goneril and Regan, unnatural daughters, as he must call them. Edmund, in total contrast, hardly regards love as natural, even as he grimly exults in being the natural son of Gloucester. But even that contrast hardly accounts for the curious sense we have that Edmund somehow is not in the same play as Lear and Cordelia.

When Goneril kisses Edmund (Act IV, scene ii, line 22), he gallantly accepts it as a kind of literal kiss-of-death, since he is too grand an ironist not to appreciate his own pledge: "Yours in the ranks of death." Still more remarkable is his soliloquy that closes Act V, scene i:

> To both these sisters have I sworn my love;
> Each jealous of the other, as the stung
> Are of the adder. Which of them shall I take?
> Both? one? or neither? Neither can be enjoy'd
> If both remain alive: to take the widow
> Exasperates, makes mad her sister Goneril;
> And hardly shall I carry out my side,
> Her husband being alive. Now then, we'll use
> His countenance for the battle; which being done,
> Let her who would be rid of him devise
> His speedy taking off. As for the mercy
> Which he intends to Lear and to Cordelia,
> The battle done, and they within our power
> Shall never see his pardon; for my state
> Stands on me to defend, not to debate.

So cool a negativity is unique, even in Shakespeare. Edmund is superbly sincere when he asks the absolutely open questions: "Which of them shall I take? / Both? one? or neither?" His insouciance is sublime, the questions being tossed off in the spirit of a light event, as though a modern young nobleman might ask whether he should take two princesses, one, or none out to dinner? A double date with Goneril and Regan should daunt any libertine, but the negation named Edmund is something very enigmatic. Iago's negative theology is predicated upon an initial worship of Othello, but Edmund is amazingly free of all connection, all affect, whether towards his two adder- or shark-like royal princesses, or towards his half-brother, or towards Gloucester, in particular. Gloucester is in the way, in rather the same sense that Lear and Cordelia are in the way. Edmund evidently would just as soon not watch his father's eyes put out, but this delicacy does not mean that he cares at all about the event, one way or another. Yet, as Hazlitt pointed out, Edmund does not share in the hypocrisy of Goneril and Regan: his Machiavellianism is absolutely pure, and lacks an Oedipal motive. Freud's vision of family romances simply does not apply to Edmund. Iago is free to reinvent himself every minute, yet Iago has strong passions, however negative. Edmund has no passions whatsoever; he has never loved anyone, and he never will. In that respect, he is Shakespeare's most original character.

There remains the enigma of why this cold negation is so attractive, which returns us usefully to his absolute contrast with Lear, and with Lear's uncanny Fool. Edmund's desire is only for power, and yet one wonders if desire is at all the right word in connection with Edmund. Richard II lusts for power; Iago quests for it over Othello, so as to uncreate Othello, to reduce the mortal god of war into a chaos. Ulysses certainly seeks power over Achilles, in order to get on with the destruction of Troy. Edmund is the most Marlovian of these grand negations, since the soldier Macbeth does not so much will to usurp power, as he is overcome by his own imagination of usurpation. Edmund accepts the overdetermination of being a bastard, indeed he over-accepts it, and glorifies in it, but he accepts nothing else. He is convinced of his natural superiority, which extends to his command of manipulative language, and yet he is not a Marlovian rhetorician, like Tamburlaine, nor is he intoxicated with his own villainy, like Richard II and Barabas. He is a Marlovian figure not in that he resembles a character in a play by Marlowe, but because I suspect he was intended to resemble Christopher Marlowe himself. Marlowe died, aged twenty-nine, in 1593, at about the time that Shakespeare composed *Richard III*, with its Marlovian protagonist, and just before the writing of *Titus Andronicus* with its Marlovian parody in Aaron the Moor. By 1605, when *King Lear* was written, Marlowe had been dead for twelve years, but *As You Like It*, composed in 1599, is curiously replete with wry allusions to Marlowe. We have no contemporary anecdotes connecting Shakespeare to Marlowe, but it seems quite unlikely that Shakespeare never met his exact contemporary, and nearest precursor, the inventor of English blank-verse tragedy. Edmund, in the pre-Christian context of *King Lear*, is certainly a pagan atheist and libertine naturalist, as Elton emphasizes, and these are the roles that Marlowe's life exemplified for his contemporaries. Marlowe the man, or rather Shakespeare's memory of him, may be the clue to Edmund's strange glamour, the charismatic qualities that make it so difficult for us not to like him.

Whether or not an identification of Marlowe and Edmund is purely my critical trope, even as trope it suggests that Edmund's driving force is Marlovian nihilism, revolt against authority and tradition for revolt's own sake, since revolt and nature are thus made one. Revolt is heroic for Edmund, and he works his plots so that his natural superiority will make him king, whether as consort either to Regan or to Goneril, or as a solitary figure, should they slay one another. After Goneril first has murdered Regan, and then killed herself, Edmund undergoes his radical transformation. What is exposed first is his acute overdetermination by his status as bastard. On knowing that his death-wound is from Edgar, at least his social equal, he begins to be reconciled to the life being left behind him, the great line of acceptance being the famous:

The wheel is come full circle: I am here.

"I am here" reverberates with the dark undertone that here I started originally, that to have been born a bastard was to start with a death-wound. Edmund is quite dispassionate about his own dying, but he is not doom-eager, unlike Goneril and Regan, both of whom seem to have been in love with him precisely because they sought a death-wound. Nowhere else even in Shakespeare are we racked by the Hitchcockian suspense that attends Edmund's slow change as he dies, a change that comes too late to save Cordelia. Edmund, reacting to Edgar's extraordinary account of their father's death, confesses to being moved, and hesitates on the verge of reprieving Cordelia. He does not get past that hesitation until the bodies of Goneril and Regan are brought in, and then his reaction constitutes the paradigmatic moment of change in all of Shakespeare:

Yet Edmund was beloved:
The one the other poisoned for my sake,
And after slew herself.

Out of context this is outrageous enough to be hilarious. The dying nihilist reminds himself that in spite of all he was and did, he *was* beloved, albeit by these two monsters of the deep. He does not say that he cared for either, or for anyone else, and yet this evidence of connection moves him. In context, its mimetic form is enormous. An intellect as cold, powerful, and triumphant as Iago's is suddenly startled by overhearing itself, and the will to change comes upon Edmund. The good he means to do will be "despite of mine own nature," he tells us, so that his final judgment must be that he has not changed, more a Marlovian than a Shakespearean stance. And yet he is finally mistaken, for his nature has altered, too late to avoid the play's tragic catastrophe. Unlike Iago, Edmund has ceased to be a pure or grand negation. It is an irony of Shakespearean representation that we like Edmund least when he turns so belatedly towards the good. The change is persuasive, but by it Edmund ceases to be Edmund. Hamlet dies into apotheosis; Iago will die stubbornly Iago, in silence. We do not know who Edmund is, as he dies, and he does not know either.

IV

No other tragedy by Shakespeare risks a final pathos as terrible as Lear's. His entrance with the dead Cordelia in his arms is a spectacle scarcely to be borne; Dr. Samuel Johnson could not tolerate it. We are not given any finality in regard to the Fool; he vanishes from the play, almost as though Shakespeare has forgotten him. Edmund's enormous transformation has no pragmatic consequences; his change of orders comes too late, and his death affects no one. Lear's death is something like an apocalypse for Edgar, Albany, and Kent, and scarcely less than that for us. Hamlet's death has elements in it of a transcendental release, while Lear's offers us no solace, aesthetic or metaphysical. The three survivors—Albany, Kent, and Edgar—are left standing on stage like so many waifs, lamenting a father-god lost forever to them. Albany, astonishingly but persuasively, attempts to yield rule to Kent and Edgar, but Kent indicates that he expects to follow Lear into death soon enough, while Edgar concludes with a plangent couplet that intimates a universal decline:

> The oldest hath borne most: we that are young
> Shall never see so much, nor live so long.

It is as if the death of the father-king-god has removed the only figuration that participated neither in origin nor in end. William R. Elton persuasively sees the tragedy as non-Christian, in harmony with its pre-Christian paganism, set as it is in a Britain contemporaneous with the Book of Job. Lear dies in despair of the pagan gods, and his survivors echo his despair, but in that echo Shakespeare blends overtones of Biblical apocalypse. Nothing becomes the Creation, in the Bible, and never can be reduced to nothing again, even in apocalypse. But in Lear's tragedy, nothing does come of nothing, and so nothing is at last both origin and end. Had Lear not abdicated, a middle ground might have been kept for a while longer, but even in the opening scene the center must give way. The greatness of Lear's nature is always beheld by us, since his rages, his opacities, his blindnesses are on a cosmological scale. He derives from the Yahweh of the Sinai theophany, but also from the half-mad Yahweh who leads a half-mad rabblement through the Wilderness in Numbers. I return to the ways in which his qualities are exposed by his Fool and by Edmund, since they are the nothings of origin and of end that he ought to have labored to keep back, to fend off from his kingdom.

The Fool's ambivalence towards Lear may not be primal, but pragmatically it becomes so. Edmund, beyond all affect until his dying change, seems indifferent to the king, and never expresses any reaction to Lear. We need expect none, since Edmund is so passionless in regard to his own father, Gloucester. Yet Edmund's whole being is a critique of Lear's passionate being, of a kingly father who cannot control any element whatsoever in his own self. Perfectly controlled to a preternatural degree, Edmund represents a nature that is precisely a knowing nothingness. We never would believe that Lear incarnates nothing and represents nothing, inadequate as he is in self-knowledge. He is the image of authentic authority, and though he himself will mock that image, we agree with Kent, who always seeks out and serves that authority.

Edmund cannot love anyone. The Fool loves Cordelia, and more ambivalently Lear. What the uncanniness of both figures highlight in the king is his furious, hyperbolical capacity to love, and to be loved. Lear's love for the Fool is a shadow of his thwarted love for Cordelia, thwarted not so much by her reticence as by his own excess, his bewilderment at the burden of something inexpressible in his love for her. Despite Lear's enormous eloquence, his very sublimity perpetually places him upon the frontiers of what cannot be said. Again, the contrast both to the Fool and to Edmund is overwhelming. The Fool strikes home with every phrase, and Edmund surpasses even Iago as a manipulative rhetorician, invariably enabled by nature to say exactly what he intends to say. But Lear is always beyond his own intentions, always beyond the sayable. He persuades us of his Jobean dilemmas even though they are not truly Jobean. His rashness is matched by his furious sincerity, and overmatched only by his mysterious authority, an eminence that survives madness and petulance, and every error of his palpable bad judgments. The Fool is uncannily accurate; Edmund cannot make a mistake; Lear is gigantically wrong, but never less than titanic, at least a daemon and sometimes a hint of something larger, a man who is also a god.

The gods, in this play, are nothing admirable, and yet they are the only gods in existence. What Edmund helps us see in Lear's character is that the king's elements of greatness are subdued neither by their antitheses in the bastard's analytical nihilism or by the monarch's own developing skepticism as to divine justice. What the Fool helps us see is that wisdom, however bitter, also does not diminish Lear's greatness, even when that is manifested only as a great unwisdom. Except for the Yahweh of the original portions of what are now called Genesis, Exodus, and Numbers, Lear remains the largest Western instance of a literary character raised to the heights, to the Sublime.

—H. B.

CRITICAL EXTRACTS

NAHUM TATE

Nothing but the Power of your Perswasion, and my Zeal for all the Remains of *Shakespear*, could have wrought me to so bold an Undertaking. I found that the New-modelling of this Story, wou'd force me sometimes on the difficult Task of making the chiefest Persons speak something like their Character, on Matter whereof I had no Ground in my Author. *Lear's* real, and *Edgar's* pretended Madness have so much of *extravagant Nature* (I know not how else to express it) as cou'd never have started but from our *Shakespear's* Creating Fancy. The Images and Language are so odd and surprizing, and yet so agreeable and proper, that whilst we grant that none but *Shakespear* cou'd have form'd such Conceptions, yet we are satisfied that they were the only Things in the World that ought to be said on those Occasions. I found the whole to answer your Account of it, a Heap of Jewels, unstrung and unpolisht; yet so dazling in their Disorder, that I soon perceiv'd I had seiz'd a Treasure. 'Twas my good Fortune to light on one Expedient to rectifie what was wanting in the Regularity and Probability of the Tale, which was to run through the whole A *Love* betwixt *Edgar* and *Cordelia*, that never chang'd word with each other in the Original. This renders *Cordelia's* Indifference and her Father's Passion in the first scene Probable. It likewise gives Countenance to *Edgar's* Disguise, making that a generous Design that was before a poor Shift to save his Life. The Distress of the Story is evidently heightned by it; and it particularly gave Occasion of a New Scene or Two, of more Success (perhaps) than Merit. This Method necessarily threw me on making the Tale conclude in a Success to the innocent distrest Persons: Otherwise I must have incumbred the Stage with dead Bodies, which Conduct makes many Tragedies conclude with unseasonable Jests.

—NAHUM TATE, "The Epistle Dedicatory" to *The History of King Lear*
(London: Printed for E. Flesher, 1681)

AARON HILL

King Lear's most discriminating mark is the violent impatience of his temper. He is obstinate, rash, and vindictive, measuring the merit of all things by their conformity to his will. He cannot bear contradiction, catches fire at first impressions and inflames himself into a frenzy by the rage of his imagination. Hence, all his misfortunes. He has mercy, liberality, courage, wisdom, and humanity, but his virtues are eclipsed and made useless by the gusts which break out in his transports. He dotes on Cordelia yet disinherits and leaves her to misery, in the heat of an ill-grounded resentment, for a fault of no purpose or consequence, and to punish his rashness, by its effects on himself, was the moral and drift of all those wrongs which are done him.

It is plain, then, that an actor who would present him as the poet has drawn him, should preserve with the strictest care that chief point of likeness—his impatience. He should be turbulent in his passions, sharp and troubled in his voice, torn and anguished in his looks, majestically broken in his air, and discomposed, interrupted, and restless in his motions. Instead of all this, the unquickened serenity of this popular player seemed to paint him as an object of pity, not so much from the ingratitude of his unnatural daughters, as from the calmness and resignation wherewith he submitted to his sufferings. We saw in his action, we heard in his voice, the affliction of the father, without the indignation; the serenity of the monarch, without the superiority; and the wrongs of the angry man, without their resentment.

Let his provocations be weighed. They will give us a measure whereby to judge of his behavior. After having been insulted, almost to madness, by his daughter Goneril, on whom he had newly bestowed half his kingdom, he comes (labouring with a meditated complaint) to Regan, in possession of the other half, fully convinced she would atone her sister's guilt by an excess of submission and tenderness. Here, instead of the duty he expected, he finds his first wrongs made light of and more than doubled by new ones—his messenger put in the stocks, and his daughter and her husband refusing him admission under pretence of being weary by travelling. Remember the qualities of the king thus provoked. Remember that impatience and peevishness are the marks of his character. Remember that you have seen him, but just before, casting out to destruction his most favourite and virtuous Cordelia only for expressing her apprehension that her sisters had flattered him. What storms of just rage are not now to be looked for from this violent, this ungovernable man, so beyond human patience insulted! so despised! so ill treated! See what Shakespeare makes him answer when Gloucester but puts him in mind of the Duke of Cornwall's fiery temper.

> Vengeance! Plague! Death! Confusion!
> FIERY!—*What* fiery Quality?—Breath, and Blood!
> Fiery!—the FIERY Duke!
> Go—tell the *Duke* and's *Wife*—I'd *speak* with 'em;
> *Now*—*presently*—Bid 'em come *forth*, and *hear* me:
> Or, at their Chamber Door, I'll *beat* the *Drum*,
> Till it cry, *Sleep to* DEATH.

When we see such starts of impetuosity hushed unfeelingly over and delivered without fire, without energy, with a look of affliction rather than astonishment, and a voice of patient restraint instead of overwhelming indignation, we may know by the calmness which we feel in our blood that the actor's is not enough agitated.

In fine, wherever King Lear called for the bass of his representor's voice, all possible justice was done him. When he mourned, prayed, repented, complained, or excited compassion, there was nothing deficient. But upon every occasion that required the sharp and the elevated, the stretched note and the exclamatory, the king *mistook*, like a dog in a dream, that does but sigh when he thinks he is barking.

I wish I could effectually recommend to so excellent yet unexerted a voice a deliberate examination into the meanings of Shakespeare in his first lines above quoted. The music and compass of an organ might be the infallible reward of his labour, did he but once accustom his nerves to that sensation which impresses (*mechanically*, and by inevitable *necessity*) the whole frame, speech, and spirit with the requisites of every character. But (I appeal to the sincerity of his own private reflection) he neither, according to the mentioned advice, stiffened the sinews, nor summoned up the blood, nor let a terrible look to the eye, nor set the teeth, nor stretched the nostrils wide, nor held the breath hard—by which last, Shakespeare had in his view a certain out-of-breath struggle in the delivery of the words when angry, which is not only natural, but disorders and stimulates the body with the most alarming resemblance of reality.

Another thing which I must recommend to his notice is that he loses an advantage he might draw from these swellings and hurricanes of the voice in places where proper, compared with such opposite beauties as its fall, its articulate soft-ness, its clear depth and mellowness, all which he is famed for already. These contrasts are in acting as necessary as in painting. All light, or all shade, never finished a picture.

I am loath to speak of absurdities, since I touch but upon errors, with a view to do service. Yet, in one single remark, I will indulge myself for that reason—it being an unavoidable consequence, when men *resolve* before they have *reflected*, that they must be sometimes ridiculous as well as mistaken.

The poor king, in the distraction of his spirits, amidst the agonies of ungov-erned sorrow, provoked, inflamed, ashamed, astonished, and vindictive, bursts out into a succession of curses against the unnatural objects of his fury, striving to ease an over-burthened heart in the following torrent of rash wishes.

All the *Stored Vengeances of Heaven* fall
On her ungrateful Head—*Strike* her young Bones.
Ye *taking* Airs, with *Lameness*—
Ye nimble Lightnings, *dart* your blinding *Flames*,
Into her Scornful *Eyes!*—&c.—

An actor who in this place, misled by his love of weight and composure, instead of grinding out the curses from between his teeth, amidst the rage and agitations of a man who has been wronged into madness, advances deliberately, forward, to the lamps in front of the pit, kneels, with elevated eyes and arms, and pronounces, with the calmness and reverence of a prayer, such a meditated string of curses in the face of heaven—that actor must destroy the pity which he labours, so injudiciously, to attract, since the audience, instead of partaking his agonies, and imputing his words to his wrongs, which they would have done, had they seen him in torture and transported out of his reason, now *mispoint* their concern, and in place of hating the daughter for reducing to such extremities a father so indulgent and generous, condemn and are scandalized at a father who with a malice so undisturbed and serene can invent all those curses for his daughter. Of such extensive importance are the mistakes of a player as even to pervert and destroy the purpose for which the poet has written!

—AARON HILL, *The Prompter* No. 95 (October 7, 1735)

SAMUEL JOHNSON

The tragedy of Lear is deservedly celebrated among the dramas of Shakespeare. There is perhaps no play which keeps the attention so strongly fixed; which so much agitates our passions and interests our curiosity. The artful involutions of distinct interests, the striking opposition of contrary characters, the sudden changes of fortune, and the quick succession of events, fill the mind with a perpetual tumult of indignation, pity, and hope. There is no scene which does not contribute to the aggravation of the distress or conduct of the action, and scarce a line which does not conduce to the progress of the scene. So powerful is the current of the poet's imagination, that the mind, which once ventures within it, is hurried irresistibly along.

On the seeming improbability of Lear's conduct it may be observed, that he is represented according to histories at that time vulgarly received as true. And perhaps if we turn our thoughts upon the barbarity and ignorance of the age to which this story is referred, it will appear not so unlikely as while we estimate Lear's manners by our own. Such preference of one daughter to another, or resignation of dominion on such conditions, would be yet credible, if told of a pretty prince of Guinea or Madagascar. Shakespeare, indeed, by the mention of his earls and dukes, has given us the idea of times more civilised, and of life regulated by softer manners; and the truth is, that though he so nicely discriminates, and so minutely describes the characters of men, he commonly neglects and confounds the characters of ages, by mingling customs ancient and modern, English and foreign.

My learned friend Mr. Warton, who has in the *Adventurer* very minutely criticised this play, remarks, that the instances of cruelty are too savage and shocking, and that the intervention of Edmund destroys the simplicity of the story. These objections, may, I think, be answered, by repeating, that the cruelty of the daughters is an historical fact, to which the poet has added little, having only drawn it into a series by dialogue and action. But I am not able to apologise with equal plausibility for the extrusion of Gloucester's eyes, which seems an act too horrid to be endured in dramatick exhibition, and such as must always compel the mind to relieve its distress by incredulity. Yet let it be remembered that our authour well knew what would please the audience for which he wrote.

The injury done by Edmund to the simplicity of the action is abundantly recompensed by the addition of variety, by the art with which he is made to co-operate with the chief design, and the opportunity which he gives the poet of combining perfidy with perfidy, and connecting the wicked son with the wicked daughters, to impress this important moral, that villany is never at a stop, that crimes lead to crimes, and at last terminate in ruin.

But though this moral be incidentally enforced, Shakespeare has suffered the virtue of Cordelia to perish in a just cause, contrary to the natural ideas of justice, to the hope of the reader, and, what is yet more strange, to the faith of chronicles. Yet this conduct is justified by the Spectator, who blames Tate for giving Cordelia success and happiness in his alteration, and declares, that, in his opinion, "the tragedy has lost half its beauty." Dennis has remarked, whether justly or not, that, to secure the favourable reception of *Cato*, "the town was poisoned with much false and abominable criticism," and that endeavours had been used to discredit and decry poetical justice. A play in which the wicked prosper, and the virtuous miscarry, may doubtless be good, because it is a just representation of the common events of human life: but since all reasonable beings naturally love justice, I cannot easily be persuaded, that the observation of justice makes a play worse; or, that if other excellencies are equal, the audience will not always rise better pleased from the final triumph of persecuted virtue.

In the present case the publick has decided. Cordelia, from the time of Tate, has always retired with victory and felicity. And, if my sensations could add any thing to the general suffrage, I might relate, that I was many years ago so shocked by Cordelia's death, that I know not whether I ever endured to read again the last scenes of the play till I undertook to revise them as an editor.

There is another controversy among the criticks concerning this play. It is disputed whether the predominant image in Lear's disordered mind be the loss of his kingdom or the cruelty of his daughters. Mr. Murphy, a very judicious critick, has evinced by induction of particular passages, that the cruelty of his daughters is the primary source of his distress, and that the loss of royalty affects him only as a secondary and subordinate evil; he observed with great justness, that Lear would move our compassion but little, but did we not rather consider the injured father than the degraded king.

—SAMUEL JOHNSON, *The Plays of William Shakespeare*
(London: J. & R. Tonson, 1768), Vol. 6, p. 158

WILLIAM RICHARDSON

Lear, thus extravagant, inconsistent, inconstant, capricious, variable, irresolute, and impetuously vindictive, is almost an object of disapprobation. But our poet, with his usual skill, blends the disagreeable qualities with such circumstances as correct this effect, and form one delightful assemblage. Lear, in his good intentions, was without deceit; his violence is not the effect of premeditated malignity; his weaknesses are not crimes, but often the effects of misruled affections. This is not all: he is an old man; an old king; an aged father; and the instruments of his suffering are undutiful children. He is justly entitled to our compassion; and the incidents last mentioned, though they imply no merit, yet procure some respect. Add to all this, that he becomes more and more interesting towards the close of the drama; not merely because he is more and more unhappy, but because he becomes really more deserving of our esteem. His misfortunes correct his misconduct; they rouse *reflection,* and lead him to that *reformation which we approve.* We see the commencement of this reformation, after he has been dismissed by Goneril, and meets with symptoms of disaffection in Regan. He who abandoned Cordelia with impetuous outrage, and banished Kent for offering an apology in her behalf; feeling his servant grossly maltreated, and his own arrival unwelcomed, has already sustained some chastisement: he does not express that ungoverned violence which his preceding conduct might lead us to expect. He strains his emotion in its first ebullition, and reasons concerning the probable causes of what seemed so inauspicious.

> LEAR: The King would speak with Cornwall; the dear father
> Would with his daughter speak, commands her service:
> Are they inform'd of this?—My breath and blood!—
> Fiery—the fiery Duke? Tell the hot Duke that—
> No—but not yet—may be he is not well—
> Infirmity doth still neglect all office,
> Whereto our health is bound: we're not ourselves
> When nature, being oppress'd, commands the mind
> To suffer with the body—I'll forbear;
> And am fallen out with my more heady will,
> To take the indispos'd and sickly fit,
> For the sound man.

As his misfortunes increase, we find him still more inclined to reflect on his situation. He does not, indeed, express blame of himself; yet he expresses no sentiment whatever of overweening conceit. He seems rational and modest; and the application to himself is extremely pathetic:

> Close pent up guilts,
> Rive your concealing continents, and cry
> These dreadful summoners grace.—I am a man
> More sinn'd against than sinning.

Soon after, we find him actually pronouncing censure upon himself. Hitherto he had been the mere creature of sensibility; he now begins to reflect; and grieves that he had not done so before.

Poor naked wretches, wheresoe'er you are,
That bide the pelting of this pitiless storm!
How shall your houseless heads, and unfed sides,
Your loop'd and window'd raggedness defend you
From seasons such as these?—Oh, I have ta'en
Too little care of this! Take physic, pomp;
Expose thyself to feel what wretches feel,
That thou may'st shake the superflux to them,
And shew the heavens more just.

At last, he is in a state of perfect contrition, and expresses less resentment against Goneril and Regan, than self-condemnation for his treatment of Cordelia, and a perfect, but not extravagant sense of her affection.

KENT: The poor distressed Lear is i' the town,
Who sometime, in his better tune, remembers
What we are come about, and by no means
Will yield to see his daughter.
GENT.: Why, good Sir?
KENT: A sovereign shame so elbows him, his unkindness,
That stript her from his benediction, turn'd her
To foreign casualties, gave her dear rights
To his dog-hearted daughters: these things sting
His mind so venomously, that burning shame
Detains him from Cordelia.

I have thus endeavoured to shew, that mere sensibility, undirected by reflection, leads men to an extravagant expression both of social or unsocial feelings; renders them capriciously inconstant in their affections; variable, and of course irresolute, in their conduct. These things, together with the miseries entailed by such deportment, seem to me well illustrated by Shakespeare, in his Dramatic Character of King Lear.

—WILLIAM RICHARDSON, "On the Dramatic Character of King Lear,"
Essays on Some of Shakespeare's Dramatic Characters (London:
J. Murray & S. Highey, 1784), pp. 308–12

CHARLES LAMB

〈...〉 to see Lear acted,—to see an old man tottering about the stage with a walking-stick, turned out of doors by his daughters in a rainy night, has nothing in it but what is painful and disgusting. We want to take him into shelter and relieve him. That is all the feeling which the acting of Lear ever produced in me. But the Lear of Shakspeare cannot be acted. The contemptible machinery by which they mimic the storm which he goes out in, is not more inadequate to represent the horrors of the real elements, than any actor can be to represent Lear: they might more easily propose to personate the Satan of Milton upon a stage, or one of Michael Angelo's terrible figures. The greatness of Lear is not in corporal dimension, but in intellectual: the explosions of his passion are terrible as a volcano: they are storms turning up and disclosing to the bottom that sea, his mind, with all its vast riches. It is his mind which is laid bare. This case of flesh and blood seems too insignificant to be thought on; even as he himself neglects it. On the stage we see nothing but corporal infirmities and weakness, the impotence of rage; while we read it, we see not Lear, but we are Lear,—we are in his mind, we are sustained by a grandeur which baffles the malice of daughters and storms; in the aberrations of his reason, we discover a mighty irregular power of reasoning, immethodized from the ordinary purposes of life, but exerting its powers, as the wind blows where it listeth, at will upon the corruptions and abuses of mankind. What have looks, or tones, to do with that sublime identification of his age with that of the *heavens themselves,* when in his reproaches to them for conniving at the injustice of his children, he reminds them that "they themselves are old." What gesture shall we appropriate to this? What has the voice or the eye to do with such things? But the play is beyond all art, as the tamperings with it shew: it is too hard and stony; it must have love-scenes, and a happy ending. It is not enough that Cordelia is a daughter, she must shine as a lover, too. Tate has put his hook in the nostrils of this Leviathan, for Garrick and his followers, the showmen of the scene, to draw the mighty beast about more easily. A happy ending!—as if the living martyrdom that Lear had gone through,—the flaying of his feelings alive, did not make a fair dismissal from the stage of life the only decorous thing for him. If he is to live and be happy after, if he could sustain the world's burden after, why all this pudder and preparation,—why torment us with all this unnecessary sympathy? As if the childish pleasure of getting his gilt robes and sceptre again could tempt him to act over again his misused station,—as if at his years, and with his experience, anything was left but to die.

Lear is essentially impossible to be represented on a stage.

—CHARLES LAMB, "On the Tragedies of Shakspeare, Considered with
Reference to Their Fitness for Stage Representation" (1812),
The Works of Charles and Mary Lamb, ed. E. V. Lucas
(London: Methuen, 1903), Vol. 1, p. 107

WILLIAM HAZLITT

We wish that we could pass this play over, and say nothing about it. All that we can say must fall far short of the subject; or even of what we ourselves conceive of it. To attempt to give a description of the play itself or of its effect upon the mind, is mere impertinence: yet we must say something.—It is then the best of all Shakespear's plays, for it is the one in which he was the most in earnest. He was here fairly caught in the web of his own imagination. The passion which he has taken as his subject is that which strikes its root deepest into the human heart; of which the bond is the hardest to be unloosed; and the cancelling and tearing to pieces of which gives the greatest revulsion to the frame. This depth of nature, this force of passion, this tug and war of the elements of our being, this firm faith in filial piety, and the giddy anarchy and whirling tumult of the thoughts at finding this prop flailing it, the contrast between the fixed, immoveable basis of natural affection, and the rapid, irregular starts of imagination, suddenly wrenched from all its accustomed holds and resting-places in the soul, this is what Shakespear has given, and what nobody else but he could give. So we believe.—The mind of Lear, staggering between the weight of attachment and the hurried movements of passion, is like a tall ship driven about by the winds, buffetted by the furious waves, but that still rides above the storm, having its anchor fixed in the bottom of the sea; or it is like the sharp rock circled by the eddying whirlpool that foams and beats against it, or like the solid promontory pushed from its basis by the force of an earthquake.

The character of Lear itself is finely conceived for the purpose. It is the only ground on which such a story could be built with the greatest truth and effect. It is his rash haste, his violent impetuosity, his blindness to every thing but the dictates of his passions or affections, that produces all his misfortunes, that aggravates his impatience of them, that enforces our pity for him. The part which Cordelia bears in the scene is extremely beautiful: the story is almost told in the first words she utters. We see at once the precipice on which the poor old king stands from his own extravagant and credulous importunity, the indiscreet simplicity of her love (which, to be sure, has a little of her father's obstinacy in it) and the hollowness of her sisters' pretensions. Almost the first burst of that noble tide of passion, which runs through the play, is in the remonstrance of Kent to his royal master on the injustice of his sentence against his youngest daughter—'Be Kent unmannerly, when Lear is mad!' This manly plainness, which draws down on him the displeasure of the unadvised king, is worthy of the fidelity with which he adheres to his fallen fortunes. The true character of the two eldest daughters, Regan and Gonerill (they are so thoroughly hateful that we do not even like to repeat their names) breaks out in their answer to Cordelia who desires them to treat their father well—'Prescribe not us our duties'—their hatred of advice being in proportion to their determination to do wrong, and to their hypocritical pretensions to do right. Their deliberate hypocrisy adds the last finishing to the odiousness of their characters. It is the absence of this detestable quality that is the only relief in the character of Edmund the Bastard, and that at times reconciles us to him. We are not tempted to exaggerate the guilt of his conduct, when he himself gives it up as a bad business, and writes himself down 'plain villain.' Nothing more can be said about it. His religious honesty in this respect is admirable. One speech of his is worth a million. His father, Gloster, whom he has just deluded with a forged story of his brother Edgar's designs against his life, accounts for his unnatural behaviour and the strange depravity of the times from the late eclipses in the sun and moon. Edmund, who is in the secret, says when he is gone—'This is the excellent foppery of the world, that when we are sick in fortune (often the surfeits of our own behaviour) we make guilty of our disasters the sun, the moon, and stars: as if we were villains on necessity; fools by heavenly compulsion; knaves, thieves, and treacherous by spherical predominance; drunkards, liars, and adulterers by an enforced obedience of planetary influence; and all that we are evil in, by a divine thrusting on. An admirable evasion of whore-master man, to lay his goatish disposition on the charge of a star! My father compounded with my mother under the Dragon's tail, and my nativity was under Ursa Major: so that it follows, I am rough and lecherous. Tut! I should have been what I am, had the maidenliest star in the firmament twinkled on my bastardising.'—The whole character, its careless, light-hearted villainy, contrasted with the sullen, rancorous malignity of Regan and Gonerill, its connection with the conduct of the under-plot, in which Gloster's persecution of one of his sons and the ingratitude of another, form a counterpart to the mistakes and misfortunes of Lear,—his double amour with the two sisters, and the share which he has in bringing about the fatal catastrophe, are all managed with an uncommon degree of skill and power.

—WILLIAM HAZLITT, *Characters of Shakespear's Plays*
(London: C. H. Reynell, 1817)

SAMUEL TAYLOR COLERIDGE

Of all Shakspeare's plays *Macbeth* is the most rapid, *Hamlet* the slowest, in movement. *Lear* combines length with rapidity,—like the hurricane and the whirlpool, absorbing while it advances. It begins as a stormy day in summer, with brightness; but that brightness is lurid, and anticipates the tempest.

It was not without forethought, nor is it without its due significance, that the division of Lear's kingdom is in the first six lines of the play stated as a thing already determined in all its particulars, previously to the trial of professions, as the relative rewards of which the daughters were to be made to consider their several portions. The strange, yet by no means unnatural, mixture of selfishness, sensibility, and habit of feeling derived from, and fostered by, the particular rank and usages of the individual;—the intense desire of being intensely beloved,—selfish, and yet characteristic of the selfishness of a loving and kindly nature alone;—the self-supportless leaning for all pleasure on another's breast;—the craving after sympathy with a prodigal disinterestedness, frustrated by its own ostentation, and the mode and nature of its claims;—the anxiety, the distrust, the jealousy, which more or less accompany all selfish affections, and are amongst the surest contradistinctions of mere fondness from true love, and which originate Lear's eager wish to enjoy his daughter's violent professions, whilst the inveterate habits of sovereignty convert the wish into claim and positive right, and an incompliance with it into crime and treason;—these facts, these passions, these moral verities, on which the whole tragedy is founded, are all prepared for, and will to the retrospect be found implied, in these first four or five lines of the play. They let us know that the trial is but a trick; and that the grossness of the old king's rage is in part the natural result of a silly trick suddenly and most unexpectedly baffled and disappointed.

It may here be worthy of notice, that Lear is the only serious performance of Shakspeare, the interest and situations of which are derived from the assumption of a gross improbability; whereas Beaumont and Fletcher's tragedies are, almost all of them, founded on some out of the way accident or exception to the general experience of mankind. But observe the matchless judgment of our Shakespeare. First, improbable as the conduct of Lear is in the first scene, yet it was an old story rooted in the popular faith,—a thing taken for granted already, and consequently without any of the effects of improbability. Secondly, it is merely the canvass for the characters and passions,—a mere occasion for,—and not, in the manner of Beaumont and Fletcher, perpetually recurring as the cause, and sine qua non of,—the incidents and emotions. Let the first scene of this play have been lost, and let it only be understood that a fond father had been duped by hypocritical professions of love and duty on the part of two daughters to disinherit the third, previously, and deservedly, more dear to him;—and all the rest of the tragedy would retain its interest undiminished, and be perfectly intelligible. The accidental is no where the groundwork of the passions, but that which is catholic, which in all ages has been, and ever will be, close and native to the heart of man,—parental anguish from filial ingratitude, the genuineness of worth, though coffined in bluntness, and the execrable vileness of a smooth iniquity.

—SAMUEL TAYLOR COLERIDGE, "Lear" (1819), Literary Remains, ed. Henry Nelson Coleridge (London: William Pickering, 1836), Vol. 2, pp. 185–88

CHARLES DICKENS

What we ventured to anticipate when Mr. Macready assumed the management of Covent Garden Theatre, has been every way realised. But the last of his well-directed efforts to vindicate the higher objects and uses of the drama has proved the most brilliant and the most successful. He has restored to the stage Shakespeare's true Lear, banished from it, by impudent ignorance, for upwards of a hundred and fifty years.

A person of the name of Boteler has the infamous repute of having recommended to a notorious poet-laureate, Mr. Nahum Tate, the 'new modelling' of Lear. 'I found the whole,' quoth Mr. Tate, addressing the aforesaid Boteler in his dedication, 'to answer your account of it; a heap of jewels unstrung and unpolished, yet so dazzling in their disorder, that I soon perceived I had seized a treasure.' And accordingly to work set Nahum very busily indeed: strung the jewels and polished them with a vengeance; omitted the grandest thing, the Fool among them; polished all that remained into commonplace; interlarded love-scenes; sent Cordelia into a comfortable cave with her lover, to dry her clothes and get warm, while her distracted and homeless old father was still left wandering without, amid all the pelting of the pitiless storm; and finally, rewarded the poor old man in his turn, and repaid him for all his suffering, by giving him back again his gilt robes and tinsel sceptre!

Betterton was the last great actor who played Lear before the commission of this outrage. His performances of it between the years 1663 and 1671 are recorded to have been the greatest efforts of his genius. Ten years after the latter date, Mr. Tate published his disgusting version, and this was adopted successively by Boheme, Quin, Booth, Barry, Garrick, Henderson, Kemble, Kean. Mr. Macready has now, to his lasting honour, restored the text of Shakespeare, and we shall be glad to hear of the actor foolhardy enough to attempt another restoration of the text of Mr. Tate! Mr. Macready's success has banished that disgrace from the stage for ever.

The *Fool* in the tragedy of *Lear* is one of the most wonderful creations of Shakespeare's genius. The picture of his quick and pregnant sarcasm, of his loving devotion, of his acute sensibility, of his despairing mirth, of his heartbroken silence—contrasted with the rigid sublimity of *Lear's* suffering, with the huge desolation of *Lear's* sorrow, with the vast and outraged image of *Lear's* madness—is the noblest thought that ever entered into the heart and mind of man. Nor is it a noble thought alone. Three crowded houses in Covent Garden Theatre have now proved by something better than even the deepest attention that it is for action, for representation; that it is necessary to an audience as tears are to an overcharged heart; and necessary to *Lear* himself as the recollections of his kingdom, or as the worn and faded garments of his power. We predicted some years since that this would be felt, and we have the better right to repeat it now. We take leave again to say that Shakespeare would have as soon consented to the banishment of *Lear* from the tragedy as to the banishment of his *Fool*. We may fancy him, while planning his immortal work, feeling suddenly, with an instinct of divinest genius, that its gigantic sorrows could never be presented on the stage without a suffering too frightful, a sublimity too remote, a grandeur too terrible—unless relieved by quiet pathos, and in some way brought home to the apprehensions of the audience by homely and familiar illustration. At such a moment that *Fool* rose to his mind, and not till then could he have contemplated his marvellous work in the greatness and beauty of its final completion.

The *Fool* in *Lear* is the solitary instance of such a character, in all the writings of Shakespeare, being identified with the pathos and passion of the scene. He is interwoven with *Lear,* he is the link that still associates him with *Cordelia's* love, and the presence of the regal estate he has surrendered. The rage of the wolf *Goneril* is first stirred by a report that her favourite gentleman had been struck by her father 'for chiding of his fool,'—and the first impatient questions we hear from the dethroned old man are: 'Where's my knave—my fool? Go you and call my fool hither.'—'Where's my fool? Ho! I think the world's asleep.'—'But where's my fool? I have not seen him these two days.'—'Go you and call hither my fool,'—all which prepare us for that affecting answer stammered forth at last by the knight in attendance: 'Since my young lady's going into France, sir, the fool hath much pined away.' Mr. Macready's manner of turning off at this with an expression of half impatience, half ill-repressed emotion—'No more of that, I *have noted it well*'—was inexpressibly touching. We saw him, in the secret corner of his heart, still clinging to the memory of her who was used to be his best object, the argument of his praise, balm of his age, 'most best, most dearest.' And in the same noble and affecting spirit was his manner of fondling the *Fool* when he sees him first, and asks him with earnest care, 'How now, my pretty knave? *How dost thou?*' Can there be a doubt, after this, that his love for the *Fool* is associated with *Cordelia*, who had been kind to the poor boy, and for the loss of whom he pines away? And are we not even then prepared for the sublime pathos of the close, when *Lear*, bending over the dead body of all he had left to love upon the earth, connects with her the memory of that other gentle, faithful, and loving being who had passed from his side—unites, in that moment of final agony, the two hearts that had been broken in his service, and exclaims, 'And my poor fool is hanged!'

Mr. Macready's *Lear*, remarkable before for a masterly completeness of conception, is heightened by this introduction of the *Fool* to a surprising degree. It accords exactly with the view he seeks to present of *Lear's* character. The passages we have named, for instance, had even received illustration in the first scene, where something beyond the turbulent greatness or royal impatience of *Lear* had been presented—something to redeem him from his treatment of *Cordelia*. The bewildered pause after giving his 'father's heart' away—the hurry yet hesitation of his manner as he orders *France* to be called—'Who stirs? Call *Burgundy*'—had told us at once how much consideration he needed, how much pity, of how little of himself he was indeed the master, how crushing and irrepressible was the strength of his sharp impatience. We saw no material change in his style of playing the first great scene with *Goneril*, which fills the stage with true and appalling touches of nature. In that scene he ascends indeed with the heights of *Lear's* passion; through all its changes of agony, of anger, of impatience, of turbulent assertion, of despair, and mighty grief, till on his knees, with arms upraised and head thrown back, the tremendous Curse bursts from him amid heaving and reluctant throes of suffering and anguish. The great scene of the second act had also its great passages of power and beauty: his self-persuading utterance of 'hysterias passio'—his anxious and fearful tenderness to *Regan*—the elevated grandeur of his appeal to the heavens—his terrible suppressed efforts, his pauses, his reluctant pangs of passion, in the speech 'I will not trouble thee, my child,'—and surpassing the whole, as we think, in deep simplicity as well as agony of pathos, that noble conception of shame as he *hides his face* on the arm of *Goneril* and says—

> I'll go with thee;
> Thy fifty yet doth double five and twenty,
> And thou art twice her love!

The *Fool's* presence then enabled him to give an effect, unattempted before, to those little words which close the scene, when, in the effort of bewildering passion with which he strives to burst through the phalanx of amazed horrors that have closed him round, he feels that his intellect is shaking, and suddenly exclaims, 'O *Fool!* I shall go mad!' This is better than hitting the forehead and ranting out a self-reproach.

But the presence of the *Fool* in the storm-scene! The reader must witness this to judge its power and observe the deep impression with which it affects the audience. Every resource that the art of the painter and the mechanist can afford is called in aid of this scene—every illustration is thrown on it of which the great actor of *Lear* is capable, but these are nothing to that simple presence of the *Fool!* He has changed his character there. So long as hope existed, he had sought by his hectic merriment and sarcasms to win *Lear* back to love and reason, but that half of his work is now over, and all that remains for him is to soothe and lessen the certainty of the worst. *Kent* asks who is with *Lear* in the storm, and is answered—

> None but the *Fool*, who labours to outjest
> His heart-struck injuries!

When all his attempts have failed, either to soothe or to outjest these injuries, he sings, in the shivering cold, about the necessity of 'going to bed at noon.' He leaves the stage to die in his youth, and we hear of him no more till we hear the sublime touch of pathos over the dead body of the hanged *Cordelia.*

The fittest passage of Mr. Macready's scenes upon the heath is his remembrance of the 'poor naked wretches,' wherein a new world seems indeed to have broken upon his mind. Other parts of these scenes wanted more of tumultuous extravagance, more of a preternatural cast of wildness. We should always be made to feel something beyond physical distress predominant here. His colloquy with *Mad Tom,* however, was touching in the last degree, and so were the two last scenes, the recognition of *Cordelia* and the death, which elicited from the audience the truest and best of all tributes to their beauty and pathos. Mr. Macready's representation of the father at the end, broken down to his last despairing struggle, his heart swelling gradually upwards till it burst in its closing sigh, completed the only perfect picture that we have had of *Lear* since the age of Betterton.

> —CHARLES DICKENS, "The Restoration of Shakespeare's *Lear* to the Stage"
> (1838), *The Works of Charles Dickens* (London: Chapman & Hall, 1914),
> Vol. 13, pp. 71–75

VICTOR HUGO

Lear is the occasion for Cordelia. Maternity of the daughter toward the father. Profound subject! A maternity venerable among all other maternities, so admirably translated by the legend of that Roman girl who in the depth of a prison nurses her old father. The young breast near the white beard: there is no holier sight! Such a filial breast is Cordelia!

Once this figure dreamed of and found, Shakespeare created his drama. Where should he put this consoling vision? In an obscure age. Shakespeare has taken the year of the world 3105, the time when Joash was king of Judah, Aganippus king of France, and Leir king of England. The whole earth was at that time mysterious. Picture to yourself that epoch. The temple of Jerusalem is still quite new; the gardens of Semiramis, constructed nine hundred years before, are beginning to crumble; the first gold coin appears in Ægina; the first balance is made by Phydon, tyrant of Argos; the eclipse of the sun is calculated by the Chinese; three hundred and twelve years have passed since Orestes, accused by the Eumenides before the Areopagus, was acquitted; Hesiod is just dead; Homer, if he still lives, is a hundred years old; Lycurgus, thoughtful traveller, re-enters Sparta; and one of may perceive in the depth of the sombre cloud of the Orient the chariot of fire which carries Elijah away: it is at that period that Leir—Lear—lives, and reigns over the dark islands. Jonas, Holofernes, Draco, Solon, Thespis, Nebuchadnezzar, Anaximenes who is to invent the signs of the zodiac, Cyrus, Zorobabel, Tarquin, Pythagoras, Æschylus, are not yet born; Coriolanus, Xerxes, Cincinnatus, Pericles, Socrates, Brennus, Aristotle, Timoleon, Demosthenes, Alexander, Epicurus, Hannibal, are ghosts awaiting their hour to enter among men; Judas Maccabæus, Viriatus, Popilius, Jugurtha, Mithridates, Marius, and Sylla, Cæsar and Pompey, Cleopatra and Antony, are far away in the future; and at the moment when Lear is king of Britain and of Iceland, there must pass away eight hundred and ninety-five years before Virgil says, "Penitus toto divisos orbe Britannos," and nine hundred and fifty years before Seneca says "Ultima Thule." The Picts and the Celts (the Scotch and the English) are tattooed. A redskin of the present day gives a vague idea of an Englishman then. It is this twilight that Shakespeare has chosen,—a long, dreamy night in which the inventor is free to put anything he likes: this King Lear, and then a king of France, a duke of Burgundy, a duke of Cornwall, a duke of Albany, an earl of Kent, and an earl of Gloucester. What matters your history to him who has humanity? Besides, he has with him the legend, which is also a kind of science, and as true as history, perhaps, although from another point of view. Shakespeare agrees with Walter Mapes, archdeacon of Oxford,—that is something; he admits, from Brutus to Cadwalla, the ninety-nine Celtic kings who have preceded the Scandinavian Hengist and the Saxon Horsa: and since he believes in Mulmutius, Cinigisil, Ceolulf, Cassibelan, Cymbeline, Cynulphus, Arviragus, Guiderius, Escuin, Cudred, Vortigern, Arthur, Uther Pendragon, he has every right to believe in King Lear and to create Cordelia. This site adopted, the place for the scene marked out, the foundation laid deep, he takes all in hand and builds his work,—unheard-of edifice. He takes tyranny, of which at a later period he will make weakness,—Lear; he takes treason,—Edmund; he takes devotion,—Kent; he takes Ingratitude, which begins with a caress, and he gives to this monster two heads,—Goneril, whom the legend calls Gornerille, and Regan, whom the legend calls Ragaü; he takes paternity; he takes royalty; he takes feudality; he takes ambition; he takes madness, which he divides, and he places face to face three madmen—the King's buffoon, madman by trade; Edgar of Gloucester, mad for prudence' sake; the King, mad through misery. It is at the summit of this tragic pile that he sets the bending form of Cordelia.

There are some formidable cathedral towers,—as, for instance, the Giralda of Seville,—which seem made all complete, with their spirals, their staircases, their sculptures, their cellars, their cæcums, their aërial cells, their sounding chambers, their bells, their wailing, and their mass and their spire, and all their vastness, in order to support at their summit an angel spreading its golden wings. Such is the drama, *King Lear*.

The father is the pretext for the daughter. That admirable human creature, Lear, serves as a support to this ineffable divine creation, Cordelia. All that chaos of crimes, vices, manias, and miseries finds its justification in this shining vision of virtue. Shakespeare, bearing Cordelia in his brain, in creating this tragedy was like a god who, having an Aurora to establish, should make a world to put her in.

And what a figure is that father! What a caryatid! It is man stooping. He does nothing but shift his burdens for others that are heavier. The more the old man becomes enfeebled, the more his load augments. He lives under an overburden. He bears at first power, then ingratitude, then isolation, then despair, then hunger and thirst, then madness, then all Nature. Clouds overcast him, forests heap their shadow upon him, the hurricane swoops down upon the nape of his neck, the tempest makes his mantle heavy as lead, the rain weighs upon his shoulders, he walks bent and haggard as if he had the two knees of Night upon his back. Dismayed and yet colossal, he flings to the winds and to the hail this epic cry: "Why do ye hate me, tempests? Why do ye persecute me? *Ye are not my daughters.*" And then all is over; the light is extinguished; Reason loses courage, and leaves him; Lear is in his dotage. This old man, being childish, requires a mother. His daughter appears, his only daughter, Cordelia. For the two others, Regan and Goneril, are not longer his daughters,—save so far as to entitle them to the name of parricides.

Cordelia approaches,—"Sir, do you know me?" "You are a spirit, I know," replies the old man, with the sublime clairvoyance of frenzy. From this moment the filial nursing begins. Cordelia applies herself to nursing this old despairing soul, dying of inanition in hatred. Cordelia nourishes Lear with love, and his courage revives; she nourishes him with respect, and the smile returns; she nourishes him with hope, and confidence is restored; she nourishes him with wisdom, and reason awakens. Lear, convalescent, rises again, and step by step returns again to life; the child becomes again an old man, the old man becomes a man again. And behold him happy, this wretched one! It is upon this expansion of happiness that the catastrophe is hurled down. Alas! there are traitors, there are perjurers, there are murderers. Cordelia dies. Nothing more heart-rending than this. The old man is stunned; he no longer understands anything; and, embracing her corpse, he expires. He dies upon his daughter's breast. He is saved from the supreme despair of remaining behind her among the living, a poor shadow, to feel the place in his heart empty, and to seek for his soul, carried away by that sweet being who is departed. O God! those whom Thou lovest Thou takest away.

To live after the flight of the angel; to be the father orphaned of his child; to be the eye that no longer has light; to be the deadened heart that knows no more joy; from time to time to stretch the hands into obscurity and try to reclasp a being who was there (where, then, can she be?); to feel himself forgotten in that departure; to have lost all reason for being here below; to be henceforth a man who goes to and fro before a sepulchre, not received, not admitted,—this is indeed a gloomy destiny. Thou hast done well, poet, to kill this old man.

—VICTOR HUGO, *William Shakespeare* [1864], tr. Melville B. Anderson
(Chicago: A. C. McClurg, 1887), pp. 244–49

LEO TOLSTOY

It is not enough to say that Shakespeare's characters are placed in tragic positions which are impossible, do not flow from the course of events, are inappropriate to time and space. These personages, besides this, act in a way that is out of keeping with their definite characters, and is quite arbitrary. It is generally asserted that in Shakespeare's dramas the characters are especially well expressed, that, notwithstanding their vividness, they are many-sided, like those of living people; that, whilst exhibiting the characteristics of a given individual, they at the same time wear the features of man in general; it is usual to say that the delineation of character in Shakespeare is the height of perfection.

This is asserted with much confidence, and repeated by all as indisputable truth; but, however much I endeavoured to find confirmation of this in Shakespeare's dramas, I always found the opposite. In reading any of Shakespeare's dramas whatever I was, from the very first, instantly convinced that he was lacking in the most important, if not the only, means of portraying characters—individuality of language, *i.e.*, the style of speech of every person being natural to his character. This is absent from Shakespeare. All his characters speak, not their own, but always one and the same Shakespearean pretentious and unnatural language, in which not only they could not speak, but in which no living man ever has spoken or does speak.

No living men could or can say as Lear says—that he would divorce his wife in the grave should Regan not receive him; or that the heavens would crack with shouting; or that the winds would burst; or that the wind wishes to blow the land into the sea; or that the curled waters wish to flood the shore, as the gentleman describes the storm; or that it is easier to bear one's grief; and the soul leaps over many sufferings when grief finds fellowship; or that Lear has become childless whilst I am fatherless, as Edgar says, or use similar unnatural expressions with which the speeches of all the characters in all Shakespeare's dramas overflow.

Again, it is not enough that all the characters speak in a way in which no living men ever did or could speak—they all suffer from a common intemperance of language. Those who are in love, who are preparing for death, who are fighting, who are dying, all alike speak much and unexpectedly about subjects utterly inappropriate to the occasion, being evidently guided rather by consonances and play of words than by thoughts. They speak all alike. Lear raves exactly as does Edgar when feigning madness. Both Kent and the fool speak alike. The words of one of the personages might be placed in the mouth of another, and by the character of the speech it would be impossible to distinguish who speaks. If there is a difference in the speech of Shakespeare's various characters, it lies merely in the different dialogues which are pronounced for these characters again by Shakespeare and not by themselves. Thus Shakespeare always speaks for Kings in one and the same inflated, empty language. Also in one and the same Shakespearean, artificially sentimental language speak all the women who are intended to be poetic—Juliet, Desdemona, Cordelia, Imogen, Marina. In the same way also it is Shakespeare alone who speaks for his villains—Richard, Edmund, Iago, Macbeth, expressing for them those vicious feelings which villains never express. Yet more similar are the speeches of the madmen with their horrible words and those of fools with their mirthless puns. So that in Shakespeare there is no language of living individuals—that language which in the drama is the chief means of setting forth characters. If gesticulation be also a means of expressing character, as in *ballets*, this is only a secondary means. Moreover, if the characters speak at random and in a random way, and all in one and the same diction, as is the case in Shakespeare's work, then even the action of gesticulation is wasted. Therefore, whatever the blind panegyrists of Shakespeare may say, in Shakespeare there is no expression of character. Those personages who in his dramas stand out as characters, are characters borrowed by him from former works which served as the foundation of his dramas, and they are mostly depicted, not only by the dramatic method, which consists in making each person speak with his own diction, but in the epic method of one person describing the features of another.

The perfection with which Shakespeare expresses character is asserted chiefly on the ground of the characters of Lear, Cordelia, Othello, Desdemona, Falstaff, Hamlet. But all these characters, as well as all the others, instead of belonging to Shakespeare, are taken by him from dramas, chronicles, and romances anterior to him. All these characters not only are not rendered more powerful by him, but in most cases they are weakened and spoilt. This is very striking in this drama of *King Lear*, which we are examining, taken by him from the drama *King Leir*, by an unknown author. The characters of this drama, that of King Leir, and especially of Cordelia, not only were not created by Shakespeare, but have been strikingly weakened and deprived of force by him, as compared with their appearance in the older drama.

In the older drama Leir abdicates because, having become a widower, he thinks only of saving his soul. He asks his daughters as to their love for him—that by means of a certain device he has invented he may retain his favourite daughter on his island. The elder daughters are betrothed, while the youngest does not wish to contract a loveless union with any of the neighbouring suitors whom Leir proposes to her, and he is afraid that she may marry some distant potentate.

The device which he has invented, as he informs his courtier, Perillus (Shakespeare's Kent), is this, that when Cordelia tells him that she loves him more than anyone, or as much as her elder sisters do, he will tell her that she must, in proof of her love, marry the prince he will indicate on his island.

All these motives for Leir's conduct are absent in Shakespeare's play. Then, when according to the old drama Leir asks his daughters about their love to him, Cordelia does not say, as Shakespeare has it, that she will not give her father all her love, but will love her husband too, should she marry—which is quite unnatural—but simply says that she cannot express her love in words, but hopes that her actions will prove it. Goneril and Regan remark that Cordelia's answer is not an answer, and that the father cannot meekly accept such indifference; so that what is wanting in Shakespeare, *i.e.*, the explanation of Lear's anger which caused him to disinherit his youngest daughter, exists in the old drama. Leir is annoyed by the failure of his scheme, and the poisonous words of his elder daughters irritate him still more. After the division of the kingdom between the elder daughters there follows in the older drama a scene between Cordelia and the King of Gaul, setting forth, instead of the colourless Cordelia of Shakespeare, a very definite and attractive character of the truthful, tender, and self-sacrificing youngest daughter. While Cordelia, without grieving that she has been deprived of a portion of her heritage, sits sorrowing at having lost her father's love, and looking forward to earn her bread by her labour, there comes the King of Gaul, who, in the disguise of a pilgrim, desires to choose a bride from amongst Leir's daughters. He asks Cordelia why she is sad. She tells him the cause of her grief. The King of Gaul, still in the guise of a pilgrim, falls in love with her, and offers to arrange a marriage for her with the King of Gaul, but she says she will marry only a man whom she loves. Then the pilgrim, still disguised, offers her his hand and heart, and Cordelia confesses that she loves the pilgrim and consents to marry him, notwithstanding the poverty that awaits her. Thereupon the pilgrim discloses to her that he it is who is the King of Gaul, and Cordelia marries him. Instead of this scene, Lear, according to Shakespeare, proposes to Cordelia's two suitors to take her without dowry, and one cynically refuses, whilst the other, one does not know why, accepts her. After this, in the old drama, as in Shakespeare's, Leir undergoes the insults of Goneril, into whose house he has removed, but he bears these insults in a very different way from that represented by Shakespeare: he feels that by his conduct towards Cordelia he has deserved this, and humbly submits. As in Shakespeare's drama, so also in the older drama, the courtier, Perillus—Kent—who had interceded for Cordelia and was therefore banished—comes to Leir and assures him of his love, but under no disguise, simply as a faithful old servant who does not abandon his king in a moment of need. Lear tells him what, according to Shakespeare, he tells Cordelia in the last scene—that, if the daughters whom he has benefited hate him, a retainer to whom he has done no good cannot love him? But Perillus—Kent—assures the King of his love towards him, and Leir, pacified, goes on to Regan. In the older drama there are no tempests nor tearing out of grey hairs, but there is the weakened and humbled old man, Leir, overpowered with grief, and banished by his other daughter also, who even wishes to kill him. Turned out by his elder daughters, Leir, according to the older drama, as a last resource, goes with Perillus to Cordelia. Instead of the unnatural banishment of Lear during the tempest, and his roaming about the heath, Leir, with Perillus, in the older drama, during their journey to France, very naturally reach the last degree of destitution, sell their clothes in order to pay for their crossing over the sea, and, in the attire of fishermen, exhausted by cold and hunger, approach Cordelia's house. Here again, instead of the unnatural combined ravings of the fool, Lear and Edgar, as represented by Shakespeare, there follows in the older drama a natural scene of reunion between the daughter and the father. Cordelia, who, notwithstanding her happiness, has all the time been grieving about her father and praying God to forgive her sisters who had done him so much wrong, meets her father in his extreme want, and wishes immediately to disclose herself to him, but her husband advises her not to do this, in order not to agitate her weak father. She accepts the counsel, and takes Leir into her house without disclosing herself to him, and nurses him. Leir gradually revives, and then the daughter asks him who he is, and how he lived formerly.

If from the first,

says Leir,

> I should relate the cause,
> I would make a heart of adamant weep.
> And thou, poor soul, kind-hearted as thou art,
> Dost weep already, ere I do begin.

Cordelia:—

> For God's love tell it, and when you have done
> I'll tell the reason why I weep so soon.

And Leir relates all he has suffered from his elder daughters, and says that now he wishes to find shelter with the child who would be in the right even were she to condemn him to death. "If, however," he says, "she will receive me with love, it will be God's and her work, but not my merit." To this Cordelia says, "Oh, I know for certain that thy daughter will lovingly receive thee." "How canst thou know this without knowing her?" says Leir. "I know," says Cordelia, "because not far from here I had a father who acted towards me as badly as thou hast acted towards her, yet if I were only to see his white head, I would creep to meet him on my knees." "No, this cannot be," says Leir, "for there are no children in the world so cruel as mine." Do not condemn all for the sins of some," says Cordelia, and falls on her knees. "Look here, dear father," she says, "look at me: I am thy loving daughter." The father recognises her, and says: "It is not for thee, but for me to beg thy pardon on my knees for all my sins towards thee."

Is there anything approaching this exquisite scene in Shakespeare's drama?

However strange this opinion may seem to worshippers of Shakespeare, yet the whole of this old drama is incomparably and in every respect superior to Shakespeare's adaptation. It is so first because it has not got the utterly superfluous characters of the villain Edmund, and unlifelike Gloucester and Edgar, who only distract one's attention; secondly, because it has not got the completely false "effects" of Lear running about the heath, his conversations with the fool and all these impossible disguises, failures to recognise and accumulated deaths; and, above all, because in this drama there is the simple, natural, and deeply touching character of Leir, and the yet more touching and clearly-defined character of Cordelia, both absent in Shakespeare. Therefore, there is in the older drama, instead of Shakespeare's long-drawn scene of Lear's interview with Cordelia and of Cordelia's unnecessary murder, the exquisite scene of the interview between Leir and Cordelia, unequalled by any in all Shakespeare's dramas.

The old drama also terminates more naturally and more in accordance with the moral demands of the spectator than does Shakespeare's, namely, by the King of the Gauls conquering the husbands of the elder sisters and Cordelia, instead of being killed, restoring Leir to his former position.

—LEO TOLSTOY, "On Shakespeare and the Drama" (Part II), tr. V. Tchertkoff and E. A., *Fortnightly Review* 87, No. 1 (January 1907): 62–67

STOPFORD A. BROOKE

There is a drawing by Ford Madox Brown of Lear in ⟨the⟩ first scene. He is represented as a huge old man, half-sunk in his great chair, unable to move, a ruin of a man. I have seen Irving represent Lear, and all through this first scene he shook like a man who had suffered from palsy. Irving pictured a broken man. But Shakespeare did not mean Lear to resemble either of these impersonations. Lear was one of an early race of men, strong even in old age. All his life he had lived in the open. Age had not weakened his body any more than his mind. There is no physical feebleness suggested in this first scene; and when we meet him again he comes home from a hunting with his hundred knights, vigorous, and ready for feasting and drinking. 'Let me not stay, he shouts, 'a jot for dinner; go, get it ready.' And this hunting and feasting has been going on for a fortnight. This was the Lear of Shakespeare, and that he made him a hale, strong old man deepens the tragedy of his breaking-up, accounts for the protracted struggle he makes against his sorrows, for the awful agony he undergoes in the struggle, and afterwards for the fury and strength, as of a wounded Titan, with which he outfaces and outdoes the rage of the storm. It was no half-paralysed old man, but a giant smitten to the heart, who is finally broken down. This, I think, is what the actor should embody.

—STOPFORD A. BROOKE, *"King Lear,"* Ten More Plays of Shakespeare (London: Constable, 1913), p. 209

SIGMUND FREUD

To avoid misunderstandings, I wish to say that I have no intention of denying that the drama of *King Lear* inculcates the two prudent maxims: that one should not forgo one's possessions and privileges in one's lifetime and that one must guard against accepting flattery as genuine. These and similar warnings do undoubtedly arise from the play; but it seems to me quite impossible to explain the overpowering effect of *Lear* from the impression that such a train of thought would produce, or to assume that the poet's own creative instincts would not carry him further than the impulse to illustrate these maxims. Moreover, even though we are told that the poet's intention was to present the tragedy of ingratitude, the sting of which he probably felt in his own heart, and that the effect of the play depends on the purely formal element, its artistic trappings, it seems to me that this information cannot compete with the comprehension that dawns upon us after our study of the theme of a choice between the three sisters.

Lear is an old man. We said before that this is why the three sisters appear as his daughters. The paternal relationship, out of which so many fruitful dramatic situations might arise, is not turned to further account in the drama. But Lear is not only an old man; he is a dying man. The extraordinary project of dividing the inheritance thus loses its strangeness. The doomed man is nevertheless not willing to renounce the love of women; he insists on hearing how much he is loved. Let us now recall that most moving last scene, one of the culminating points reached in modern tragic drama: 'Enter Lear with Cordelia dead in his arms'. Cordelia is Death. Reverse the situation and it becomes intelligible and familiar to us—the Death-goddess bearing away the dead hero from the place of battle, like the Valkyr in German mythology. Eternal wisdom, in the garb of primitive myth, bids the old man renounce love, choose death and make friends with the necessity of dying.

The poet brings us very near to the ancient idea by making the man who accomplishes the choice between the three sisters aged and dying. The regressive treatment he has thus undertaken with the myth, which was disguised by the reversal of the wish, allows its original meaning so far to appear that perhaps a superficial allegorical interpretation of the three female figures in the theme becomes possible as well. One might say that the three inevitable relations man has with woman are here represented: that with the mother who bears him, with the companion of his bed and board, and with the destroyer. Or it is the three forms taken on by the figure of the mother as life proceeds: the mother herself, the beloved who is chosen after her pattern, and finally the Mother Earth who receives him again. But it is in vain that the old man yearns after the love of woman as once he had it from his mother; the third of the Fates alone, the silent goddess of Death, will take him into her arms.

—SIGMUND FREUD, "The Theme of the Three Caskets" (1913),
Collected Papers, tr. Joan Riviere (New York: Basic Books, 1959),
Vol. 4, pp. 255–56

G. WILSON KNIGHT

Lear himself shows, as I have already indicated, an excessive naturalism in point of religion. His early curses and prayers are addressed to natural objects, or nature personified. The 'heavens' he cries to are natural rather than eschatological: they are, like the earth, 'old'. He invokes 'blasts and fogs', 'nimble lightnings', 'fen-suck'd fogs' to avenge him (p. 183). He wishes 'the plagues that in the pendulous air hang fated o'er men's faults' to punish poor Tom's supposed 'daughters' (III. iv. 66). These natural deities he prays to execute natural punishment: Regan's young bones are to be struck with lameness, goddess nature is to convey sterility into Goneril's womb. He thinks purely in terms of the natural order. In these speeches his religion is pagan, naturalistic. It is, in fact, nearer primitive magic than religion. He swears by

> the sacred radiance of the sun,
> The mysteries of Hecate, and the night;
> By all the operation of the orbs
> From whom we do exist and cease to be ...   (I. i. 111)

His early gods are classical: Apollo, Jupiter—used, however, purely as oaths; and, once, 'high-judging Jove', with a sense of conviction (II, iv, 231). In the middle scenes he apostrophizes the elements as living beings. His early primitivism gives place, however, to something more definite in the thought of 'the great gods who keep this dreadful pother o'er our heads', whose 'enemies' are wicked men (III. ii. 49). Thoughts of morality are being added to his first pagan selfishness. He questions the justice of 'the heavens' towards naked poverty (III. iv. 28). He thinks of fiends in his madness:

> To have a thousand with red burning spits
> Come hizzing in upon 'em—   (III. vi. 17)

Of women, he says:

> But to the girdle do the gods inherit,
> Beneath is all the fiend's.   (IV. vi. 129)

These are transition thoughts from his early passionate paganism. The return to nature which he endures in the play's progress paradoxically builds in him a less naturalistic theology. At the end, he can speak to Cordelia those blazing lines:

> You do me wrong and take me out o' the grave:
> Thou art a soul in bliss; but I am bound
> Upon a wheel of fire, that mine own tears
> Do scald like molten lead.   (IV. vii. 45)

Now 'the gods themselves' throw incense on human sacrifices (V. iii. 20). He and Cordelia will be as 'God's spies' (V. iii. 17)—here not 'the gods', but 'God's'. Slowly, painfully, emergent from the *Lear* naturalism we see a religion born of disillusionment, suffering, and sympathy: a purely spontaneous, natural growth of the human spirit, developing from nature magic to 'God'.

The emergent religion here—the stoic acceptance, the purification through sympathy, the groping after 'the gods'—all these are twined with the conception of justice. The old Hebrew problem is restated: *King Lear* is analogous to the *Book of Job*. Is justice a universal principle? The thought of justice, human and divine, is percurrent. The first sentence of the play suggests that Lear is guilty of bias:

> KENT: I thought the King had more affected the Duke of Albany than Cornwall.
>   (I. i. 1)

He is unjust to Cordelia and to Kent in the first act. His suffering is thus seen to be at least related to injustice of his own. Edmund, too, has reason to complain of injustice: the world brands him with the shame of his birth and inflames his mind. Many of the persons here attempt to execute justice. Kent punishes Oswald for his impertinence and is himself punished; Regan and Cornwall sit in judgement on Gloucester, and gouge out his eyes; a servant takes the law into his own hands and kills Cornwall; Edgar punishes Oswald and Edmund with death; France and Cordelia raise an army to right the affairs of Britain. Gloucester does his best to bring Edgar to justice. Lear is concerned with the more primitive thought of vengeance, and invokes the heavens and nature to aid him. His 'revenges' will be 'the terror of the earth' (II. iv. 285). The thought of justice burns in his mind during the storm: now can the gods 'find out their enemies'; hypocrites, with 'crimes unwhipp'd of justice' must tremble before 'these dreadful summoners' (III. ii. 49). He himself, however, is 'a man more sinned against than sinning' (III. ii. 60). But he next thinks of those in ragged poverty: it is well for pomp to take this tempestuous physic, exposure's misery, that so the rich may share their wealth and 'show the heavens more just' (III. iv. 36). His mind thus beating on 'justice', the old man's reason breaks and the same thought is expressed now in lunatic action. He holds his mock-trial of Goneril and Regan, with poor Tom as 'learned justicer' (III. vi. 24):

> I'll see their trial first. Bring in the evidence.   (III. vi. 38)

Tom is the 'robed man of justice' and the Fool his 'yoke-fellow of equity'; and Kent is 'o' the commission'. The 'honourable assembly' proves corrupt:

> Corruption in the place!
> False justicer, why hast thou let her 'scape?   (III. vi. 58)

When we meet Lear again in madness (IV. vi.) we find him still on the same theme. He thinks himself in judicial authority:

> When I do stare, see how the subject quakes.
> I pardon that man's life. What was thy cause?
> Adultery?
> Thou shalt not die: die for adultery! No:
> The wren goes to't, and the small gilded fly
> Does lecher in my sight.   (IV. vi. 111)

He remembers that 'Gloucester's bastard son' was kinder, as he thinks, to his father than his legitimate brother. Lear's mind in madness is penetrating below the surface shows to the heart of human reality—that heart rooted in nature, uncivilized, instinctive as 'the small gilded fly'. The 'simpering dame', apparently pure-minded and virtuous, is yet lecherous at heart:

> The fitchew nor the soiled horse goes to't
> With a more riotous appetite.   (IV. vi. 125)

It is the old problem of *Measure for Measure:* man's ethics, his show of civilization, are surface froth only. The deep instinctive currents hold their old course, in earth, beast, and man. Man's morality, his idealism, his justice—all are false and rotten to the core. Lear's mind has, since his first mad-scene, pursued its lonely orbit into the dark chaos of insanity, and now whirls back, in the fourth act, grotesque and baleful comet, with a penetrating insight into man's nature: whereas his first mad justice thoughts at the mock-trial were born of a primitive desire to avenge himself on his daughters. Now he returns, with a new justice-philosophy. He concentrates on the mockery and futility of human justice:

> Look with thine ears; see how yond justice rails upon yond simple thief. Hark in thine ear: change places; and, handy-dandy, which is the justice, which is the thief? (IV. vi. 155)

A 'beggar' will run from a 'farmer's dog'. That is the great image, says Lear, of authority. 'A dog's obeyed in office.' The beadle lusts himself to use the whore he whips. All is corrupt:

> Robes and furr'd gowns hide all. Plate sin with gold,
> And the strong lance of justice hurtless breaks. (IV. vi. 170)

Therefore 'none does offend'. Lear's mind is ever on justice: tearing at it, worrying it, like a dog with a bone. And these thoughts of naturalistic psychology hold a profound suggestion: they are a road to recognition of the universal injustice. For when earthly justice is thus seen to be absolutely non-existent and, in fact, impossible, the concept of 'justice' is drained of meaning. How then can we impose it on the universal scheme? With a grand consistency the poet maintains this sense of universal justice up to the last terrible moment of the tragedy.

—G. WILSON KNIGHT, "The Lear Universe," The Wheel of Fire (1930; rev. ed. London: Methuen, 1949), pp. 189–93

MAUD BODKIN

In our first essay some attempt was made to show, in the dramas of Hamlet and King Lear, how the central figure, though in no way explicitly presented as super-human, yet, through the magic of poetic speech, and in relation to the tragic pattern, takes on an almost superhuman quality. In regard to Hamlet, this feeling has been expressed by Bradley when he speaks of his figure appearing

> as the symbol of a tragic mystery inherent in human nature. Whenever this mystery touches us, whenever we are forced to feel the wonder and awe of man's god-like apprehension, and his 'thoughts that wander through eternity', and at the same time are forced to see him powerless in his petty sphere of action, and powerless (it would appear) from the very divinity of his thought, we remember Hamlet.

The wonder and awe at the god-like element in man, which Bradley says may be felt in Hamlet, would seem the result of Shakespeare's poetry transfiguring the play of thought and feeling around Hamlet's inner conflict, releasing in the spectator deep reminiscence personal and racial, thus making the imagined conflict symbolic of vast forces, both terrible and glorious in their range and compelling power upon our lives.

It is the same magic of poetic speech that transforms the raving Lear into a majestic figure who seems to bear 'the imagined burden of the whole world's sorrow'. The glory that the poet's art reveals, within the old man broken to madness upon the desolate heath, may in part be traced, as I have tried to show, to the collective emotional energies vested, through personal and racial history, within the appearances of the storm, and within the person and function of a king. The power, daemonic or divine, glorifying the contemplated figure, which is also seen with perfect distinctness in its human limitations, weakness, and misery—'such a poor, bare, forked animal as thou art', 'I am a very foolish, fond old man'—moves the spectator with the authentic tragic feeling that has, among its mingled aspects, the character of a purgation, and hence an atonement. Kingly greatness, beheld in a form so broken and pitiful, is no longer a possible object of the personal self-seeking and power-craving that isolates the individual from his kind.

With the tragic glory that shines in Lear we choose to compare, as fitted above all other instances for our purpose, the strange light of a transfiguring terrible holiness that in the play of Sophocles is thrown about the figure of the aged Oedipus. There is, I believe, no other passage of Greek poetry—hardly perhaps of any literature—in which a responsive reader is so constrained to religious awe as in the closing scene of the *Oedipus Coloneus.*

As in the last scenes of *King Lear,* the destitution of the royal sufferer is poignant with the contrast of prior greatness. Upon that prior dignity had fallen the shadow of the doom of *hubris:* as on the blind wilfulness of Lear, so on the confidence of Oedipus that he—all unwittingly polluted—can bear responsibility for every soul within his realm. Now the stroke of that foreshadowed doom has been endured to the end. So in the case of Lear, the poet has used the resources of passionate speech to link with the motions of the sufferer's mind the majesty of the storm. As the Chorus speak of reversals of fortune, the mighty overthrown, the lowly exalted, thunder is heard, and as peal follows peal their words convey the terror of the por-tent, which to Oedipus but confirms the sign, 'the watchword', already received, of destiny. Empowered by the divine summons, the figure of the blind Oedipus, hith-erto seen moving timidly in physical dependence, is shown passing with firm and eager steps from the sight of the spectators. The messenger who narrates his end tells how he moved, 'guide himself unto us all'. After the description of the clinging farewell between father and daughters come the words which most powerfully con-vey the companionship of Oedipus in his last moments with the unseen:

> When they had made an end of wailing, and the sound went up no more, there was a stillness; and suddenly a voice of one who cried aloud to him, so that the hair of all stood up on their heads for sudden fear, and they were afraid. For the god called him with many callings and manifold: *'Oedipus, Oedipus, why delay we to go? Thou tarriest too long.'*

When the attendants, dismissed from the sacred scene, looked back after no long time,

Oedipus we saw nowhere any more, but the king [Theseus] alone, holding his hand before his face to screen his eyes, as if some dread sight had been seen, and such as none might endure to behold. And then, after a short space, we saw him salute the earth and the home of the gods above, both at once, in one prayer.

But by what doom Oedipus perished no man call tell, save Theseus alone. No fiery thunderbolt of the god removed him in that hour, nor any rising of storm from the sea; but either a messenger from the gods, or the world of the dead, the nether adamant, riven for him in love, without pain; for the passing of the man was not with lamentation, or in sickness and suffering, but, above mortal's, wonderful.

The austerity of this scene has been contrasted with the human tenderness that illumines the death of Lear. Lear dies with the cry on his lips of hope and joy in the love 'which does redeem all sorrows'. Oedipus has dismissed his daughters, stilling their cries of love and grief, that he may pass alone, with but the one royal witness, to his destined end. Yet, beyond the contrast, there is also likeness in the feeling conveyed. When the last pulse of hope and fear has ceased in Lear's torn heart, there remain with us the words in which Kent, the faithful servant, voices the beholder's awe and pity:

Vex not his ghost: O! let him pass; he hates him
That would upon the rack of this tough world
Stretch him out longer.

The spirit that informs these words is the same that moulds the tale of the passing of Oedipus. After such infinitude of suffering 'the grave's most holy peace' comes as the supreme boon; and with it the sense of something revealed or achieved for the world, once for all, by these sufferings:

we that are young
Shall never see so much, nor live so long.

Lear, like Oedipus, has been lifted up, a portent to mankind, but one sacred and fraught with comfort—a vision of man's essential nature and destiny, beheld under the form of eternity, from which taint of mortal sin and delusion is purged away.

The tragic hero, seen under this aspect as a figure sacrificial, profoundly representative, has a clear relation to the Christ of the Gospel story. In Christ appears pre-eminently this character felt obscurely in such heroes of poetic tragedy as Oedipus and Lear. Christ is the sacred object lifted up, fraught with comfort for man, gazing upon whom he sees, as in a transfiguring mirror, his own soul purified and delivered.

—MAUD BODKIN, "The Patterns in Sacred and in Contemporary Literature,"
Archetypal Patterns in Poetry: Psychological Studies of Imagination
(London: Oxford University Press, 1934), pp. 280–84

GEORGE ORWELL

⟨. . .⟩ why did Tolstoy, with thirty or more plays to choose from, pick out *King Lear* as his especial target? True, *Lear* is so well known and has been so much praised that it could justly be taken as representative of Shakespeare's best work: still, for the purpose of a hostile analysis Tolstoy would probably choose the play he disliked most. Is it not possible that he bore an especial enmity towards this particular play because he was aware, consciously or unconsciously, of the resemblance between Lear's story and his own? But it is better to approach this clue from the opposite direction—that is, by examining *Lear* itself, and the qualities in it that Tolstoy fails to mention.

One of the first things an English reader would notice in Tolstoy's pamphlet is that it hardly deals with Shakespeare as a poet. Shakespeare is treated as a dramatist, and in so far as his popularity is not spurious, it is held to be due to tricks of stagecraft which give good opportunities to clever actors. Now, so far as the English-speaking countries go, this is not true. Several of the plays which are most valued by lovers of Shakespeare (for instance, *Timon of Athens*) are seldom or never acted, while some of the most actable, such as *A Midsummer Night's Dream,* are the least admired. Those who care most for Shakespeare value him in the first place for his use of language, the "verbal music" which even Bernard Shaw, another hostile critic, admits to be "irresistible". Tolstoy ignores this, and does not seem to realise that a poem may have a special value for those who speak the language in which it was written. However, even if one puts oneself in Tolstoy's place and tries to think of Shakespeare as a foreign poet it is still clear that there is something that Tolstoy has left out. Poetry, it seems, is *not* solely a matter of sound and association, and valueless outside its own language-group: otherwise, how is it that some poems, including poems written in dead languages, succeed in crossing frontiers? Clearly a lyric like "Tomorrow is Saint Valentine's Day" could not be satisfactorily translated, but in Shakespeare's major work there is something describable as poetry that can be separated from the words. Tolstoy is right in saying that *Lear* is not a very good play, as a play. It is too drawn-out and has too many characters and sub-plots. One wicked daughter would have been quite enough, and Edgar is a superfluous character: indeed it would probably be a better play if Gloucester and both his sons were eliminated. Nevertheless, something, a kind of pattern, or perhaps only an atmosphere, survives the complications and the *longueurs. Lear* can be imagined as a puppet show, a mime, a ballet, a series of pictures. Part of its poetry, perhaps the most essential part, is inherent in the story and is dependent neither on any particular set of words, nor on flesh-and-blood presentation.

Shut your eyes and think of *King Lear,* if possible without calling to mind any of the dialogue. What do you see? Here at any rate is what I see: a majestic old man in a long black robe, with flowing white hair and beard, a figure out of Blake's drawings (but also, curiously enough, rather like Tolstoy), wandering through a storm and cursing the heavens, in company with a Fool and a lunatic. Presently the scene shifts, and the old man, still cursing, still understanding nothing, is holding a dead girl in his arms while the Fool dangles on a gallows somewhere in the background. This is the bare skeleton of the play, and even here Tolstoy wants to cut out most of what is essential. He objects to the storm, as being unnecessary, to the Fool, who in his eyes is simply a tedious nuisance and an excuse for making bad jokes, and to the death of Cordelia, which, as he sees it, robs the play of its moral. According to Tolstoy, the earlier play, *King Leir,* which Shakespeare adapted

> terminates more naturally and more in accordance with the moral demands of the spectator than does Shakespeare's: namely, by the King of the Gauls conquering the husbands of the elder sisters, and by Cordelia, instead of being killed, restoring Leir to his former position.

In other words the tragedy ought to have been a comedy, or perhaps a melodrama. It is doubtful whether the sense of tragedy is compatible with belief in God: at any rate, it is not compatible with disbelief in human dignity and with the kind of "moral demand" which feels cheated when virtue fails to triumph. A tragic situation exists precisely when virtue does *not* triumph but when it is still felt that man is nobler than the forces which destroy him. It is perhaps more significant that Tolstoy sees no justification for the presence of the Fool. The Fool is integral to the play. He acts not only as a sort of chorus, making the central situation clearer by commenting on it more intelligently than the other characters, but as a foil to Lear's frenzies. His jokes, riddles and scraps of rhyme, and his endless digs at Lear's high-minded folly, ranging from mere derision to a sort of melancholy poetry ("All thy other titles thou hast given away; that thou wast born with"), are like a trickle of sanity running through the play, a reminder that somewhere or other, in spite of the injustices, cruelties, intrigues, deceptions, and misunderstandings that are being enacted here, life is going on much as usual. In Tolstoy's impatience with the Fool one gets a glimpse of his deeper quarrel with Shakespeare. He objects, with some justification, to the raggedness of Shakespeare's plays, the irrelevancies, the incredible plots, the exaggerated language: but what at bottom he probably most dislikes is a sort of exuberance, a tendency to take—not so much a pleasure, as simply an interest in the actual process of life. It is a mistake to write Tolstoy off as a moralist attacking an artist. He never said that art, as such, is wicked or meaningless, nor did he even say that technical virtuosity is unimportant. But his main aim, in his later years, was to narrow the range of human consciousness. One's interests, one's points of attachment to the physical world and the day-to-day·struggle, must be as few and not as many as possible. Literature must consist of parables, stripped of detail and almost independent of language. The parables—this is where Tolstoy differs from the average vulgar puritan—must themselves be works of art, but pleasure and curiosity must be excluded from them. Science, also, must be divorced from curiosity. The business of science, he says, is not to discover what happens, but to teach men how they ought to live. So also with history and politics. Many problems (for example, the Dreyfus Case) are simply not worth solving, and he is willing to leave them as loose ends. Indeed his whole theory of "crazes" or "epidemic suggestions", in which he lumps together such things as the Crusades and the Dutch passion of tulip growing, shows a willingness to regard many human activities as mere ant-like rushings to and fro, inexplicable and uninteresting. Clearly he could have no patience with a chaotic, detailed, discursive writer like Shakespeare. His reaction is that of an irritable old man who is being pestered by a noisy child. "Why do you keep jumping up and down like that? Why can't you sit still like I do?" In a way the old man is in the right, but the trouble is that the child has a feeling in its limbs which the old man has lost. And if the old man knows of the existence of this feeling, the effect is merely to increase his irritation: he would make children senile, if he could. Tolstoy does not know, perhaps, just *what* he misses in Shakespeare, but he is aware that he misses something, and he is determined that others shall be deprived of it as well. By nature he was imperious as well as egotistical. Well after he was grown up he would still occasionally strike his servant in moments of anger, and somewhat later, according to his English biographer, Derrick Leon, he felt "a frequent desire upon the slenderest provocation to slap the faces of those with whom he disagreed". One does not necessarily get rid of that kind of temperament by undergoing religious conversion, and indeed it is obvious that the illusion of having been reborn may allow one's native vices to flourish more freely than ever, though perhaps in subtler forms. Tolstoy was capable of abjuring physical violence and of seeing what this implies, but he was not capable of tolerance or humility, and even if one knew nothing of his other writings, one could deduce his tendency towards spiritual bullying from this single pamphlet.

However, Tolstoy is not simply trying to rob others of a pleasure he does not share. He is doing that, but his quarrel with Shakespeare goes further. It is the quarrel between the religious and the humanist attitudes toward life. Here one comes back to the central theme of *King Lear,* which Tolstoy does not mention, although he sets forth the plot in some detail.

Lear is one of the minority of Shakespeare's plays that are unmistakably *about* something. As Tolstoy justly complains, much rubbish has been written about Shakespeare as a philosopher, as a psychologist, as a "great moral teacher", and what not. Shakespeare was not a systematic thinker, his most serious thoughts are uttered irrelevantly or indirectly, and we do not know to what extent he wrote with a "purpose" or even how much of the work attributed to him was actually written by him. In the Sonnets he never even refers to the plays as part of his achievement, though he does make what seems to be a half-ashamed allusion to his career as an actor. It is perfectly possible that he looked on at least half of his plays as mere pot-boilers and hardly bothered about purpose or probability so long as he could patch up something, usually from stolen material, which would more or less hang together on the stage. However, that is not the whole story. To begin with, as Tolstoy himself points out, Shakespeare has a habit of thrusting uncalled-for general reflections into the mouths of his characters. This is a serious fault in a dramatist but it does not fit in with Tolstoy's picture of Shakespeare as a vulgar hack who has no opinions of his own and merely wishes to produce the greatest effect with the least trouble. And more than this, about a dozen of his plays, written for the most part later than 1600, do unquestionably have a meaning and even a moral. They revolve around a central subject which in some cases can be reduced to a single word. For example, *Macbeth* is about ambition, *Othello* is about jealousy, and *Timon of Athens* is about money. The subject of *Lear* is renunciation, and it is only by being wilfully blind that one can fail to understand what Shakespeare is saying.

Lear renounces his throne but expects everyone to continue treating him as a king. He does not see that if he surrenders power, other people will take advantage of his weakness: also that those who flatter him the most grossly, i.e. Regan and Goneril, are exactly the ones who will turn against him. The moment he finds that he can no longer make people obey him as he did before, he falls into a rage which Tolstoy describes as "strange and unnatural", but which in fact is perfectly in character. In his madness and despair, he passes through two moods which again are natural enough in his circumstances, though in one of them it is probable that he is being used partly as a mouthpiece for Shakespeare's own opinions. One is the mood of disgust in which Lear repents, as it were, for having been a king, and grasps for the first time the rottenness of formal justice and vulgar morality. The other is a mood of impotent fury in which he wreaks imaginary revenges upon those who have wronged him. "To have a thousand with red burning spits Come hissing in upon 'em!", and:

> It were a delicate stratagem to shoe
> A troop of horse with felt: I'll put't in proof;
> And when I have stol'n upon these sons-in-law,
> Then kill, kill, kill, kill, kill!

Only at the end does he realise, as a sane man, that power, revenge and victory are not worth while:

> No, no, no, no! Come let's away to prison . . .
> . . . . and we'll wear out,
> In a wall'd prison, packs and sects of great ones
> That ebb and flow by the moon.

But by the time he makes this discovery it is too late, for his death and Cordelia's are already decided on. That is the story, and, allowing for some clumsiness in the telling, it is a very good story.

But is it not also curiously similar to the history of Tolstoy himself? There is a general resemblance which one can hardly avoid seeing, because the most impressive event in Tolstoy's life, as in Lear's, was a huge and gratuitous act of renunciation. In his old age he renounced his estate, his title and his copyrights, and made an attempt—a sincere attempt, though it was not successful—to escape from his privileged position and live the life of a peasant. But the deeper resemblance lies in the fact that Tolstoy, like Lear, acted on mistaken motives and failed to get the results he had hoped for. According to Tolstoy, the aim of every human being is happiness, and happiness can only be attained by doing the will of God. But doing the will of God means casting off all earthly pleasures and ambitions, and living only for others. Ultimately, therefore, Tolstoy renounced the world under the expectation that this would make him happier. But if there is one thing certain about his later years, it is that he was *not* happy. On the contrary, he was driven almost to the edge of madness by the behaviour of the people about him, who persecuted him precisely *because* of his renunciation. Like Lear, Tolstoy was not humble and not a good judge of character. He was inclined at moments to revert to the attitudes of an aristocrat, in spite of his peasant's blouse, and he even had two children whom he had believed in and who ultimately turned against him—though, of course, in a less sensational manner than Regan and Goneril. His exaggerated revulsion from sexuality was also distinctly similar to Lear's. Tolstoy's remark that marriage is "slavery, satiety, repulsion" and means putting up with the proximity of "ugliness, dirtiness, smell, sores", is matched by Lear's well-known outburst:

> But to the girdle do the gods inherit,
> Beneath is all the fiend's;
> There's hell, there's darkness, there's the sulphurous pit,
> Burning, scalding, stench, consumption, etc etc.

And though Tolstoy could not foresee it when he wrote his essay on Shakespeare, even the ending of his life—the sudden unplanned flight across country, accompanied only by a faithful daughter, the death in a cottage in a strange village—seems to have in it a sort of phantom reminiscence of *Lear*.

—GEORGE ORWELL, "Lear, Tolstoy and the Fool" [1947], *The Collected Essays, Journalism and Letters of George Orwell*, ed. Sonia Orwell and Ian Angus (New York: Harcourt Brace Jovanovich, 1968), Vol. 4, pp. 292–97

D. G. JAMES

Hamlet is young, thoughtful, philosophical, diposed to reflection; Lear is old, unreflective, rash, extrovert. Hamlet is highly sensitive; Lear is crass. Hamlet, one might have expected, had a mind sufficiently trained and philosophical to bear the ills of life; in fact, he was not philosophical enough. But we do not expect, we have no reason to expect, that Lear can withstand the onslaught of suffering; we know that he will be helpless, and he is. Or again, Hamlet reflects much, but hardly knows what to do; Lear knows, or thinks he knows, what to do, and without a moment's reflection. The one yields a tragedy, I will not say, of excessive reflection, but of abundant reflection which has issued in no settled principles of practice or belief; the other gives us a tragedy of unreflective desire, noble and ignoble.

But the difference between the two men is shown also when we consider their stories. Hamlet remains, in spite of much that he does, passive; he is borne along on a stream of events; he does not, eventually, change; and disaster overtakes him. Towards the end of the play, in the scene with Horatio before the duelling, he seems indeed to have come to a calm of mind; but it is only a calm of defence, which helps him to accept what he has not had the strength of mind to prevent. He remains, at bottom, the same all through; there is little development in him; he does not acquire efficacy; he becomes increasingly a 'story' to be told in a 'harsh world'.

But with Lear it is different. His world is harsh enough; but at the end he is not, to himself or anyone else, a sad 'story'. We see Lear at the end with clear eyes; but we are also looking at the dead Cordelia. But Lear has changed much before he comes to this point. He has learnt, if you will, lessons which Hamlet, with all that his philosophy dreamed on, did not learn. Hamlet's very intellectuality keeps him at a certain remove from experience; Lear's thoughtlessness plunges him into it. Hamlet plays, or half-plays, at being mad; and he gets little or nothing out of it. Lear becomes mad in all truth; but he comes out of his madness a changed man. Hamlet will exclaim, in his brilliant way, 'O God, I could be bounded in a nut-shell, and count myself a King of infinite space'; but the time comes when Lear says:

> Come, let's away to prison;
> We two alone will sing like birds i' the cage . . .

Hamlet was talking brilliantly; Lear is saying something which he feels with profound sincerity.

I put the same point in another form. Hamlet's mind is naturally thoughtful, speculative, imaginative. We are constantly made aware of the play of his great mind; the other characters we see for the bigger part as affecting him in the range and subtlety of his emotion and thought. Even Horatio remains a curiously shadowy and undefined figure; he appears comparatively little, does little, speaks little; it is what Hamlet feels about him that is at the centre. The other characters mostly inhabit life at far lower levels; a Laertes, Polonius, Ophelia, Gertrude, are simple people unable to reach up to Hamlet or to begin to understand him. Hamlet is everywhere isolated, alone in his thought; and his world of despair, doubt, speculation, is something of which the others have no sense. His problems, his questions, are his; he is encircled away from the common humanity, even of a Court. He out-tops its knowledge and ascent to him is out of the question; he is a rare and estranged spirit. But Lear is an ordinary enough fellow; he is no intellectual; he is at the level of the other characters in all essentials, if we exclude Cordelia and Edgar; he is in their world. And upon all of them the great problem of life presses; the last and metaphysical question is not only Lear's, with his

> Is there any cause in nature that makes these hard hearts?

It is Kent's with his

> It is the stars,
> The stars above us, govern our conditions . . .;

and Gloucester's, with his

> As flies to wanton boys are we to the gods;
> They kill us for their sport . . .;

and Edgar's, with his

> Think that the clearest gods, who make them honours
> Of men's impossibilities, have preserved thee;

and Albany's

> If that the heavens do not their visible spirits
> Send quickly down to tame these vile offences,
> It will come,
> Humanity must perforce prey on itself
> Like monsters of the deep.

Are there Gods, and are they just? This and other questions had pressed upon Hamlet but upon him only; it presses upon many in *King Lear* whose minds confront the mystery of the world. But again in *Hamlet* we see a mind putting high ethical and metaphysical questions; but *King Lear* is a question, or rather a number of questions; and one of the questions is

> Why should a dog, a horse, a rat, have life
> And thou no breath at all?

The question is asked about Cordelia. It was not asked about Ophelia. Ophelia dies in, so to speak, a not unpleasing poetical description; the impact of her death is softened to us. The recent film of *Hamlet* distressed us, I think, in its delineation of the death of Ophelia; but was it so far, in the falsity we felt in it, from the Queen's speech which describes it in the play? And then, later, Ophelia is the topic of a lot of ranting over her grave. But Cordelia is carried on, dead, warm from her hanging; there is here no fine gauze of poetry to beautify her in her death. 'Thou art the thing itself.'

—D. G. JAMES, "Poetic Experiment," *A Dream of Learning: An Essay on*
The Advancement of Learning, Hamlet *and* King Lear (Oxford:
Clarendon Press, 1951), pp. 71–74

HONOR MATTHEWS

King Lear, in which Shakespeare takes up and transcends the various images of justice, mercy and false-seeming which he had previously created, and fuses them into a whole of new and terrible beauty, has two early precursors of considerable interest. *Titus Andronicus*, offers an unusually vivid example of the long incubation which a thought may undergo in a poet's mind. Titus, like Lear, is an old man driven mad by the loss of his all, yet retaining in madness a clear knowledge of his own wrongs and of their perpetrators. Like Lear he has begun his own undoing by driving from him his child, Mutius, whom he unjustly kills and by trusting in the specious words of his enemies to whom he surrenders the realm of which he could have been chosen emperor. Having given them everything he is driven to madness, finally dying himself and killing the beautiful and virtuous daughter whom he loves.

Lastly, as Lear does, Titus seeks from heaven the justice denied him on earth. In a grotesque but tragic scene he addresses petitions to the gods, sending to Pluto by messenger and dispatching the other petitions by shooting them skyward on arrows. The first message is to Pluto.

Tell him, it is for justice and for aid,
And that it comes from old Andronicus.   (IV, iii, 15–16)

Publius brings answer:

                    Pluto sends you word,
If you will have Revenge from hell, you shall:
Marry, for Justice, she is so employ'd,
He thinks, with Jove in heaven, or somewhere else,
So that perforce you must needs stay a time.   (IV, iii, 37–41)

But Titus holds to his faith in heaven's justice.

And, sith there's no justice in earth nor hell,
We will solicit heaven and move the gods
To send down Justice for to wreak our wrongs.   (IV, iii, 49–51)

The arrows are sent off by his old brother, a prototype of Kent, and three loyal
friends who humour him in his madness, as Lear is humoured by Edgar and the fool.
These messages finally reach the ears of the emperor. Saturninus, unlike the evil
characters in *King Lear*, still thinks it worth while to use the 'value' words of the old
order to cloak his unscrupulous pursuit of his private ends. He protests that:

                    nought hath pass'd,
But even with law, against the wilful sons
Of old Andronicus....
What's this but libelling against the senate,
And blazoning our injustice every where?
A goodly humour, is it not, my lords?
As who would say, in Rome no justice were.   (IV, iv, 7–20)

He is, however, extraordinarily like Goneril and Regan in the down-to-earth sweet
reasonableness of his most callous statements:

                    And what an if
His sorrows have so overwhelm'd his wits,
Shall we be thus afflicted in his wreaks,
His fits, his frenzy, and his bitterness?
And now he writes to heaven for his redress:...
Sweet scrolls to fly about the streets of Rome!   (IV, iv, 9–15)

His last line is as practical and sensible as the remarks exchanged by Lear's daughters. The final parallel to 'King Lear' is the rescue of the empire, but not of Titus and
Lavinia who are both dead before the victory is assured, by an invading army led
by the old man's youngest child.

It is interesting, but not now surprising, to find a whole phrase recurring to
Shakespeare when he wrote the later play:

I am not mad; I know thee well enough;   (*Titus Andronicus*, V, i, 21) says Titus, during his terrible conversation with Tamora disguised as Revenge, and later he confesses:

> we worldly men
> Have miserable, mad, mistaking eyes.   (V, ii, 65–6)

The eye-imagery which was later to determine the course of the sub-plot in *King Lear* has here appeared side by side with the theme of justice which is thus related to the truth or falsehood of appearances in Shakespeare's earliest tragedy.

Henry VI is also a significant forerunner of King Lear, for he is a king who signally fails to fulfil his obligations, and who divides his authority among those to whom it does not belong and who are incapable of exercising it properly. Lear demanded the pomp and circumstance and personal freedom which are the concomitants of royalty, but no man can 'retain the name, and all the additions to a king' by giving away the power, along with the responsibilities of kingship, and his elementary error is obvious to the audience as well as to the Fool:

> ...I can tell why a snail has a house.... Why, to put his head in; not to give it away to his daughters, and leave his horns without a case.
> (*King Lear*, I, v, 30–3)

Henry's final error is—like Lear's first—the division of his kingdom between two 'younger strengths'. A refusal to exercise his proper power has been Henry's fault from the beginning of his reign, and the moment when Warwick and Clarence kneel before him, as Albany and Cornwall kneel before Lear, makes this statement in its most dramatically powerful form.

> Warwick and Clarence, give me both your hands:
> Now join your hands, and with your hands your hearts,
> That no dissension hinder government:
> I make you both protectors of this land,
> While I myself will lead a private life
> And in devotion spend my latter days,
> To sin's rebuke and my Creator's praise.   (3 *Henry VI*, IV, vi, 38–44)

Not only does he divide his kingdom into two instead of ruling it himself, but he bases his hopes of peace on misapprehensions very similar to Lear's.

> I have not stopp'd mine ears to their demands,
> Nor posted off their suits with slow delays;
> My pity hath been balm to heal their wounds,
> My mildness hath allay'd their swelling griefs,
> My mercy dried their water-flowing tears; ...
> Then why should they love Edward more than me?
> No, Exeter, these graces challenge grace.   (IV, viii, 39–48)

After his final defeat Henry's words to the Lieutenant of the Tower who has begged his pardon are also paralleled in *King Lear:*

For what, lieutenant? For well using me?
Nay, be thou sure I'll well requite thy kindness,
For that it made my imprisonment a pleasure;
Ay, such a pleasure as incaged birds
Conceive when after many moody thoughts
At last by notes of household harmony
They quite forget their loss of liberty. (IV, vi, 9–15)

Lastly, each of these royal victims is granted an extraordinary access of bodily vigour just before death; but while Henry uses this strength in the obvious way, to defy his enemy, Lear, although he kills the slave that was hanging Cordelia, yet uses his failing powers to carry in his arms the child he has himself sacrificed and, like an Abraham for whom there is no ram allowed in the thickets, to lay her on the ground and mourn for her, before he dies in the spiritual insight that her life and death have brought him.

—HONOR MATTHEWS, "Pardon and Punishment," *Character and Symbol in Shakespeare's Plays* (Cambridge: Cambridge University Press, 1962), pp. 139–42

WILLIAM R. ELTON

To sum up Lear's development is to rehearse the development of the play, its gigantic inversions and its complexities. From an opening scene of maximal religious confidence of a heathen sort, we move toward a testing of that confidence—Lear's love test of the opening scene begins to involve an extrafamilial, political, and cosmic love test, one which encompasses the heavens themselves (whom also he had "Made" his "guardians," as he accuses his daughters, II.iv, 253; cf. III.ii.21–24). Human love betrayed reaches into divine love betrayed; thus the question of providence obtrudes, analogically, into the question of a daughter's affection.

Lear's polytheism impinges on an animism whose deities are extensions of nature, as, for example, the sun-god, Apollo; hence, the king's devout polytheism, adoring the nature goddess, could yet embrace what would seem, to a Renaissance Christian, symptoms of naturalism and therefore skepticism. Living before the Christian revelation, as well as outside it, Lear could not know or accept the basic paradox of Creation, that God created the world out of nothing. Thus Shakespeare's ascription to him, expositionally twice-mentioned, that nothing could come of nothing, could signify, ambiguously, that Lear was a pagan, although a skeptic from a Christian standpoint; and that, although a good pagan, his expression of his belief in such terms might serve as a foreshadowing of disbelief to come.

In Acts II and III Lear's pagan devotion begins to undergo its trial, commencing that tension between belief and fear not to believe that surcharges his already strained mind. Again, the failure in humanity parallels the failure in the heavens; the storm occurs on all levels at once, cosmic, familial, and personal. And Lear's questioning of man's state above the animals is a corollary of his questioning of divine providence and justice above man. Once more, from the Christian view of Shakespeare's audience such denial of man's unique place was characteristic of skepticism; and from a pagan view Lear's doubtful defiance of the heavens is also a manifestation of a growing skepticism. The latter becomes even clearer when at one point the king dares, in his madness, to question the divine source of thunder, which to Christians, and to many pagans, was ever the dread voice of the heavens. When Lear exclaims at the midpoint of the play, "I am a man / More sinn'd against than sinning" (III.ii.59–60), we know we have proceeded to a point where a previous confidence in divine and poetic justice has become, in his own person, a bewildered sense of injustice. Ambivalence has overtaken faith.

The storm is the test of the gods. Divine justice above, Lear hopes, will be shown by human justice and charity below (III.iv.34–36); their mutual dependence is the reason for the paramount significance of the religious meaning of this play. In Act IV the maddened Lear has given up his confidence in the sense of the thunder: "when the thunder would not peace at my bidding," and this cosmic debacle involves a human one, as he continues, "there I found 'em, there I smelt 'em out" (IV.vi.103–105). As Lear hints at natural causation for the traditional voice of the gods, thunder, so he hints at natural causation for a traditional divine malady in humans, "hard hearts" (III.vi.77–79); Lear implies skepticism on the macrocosmic and microcosmic levels, operating here, as elsewhere, analogically, in thrusts which could have been evident to Shakespeare's audience but which may be lost on our own. Indeed, the measure of religious change between Shakespeare's time and the present is perhaps a measure of the incomprehensibility to modern spectators of his most cosmic tragedy.

By the end of Act IV Lear's madness has run its course, as have also the tension and breakdown caused by the failure of belief on all levels; and he is ready for "belief" of some kind, though not, of course, for anything resembling his previous tenets. Like Gloucester's, this belief has here a syncretic Christian-Stoic coloring, though there is no reason that we should not reverse the usual order and say it is Stoic-Christian, for the pagan has as great a claim to the syncretism as the Christian element. Lear's new belief is negative and exclusive, one of abnegation, *contemptus mundi*, and forfeit; it is not simply one of "salvation," which recent commentators have sought to fasten on him. It is, ironically, one whose fixity will, Lear vainly hopes, oppose all mutability, although it is immediately to be undermined. Lear's newfound "faith" is pathetically and suddenly withdrawn from him by the murder of Cordelia.

His laments against divine providence, his insistent "why?", his sense of man's reduced place in the scheme of things beneath the lowly animals, his offering of violence to "heaven's vault," are in large part motivated by an inconsolable view that death, excluding resurrection, ends all. This view, which is the premise of the play, implicit in its beginnings and never contradicted, is by definition a pagan, not a Christian, attitude to immortality. It thus explains the funereal chorus at the end of the play, which, syncretically, also invokes the Last Judgment (V.iii.263–264), while at the same time it heathenishly denies that any immortality is possible; here syncretism intensifies despair, implying the disparity between pagan hopelessness and Christian possibility. The pagan attitude also disposes of modern critical contentions that Lear is "saved" or that salvation operates in the denouement. For we have, among others, the evidence of a Renaissance English bishop that Lear's attitude was explicitly and even verbally the pagan attitude toward death, with the grief consequent upon an awareness that death ends all.

Lear's last speeches thus touch on the following ideas: immortality (V.iii.270, 307); providence, general or particular (V.iii.306–307); and man's special status above the beasts. In earlier analyses I have indicated similar attitudes, questionable from the point of view of Christian orthodoxy. These deviations may, indeed, suggest that Shakespeare might have conceived Lear's views partially in relation to Renaissance outward skepticism, toward which his disabused polytheism could credibly have led him. Un-Joblike, certainly un-Christlike, the king, "Unhousel'd, disappointed, unaneled," goes to a reward the premises for whose existence he has just vehemently questioned; in his case, rather than an angelic chant in Paradisum or a Faustian exit with devils, the rest is a perplexing silence.

Finally, among other aims, this discussion has tried to show that the obstacles to an orthodox theological reading of King Lear, in which the protagonist moves from sin and suffering to redemption, are more formidable than has generally been realized. The so-called stumbling block, to the Shakespearean neo-Christianizers, of Lear's last appearance is, it may now be evident, scarcely a hapax legomenon but a carefully anticipated culmination of Lear's previously expressed tendencies.

—WILLIAM R. ELTON, "Deus Absconditus: Lear," King Lear and the Gods
(San Marino, CA: Huntington Library, 1966), pp. 260–63

EDWARD BOND

I want to say something brief about the play. Lear did not have to destroy his daughters' innocence, he does so only because he doesn't understand his situation. When he does understand he leaves Thomas and Susan unharmed. But I think he had to destroy the innocent boy. Some things were lost to us long ago as a species, but we all seem to have to live through part of the act of losing them. We have to learn to do this without guilt or rancour or callousness—or socialized morality. So Lear's ghost isn't one of the angry ghosts from Early Morning, but something different.

Apart from the ten or so main characters of the play there are about seventy other speaking parts. In a sense these are one role showing the character of a society.

Act One shows a world dominated by myth. Act Two shows the clash between myth and reality, between superstitious men and the autonomous world. Act Three shows a resolution of this, in the world we prove real by dying in it.

—EDWARD BOND, "Author's Preface" to Lear (London: Methuen, 1972),
pp. xiii–xiv

JAMES P. DRISCOLL

Lear's structured progress through three archetypal stages toward the final Christ symbol constitutes a quest for wholeness involving great suffering. C. G. Jung, whose later work was deeply preoccupied with the crucial role suffering and evil play in that task and goal he called individuation, comments on this archetypal pattern:

> The goal of psychological, as of biological development is self-realization, or individuation. But since man knows himself only as ego, and the self, as a totality, is indescribable and indistinguishable from a God-image, self-realization—to put it in religious or metaphysical terms—amounts to God's incarnation. That is already expressed in the fact that Christ is the son of God. And because individuation is an heroic and often tragic task, the most difficult of all, it involves suffering, a passion of the ego. . . . Through the Christ symbol, a man can get to know the real meaning of his suffering; he is on the way to wholeness.

Each stage in *King Lear*'s variation on the myth of the emergence of wholeness, or divine incarnation, compensates or enlarges the stages that preceded it. The lowest or initial stage is that of the wrathful, unconscious, and contradictory animal nature Yahweh exhibits—the early Lear. The sea monster emblematizes Yahweh's terrible *anima*—Goneril. At the next stage stands Job, the man who must suffer Yahweh's injustices. Lear's mortification, torment, madness, and the journey to the unconscious it represents, together with his temporary realization of expanded consciousness in humility and patience when he reunites with Cordelia, dramatize this stage. With Cordelia's violent death Lear enters the third stage, where he fully grasps the reality of evil and suffering by becoming a defiant Promethean figure. The highest or goal stage is that of fulfillment, wholeness, or enlightenment and, as the later Jung would say, is identified with Christ as alchemical symbol. Cordelia stands at this stage.

Yahweh's paradoxical nature—his drive for unbridled power and need for love and truth, embodied in the two hostile brothers Christ and Satan—finds parallels in Lear and his relationships with Cordelia and Goneril. In *Answer to Job* Jung's discussions of this complex and bewildering archetypal symbol often cast illumination on the early Lear and his subsequent development:

> [Here was] . . . a contradictory picture of Yahweh—the picture of a God who knew no moderation in his emotions and suffered precisely from this lack of moderation. He admitted that he was eaten up with jealousy and that this knowledge was painful to him. Insight existed along with obtuseness, loving-kindness along with cruelty, creative power along with destructiveness. Everything was there and none of these qualities was an obstacle to the other. . . . A condition of this sort can only be described as amoral.

> The character thus revealed fits a personality who can only convince

himself that he exists through his relation to an object. Such dependence on the object is absolute when the subject is totally lacking in self-reflection and therefore has no insight into himself. It is as if he existed only by reason of the fact that he has an object which assures him that he is really there.

Yahweh must become man precisely because he has done man wrong. He, the guardian of justice, knows that every wrong must be expiated, and Wisdom knows that moral law is above even him. Because his creature has surpassed him he must regenerate himself.

Lear's real identity is not the same as the identity orthodox theology attributes to the Yahweh of Biblical myth (*creatio ex nihilo* is decidedly not among Lear's powers), but the real identity of the early Lear does resemble that which Jung discerns behind Yahweh enough to justify the conclusion that they both manifest the same archetype. This Lear, like Jung's Yahweh, knows no moderation, has no insight into himself, is eaten up with rage and jealousy, and is a contradictory being in whom cruelty and destructiveness exist beside loving-kindness—he contains both Cordelia and Goneril as Yahweh contains Christ and Satan. Since he totally lacks self-reflection, his sense of existing, or conscious identity, depends on recognition of his power by others—the daughters, Kent, Burgundy—and on their repeated assurance that he is everything. Belief in personal all-sufficiency provides a rationale for not examining either his real identity or the injustices he commits and allows. The injustice against Cordelia is, like the injustice Yahweh inflicts upon Job, a wrong which must be expiated. In order for Lear, the guardian of justice, to regenerate himself, he must experience as an object an arbitrary power like that of his own worst self, a power and a self he meets in Goneril.

Ordinarily, the transition from one archetypal stage to its successor comes gradually and ineluctably, like the movement from one Yeatsian gyre to another, and each stage lives in its predecessor and emerges while the other wanes to nothing. In *King Lear* we see the Job archetype gradually emerge from the Yahweh as Lear moves toward madness, until the Job archetype becomes dominant at the reunion with Cordelia. Jung observes that Yahweh's unconsciousness renders him *non compos mentis:* Kent, censuring his conduct toward Cordelia, notes the same phenomenon incipient in Lear. Lear undergoes actual madness after the evil daughters shatter his conscious identity as a godlike king and reduce him to the social nothingness of a bare, forked animal. In madness he comes to understand both the insanity behind arbitrary power and human life's tragic dimension. Likewise, after Yahweh assumes the identity of suffering man, i.e., Christ, he appears to achieve in his death cry "My God, my God, why hast thou forsaken me?" sensitivity to the tragic implications of the wrong he imposed on Job. Yahweh-Christ reaches fullest divinity at the moment he feels Job's or mortals' deepest anguish. Before his humiliation and subsequent madness, Lear, as we have seen, embodies numerous characteristics which Jung in *Answer to Job* attributes to the archetypal figure Yahweh. To assert this is not, of course, to contend that either Shakespeare or his audience would have consciously made such an association. However, as John

Holloway observes, they would have been conscious of important similarities between the Lear who has lost everything and the Biblical Job and hence alive to the concern with the problems of evil and divine justice which *King Lear* shares with the Book of Job. Shakespeare's treatment of these problems would have been illuminated no less by the differences that distinguish Lear from Job than by their similarities. Both Job and Lear suffer enormously, and both find the governing forces of the universe inexplicable; but the fact that Lear lacks Job's steadfast faith, cannot marshal patience, and never enjoys restoration to his original social identity as a powerful man suggests that *King Lear* possesses the darker theological and philosophic outlook.

The Promethean archetype dominates the final stage of Lear's quest for consciousness and of his confrontation with injustice, death, evil, and God. The manifestation the Promethean archetype takes in *King Lear* bears some important similarities to its form in Greek heroic myth. And Lear's cry, "O Regan, she hath tied / Sharp-tooth'd unkindness, like a vulture here" (II.iv.136–37), may indicate that Shakespeare used Promethean analogy deliberately. While transiting from the Yahweh to the Job archetype, Lear displays something like a Promethean stance both in denouncing the social and metaphysical evils that cause affliction and in compassion for fellow sufferers. Prometheus' name means "forethought," and he has often symbolized consciousness. Lear strives for heightened consciousness and aspires for Promethean dignity in suffering. The Lear of the last scene exhibits Prometheus' insight into cosmic justice, his sense of divine betrayal, and his defiant assertion of the dignity of human life. But the Promethean archetype derives its peculiar significance and impact from the largely unconscious way Shakespeare relates it to the Yahweh, Job, and Christ archetypes to form an overall vision of God that compensates for traditional theology's more consoling answers to the problems of enlightenment and evil. Orthodox Christian theology's characteristic emphasis on the Job stage (and the accompanying reduction of evil to *privatio boni*) inhibited movement beyond it to the unflinching recognition of evil and unrestrained protest of true Promethean consciousness. In *King Lear* evil gains recognition as a far more powerful and fundamental force than *privatio boni*, which, Jung suggests, denies dignity to tragic passion by rendering it and the evils that cause it ultimately unreal. The Promethean stage is compensatory to and higher than the Job stage because it entails full recognition for the independence of evil which allows greater dignity and truer heroism to man's struggle for wholeness. But the enhanced dignity and heroism that come to those who defiantly champion good against radical evil bring ever more intensified anguish. Lear dies the apotheosis of suffering; had he attained wholeness, he would have become, like Cordelia, fully aware of evil and the pervasive suffering it generates without agonized awareness possessing him as it does those caught in the Promethean stage.

Cordelia, like Lear, clearly has an archetypal as well as a realistic dimension. She symbolizes what Jung believed Christ represented to Renaissance Hermetic and alchemical speculators, the archetype of psychic wholeness; and Lear's quest for Cordelia's love, like the quest for those alchemical Christ symbols, the philosopher's stone and the Holy Grail, constitutes a search for wholeness.

Identification of Christ with the archetype of wholeness forms a cardinal principle in Jung's psychology of religion. The orthodox Christ, Jung maintains, excludes the dark Luciferian side of things; but the alchemical Christ, which is conceived loosely enough to accommodate compensatory light and dark psychic elements, more closely approximates the all-encompassing quality the paramount archetype possesses. To say that Cordelia represents the archetype of wholeness is to contend neither that she coincides with all Jung's conceptions about this archetype nor that she exactly resembles the orthodox Christ: an artist always has individualized perceptions of archetypes. The differences between Cordelia and traditional Christian conceptions of Christ are significant. While both embody truth and love, or *sophia* and *caritas*, these two complementary values are balanced in Cordelia, but in Christ love usually predominates. Thus, though Cordelia herself does not manifest human nature's darkest side, her uncompromisable truth will not permit denial of any evil, so that the *King Lear* myth fully recognizes the independent reality and interrelatedness of human and metaphysical evil, a recognition Jung deems either absent or muted in Christian theology with its doctrine of evil as *privatio boni*. A correlative difference involves the question of redemption. Jung maintains that, although Christ is explicitly a redemptive figure, Christianity's denial of radical evil makes true redemption impossible because no one can be redeemed where no one is willing to understand what man is to be redeemed from. Cordelia, on the other hand, is not explicitly a redemptive figure, and the presence of radical evil in *King Lear* makes it impossible for man to redeem all the sorrows he has ever felt; nonetheless, her truth, which recognizes evil, makes redemption from inauthenticity possible.

Lear's love test establishes the parallel between Cordelia and Christ. Christ on trial before Pilate defines his identity as he declares the purpose of his being; "To this end I was born, and for this cause came I into the world, that I should bear witness to the truth" (John 18:37). When Lear puts Cordelia's love on trial, she also bears witness to the truth. In so doing she, like Christ, demonstrates the highest love. The imagery and ending of *King Lear* furnish keys to the crucial differences that separate Cordelia and Christ. Caroline Spurgeon has pointed out that the play is dominated by a single, overpowering, continuous image: "a human body in anguished movement, tugged, wrenched, beaten, pierced, stung, scourged, dislocated, flayed, gashed, scalded, tortured and finally broken on the rack." Miss Spurgeon does not draw this inference; yet her findings seem to support the conclusion that *King Lear* abounds with crucifixion imagery. Although Cordelia is hanged, none of the play's imagery encourages us, even indirectly, to envision her suffering overwhelming physical or psychological pain. It is Lear who has been stretched out on the rack of this tough world, has been spoiled by crosses, and has born the most. If anyone is crucified, surely it is he. The other striking difference between Christ and Cordelia is that her story offers no happy ending in a resurrection. The most terrifying fact the play presents lies in the irrevocable finality her death holds, and Lear's response to it forms the most painful event in all Shakespeare.

There is a hidden philosophy behind the archetypal patterns, stages and symbols in *King Lear,* and it comprises an unflinching revelation of existential truths about man's condition and identity and about the gods. It suggests every man's highest possibility, ideal identity, or wholeness, in the figure of Cordelia. With both Lear and Cordelia, identity relates to conceptions about divinity. Jung notes the connection between the God-image and the primal source of man's identity, the self:

> It is the same problem as in Job. As the highest and supreme dominant in the psychic hierarchy, the God-image is immediately related to, or identical with, the self, and everything that happens to the God-image has an effect on the latter.

The conscious identity Lear exhibits, as William R. Elton has shown, directly relates to his beliefs about the gods. Furthermore, through the operation of those archetypes which inform his character, his real identity represents symbolically western man's images of God, and in many instances his development recapitulates the development these images have undergone. The hidden philosophy behind the vision of *King Lear* speaks through archetype and symbol to both the conscious and the unconscious mind. Critical interpretation which outlines the play's basic archetypal patterns, stages, and symbols can throw its philosophy into bolder relief and show more clearly the origins and significance of its vision.

Archetypal psychology offers new ways to explore the dark, hidden regions of the play's philosophic and theological outlook by giving a fuller picture of Lear (and Cordelia) than can be furnished by traditional approaches which limit critical investigation to the supposed conscious intentions and attitudes of the author and his original audience. Assuming the activation of archetypes within the unconscious to be an energy underlying artistic creation, an assumption that seems to hold particular validity in works like *King Lear*, where the mythic import and folkloric quality are indisputable, we can see Lear as a figure initially like Yahweh who, forced to experience the suffering humanity of a Job, at last turns with Promethean defiance to cry for justice from a universe whose government seems no less arbitrary than his own will has been. If we look from a slightly different perspective, we can perceive *King Lear* as a vision of Yahweh's passion and crucifixion.

The identification of Yahweh, Job, and Prometheus with three formative stages in the process of divine incarnation, and Christ with its final goal, is original to my reading of *King Lear*. However, Jung's work with alchemical literature treating myths about kings and his *Answer to Job* and *Aion* often closely parallel my position. In the alchemical literature he contends that because the king represents an exalted personality, he becomes the carrier of myth—statements from the collective unconscious—and represents the self and God. Like every archetype, Jung maintains, the king is no static image: "... he signifies a dynamic process whereby the human carrier of the mystery is included in the mysterious drama of God's incarnation" (p. 265). Jung gives a detailed analysis of Sir George Ripley's (1415–90) *Cantilena*, a verse rendering of alchemical myths about the regeneration of the aged king (God) which shares numerous archetypal elements with *King Lear*. Those who like to hunt allusions will be struck by Ripley's association of his decrepit king with the "Ancient of Days" (from Daniel 7:9) whose throne is mounted on "wheels of burning fire" (pp. 279–81). Shakespeare's imagination may have re-turned to the same Biblical image when he made the aged Lear place himself on a figurative "wheel of fire". Lear differs from the "Ancient of Days," the king in Ripley, and similar accounts in that Lear's fiery wheel symbolizes torture, not triumph, and his renewal proves only a teasing respite before an agonized death. While the ending of *King Lear* is darker than those of its alchemical analogues, the preceding events—the dissolution of Lear's pride and identity in madness and the rebirth of a sane and humble Lear—illustrate the alchemical pattern of dissolution and rebirth into a purified state. The alchemical renewal, Jung points out, comes after the king descends into inner darkness, where he is reminded about his blood relationship to the evil principle (Goneril in Lear's case—see II.iv.224–29). Thus, *King Lear*, to probe the Godhead, employs a complex imaginative mode which usually deepens realism with archetypal symbolism and sometimes becomes distinctively archetypal.

—JAMES P. DRISCOLL, "The Vision of *King Lear,*" *Shakespeare Studies* 10
(1977): 159–66

HOWARD FELPERIN

Th(e) breakdown of the morality forms by which the social order and the individual mind maintain their stability conditions not only Lear's madness in particular but Shakespearean madness in general. For the roles and forms of morality convention, as we have repeatedly seen, are employed by Shakespeare's characters as a pro-tection against the confusion of raw experience, a screen that selectively permits only that which can be made sense of within a predetermined order to reach the perceiving mind. But it is an inflexible screen, whose very rigidity renders it break-able, exposing the self to that which it can no longer process. It is only Shakespeare's protagonists—Hamlet, Othello, Lear, and Lady Macbeth—as characters whose role-playing is precarious and whose naked humanity is therefore most vulnerable, who are capable of true madness. Their foils are immune to madness, precisely because they are too thoroughly engrossed in their protective roles for an under-lying self ever to be exposed in its naked frailty. Lear in his madness thus stands in contrast to Gloucester, who naively wishes he could go mad like Lear, mistaking madness for a protection against pain when it is in fact an exposure to it:

> The King is mad: how stiff is my vile sense,
> That I stand up, and have ingenious feeling
> Of my huge sorrows! Better I were distract:
> So should my thoughts be severed from my griefs,
> And woes by wrong imaginations lose
> The knowledge of themselves. (IV.vi.284–289)

Like his nakedness—to which it is the psychological correlative—Lear's madness also stands in contrast to Edgar's stagy and conventional madtalk of "sin" and "foul fiends." Edgar's "madness," as a role based upon a wholly traditional and external view of madness as demonic possession, is actually the antithesis of the true madness of Lear, since the latter arises from the breakdown of roles whereas the former is itself a role and therefore a protection against a maddening overperception. Like Edgar's mock-beggary, also deriving from a long tradition of moral iconography, his mock-madness is thus a shadow or parody of "the thing itself." It has the status of a sign emptied of its significance and divorced from the realities of nakedness and madness to which it refers, the absent referent in both cases being supplied by Lear. Within the universe of Shakespearean tragedy, madness is thus the opposite pole to morality, a vision of undifferentiated anarchy as opposed to one of a wholly mapped-out order.

The temptation at this point is to grant this vision of madness and absurdity a privileged status and equate it with the meaning of the play. But this tendency is only the modernist counterpart of the archaeological tendency to do the same with the earlier vision of morality, and is no more valid. Because Lear's vision of madness is an inversion of his vision of morality, it remains dependent on it, derives its terms from it, and is capable of being turned back into it. This is exactly what happens, for neither morality nor madness constitutes a resting-point for Lear or Shakespeare, and both are left behind on the way to a truer, more austere mimesis. The fact is that Lear is able to maintain neither the complacent vision he shared with his society at the beginning nor the painful counter-vision he comes to in his alienation, though he tries desperately to maintain each in turn. For when he awakens from his ordeal in the presence of Cordelia, he would seem to have renounced his restless probing for a demystified and naturalistic explanation of his world. Cordelia seems to him "a soul in bliss," his madness the infernal or purgatorial punishment of "a wheel of fire," and his recovery nothing less than a resurrection wrought by this "spirit" to whom he now kneels and prays for benediction. Not only has Lear renounced his maddening effort to explain the world, to find out its true causes, he has renounced the world itself. In a spirit of *contemptus mundi,* he resigns all interest in the vindication he had formerly tried to call down on his persecutors, leaving them to "The good years" (V.iii.24) of plague and pestilence to be devoured in due course. He welcomes his life with Cordelia in prison with a religious joy, as if it were a posthumous or monastic existence removed from the mutability of earthly life. Indeed, Lear has awakened to find himself, like several converted morality protagonists before him, clothed in the fresh garments traditionally emblematic of an inner and spiritual reaccommodation. Nowhere in the play is the return to an older morality vision so pure and complete, so strenuously and extravagantly reenacted— for we are still in the realm of histrionic recreation—as it is by Lear himself at the start of the final act. The play has all but reunited with its prototype, the wheel of interpretation come full circle.

If *King Lear* had ended here, we should still have had to say that Shakespeare has altered his sources significantly and, in so doing, achieved a representation of human depth and complexity quite beyond them and very much of the order of displaced Christian vision ascribed to the play by Bradley and Mack. But the final stage in the process of mimetic realization toward which the play moves consists in a still more radical putting into question of all prior visions—the vision of morality taken over from its sources and the counter-vision of madness introduced by Shakespeare alike—and that process has at this point only begun. For when Lear reenters shortly afterward with Cordelia in his arms, he no longer speaks in the recovered language of morality but in his early language of madness: "Howl, howl, howl, howl . . . / I know when one is dead and when one lives; / She's dead as earth" (V.iii.259–263). Yet by the end of this speech, he is calling for a looking-glass in the hope of life, which he then discovers in the very terms of Christian mystery: "This feather stirs; she lives. If it be so, / It is a chance which does redeem all sorrows / That ever I have felt" (V.iii.267–269). Again, the play might well have ended here on this act of recuperation, however tentative, of the older vision. But it does not: "A plague upon you, murderers, traitors all! / I might have saved her. . . ." Or it could have ended soon afterward with Albany's assertion, however muted, of a restored justice of rewards and punishments. But it does not:

> And my poor fool is hanged: no, no, no life?
> Why should a dog, a horse, a rat have life,
> And thou no breath at all? Thou'lt come no more,
> Never, never, never, never, never.
> Pray you, undo this button. Thank you, sir.   (V.iii.307–311)

Lear's fluctuation between the visions of morality and madness, meaning and absurdity, accommodation and disaccommodation becomes dizzying in its intensity. But still it seems to go on: "Do you see this? Look on her. Look, her lips, / Look there, look there." These parting lines might well be interpreted as another and final access of faith or delusion, yet they are themselves remarkably free of the mythologizations of either morality or madness, which have been only preludes to this moment and are now left behind. Lear's language and gesture now proceed not out of a convention of vision but out of a depth and fullness of feeling that is unquestionably "there" but unfathomable in its inwardness. His last lines merely point to a form that has also been "there" all along, though repeatedly misconstrued and overlooked, with no longer any attempt to define it. In the end, the play renounces its own mediations of morality and madness alike and redirects our attention to an undetermined reality that exists prior to and remains unavailable to both.

In the play that has come to be regarded as the definitive achievement of Shakespearean tragedy, Shakespeare has certainly not made things easy for us. For he leaves us in the end with not a choice of *either* morality and meaning *or* madness and absurdity, but more like an ultimatum of *neither* morality and meaning *nor* madness and absurdity, an ultimatum that becomes inescapable as a result of Lear's own strenuous and futile effort to remain within the realm of choice. Lear enacts in advance our own dilemma as interpreters, alternating between antithetical visions of experience, only to abandon both in favor of a pure and simple pointing to the thing itself. Interpreters of the play, like Albany, Kent, and Edgar within it, have been understandably reluctant to follow him into this state of aporia, of being completely at a loss, so peremptory is the human need to make sense of things, to find unity, coherence, resolution in the world of the text and the text of the world. Yet the aporia toward which not only *Lear*, but Shakespeare's other great tragedies, move represents the very negation of the possibility of unity, coherence, and resolution, of the accommodation that all our systems of explanation provide, be they pious or modernist, consoling or painful, older or newer. In his dizzying fluctuation between contradictory meanings, Lear reenacts the intense shifting between de-mystification and remystification of the self we saw in Othello's closing speech, which also ends with an act of pointing. We saw a similar movement in Hamlet's division between a last-gasp impulse to shape and tell his story—"O, I could tell you!"—and his equal and opposite impulse to repudiate self-mythologization alto-gether and return his play to the status of the most inexplicable dumb-show of all—"The rest is silence." Yet this very process of casting off inherited forms and imposed meanings to point to the thing itself only invites their reimposition. Like Horatio and Fortinbras, Cassio and Lodovico, Edgar and Albany, we feel we still can and must report Hamlet's story to the world and tell Othello and Lear who they are, even though they themselves, possessed of larger, tougher, and finer minds than we, have anticipated our attempt and thrown up their hands. The characters we *can* denote truly—Laertes, Cassio, Gloucester—do not ask to be told who they are, for such characters are content to remain within the defining forms that tradition provides and that society, with the wisdom of self-preservation, maintains as "true." Unlike his interpreters and his own choric commentators, however, Shakespeare never succumbs to the rhetorical pressure of the traditional forms he employs, to their built-in claim to have made sense of the world, but keeps them always in brackets and puts them ultimately into question. The Shakespearean text remains a step ahead of its critics, even at the very moment we think we have caught up with it.

—HOWARD FELPERIN, "Plays within Plays: *Othello, King Lear, Antony and Cleopatra,*" *Shakespearean Representation: Mimesis and Modernity in Elizabethan Tragedy* (Princeton: Princeton University Press, 1977), pp. 100–106

BENEDICT NIGHTINGALE

Shakespeare's *King Lear* is a play Bond enormously admires, but one he thinks crucially flawed. In particular, he dislikes its stoicism. 'To endure till in time the world will be made right' is, he says, a dangerous moral, especially for a world whose time may be running out. Indeed, the play is a little comfortable: 'You don't have to question yourself or change your society'. His job, therefore, was to rewrite it 'for ourselves, for our own society, for our time, for our problems'.

The execution turned out to be as bold as the intention. We are shown a semi-mythic, semi-modern Britain ruled by Lear, a paternalist tyrant using slave labour to build a great wall which will keep his enemies out and guarantee eventual 'peace' and 'freedom' inside. His daughters, Bodice and Fontanelle, at first sound sensible, like their prototypes, Goneril and Regan. They will marry Lear's hereditary

enemies, the Dukes of Cornwall and North, and raze the wall. Before long, however, they have overthrown their father and instituted a régime even more vicious
than his. In time, they too are overthrown, by a revolutionary army led by one
Cordelia, whose husband has been murdered for harbouring the fugitive Lear. But
this, it appears, is only to substitute Stalinism for arbitrary Tsarism. Means are
subordinated to ends; 'political officers' interrogate the prisoners of the old régime,
and 'undesirables' are shot; Fontanelle and Bodice are killed without trial; a petty
swindler is hanged because 'certain economic offences have been made capital with
retrospective effect' and he is a 'social liability'; and people are once again press-
ganged to build the selfsame wall. Many of the old atrocities are perpetrated, but
this time more calculatedly and coldly. Lear himself is blinded in an attempt to make
him politically ineffective, with what the horribly considerate doctor performing the
operation calls 'not an instrument of torture, but a scientific device'. In 1971, when
the play was first performed, Bond manifestly took a more sceptical view of violent
revolution than now and, as we'll see, tended to regard the winning of hearts and
minds as the prime way of achieving social change.

Shakespeare's Lear makes a spiritual journey, Bond's a more political one. In
defeat, he's at first maddish, self-pitying, vindictive: he has been 'too trusting, too
lenient'. But when he is captured by his daughters' soldiers, he shows a genuine
altruism by trying, unsuccessfully, to protect those who have protected him. In
captivity he begins to elaborate what's to become the play's central metaphor, that
of an animal in a cage, clawing to escape. Like Shakespeare's Lear, he achieves sanity
in apparent madness, and, like Gloucester, he sees clearly only when he is blind. He
denounces evil, especially that done in the name of order, justice and good. He
learns compassion, and eventually he learns that compassion is not enough.

Here's the relevance of one of the play's odder inventions, the ghost of the
character who originally offered Lear sanctuary, the 'gravedigger's boy'. He attaches
himself to the deposed king, and at first serves a similar function to Shakespeare's
disguised Edgar. His presence helps instruct the old man in pity. But Bond, the first
dramatist since the Jacobeans to make widespread use of them, has said that ghosts
are 'always nasty and corrupt'; and this one becomes hardly less so than the spectral
cannibals of Early Morning. He wants Lear to return to his old farm and withdraw
with him into an essentially private world. As the play proceeds, he becomes more
and more importunate, and also thinner, more wasted, more obviously representative of a kind of living death. Lear, explains Bond, 'has a clear vision of a golden
age which his political activities have helped to destroy, but he has to recognize that
its loss is irrecoverable, and there are great dangers in romanticizing and clinging to
the impossible'. 'Some things are dead, but they die with difficulty,' he says, and adds
elsewhere, 'When Lear tries to hug this image of the past, it becomes evil . . . So that
if you have aspirations and do nothing to make them real, then you aren't really
thinking of utopia, you're just wasting your time in some sort of daydream.'

So Lear learns he must act, and act now. At first he delivers social parables to
pilgrims visiting the Tolstoyan homestead where he lives with his disciples. But the
government finds his enthusiasm for disarmament dangerous, and prepares to

execute him, whereupon he comes to a decision that coincides with the second and final death of the gravedigger's boy, who (significantly) is savaged by the pigs he wanted Lear to spend his old age serenely tending. He travels to the wall and is shot as he begins to dismantle it: his belief, his exemplary commitment, will presumably survive.

In his author's word, he 'makes a gesture in which he accepts responsibility for his life and commits himself to action'; and 'responsibility', as often in Bond's work, seems a key concept. We must learn to take our share of responsibility for the future, for the present that will determine it, and, hardly less importantly, for the past that has fashioned the present. There is a curious scene in which Lear rhapsodizes over Fontanelle's body, which is undergoing an autopsy: the point, as he recognizes, is that he himself irreparably damaged what might have been the outer expression of that inner order and beauty. He 'destroyed' her. One of the things that worries Bond about Shakespeare's original is its failure to recognize that Lear helped cause Goneril and Regan; and he attempts to fill this supposed gap both here, and by bringing on Bodice and Fontanelle as they were as children, to offer an impressionistic memory of dead soldiers and a 'terrible bell'. No wonder they turned into loveless, destructive adults.

Bond's less attractive characters are always corrupted rather than corrupt. Cordelia, too, is what she is because her father was a 'priest' who 'taught her everything'. At first, she strikes us as withdrawn, unfriendly, neurotic; later, she sacrifices all to an arrogant vision of what's right. For Bond, she is 'a moralized person, and moralized people are not good people ... She always has the words "good" and "justice" on her lips. And she is an absolute disaster for any society. So I very much wanted to convey through that figure that the people who have manipulated and taken over the language of ethics in our society are in fact very violent and destructive people.' Indeed, the play is substantially about upbringing and education. Many have been irrevocably twisted by their backgrounds, and some go on to try to indoctrinate others. Suffering and the ability to identify with others' suffering enables Lear to break the cycle. 'I must become a child ... I must open my eyes and see,' he declares over Fontanelle's entrails: he ditches his old intellectual luggage, re-educates himself, and becomes a seer, instructing eager acolytes in Bond's view of the world.

Of course, not everyone will endorse that view, and even those who do may feel the gap between our own world and the one shown here is too wide for his purposes. We can hardly disclaim the play's atrocities, which include, not only Lear's blinding, but a scene in which Bodice destroys the eardrums of a tongueless captive with her knitting needle while Fontanelle screeches, 'Kill his hands! Kill his feet ... I want to sit on his lungs.' More sadistic things have been done on and off the world's battlefields in our own era. But it seems that Bond wants us to identify his overt violence with the more covert violence he believes to be institutionalized in a society in which, as Lear says, we 'send our children to a school in the graveyard', 'jackals and wolves' rend the poor and hungry, and 'good, decent, honest, upright, lawful men who believe in order ... devour the earth'. Indeed, he would specifically compare Cordelia with Mary Whitehouse, the celebrated propagandist for moral cleanliness. But doesn't it take an exorbitant effort of imagination and will to witness the play's savageries and detachedly extrapolate truths about our own predicament from them?

Still, the play remains an impressive achievement. Some bardophiles may feel that Bond unjustly patronizes Shakespeare for the crime of having lived before Marx; and they may reasonably attack him in turn for the relative thinness of those passages in which his chopped, exact style becomes metaphoric, 'poetic'. Compare, for instance, his Lear's 'Who shut that animal in a glass cage? O God, there's no pity in this world. You let it lick the blood from its hair in the corner of a cage with nowhere to hide from its tormentors' with 'Poor naked wretches, whereso'er you are, that bide the pelting of this pitiless storm . . .'. Yet the very fact we make such comparisons shows that Bond is writing with an audacity, ambition and scope too rare in the contemporary theatre. How many modern plays contain seventy speaking parts, involve the clash and collapse of civilizations, and force us to ask ourselves such large questions as how we should hope to be governed, how rightly to live in an unjust world? Very few; and most of them are by Edward Bond.

—BENEDICT NIGHTINGALE, *"Lear,"* A Reader's Guide to Fifty Modern British Plays (London: Heinemann Educational Books, 1982), pp. 401–5

EDGAR SCHELL

The speech in which Lear assures Cordelia that they will transform their prison into a retreat is defined as a sentimental fancy even before he makes it. At the end of act 5, scene 1, Edmund had promised that if Lear and Cordelia came into his power he would kill them; and as soon as they leave the stage in scene 3, guarded, he sends the captain off with orders for their deaths. If we set that aside for a moment, however, just as Shakespeare does by means of the distracting interlude of Goneril and Regan's bickering over Edmund, which is followed by the combat between Edmund and Edgar and their mutual confessions, we can see that Lear's fancy is one of the promised endings of the play. His failure to value Cordelia's plain expression of love properly had led to all the imbalances in the narrative—Cordelia's banishment and Kent's, as well as Lear's impulsive transfer of all that he had to Goneril and Regan—and now that failure has been corrected and most of the imbalances have been set right. Lear has discovered that to be loved according to the bond that unites him with his daughter is not to be loved coldly and grudgingly, as he had thought, but to be loved constantly and inexhaustibly. And so he has come to value Cordelia above all the world.

Still holding Edmund's counterplot at bay, we can see that there are other senses in which the state of restored and enhanced happiness expressed in Lear's fancy is also promised. Alan Young has argued, for example, that the promise is made in one form by all the cognate stories in folklore that end happily and so establish a generalized expectation, triggered as soon as we recognize the form of the Lear story, that Shakespeare's play will also have a happy ending. The fact that every other version of the Lear story ends happily leads F. T. Flahiff to imagine that Shakespeare's original audiences must have felt "shock and surprise . . . when they did not witness Lear's happy restoration to the throne, his peaceful death, or his succession by Cordelia." The title given to the play in the quarto edition (*M. William Shakespeare: His True Chronicle Historie . . .*) implies for Flahiff that his audiences were "invited to attend Shakespeare's reworking of familiar history," only to see instead his "disaccommodation of history."

There are also reasons closer to home, within the play itself, why one might conclude that shock and surprise were the ends at which Shakespeare deliberately aimed. As soon as it becomes clear that Goneril and Regan mean to reduce Lear to their authority or dispossess him, we begin to hear that Cordelia is coming to rescue him, and these assurances become more specific, more pointed and weighty, as we move toward their reconciliation. So the roots of the structural association of Cordelia with redemptive grace are planted early and grow through the narrative. The letter that Kent reads in the stocks early in act 2 is no more than a vague promise ("shall find time from this enormous state—seeking to give losses their remedies"); but at the beginning of act 3 we hear that the French have indeed landed and are almost ready to show themselves, and two scenes later Gloucester assures us that "these injuries the king now bears will be reveng'd home; there is part of a power already footed." Even "tied to the stake" by Regan and Cornwall at the end of act 3, he is confident that he will "see / The winged vengeance overtake such children." We may find ourselves to be as confident as he that justice will prove out (with the same ironic result), encouraged as we are by the idealizing language that plays around Cordelia like a corona, absolutizing her virtues and implicitly associating her with Christ ("O dear father, / It is thy business that I go about"), with redeemed souls ("Thou art a soul in bliss"), and with redemptive grace ("Thou hast one daughter / Who redeems nature from the general curse / Which twain have brought her to").

These implications fail at last, but, before they do, the verbal and structural associations of Cordelia and Christian grace function in another way; and to my mind the most telling promise made by the play that its ending will be in some sense happy is the promise implied by Shakespeare's detailed restructuring of the old story around the action of life's pilgrimage. In every other version of the story, the Lear who suffers at the hands of his daughters is merely a pathetic victim; only in Shakespeare's is his suffering treated as part of a spiritual pilgrimage in which, by pursuing all his follies to the disillusioning ends they imply, he discovers what his nature truly requires. From the beginning our understanding of the story is guided along familiar lines by Kent and the Fool, by Edgar, even by Goneril and Regan, who, no less than the others, keep us aware of the familiar forms of moral action that shape Lear's pilgrimage. Regan's remark when Lear rushes out into the storm, that "to willful men / The injuries that they themselves procure / Must be their schoolmasters," though it convicts her as smug and coldhearted, given the circumstances, is a moral commonplace we have often heard before. And when the storm persuades Lear that he has taken too little care of the poor, and when Gloucester, blinded, discovers that "our means secure us, and our mere defects / Prove our commodities," it turns out to be true in precisely the same sense in which it has always been true—though that sense is more profound than Regan could have imagined.

Set to think along familiar lines by the pattern of changes Shakespeare has made in his sources, we are, I believe, positively encouraged, as part of the design of the play, to expect that these lines will be played out to their familiar ends: that, having brought him through suffering and repentance to the beginnings of understanding, Lear's pilgrimage will end, not with everyone living happily ever after, perhaps, but with some sort of assurance that he has won through to a secure spiritual state. Even Lear's fancy that he and Cordelia, imprisoned, will take on "the mystery of things" and "wear out . . . packs and sects of great ones / That ebb and flow by th'moon" may seem to further this expectation in a curiously teasing fashion. For the Pilgrim, Filius Regis, and Mankind are all sent off to secure castles after they have been recovered from the land of unlikeness, and they are sequestered from the world and provided with knowledge of eternal things. These castles, too, are assaulted and even breached, as we know that Lear's prison / retreat will be breached by Edmund's order; but the assaults all fail in the end because the strength of the castles—which is to say the integrity of the moral knowledge they enclose—is secured by the grace with which Cordelia has been associated. So even Edmund's plot against Cordelia's life, flatly revealed to us, may be ironically encouraging and lead us further down the garden path.

But not for long. Within two hundred lines, scarcely fifteen minutes' playing time, Lear enters with Cordelia dead in his arms, shattering whatever expectations the form of the story may have generated. He has fallen back into madness again, deeper and more terrible than the madness from which Cordelia had recovered him, because, where that had come from the loss of illusions, this comes from the loss of a painfully acquired truth. And, fifty lines later, he dies himself, asking what sense there is in Cordelia's death.

This has long been the crux of every interpretation of *King Lear*—the relationship between the action, as it is developed through the reconciliation of Lear and Cordelia, with all the formal expectations generated by that development, and the tragic ending that Shakespeare, in distinction from everyone else who has told the story, finds appropriate for it. Explanations of the sense to be found in Cordelia's death cover the whole philosophical spectrum, from Christian optimism to the bleakest nihilism; but almost everyone who has commented on it has noted some element of misdirection, even of gratuitousness, in its presentation. Bradley said that Cordelia's murder seems "especially designed to fall like a bolt from a sky cleared by the vanished storm," and there has been little disagreement about that. Lear's anguished death is rooted in Cordelia's, and hers seems unarguably an expression of a vision that what is inescapably tragic is not life lived foolishly or badly, as in the allegorical tradition that Shakespeare drew on in constructing the play, but simply life lived, even to the highest pitch of integrity. The world revealed at the end of *King Lear* seems to have been constructed as a challenge to the earlier part of the play; as such, it indirectly challenges the rational and optimistic assumptions that underlie the figure of life's pilgrimage, for in the world of *Lear* it is possible to follow the pilgrim's route to the very end only to have everything snatched away by what is made to look very much like an accident. Shakespeare moves the responsibility for Cordelia's death around like a pea in a shell game, obscuring it almost as soon as he has revealed it. Edmund considers his intention to have Lear and Cordelia killed only toward the end of act 5, scene I, about forty lines before he sends the captain off to do it. And by the time we learn that his order has been carried out, he no longer wants them dead but is urging Albany to hurry and save their lives. Moreover, the scheme that Edmund has now disowned is given a chance to work only because Albany's attention has been deflected from Lear and Cordelia, first by Edmund's presumption and then by the combat between Edmund and Edgar. The result, when Albany is recalled to the major issue of the play by Kent's inquiry for Lear, may be the most astonishing cue for a tragic entrance to be found in any literature: "Great thing of us forgot!"

Of course, the whole sequence might have been as plausibly handled in a different manner. But Shakespeare's use of Albany in the design of the scene seems clearly intended to throw into high relief the quality of accident in Cordelia's murder: committed after the man who ordered that it be done has repented; permitted only because the objects of a great battle were simply forgotten in its aftermath. With will and purpose canceled in advance and the occasion provided by inadvertence, Cordelia's death and Lear's are left almost opaque, challenging attempts to reduce them to form and order.

The problem of making sense of events, particularly moral sense, is thus built aggressively into the tragic ending of the play. In truth, of course, the problem has been there all along, a softly whispered and diffused threat of a different and bleaker end; but it is only in the last scene that we are forced to confront it. As Shakespeare has constructed it, Lear's entrance with Cordelia's body forms the final term in a dialectic between different ways of understanding experience, medieval and modern, broadly Thomist and even more broadly Calvinist, that has been woven lightly through the narrative from the first. On one side there are characters who imagine that good will regularly come from good and evil from evil, who expect, with Aquinas and Hooker, that they will find in the form of experience itself the evidence of a divine and intelligible order. On the other side there are the strange twistings and turnings of events that sometimes directly, more often indirectly, challenge that expectation by implying that, if there is a divine order, it may not easily or certainly be known. An assumption that the values of the gods are regular and knowable and woven as laws into the tissue of human experience shapes the common language of characters like Lear and Kent and Albany, revealing itself in inferences and judgments, blessings and curses, that turn out either not to be answered at all, as in Lear's case, or answered in ironic and equivocal ways. Kent's benedictory wish in act I, scene I, that "the gods to their dear shelter take [Cordelia] / That justly think'st and hast most rightly said," seems to be answered directly when France's love is "kindled to inflamed respect" by Cordelia's virtue and he makes her his queen, and it appears to be answered even more fully when she is reconciled with her father. But her accidental murder calls everything into doubt. An ironic answer to Kent's wish that "the gods reward" Gloucester for helping Lear comes more swiftly—Cornwall and Regan pluck out his eyes in the very next scene, while Gloucester swears by the "kind gods"; but it turns out to be no less equivocal a reply when Gloucester discovers that he "stumbled when he saw" but that blind, he recognizes his true son. Are the gods indifferent or malevolent? Or do they answer in their own obscure ways, providing, in the words of the *Book of Common Prayer,* what is "most needful" for men? Uncertainty about this is built into even the verbal rhythms of the play. When Albany is told that Cornwall was mortally wounded by his own servant after he had plucked out one of Gloucester's eyes, he takes that revolt from within Cornwall's extended body to be evidence of the swiftness of divine justice, as might any Elizabethan steeped in the Scholastic doctrine that the punishment for evil is immanent in the act itself. But then he is told that Cornwall went on, nonetheless, to pluck out the other eye. Edgar extracts from the fates of Gloucester and Edmund an example of moral economy that Hooker might have seen as a fair poetic image of the working of natural law: "The gods are just, and of our pleasant vices / Make instruments to plague us: / The dark and vicious place where thee he got / Cost him his eyes." But as Rosalie Colie notes, that "dark and vicious place" will, in less than a hundred lines, cost Cordelia her life and Lear his peace. Patterns that seem to reveal an immanent moral order may dissolve in a moment to challenge it. This equivocal irony is brought into direct and theatrical focus when the dead bodies of Goneril and Regan and Cordelia are laid side by side on the stage. The corpses of Goneril and Regan provide Albany with an image of the awesome "judgement of the heavens," but, fifteen lines later, his complementary prayer, that the heavens defend Cordelia, is answered only by Lear's "howl" as he enters with her body.

The dialectic remains unresolved. Life as it is imagined by the play may be inescapably tragic, even, on the evidence of Cordelia's murder, randomly tragic; yet there is clearly some sort of retributive force at work in the play, and its operations are regularly pointed out to us. This force may not seem to be economical or precise, but it is sufficiently sure to warrant Albany's belief that there are justicers above and thus, by implication, to underpin the social order that seemed imperiled when it seemed that Goneril and Regan were triumphant. The wages of evil are certainly death. But what the gods do not guarantee, either within the world of the play or by any clear implication beyond it, are the wages of virtue. They are paid, if at all, only in the hazard that being true to oneself may be more likely to succeed than being false. There is no hint of transcendence or affirmation in Cordelia's death, no clue as to what we are to make now of those teasing allusions to grace. We are directed instead toward its finality: "She's dead as earth." "She's gone for ever." She will "come no more, / Never, never, never, never, never."

There are critics who have suggested that to find the manner of Cordelia's death morally significant is naïve. We all know, they remind us, as Shakespeare's contemporaries did, that life has never been fair. But to take Cordelia's death as merely realistic, no more a challenge to moral perception than tragic accidents in life, is to trivialize it as art, which has the advantage over life of being free of accidents. Accidents in art are not morally indigestible lumps of experience; they are inevitably part of the complex perception of moral order that a work embodies, positive assertions that experience cannot be completely digested by rational moral categories. The passage that Bradley thought summed up the meaning of the play—" 'The gods defend her.' [*Enter Lear with Cordelia in his arms.*]"—is the clearest form of a challenge, made over and over in the play, to those who think they know exactly what the gods will reward, shelter, cherish, and defend; it teases them out of thought, disarms authority, leaves them only with what they feel, not what they ought to say. While it may be going too far to conclude, as one recent critic has put it, that Shakespeare has "broken the Elizabethan dramatist's teleological link between the world of the play and a beneficent divine order, and set the play world terrifyingly adrift," there seems every reason to think that our capacity to see and to understand that link is made problematic by the play's design.

King Lear may, indeed, be Shakespeare's most Shavian play in the way that it turns a familiar dramatic form against itself and the assumptions it embodies. Just as Shaw appropriates the narrative conventions of nineteenth-century melodrama in order to bring melodramatizing thought to the surface and set its romantic fictions against reality, so Shakespeare reworks the Lear story along the lines of dramatic moral allegory and draws out the forms of thought associated with it, only to confront allegory with tragic reality. The result is that what we once thought of as moral allegory we must now think of as moral romance.

The problem posed by Shakespeare's peculiar construction of the ending of King Lear is thus essentially an epistemological problem, and the terrible poise with which the play addresses this problem dramatizes the epistemological crisis of its time. The Scholastic image of the universe and man's place in it, the image assumed and articulated by Aquinas and Hooker and embodied in all the plays we have been examining, was in the process of being dismantled at the turn of the century—in philosophy by a resurgent nominalism, in religion by the voluntarism of Luther and Calvin and the skeptical materialism of Bacon and Montaigne. Aquinas' God, whose justice was immanent in the laws of man's nature—the God assumed in the Bernardine figure of the land of unlikeness—had begun to retreat behind the clouds of his heaven, driven there by Calvin's insistence that for men to imagine they could trace his ways further than he had explicitly chosen to reveal them was presumptuous: God's ways are just simply because they are his ways; but "the reason of the divine justice," Calvin said, "is too high to be measured by a human standard or comprehended by the littleness of the human mind." So, for Montaigne, "it is enough for a Christian to believe that all things come from God and to receive them with acknowledgement of his divine and inscrutable wisdom," but to go further and expect that his wisdom will make itself scrutable to man is to diminish and falsify God, who "allots and handles the fortunes and misfortunes of the world according to his occult disposition." It is this hidden and inscrutable disposition of whatever gods rule the world of the play that we are made to confront in the final tableau—not a terrible void or an imbecile universe but a puzzle that has come to be all too familiar. The dominant rhetorical mode of the last moments of the play is interrogative, and the questions are all variations on one: What are we to make of this? It is in that sense, I think, that *King Lear* is, not a moral tragedy but a tragedy of a moral system. Lear's entrance with Cordelia's body virtually marks the end of a long-lived way of understanding experience and of the dramatic form created to express it.

—EDGAR SCHELL, "The Skeptical Traveler: *King Lear* and the End of the Pilgrimage," *Strangers and Pilgrims: From* The Castle of Perseverance *to* King Lear (Chicago: University of Chicago Press, 1983), pp. 188–95

PETER ERICKSON

King Lear elaborates further the dramatic possibilities of the two extreme versions of women between which Othello shuttles. The opening scene makes clear that Lear himself is the major source of this splitting, for he initiates the contest that provokes the division into good and bad daughters. Though they respond differently to this provocation, all three daughters share the common purpose of protecting themselves against the father's total claim on them. Lear subsequently satisfies his need to make a total claim through the absolute, unquestioning loyalty and devotion of the disguised Kent. Frustrated by women, Lear "sets his rest" on the "kind nursery" of male bonding (1.1.123–24). ⟨. . .⟩

To counter his daughters' "unkindness" (3.2.16), Lear assembles a ragged band of brothers and fashions a male refuge on the exposed heath. Kent, the Fool, and Edgar are Lear's shadows, who try to tell him who he is (1.4.230–31). In Kent's version, Lear's authority rests on masculine firmness backed by the willingness to use force. Kent devotes himself to restoring Lear's "frame of nature" to "the fix'd place" of "manhood" (268,269,297). As Lear's surrogate, Kent displays the aggressiveness in which Lear himself has been deficient. Kent's aggression in the service of goodness is instantly recognized by Lear as "love" (88) and rewarded (94) when the disguised Kent trips up the "base football player" (86) Oswald, Goneril's steward. Kent again courts violence with the verbal and physical attack on Oswald (now "the son and heir of a mungril bitch" [2.2.22]) that lands him in the stocks. Kent's antagonism, which elicits the "violent outrage" "upon respect" (2.4.24) and forces Lear into acute awareness of his diminished power, is described by both sides as a product of blunt manliness: "put upon him such a deal of man" (2.2.120) and "having more man than wit about me" (2.4.42). This manhood carries an antifemale note, for Kent's lack of vulnerability to women is one of the qualities by which he recommends himself to Lear's service: "Not so young, sir, to love a woman for singing, nor so old to dote on her for any thing" (1.4.37–38).

In the Fool, Kent's aggressive action takes the form of aggressive wit. The Fool baits both Goneril ("the Lady Brach" [1.4.112]) and Lear to bring home the powerlessness Lear has brought upon himself by disordering the traditional gender hierarchy. Relentlessly exposing Lear's weakness the better to push him toward a renewal of manhood, the Fool mocks Lear's sex. Having given "the rod" (174) to his daughters, Lear's penis is "a sheal'd peascod" (200), an empty symbol of masculine power that makes him a woman: "now thou art an O without a figure" (192–93). The Fool's pointed humor has a misogynist edge: "For there was never yet fair woman but she made mouths in a glass" (3.2.35–36). Edgar, the third member of Lear's male chorus, picks up the antifeminist line when he warns against "the act of darkness" (3.4.87): "Let not the creaking of shoes nor the rustling of silks betray thy poor heart to woman. Keep thy foot out of brothels; thy hand out of plackets" (94–97). However, while Kent and the Fool press their single-minded attempt to shore up Lear's masculinity, Edgar evokes in Lear a more complicated response.

Lear's immediate identification with Edgar—"Didst thou give all to thy daughters? And art thou come to this?" (3.4.49–50)—can be explained in part as a projection that reinforces tough-minded hostility toward women. But Edgar's status as a beggar implies vulnerability—his "presented nakedness" hopes to "enforce their charity" (2.3.11, 20)—as well as defiance. Edgar answers to the self-image of beggar that Lear has already begun to adopt for himself:

> "On my knees I beg
> That you'll vouchsafe me raiment, bed, and food."   (2.4.155–56)

> Why, the hot-bloodied France, that dowerless took
> Our youngest born, I could as well be brought
> To knee his throne, and squire-like, pension beg
> To keep base life afoot. Return with her?
> Persuade me rather to be slave and sumpter
> To this detested groom.   (212–17)

> O, reason not the need! our basest beggars
> Are in the poorest thing superfluous.   (264–65)

Once on the heath, Lear ceases to resist the beggar image and instead seeks it:

> Poor naked wretches, wheresoe'er you are,
> That bide the pelting of this pitiless storm,
> How shall your houseless heads and unfed sides,
> Your loop'd and window'd raggedness, defend you
> From seasons such as these?   (3.4.28–32)

Lear's prayer (27) is answered by Edgar's voice calling from within the hovel and, shortly, by the actual presence of his "uncover'd body" (102), a physical state to which Lear exposes himself: "Thou art the thing itself: unaccommodated man is no more but such a poor, bare, fork'd animal as thou art. Off, off, you lendings! Come, unbutton here" (106–9). In his guise as beggar, Edgar performs a service for Lear, of which neither Kent nor the Fool was capable, by facilitating Lear's openness to vulnerability.

Nonetheless, this openly acknowledged vulnerability exacerbates the distrust of women. This moment in act 3, scene 4, can be too easily cited as evidence that Lear learns from his suffering according to the beneficent tragic view: "The art of our necessities is strange / And can make vild things precious" (3.2.70–71). But the newfound preciousness of "unaccommodated man" bespeaks a humanism that coexists with hatred of women, for Lear has two separate visions of the human body, depending on whether "the thing itself" is male or female. One crux of the play lies in the juxtaposition of the "poor, bare, fork'd animal" that Edgar presents with the "simp'ring dame, / Whose face between her forks presages snow" (4.6.60–67) that Lear "anatomizes" (3.6.76) with all the sanctimony he can summon:

> But to the girdle do the gods inherit,
> Beneath is all the fiend's: there's hell, there's darkness,
> There is the sulphurous pit, burning, scalding,
> Stench, consumption. (4.6.126–29)

Just as the Edgar who occasions Lear's humanist revelation becomes the "most learned justicer" (3.6.21) who helps Lear prosecute Goneril and Regan in the mock trial on the heath, so Lear uses the Gloucester who "sees feelingly" (4.6.149) as an ally in taking revenge against women. Lear's critique of justice—"Why dost thou lash that whore?" (161)—applies to his own rhetorical assault on the female body, but he is blissfully unaware of the self-application.

The "darkness" (4.6.127) of the vagina is synonymous with heterosexual intercourse: "the act of darkness" (3.4.87) is the woman's "dark and vicious place" (5.3.173). Displaced from the male body and projected exclusively onto the female, sexuality becomes female sexuality; "copulation" (4.6.114) becomes a province for which women, not men, are responsible. In this view, the normal superiority of civilization to nature is reversed, transposed into an opposition between male necessity and female "luxury" (117); and between Edgar's salutary nakedness and the bad daughters' "plighted cunning" (1.1.280), literally imaged in their extravagant clothes (2.4.267–70) or in the verbal flattery by which Regan's "most precious square of sense" (1.1.74) disguises her "sulphurous pit" (4.6.128). Male perturbation with sexuality is greater here than in *Othello* because the sexual act is bound up with procreation. However repulsive the image of "making the beast with two backs" (*Othello*, 1.1.116–17), however convulsed Othello is by the thought of Desdemona "topp'd" (3.3.396)—"It is not words that shakes me thus. Pish! Noses, ears, and lips" (4.1.41–42)—there is nothing in *Othello* so alienated as Lear's life-denying curse against Goneril.

Lear takes revenge in a direct attack on her powers of gestation. Into her "sulphurous pit," he would "convey sterility" (1.4.278). If he cannot make her infertile, he condemns her to reproduce the filial ingratitude she has inflicted on him: "Turn all her mother's pains and benefits / To laugher and contempt" (286–87). Lear's earlier curse against Cordelia also strikes against procreation: "Better thou / Hadst not been born than not t' have pleased me better" (1.1.233–34). Lear finds particularly galling the physical intimacy of the blood connection that makes parent and child one flesh: "But yet thou art my flesh, my blood, my daughter— / Or rather a disease that's in my flesh, / Which I must needs call mine" (2.4.221–23). He employs several stratagems to try to sever this indissoluble bond. First, he banishes and disinherits: "Here I disclaim all my paternal care" (1.1.113). Cordelia is now "my sometime daughter" (120), "Unfriended, new adopted to our hate, / Dower'd with our curse, and stranger'd with our oath" (203–4), "for we / Have no such daughter" (262–63).

Second, he attempts a mortification of the flesh, analogous to the self-mutilation proposed by Edgar—"Strike in their numb'd and mortified arms / Pins, wooden pricks, nails, sprigs of rosemary" (2.3.15–16). When Lear calls the storm down upon his head, he punishes his body in order to purify it while at the same time destroying the universal power of procreation that corrupted him: "Crack nature's moulds, all germains spill at once" (3.2.9). Ultimately, the separation of male spirit from female flesh is achieved by the death of the woman. The play comes to rest when the threat posed by the female body is ended: "Produce the bodies" (5.3.231), "seest thou this object?" (239). The potency of the "sulphurous pit" has been canceled, as the exhibition of silent bodies bears witness.

The motif of the missing mother is only a decoy, for the play's "darker purpose" produces mother figures to fill the vacuum left by the absence of Lear's wife. He asks for trouble by turning his daughters into mothers, as the Fool indicates after the fact. Lear's divestment of his authority initiates the dismantling of patriarchal order and the reinstatement of maternal power. A confusion in the ideal of male beneficence emerges: Lear retains the self-pitying image as "Your old kind father, whose frank heart gave all" (3.4.20), when actually he had used giving all as a means to receive all. He makes clear, in retrospect, the terms of the bargain when he desperately appeals to "tender-hefted" Regan to show "The offices of nature, bond of childhood, / Effects of courtesy, dues of gratitude" (2.4.178–79) by immediately reminding her of the gift by which he purchased these dues: "Thy half o' th' kingdom hast thou not forgot, / Wherein I thee endow'd" (180–81). But more often Lear suppresses the logic that connects "So kind a father" (1.5.32) to his desire for "kind nursery" (1.1.124). In the candor prompted by extreme disappointment, Lear admits that he was maneuvering "to set my rest" (123) on Cordelia's care of him. Instead of the maternal comfort he had sought, he inadvertently recreates the pain of maternal abandonment. When he renounces Cordelia after she has denied her undivided affection, Lear elevates his rage to the heroic proportions of the "barbarous Scythian" (116) and the "dragon" (122). But Lear's image of the angry, devouring father is preceded by his invocation of a dangerous goddess—"The mysteries of Hecat and the night" (110)—who modulates into the powerful mother whose victim is Lear.

Lear defends against this mother by standing on the ceremony of manliness (2.4.276–78). But once he has entered the open heath in a stormy night "wherein the cub-drawn bear would crouch" (3.1.12), he gives in to the all-consuming experience of his infantlike vulnerability. This is the burden of Lear's beggar imagery: the infant's needy dependence on a mother's care. Edgar as the embodiment of beggary evokes a whole range of feelings associated with this dependence—from the fear of deprivation to the hope of survival. The "unfed sides" of "poor naked wretches" (3.4.30,28) whose destitution Lear commits himself to share refers in part to the basic necessity of maternal nurturance. Yet Lear short-circuits awareness by attempting to recover an image of benevolent paternal bounty:

> O, I have ta'en
> Too little care of this! Take physic, pomp,
> Expose thyself to feel what wretches feel,
> That thou mayest shake the superflux to them,
> And show the heavens more just.   (32–36)

Patriarchal liberality that redistributes the superflux is not the appropriate "physic" for Lear's central problem; this fantasy of reparation by a reformed male authority cannot serve as a substitute for the absence of maternal generosity, the "kind nursery" to which Lear has pinned his "unburthen'd" self (1.1.41). Male bounty, independent of women, cannot be sustained.

The crucial importance of women for a sane social order is underscored by Lear's inability to release himself from misogynist rage. Only Cordelia's intervention provides him with the "sweetened imagination" he needs (4.6.131). Cordelia is the "daughter / Who redeems nature from the general curse / Which twain have brought her to" (205–7) because she is both maternal and virginal. The elimination from the play of her husband (4.3.1–6) ensures her exclusive devotion to Lear. Her "organs of increase" (1.4.279) are not at issue because, despite her maternal ambience, she is kept from association with literal child bearing. Upon her reentry to the play, she obliges Lear in the role of the good, comforting mother, to which he had originally assigned her. The maternal aspect of her rescue is implied by her image as "Our foster-nurse of nature" (4.4.12); this physic is hers to bestow, not the doctor's. Cordelia's reference to "our sustaining corn" (6) is linked metaphorically to the natural restorative power of her tears: "All blest secrets, / All you unpublish'd virtues of the earth, / Spring with my tears; be aidant and remediate / In the good man's distress" (15–18).

The image of a patriarchal "pomp" that makes restitution by "shaking" its "superflux" cannot hold a candle to Cordelia's maternal kindness, so necessary to Lear's restoration. However poignant the relations among Lear's company of supportive men, this male bonding is finally a minor resource compared with the unequivocal centrality of Cordelia for Lear—a centrality that dominates the play after her reappearance in act 4, scene 4. This is the significance of Lear's nonrecognition of Kent (5.3.279–95) and of his inattention to the Duke of Albany's scheme for patriarchal justice (297–305). Such consolations are irrelevant to Lear's desolation: Cordelia's death makes it impossible for him to "taste" her "cup" (303, 305). The gods do not exist who can revive the "miracle" of her life so as to "make them honors / Of men's impossibilities" (4.6.55, 73–74). In contrast to *Othello, King*

Lear places greater structural emphasis on the final phase in which the male protagonist regains his perception of the woman's innocence. The dramatic potential is
increased because Lear is permitted, as Othello is not, to reunite with her while she
is still alive and to ask her forgiveness.

This is not to say that Lear's reconciliation with Cordelia is entirely positive; on
the contrary, it is irredeemably tragic. The play cautions us against false optimism
by undercutting Edgar's premature, sententious "The lamentable change is from the
best, / The worst returns to laughter" (4.1.5–6). But Edgar's optimism is incurable;
he thinks he can "cure despair" (4.6.33–34; 5.3.192) and returns "the worst" to
laughter by means of an upbeat narrative closure: "Burst smilingly" (5.3.200). The
main plot, however, defies Edgar's efforts to fashion a happy ending. In Lear's case,
the comic rebirth prepared for him "closes the eye of anguish" (4.4.15) in a way that
has negative as well as positive implications. Gloucester, misapprehending Lear's
madness, desires it to escape his own "ingenious feeling" (4.6.280):

> Better I were distract,
> So should my thoughts be sever'd from my griefs,
> And woes by wrong imaginations lose
> The knowledge of themselves.   (281–84)

But for Lear the reverse is more nearly true. His madness has shown the way to
sharpened awareness; his "repose" (4.4.12) leads to some loss of this acute consciousness.

The correct identification of "good" and "bad" daughters is not enough because Lear proceeds to take advantage of Cordelia's goodness. In the reconciliation
scene, Lear discovers that he is to "drink" not the "poison" of Cordelia's revenge as
he had expected (4.7.71) but rather her unconditional mercy. Yet the play's final
scene begins with Lear's transformation of the original moment of forgiveness into
a commemorative routine: "We two alone will sing like birds i' th' cage; / When
thou dost ask me blessing, I'll kneel down / And ask of thee forgiveness" (5.3.9–11).
His momentary openness to human contact—"Be your tears wet? Yes, faith"
(4.7.70)—is superseded by a withdrawal into the hollow posture of omnipotent
fantasy, hollow because it denies not only Edgar's reality but also Cordelia's. Authentic communication between father and daughter has ceased. To Cordelia's
gentle nudge "Shall we not see these daughters and these sisters?" (5.3.7), Lear can
offer only flat resistance: "No, no, no, no!" (8). Cordelia is subsumed in the escapist
vision Lear constructs for both of them; she is not consulted: her part is once again
to "Love, and be silent" (1.1.62). This appropriation of Cordelia is not an act of love
but a violation of it that echoes and repeats Lear's ritual of possessiveness in the
opening scene.

The sacrificial nature of Cordelia's role is explicit: "Upon such sacrifices, my
Cordelia, / The gods themselves throw incense. Have I caught thee?" (5.3.20–21).
Her compliance thus caught, verbal assent is unnecessary; Cordelia accepts her
"plight" (1.1.101) by crying. But Lear insists that she stifle her tears as he lapses into
the mode of vengeful defiance that blots self-awareness: "Wipe thine eyes; / The

good-years shall devour them, flesh and fell, / Ere they shall make us weep! We'll see 'em starved first" (5.3.23–25). Having secured the maternal symbiosis of "kind nursery," Lear redirects the mother's punishments of "starving" and "devouring" against his enemies. Superficially, the tragic ending is the result of external evil forces now beyond Lear's control. Yet the tragedy cannot be made to hinge on the technicality of failing to save Cordelia in time (237–57). To give credence to the possibility of a last-minute rescue is to hold out too much melodramatic faith in a benign resolution and to avoid feeling the depth of the tragic horror. Lear's entrance with Cordelia dead in his arms answers directly to his own evocation of "sacrifices" at the beginning of the scene. Though we are moved by the agony of Lear's deprivation, we must nonetheless question the political way in which he had expected her to "redeem all sorrows / That ever I have felt" (267–68), as his ready conversion of Cordelia's forgiveness into her sacrifice has just demonstrated. Lear recognizes his immense loss and his initial error, but he repeats the error and never fully understands his contribution to the tragic outcome nor acknowledges his responsibility. He can win from one daughter a suspension of tragic causation—"No cause, no cause" (4.7.75). But another speaks the harsh truth: "The injuries that they themselves procure / Must be their schoolmasters" (2.4.303–4). The play's rigorous tragic logic insists on the necessity that Lear pay the price for the continuing self-evasion exemplified by the dream vision of imprisonment with Cordelia. Though Lear does not want to hear the lesson taught by the stern schoolmaster tragedy, we must.

—PETER ERICKSON, "Maternal Images and Male Bonds in *Hamlet*, *Othello*, and *King Lear*," *Patriarchal Structures in Shakespeare's Drama* (Berkeley: University of California Press, 1985), pp. 103–4, 106–15

BARBARA L. ESTRIN

King Lear twice comes close to the foundling experience, nestling a small haven of reconciliation between the larger contexts of exposure in the opening and concluding acts. The larger story reverses the order of the formula. It begins with the art of the adoptive interlude—in Lear's wish that his daughters would mother him while he, infantile, "crawls[s] ... unburthen'd" (1.1.41). It ends with the voracious nature usually inaugurating foundling plots (in the final sacrifice of Cordelia). At first Lear creates a fictional pastoral, demanding that his daughters fulfill his philosophical concept of love. The nature he denies with that artifice comes back at the end to assert itself all the more cruelly.

But between that artificial beginning and the brutal end is a foundling story based on the role reversal of Lear and his daughters. On the heath, Lear is the exposed child who experiences a more persuasive semblance for the adoptive interlude—both its primitive surroundings and, with Edgar and Kent, its nurturing humanity. After his humbling conversion, he is reconciled to the daughter he condemned and restored by her to his former stature. For a moment in act 4 and the beginning of act 5, the man who at first sought to be a child and give away his power becomes once more a father and a king. The happiness of that restoration is only momentary, partly because of the all-pervading violence at the end and partly because Lear is blinded, as he was earlier, by his need to possess Cordelia in a world he imagines. Thus, the second foundling story climaxes in the original artifice of Lear's dominion as he anticipates an extended prospect of "blessing" and "forgiveness" (5.3.10,11) in prison. Seeking again to monopolize his child, Lear stymies the dynasty that would complete the formula. If, in the enclosed story, Lear becomes the abandoned child, experiencing, on the heath with Edgar and Kent, the pastoral renewal that enables him to become the found parent of act 4, in acts 1 and 5 he is the arbitrary father, exposing Cordelia to the fantasy of his domination. As father and as king, Lear believes that he can—by an art he invents (in act 1 through an arbitrary command, in act 5 through a pathetic dependency)—force his vision on the world.

During the opening moments of the play, Lear places himself in a fictional country, trusting in the dream of a supportive realm as he releases the remnants of his personal power. The dream is based not on created reality (nature) but on invented substance (art). Lear confers on his children the land of his mind in exchange for the love of their devising. If Goneril and Regan vie for the opulence of "shadowy forests with champains rich'd / With plenteous rivers and wide-skirted meads" (1.1.63–64) never seen in the play, they match in hyperbolic gesture the poetic vistas they receive. What Lear gives is what he gets—an art of nature, a pastoral world of "shadowy forests and plenteous rivers" for a romanticized sign of filial devotion. He bequeaths an imagined territory; he accepts a professed love—because both fit a picture he wants to believe. Fantasizing about his kingdom and making his children his parents, he invents the pastoral realms and the nurturing substitutes of the adoptive interlude. Promising "our largest bounty may extend / Where nature doth with merit challenge" (1.1.52), Lear speaks of what is given ("bounty") in terms of what is earned ("merit"). Such a philosophy finally discounts an externally created universe, making man's words equal in their seminal power to God's.

Lear's quibble about nothing manifests this philosophy. When Cordelia is silent, Lear answers with the famous rejection: "Nothing will come of nothing" (1.1.90). Threatening his daughter with extinction, Lear places the source of her failure to acquire in the obstinance of her refusal to utter the words reaping riches. The context for creativity is the mind, out of which words flow and empires follow. Without those words, Cordelia's sphere is barren. She can pull nothing to her. No thoughts (no words) equal no worlds (no things). Lear repeats this position in response to the Fool's questions about practicality:

FOOL: Can you make no use of nothing, Nuncle?
LEAR: Why, no, boy; nothing can be made out of nothing.   (1.4.136–37)

Man's intellect propels the idea that forms a concrete entity, just as in Genesis God's spirit "moves" on the face of the waters to make land. Lear considers himself the guiding force in his firmament.

The Fool mocks this belief when he shows Lear how he squandered his dominion:

FOOL: Nuncle, give me an egg, and I'll give thee two crowns.

LEAR: What two crowns shall they be?

FOOL: Why, after I have cut the egg i' th' middle and eat up the meat, the two crowns of the egg. When thou clovest thy crown i' th' middle, and gav'st away both parts, thou bor'st thine ass on thy back o'er the dirt: thou hadst little wit in thy bald crown when thou gav'st thy golden one away.

(1.4.160–71)

Having given away his crown and the concrete wealth it represented, Lear cut out his brain (crown) and the abstract ideas it formulated. Since the land, as Lear defines it, is measured by the mind that makes it, to empty the container (crown) is to flush out the thing contained (wit). The egg white corroborates, in its absence of color, the truth of Lear's hollowness. He has destroyed the golden—the substance—and is left with only the blankness—the abstraction.

Without his crown and its accompanying power, Lear is bald, shorn of the wit he once had because his center—as the vanished egg yolk shows—is eaten. In the voracious image that follows, the Fool ties the eaters to the daughters:

For you know, Nuncle,
The hedge-sparrow fed the cuckoo so long,
That it's had it head bit off by it young.
So out went the candle, and we were left darkling.   (1.4.222–26)

Like Error's children devouring their dam in *The Faerie Queene,* Goneril and Regan swallow Lear, reversing the process of confinement he initially imposed on them. Reduced, he is left groping for wit, searching for love, emptied of the enlightening power out of which his world grew. If Lear believes the world to be made by man, the fool convinces him that without evidence "out there" to objectify it, nothing remains "in here" to originate it. Having snuffed the candle of reason, Lear is left "darkling," derived of the light in the self that would in turn illuminate nature. To be witless is to be worldless. Strengthening his daughters, he weakened himself, converting them into the custodians of his life:

LEAR: I should be false persuaded I had daughters.

FOOL: Which they will make an obedient father.   (1.4.241–42)

Goneril and Regan emerge mothers to his self, definers of his being. Reduced to nothing, Lear becomes the controlled object of his daughters' imaginations. Having cast himself out, Lear wills his decline. He has been taught by the Fool, forced by his daughters, to pronounce the failure of his art.

When he understands his diminution, the first frame of the play ends and Lear—the proud parent—becomes the humbled child of the enclosed story. Forfeiting his crown of art, he has lost his power in nature. The second story begins on the heath as Lear reaches the bottom he feared and discovers, in accepting the nature he formerly denied, that he can touch and be touched. In his defense of the storm, Lear's new being surfaces:

> But where the greater malady is fix'd,
> The lesser is scarce felt. Thou'ldst shun a bear;
> But if thy flight lay toward the roaring sea,
> Thou'ldst meet the bear i' th' mouth. When the mind's free
> The body's delicate.   (3.4.7–11)

Formerly a believer in absolutes ("all" or "nothing"), Lear affirms the relative. While the sea can overwhelm, the bear might still be tamed, cajoled. When the mind is free from raging passion, the body emerges "delicate," trainable, young. Thus, what at first seemed impossible (the wild animal) becomes containable—not so threatening. Meeting the bear in the mouth, Lear promises to "endure" (3.4.18). Taking his chances with the bestial he finds, as the rain pelts and pours, what remains when everything seems to have slid over the cataract: that something in himself existing to fight back. He comes to rest with the strength of the human form, what it suffers, what it fears, what it touches. The Lear who started out as a god, making and measuring the world, begins as a child. In the storm, Lear earns his position as foundling. Lost on the heath, he acquires a radical innocence and establishes his brotherhood with man. When he promises to "endure," Lear, like Cleopatra, recognizes humanity at its simplest level. The "poor naked wretches" are Lear's equivalent to the milkmaid Cleopatra tried to become. Befriending poor Tom, Lear defines man as one rung lower on the chain of being:

> Thou wert better in a grave than to answer with thy uncover'd body this extremity of the skies. Is man no more than this? Consider him well. Thou ow'st the worm no silk, the beast no hide, the sheep no wool, the cat no perfume. Ha! here's three on's are sophisticated; thou art the thing itself; unaccommodated man is no more but such a poor, bare, forked animal as thou art. Off, off, you lendings! Come; unbutton here. (3.4.103–12)

When he asks, "Is man no more than this?" he mediates between the death of self he saw as the nothing and the new something he finds—the thing itself. Man is more than an extension of the gods (the trembling extremity) and more than the things he adds from nature (the temporary lendings). The first image denies man's wit by making him the bearer of a foreign internal force; the second hides his substance by transforming him into the wearer of an appropriated external trim. To add is to detract from the self, to confuse the subject with the objects it manifests. Calling Tom a beast, Lear aligns himself with him. To be the thing itself is to be undisguised by show, unswayed by force. The poor bare animal is steadfast, planting himself with "forked" legs in the earth, enduring because he can, an animal himself, confront the bear. Unbuttoning, Lear removes the accommodations of man and emerges "delicate." Ridding himself of "lendings," Lear finds new origins, establishing himself—with the forked animal—on the ground he earlier denied.

This alliance with the earth and unaccommodated man provides the adoptive interlude that makes possible the actual reconciliation within the play. Joining with Edgar, Lear is nurtured by the minimalist surroundings—the bare animal, the plain heath—that contrast to the false opulence (both of the wealthy court and of the adorned mind) with which he began. Promising to endure, Lear recognizes in the bear a nature from which he initially thought he was exempt. This double opening, both to the existence and experience of the animal, helps Lear become the chastised man Cordelia protects. When she finds him, she restores him to that better place he has learned, through what he has lived, to appreciate. Removing his thorns and changing his clothes, Cordelia attempts to revive in her father the eminence he lost in the duration of his trial. Cordelia's rage translates into more than a praise for endurance; it resounds with an insistence on reparation. If Lear on the heath was reduced, through his relationship with Kent and his "unbuttoning" with Edgar, to the naked babe of fortune, Cordelia gives him back his former prowess, taking him in four steps beyond the stage of childhood and into his present age. When she ascends in her appellations (first) from "poor perdu" (4.7.35) to (second) "poor father" (4.7.38), she transforms Lear from child lost to man loved. When she insists (third) "No, Sir, you must not kneel" (4.7.59), she reminds him at once of his position as royalty and his role as parent. Blessing him, she begs Lear, as Joseph did Israel, to bless her, returning to her father the kingdom of supremacy he thought long ago vanished. Fourth, she places him once more on the royal pedestal, advancing in her address from child, to father, to Sir, to "Highness" (4.7.83), even as she assures him with the full force of her presence—"I am, I am" (4.7.70)—of his majesty as king.

And when the recovered Lear, in turn, commands Cordelia to "bear with" him (4.7.83), he turns to the future, imploring her to endure at his side the burden of humanity that might make it possible to bloom together ("bear") in a revival he henceforth can anticipate. That shared expectation is what Lear sought on the heath and what he finds now. Finally, when he prays to Cordelia, empowering her to act as God, commanding her to obey as child (4.7.84), he removes the past, lifting with the "forget and forgive" any burden of personal guilt. If he is now old and foolish, perhaps he was so "then." The release makes it possible to see his daughter at once as young child he can direct (bear with) and as fellow creature who can help (bear him up). A "fool" (4.7.60), Lear arrives at the stage of helplessness that still has hope, having survived the tears of birth and reached ancient renewal. The enclosed story ends there. Restored to his kingship, Lear returns, in act 5, to his early self.

When Cordelia revives her father, she reinstills his initial possessiveness; bolstered by the exhilaration of his recovery, Lear imagines his independence by denying Cordelia hers. Even as he vows to defy his enemies by creating a psychological freedom within the prison's confines, he deprives Cordelia of her own voice. Her future, her capacity to bear her own life, have her own children, is forgotten. She can now only "bear with" (sustain) her father:

> Come, let's away to prison;
> We two alone will sing like birds i' th' cage:
> When thou dost ask me blessing, I'll kneel down,
> And ask of thee forgiveness: so we'll live,
> And pray, and sing, and tell old tales, and laugh
> At gilded butterflies ...
> . . . .
> Upon such sacrifices, my Cordelia,
> The Gods themselves throw incense. Have I caught thee? (5.3.8–13; 20–21)

With the redundant "two" of his opening he reveals how Cordelia fortifies him. With the "alone," he speaks as if the two of them were the last people on earth, on yet another island of imposed love. After he assures Cordelia of the gods' assent, Lear turns and asks, "Have I caught thee?" With that question, he confesses how his vision of protection is buttressed by his daughter. If Lear is imprisoned by Edmund, Cordelia is confined by Lear. He captures his bird, enticing it into the cage by a combination of rhetorical logic and physical embrace. Lear has "caught" Cordelia, inspiring her and holding her with him as a wall within the enclave of the world he now anticipates. There, he seeks to preserve the "blessing and forgiving" of his recovery by perpetually repeating it. He creates a tableau, a picture of kneeling parent and importuned child, which will "wear out" those who "ebb and flow by the moon." Those who so ebb and flow are those whose earthly fortunes change—the gilded butterflies and the court fools. But they are also those who live by the changing process of time and seek, in the generational cycle, a continuance that also depends, in its monthly progress, on the moon. In his image of what he and Cordelia will do, Lear creates an artistic empire (tiny as it is) that transcends (in his mind) both the peaceful flow—and the flooding tides—of nature outside. As Spenser "holds" his characters, Lear "catches" his daughter in a moment of reconciling arrest that impedes the dynastic renewal so important to the foundling formula.

In his exaltation Lear, returned to his beginnings, reiterates the fatal flaw of his initiation—the belief in a picture of love that is self-sustaining. For the rich pastures of the opening, he substitutes a little cage, content with the simplicity he has learned to endure during his trial. But that happy isolation sets him off once more into a false pastoral interlude, a fantasy realm within the same court he initially transformed. No wonder, then, that the beast he originally denied rises once again to its monstrosity, leaving (as it did in *Hamlet*) a stage of corpses and raising (as it did not in the end for Hamlet) the specter of nothingness. When Cordelia is hanged, Lear's faith is wrenched away. He ends where he began, discerning neither object in space—"no, no, no life" (5.7.305)—nor proof in time—"never" (5.3.308). If Cordelia does not breathe, what is left is carnivorous nature—a dog, a horse, a rat—obliterating living man. There is no thing in itself, no returning sign of the humanity Lear lost and then found. He has not caught Cordelia; he cannot hold her still in his arms. Nothing remains to face the bear in the mouth. Believing, as he once did, in the goodness of art, even if it is a better art than he earlier espoused, Lear is left with only the evil in nature—an evil, moreover, that he, both through paternity and philosophy, engendered.

Lear at the end is to Cordelia what the ghost was to Hamlet in the beginning, imposing on her a vision of filial forgiveness as the ghost forced on his son an obligation for familial revenge. Like the ghost, Lear calls his child back to himself, "catching" her without casting her forward into the generations. Both tragedies end in lost dynasties. Each hero is given a moment of recovered beginnings (Hamlet's restoration of his childhood, Lear's reconciliation with Cordelia) that cannot last. The generational continuity—so vital to the foundling formula—is left for someone else to fulfill. The vision of *King Lear* is barren, its emptiness heightened by the false hopes of the temporary reconciliation. Lear's tragedy is precipitated in the first act by his failure to appreciate the needs of his children. When he demands that Cordelia love her father "all" (1.1.94), he denies her the right, as she answers, to make a future with her husband. When the restored Lear ignores that future again by reviving the parental possessiveness that caused his downfall in the first place, he destroys the dynastic sequence that should follow the forgiving and blessing in the foundling experience. Proselytizing the fictional realm of "old tales" (5.3.12), as he had earlier boasted about his "champains rich" (1.1.64), Lear reverses the foundling formula. The art of the lost interlude rises at the beginning and at the end, both times unleashing an absolutely savage nature. The relatively benign nature of the enclosed story, a nature that could sustain the belief in return corroborated by Cordelia's coronation speech in act 4, will "come no more" (5.3.307) to sustain Lear. Despite the brief recovery of his child, he is left with "nothing." He cannot keep—or be kept by—his family.

> —BARBARA L. ESTRIN, "A World Within: Found Enclosure and Final Exposure in *King Lear*," *The Raven and the Lark: Lost Children in Literature of the English Renaissance* (Lewisburg, PA: Bucknell University Press, 1985), pp. 170–77

YVES BONNEFOY

The historical context of *Lear* is not without certain resemblances to the earlier play (*Hamlet*), since the work is set in an England at least as archaic as the Denmark of Hamlet's father—it is even a pagan world, closely watched over by its gods—and yet here, too, one discovers signs that seem to announce new modes of being. And in *Lear* there also emerges a character one can sense from the outset incapable of recognizing that the world is an order, rich in meaning—Edmund, second son of the Earl of Gloucester. A son, then, like the prince of Denmark, and one who has, like Hamlet, reasons for doubt about what will be his heritage. But the resemblance between Edmund and Hamlet stops there, for the painful plight of the son, which Hamlet has lived through with honesty and with the burning desire to do what is right, is now studied in one who is clearly evil, and with conceptual categories that remain essentially medieval. One might, at first sight, consider modern this certainly noncomformist personality who scoffs at astrological explanations, at the superstitions of those who surround him, and even at the values of common morality. But it should be observed that Edmund's speeches are accompanied by none of those indications—such as the actors, Wittenberg, the presence of Horatio—which in *Hamlet* serve to mark, by outward sign, that one is approaching the modern era. What makes Edmund an outsider, far from being seen as symptomatic of crisis, is rather set very explicitly by Shakespeare in the context of one of the convictions advanced by the medieval understanding of man: if Edmund would usurp his brother's place, if he longs to see his father dead, if he thus shows how far he is from the most universal human feelings, it is because he is a bastard, born out of wedlock, the fruit himself of sin. And it is in complete agreement with traditional Christian teaching that *King Lear* asks us to understand that this sin, this adultery, is precisely the occasion that evil, ever unvanquished, even if always repelled, has been waiting for—the chance to invade once again the order established by God, which order will nonetheless in the end emerge triumphant once more, thanks to the intervention of a few righteous souls. And this being the case, if Edmund evokes nature as his one guiding principle, as the law to which his services are bound, one should not see in this a reflection of the Renaissance humanist for whom the study of matter is unbiased activity of mind, but rather the relevation of the baseness of a soul, influenced, on the contrary, by black magic—a soul that feels at home nowhere so much as amidst the most frankly animal realities. Edmund's actions do not disclose the ultimate crisis of the sacred order, but rather its innermost weakness. And one knows from the very outset of the action that he will perish—unmistakably, without a trace of uneasiness or regret, without a future in the new forms of consciousness, as soon as the forces of goodness he has caught off guard have reestablished their power.

Far from signifying, then, that Shakespeare's attention is focused on the problems of modernity as such, as was the case in *Hamlet,* the character of the son in *King Lear* serves rather to reinforce the notion that the old order remains the uncontested frame of reference in the play, the determining factor in the outcome of the drama, the truth that will be reaffirmed after a moment of crisis. And it is clearly for this reason that there emerges in the foreground of the play a figure missing in *Hamlet,* since neither Laertes nor Fortinbras ever attains truly spiritual stature, the figure of the child—girl or boy, since it is as true of Cordelia, third daughter of Lear, as of Edgar, firstborn son of Gloucester—whose purity and moral determination find the means of thwarting the traitors' schemes. In fact, more even than Cordelia, whose somewhat cool and arid virtuousness keeps a certain distance from those violent, contradictory words, mingled with both love and hatred, through which the action of the play is developed and resolved, the agent of redemption for the imperilled group is Edgar who, at the very moment when he might have yielded to despair or given in to cynicism—hasn't he been falsely accused, attacked by his own brother, misjudged without cause, by his father?—gives proof, on the contrary, to those reserves of compassion, of lucidity, of resolute understanding of the darkest depths of the souls of others, that can be found in anyone, even quite early in life and without special preparation. Struck in a completely unforseeable way by what appears to be the purest form of evil, this still very young man, who only the day before was rich, pampered, assured of a future place among the most powerful of the land, chooses at once to plunge into the very depths of adversity, taking on the semblance of a beggar and the speech of a fool to shatter at the outset the too narrow framework of his own personal drama and to bring his inquiry to bear on all injustices, all the miseries, all the forms of madness that afflict society. He understands instinctively—and here is clearly a sign that this world is still alive—that he will be able to achieve his salvation only by working for the salvation of others, each man needing as much as another to free himself from his egotism, from his excesses, from his pride so that true exchange might begin once more.

In spite of everything, however, the hero of *King Lear* remains the one for whom the play is named—the old King—since unlike Edmund who has been marked from the outset by the sin involved in his birth, and in contrast to Edgar who emerges into his maturity through the crimes of another, Lear is thrown into his troubles by his own free act, and thus his punishment and his folly, his gradual discovery of those truths and realities he had neglected before, become a succession of events all the more deeply convincing and touching. Lear begins, not with something rotten in the state, as was the case for Hamlet, but rather with a mysterious sickness in the soul, and in this case, with pride. Lear admires himself, prefers himself; he is interested in others only to the extent that they are interested in him, and thus he is blind to their own true being; he therefore does not truly love others, in spite of what he might think: and so the ground is laid for the catastrophic act that will refuse to recognize true value, that will deprive the righteous of their due, and that will spread disorder and sorrow everywhere and give the devil the chance he has been waiting for in the son born of adultery. Lear—even more than Gloucester whose only sins are sins of the flesh—has relived, has reactivated the original sin of men, and thus he represents, more than any other character in the play, our condition in its most radical form, which is imperfection, but also struggle, the will to self-mastery. When, on the basis of those values he has never denied but has understood so poorly and lived so little, he learns to recognize that his kingly self-assurance is pure pretension, his love a mere illusion, and when he learns what true love is, what happiness could be, one feels all the more deeply moved as his initial blindness belongs to all of us, more or less: he speaks to the universal. And yet, even though he occupies the foreground from beginning to end of the play, Lear cannot and must not hold our attention simply because of what he is, or merely on the basis of his own particular individuality, since his spiritual progress comes precisely from having rediscovered the path toward others and from having thereafter forgotten about himself in the fullness of this exchange. It is in the modern era, the era of Hamlet, that the individual—separated from everything and from everybody, incapable of checking his solitude, and trying to remedy what is missing through the proliferation of his desires, his dreams, and his thoughts—will slowly assume that extraordinary prominence, the end point of which is Romanticism. In *King Lear*—as on the gothic fresco which is always more or less the *danse macabre*—no one has greater worth merely because of what sets him apart from others, however singular or extreme this difference might be. The soul, studied from the point of view of its free will, which is the same in every man, is less the object of descriptions that note differences than it is the very stage of the action, and from the outset the only stage: and what appears in the play, what finds expression there, are the great key figures of the society, such as the king and his fool, the powerful lord and the poor man, and those categories of common experience such as Fortune or charity, or the deadly sins that Marlowe, in his *Doctor Faustus*, scarcely ten years earlier, had not been reluctant to keep on stage. In short, behind this character who is remarkable, but whose uncommon sides are above all signs of the extent of the dangers that menace us—and the extent of the resources at our disposition as well—the true object of Shakespeare's attention, the true presence that emerges and runs the risk of being overwhelmed, but triumphs in the end, is that life of the spirit to which Lear, and Edgar as well, and also to a certain extent Gloucester and even Albany all bear witness—what is designated by the word *ripeness*.

Ripeness, maturation, the acceptance of death as in *Hamlet*, but no longer in this case because death would be the sign, par excellence, of the indifference of the world, the lack of meaning—no, rather because acceptance of death could be the occasion for rising to a truly inner understanding of the real laws governing being, for freeing oneself from illusion, from vain pursuits, for opening oneself to a conception of Presence which, mirrored in our fundamental acts, will guarantee a living place to the individual in the evidence of All. One can only understand *King Lear* if one has learned to place this consideration in the foreground, if one has come to see that this is the thread that binds everything together, not only the young man with the old one whose soul is ravaged but intact, but with them the Fool, for instance, who represents in medieval thought the outermost edge of our uncertain condition; and this consideration must be seen to dominate even in a context in which the forces of night seem so powerful, in which the Christian promise has not yet resounded—although its structures are already there, since it is Shakespeare who is writing; one can therefore sense in them an indication of change, a reason for hope. *Ripeness* emerges in *Lear* as a potentiality for everyone, as the existential starting point from which the protagonists of this tragedy of false appearances begin to be something more than mere shadows; and from the Fool to Lear, from Edgar to his father, from Cordelia, from Kent, from Gloucester to their sovereign, even from an obscure servant to his lord when the latter has his eyes plucked out, it is what gives the only real substance to human exchange which is otherwise reduced to concerns and desires that are only hypocrisy or illusion. This primacy accorded to the inner life of men, with the inevitable shaking of the foundations that comes with it, is what gives meaning to the most famous scene in *Lear* in which one sees Edgar, disguised as a fool, with the fool who is a fool by profession, and Lear, who is losing his mind, all raving together—or at least so it seems—beneath the stormy skies. Those blasting winds and bursts of lightning, that crackling of the cosmos, might well seem to suggest the collapse of meaning, the true state of a world we once had thought of as our home; but let us not forget that in that hovel, and under the semblance of solitude, misfortune, and weariness, the irrational powers that tend to reestablish truth are working much more freely than ever they could in the castles of only a moment before. It is here that true reflection begins again, here that the idea of justice takes shape once more. This stormy night speaks to us of dawn. The brutality of the gods and of men, the fragility of life, are as nothing against a showing of instinctive solidarity that brings things together and provides comfort. And let us also remember that nothing of this sort appears in *Hamlet*, where, if one excepts Horatio, who in fact withdraws from the action, and Ophelia, who, unable to be what she truly wants to be, becomes mad and kills herself, everything in the relationship between people is cynical, harsh, and joyless: let us not forget, for instance, the way in which Hamlet himself gets rid of Rosencrantz and Guilden-stern—"They are not near my conscience." It is not the universe of *Lear*—however bloody it might seem—that contains the most darkness. This "tragedy"—but in an entirely different sense from the Greek understanding of the term—is, with com-parison to *Hamlet*, an act of faith. We meet in an arena of error, of crime, of dreadfully unjust death, in which even the very idea of Heaven seems missing; and yet, "the center holds," meaning manages to survive and even to take on new depth, assuring values, calling forth sacrifice and devotion, allowing for moral in-tegrity, for dignity, and for a relation to oneself that one might term plenary if not blissful. Here we learn that the structures of meaning are but a bridge of thread thrown over frightful depths; but these threads are made of steel.

—YVES BONNEFOY, "Readiness, Ripeness: *Hamlet, Lear,*" tr. John T. McNaughton, *New Literary History* 17, No. 3 (Spring 1986): 485–91

BENNETT SIMON, M.D.

Lear demands, Lear commands; he does not listen. Only as his suffering and his learning proceed do we sense a gradual shift from the imperative to the interroga-tive, from the imperious to the attentive. His ability to relinquish his illusions, partial at best, allows him to accept some passivity and limitation. His plaint late in the play, "they told me I was everything: 'tis a lie, I am not ague-proof" (4.6.106–07), reflects both his grandiosity and the glimmers of what he has so painfully learned. Clearly, Lear's madness involves a megalomaniac contest with the forces of nature, a de-lusion about his ability to control and command everything. For many viewers and readers, his behavior before his florid madness similarly involves an assumption, characterological rather than psychotic, that he can forestall some of life's inevita-bilities. These include not only the consequences of growing old and having to relinquish power, but the belief that one can control the separations, divisions, and differentiations that are entailed in parent-child and sibling relationships and in political matters. His demand of Cordelia that she "love her father all" is as grandiose as the wrenching final scene of the play in which Lear recognizes that Cordelia is dead and still insists that she might breathe and live.

> I know when one is dead and when one lives;
> She's dead as earth. Lend me a looking glass. (5.3.262–63)

Heinz Kohut once defined narcissism, the narcissistic conception of the people in one's life, as the belief that the other should obey you as does your right arm (1971, p. 33). Lear's definition of the outrage inflicted on him by Goneril and Regan is:

> Filial ingratitude,
> Is it not as this mouth should tear this hand
> For lifting foot to 't? (3.4.14–16)

Lear cannot let go. His attempt to relinquish temporal responsibility is not combined with a realistic appraisal of the necessary loss of privilege. Goneril and Regan torture him by quite specifically understanding his vulnerability and finding every way to strip him of power and remind him of his helpless dependency upon them. The Fool taunts Lear, torturing him in his own way, with reminders that Lear does not know the difference between commonsense holding and commonsense giving away. Lear's childish expectations lead to the dramatic and tragic reversals of the play, in which children become mothers and fathers to their parents. Edgar's "He childed as I fathered" (3.6.109) epitomizes these unnatural reversals, as do the Fool's taunts, "thou mad'st thy daughters thy mothers...thou gav'st them the rod, and put'st down thine own breeches" (1.4.176–78).

Lear does not understand that authority and affection rest on a complex and subtle matrix of obligation, power, loyalty, reciprocal need, and love. None of these is absolute. Cordelia in vain tries to explain:

> Good my lord,
> You have begot me, bred me, and loved me. I
> Return those duties back as are right fit,
> Obey you, love you, and most honor you.
> Why have my sisters husbands, if they say
> They love you all? Haply, when I shall wed,
> That lord whose hand must take my plight shall carry
> Half my love with him, half my care and duty.
> Sure I shall never marry like my sisters,
> To love my father all. (1.1.98–106)

Lear's response to this speech is to proclaim, simultaneously, infinite distance between parent and child and no distance at all. He disowns and banishes Cordelia and then collapses generational distances and distinctions by means of a cannibalistic image of merger:

> The barbarous Scythian,
> Or he that makes his generation messes
> To gorge his appetite, shall to my bosom
> Be as well neighbored, pitied, and relieved,
> As thou my sometime daughter.   (1.1.118–23)

His disappointment in Cordelia is in proportion to how much he had counted on her to be, in return for his love for her, the nurse of his old age. "I loved her most, and thought to set my rest / On her kind nursery" (1.1.125–26).

Indeed, images of cannibalism, of parent and child devouring each other, are scattered throughout the play and typically convey an ambiguity around whether closeness, union, or all-devouring rage is at work. " 'Twas this flesh begot / Those pelican daughters" (3.4.74–75) is the most famous instance of such a confusion— the pelican daughters devour their father, who begot them. In Elizabethan symbolism, the pelican is a bird that "loveth too much her children" and allows them to smite the parents in the face. In anger, the mother pelican then slays the children and "on the third day"—Christ-like—sheds her own blood onto her children, who are then quickened by the blood of the dying mother (Furness 1880, ad loc.).

In Lear's rage at his other two daughters, we encounter other forms of degradation of parent-child closeness. We see the transforming power of narcissistic rage: the child is now an internal persecutor or poisoner. Lear shouts at Goneril:

> We'll no more meet, no more see one another.
> But yet thou are my flesh, my blood, my daughter,
> Or rather a disease that's in my flesh,
> Which must needs call mine. Thou are a boil,
> A plague-sore, or embossèd carbuncle
> In my corrupted blood.   (2.4.219–23)

Lear, when all is said and done in the play, has achieved only a limited awareness of the need for differentiation and relinquishing control over one's children. One of the tenderest scenes, yet one marking Lear's tragic inability to let go, is "No, no, no, no! let's away to prison: / We two alone will sing like birds i' th' cage" (5.3.8–9). "He that parts us shall bring a brand from heaven / And fire us hence like foxes" (22–23). He ignores the fact that Cordelia is married (as does Cordelia!), just as he refuses in act 1, scene 1, to acknowledge any division of loyalty on Cordelia's part.

But inadequate separation and differentiation, the unwillingness to relinquish, is not only Lear's hallmark, it is a characteristic of the play. Cordelia, especially in the last act and according to some readings, in the first act as well, similarly has difficulty acknowledging separation. Edmund in the final act reveals that he is promised, adulterously, to both Goneril and Regan. When he learns of their deaths, as he is dying, he puns: "all three now marry in an instant" (5.3.230).

The term *pathological grief* has come to signify a refusal to acknowledge death, loss, or separation, an insistence on maintaining by denial, in fantasy or in deed, that a death (for example) has not taken place or is not final. A narcissistic relation to another person, an insistence on the other's serving primarily as an extension of the self, can also be viewed from the perspective of pathological grief as a refusal to mourn, a refusal to acknowledge separation and growth. Refusal to mourn is an important part of the play, particularly in Lear himself. Lear does not cry. If he begins to cry, he must stifle the tears; he is ashamed of his tears, curses his eyes, and threatens to pluck them out if ever they cry again (1.4.308–11). He can allude, ambiguously, to crying oneself to sleep, but this is manifestly framed as railing against Regan and her husband, Cornwall (2.4.115). He will not cry, for it is unmanly and, even worse, would involve full acknowledgment of the loss of affection and respect from Goneril and Regan.

> [You gods] ... touch me with noble anger,
> And let not women's weapons, water drops,
> Stain my man's cheeks. No, you unnatural hags!
> I will have such revenges on you both
> That all the world shall—I will do such things—
> What they are, yet I know not; but they shall be
> The terrors of the earth. You think I'll weep.
> No, I'll not weep.
>   *Storm and tempest.*
> I have full cause of weeping, but this heart
> Shall break into a hundred thousand flaws
> Or ere I'll weep. O Fool, I shall go mad!   (2.4.275–85)

Lear, in his madness, still refuses to weep, but the flood of rain in the storm actualizes in the world of nature the torrents of tears he is keeping back. In act 4, he struggles with tears several times, primarily in his encounter with Gloucester, and then in his reunion with Cordelia. In the recognition scene, when the still mad but slightly calmer Lear meets the blind Gloucester, Lear refers repeatedly to tears, but they are literally given over to Gloucester or ascribed to the generality of mankind. Lear addresses the blind Gloucester, who is crying:

> LEAR: If thou wilt weep my fortunes, take my eyes.
> I know thee well enough; thy name is Gloucester:
> Thou must be patient; we came crying hither:
> Thou know'st, the first time that we smell the air
> We wawl and cry. I will preach to thee: mark.
> GLOUCESTER: Alack, alack the day!
> LEAR: When we are born, we cry that we are come
> To this great stage of fools.   (4.6.178–85)

Lear's struggle with weeping and his need to distance himself from his own tears is seen in the conditional tense of the verb:

Why, this would make a man a man of salt,
To use his eyes for garden water-pots,
Ay, and laying autumn's dust.   (4.6.197–98)

In the scene of his awakening and reunion with Cordelia, as he is slowly coming to recognize and acknowledge her, his tears are not salt water but a dangerous and destructive liquid.

You do me wrong to take me out o' th' grave:
Thou art a soul in bliss; but I am bound
Upon a wheel of fire, that mine own tears
Do scald like molten lead.   (4.7.45–48)

He associates tears, especially his own, to poison as he explicitly names Cordelia:

LEAR: For, as I am a man, I think this lady
To be my child Cordelia.
CORDELIA: And so I am, I am.
LEAR: Be your tears wet? Yes, faith. I pray, weep not.
If you have poison for me, I will drink it. (4.7.68–72)

Tears, then, signify for Lear everything unacceptable to his fragile yet inflated sense of self: vulnerability, need for another, feminine weakness, childish attachment, caring, and, at the bottom, mortality.

Lear's inability to recognize the realities of aging, mortality, and separation and the necessary distinctions between parent and child are thus made tangible and visible around the scenes of weeping, especially thwarted weeping. Another important image of this inability is that of childish games—especially in the Fool's songs, which for Lear are a mixture of taunting and therapy. Early in the play, as Lear is beginning to see the consequences of his foolish divestments and his rejection of Cordelia, he is irritated but intrigued by the Fool:

LEAR: When were you wont to be so full of songs, sirrah?
FOOL: I have used it, Nuncle, e'er since thou mad'st thy daughters thy mothers;
        for when thou gav'st them the rod, and put'st down thine own breeches,
Then they for sudden joy did weep,
    And I for sorrow sung,
That such a king should play bo-peep,
    And go the fools among.   (1.4.176–82)

Lear has made himself into a bad child and has offered himself to be beaten by his mother. The image of the king's pulling down his pants and exposing his buttocks to be beaten has sexual reverberations as well as overtones of parental discipline. For the moment, I want to focus on the phrase "play bo-peep." Insofar as this is an allusion to the well-known nursery rhyme, "Little Bo-Peep has lost her sheep," there are several meanings condensed therein. Who is the sheep and who the shepherd is ambiguous: Lear is at once and alternately both shepherd and lost sheep. His daughters were originally his sheep, and he is lost as a leader. As a (female) shepherd, he is weak and impotent. Shall he meekly await the sheep's return home, hoping that they will be both penitent and joyful to be reconciled with him? He is also a shepherd who does not know how many sheep he has or wants. Is Cordelia one of them, or only Goneril and Regan? Is he a father or a mother—especially apt in a play where there is scarcely a mention of "Queen Lear"? Who is looking for nurturance from whom? Many other constructions and construals can arise from this line of comparison to the nursery rhyme, and I believe it is a valid and useful exegesis of what the poetic genius packed into a few words. As it happens, one cannot, strickly speaking, use "Little Bo-Peep" as a gloss on this passage, because its appearance cannot be documented before 1810, although it is probably older and may well have been Elizabethan. Though the nursery rhyme is a "modern" association to the play, the lines of meaning that emanate from using it as a gloss do correspond with features of the play as a whole.

In Elizabethan times, the meaning of "play bo-peep" corresponded more to the phrase "play peek-a-boo." This reverberates with a childhood game that has a number of different implications. In this passage, who is the nursemaid or mother, and who the baby? Lear, again, alternately takes both roles, mother and baby, playing a game of appearance and disappearance; is it permanent or is it not? It is also a game of pretending, making believe that something is not there that really is, and vice-versa. The game can generate considerable excitement, as well as anxiety, in a baby. The Fool's interpretation to Lear, then, of Lear's giving away his kingdom and disavowing a daughter is that via the excitement of a "gone-but-not-gone" game, he was seeking to "play peek-a-boo" with aging, death, loss, and necessary separation from his children. In his demand for love from them, he was also playing the game of "she loves me—she loves me not," hoping to stave off any true test of love. Other connotations of "bo-peep" in Elizabethan times are of coyness, shyness, and also lascivious looking, peeping, and peeking. The game he is playing with his daughters is thus also a sexualized one.

"Play bo-peep" enacts several kinds of childhood fantasies and fears: early mother-child separation, sexual excitement in games with mother, seduction and refusal, perpetual suspense—no ending, no culmination. In effect, the Fool's taunt is that Lear, either as a mother or as child, cannot face up to the inevitable and thereby makes things absolutely topsy-turvy.

—BENNETT SIMON, M.D., "All Germains Spill at Once: Shakespeare's
King Lear," Tragic Drama and the Family: Psychoanalytic Studies from
Aeschylus to Beckett (New Haven: Yale University Press, 1988), pp. 106–12

CRITICAL ESSAYS

A. C. Bradley

KING LEAR

I

The position of the hero in this tragedy is in one important respect peculiar. The reader of *Hamlet, Othello,* or *Macbeth,* is in no danger of forgetting, when the catastrophe is reached, the part played by the hero in bringing it on. His fatal weakness, error, wrong-doing, continues almost to the end. It is otherwise with *King Lear.* When the conclusion arrives, the old King has for a long while been passive. We have long regarded him not only as 'a man more sinned against than sinning,' but almost wholly as a sufferer, hardly at all as an agent. His sufferings too have been so cruel, and our indignation against those who inflicted them has been so intense, that recollection of the wrong he did to Cordelia, to Kent, and to his realm, has been well-nigh effaced. Lastly, for nearly four Acts he has inspired in us, together with his pity, much admiration and affection. The force of his passion has made us feel that his nature was great; and his frankness and generosity, his heroic efforts to be patient, the depth of his shame and repentance, and the ecstasy of his re-union with Cordelia, have melted our very hearts. Naturally, therefore, at the close we are in some danger of forgetting that the storm which has overwhelmed him was liberated by his own deed.

Yet it is essential that Lear's contribution to the action of the drama should be remembered; not at all in order that we may feel that he 'deserved' what he suffered, but because otherwise his fate would appear to us at best pathetic, at worst shocking, but certainly not tragic. And when we were reading the earlier scenes of the play we recognised this contribution clearly enough. At the very beginning, it is true, we are inclined to feel merely pity and misgivings. The first lines tell us that Lear's mind is beginning to fail with age.[1] Formerly he had perceived how different were the characters of Albany and Cornwall, but now he seems either to have lost this perception or to be unwisely ignoring it. The rashness of his division

From *Shakespearean Tragedy* (London: Macmillan, 1904), pp. 280–93.

of the kingdom troubles us, and we cannot but see with concern that its motive is mainly selfish. The absurdity of the pretence of making the division depend on protestations of love from his daughters, his complete blindness to the hypocrisy which is patent to us at a glance, his piteous delight in these protestations, the openness of his expressions of preference for his youngest daughter—all make us smile, but all pain us. But pity begins to give way to another feeling when we witness the precipitance, the despotism, the uncontrolled anger of his injustice to Cordelia and Kent, and the 'hideous rashness' of his persistence in dividing the kingdom after the rejection of his own dutiful child. We feel now the presence of force as well as weakness, but we feel also the presence of the tragic ὕβρις. Lear, we see, is generous and unsuspicious, of an open and free nature, like Hamlet and Othello and indeed most of Shakespeare's heroes, who in this, according to Ben Jonson, resemble the poet who made them. Lear, we see, is also choleric by temperament—the first of Shakespeare's heroes who is so. And a long life of absolute power, in which he has been flattered to the top of his bent, has produced in him that blindness to human limitations, and that presumptuous self-will, which in Greek tragedy we have so often seen stumbling against the altar of Nemesis. Our consciousness that the decay of old age contributes to this condition deepens our pity and our sense of human infirmity, but certainly does not lead us to regard the old King as irresponsible, and so to sever the tragic *nexus* which binds together his error and his calamities.

The magnitude of this first error is generally fully recognised by the reader owing to his sympathy with Cordelia, though, as we have seen, he often loses the memory of it as the play advances. But this is not so, I think, with the repetition of this error, in the quarrel with Goneril. Here the daughter excites so much detestation, and the father so much sympathy, that we often fail to receive the due impression of his violence. There is not here, of course, the *injustice* of his rejection of Cordelia, but there is precisely the same ὕβρις. This had been shown most strikingly in the first scene when, *immediately* upon the apparently cold words of Cordelia, 'So young, my lord, and true,' there comes this dreadful answer:

Let it be so; thy truth then be thy dower.
For, by the sacred radiance of the sun,
The mysteries of Hecate and the night;
By all the operation of the orbs
From whom we do exist and cease to be;
Here I disclaim all my paternal care,
Propinquity and property of blood,
And as a stranger to my heart and me
Hold thee from this for ever. The barbarous Scythian,
Or he that makes his generation messes
To gorge his appetite, shall to my bosom
Be as well neighbour'd, pitied and relieved,
As thou my sometime daughter.

Now the dramatic effect of this passage is exactly, and doubtless intentionally, repeated in the curse pronounced against Goneril. This does not come after the daughters have openly and wholly turned against their father. Up to the moment of its utterance Goneril has done no more than to require him 'a little to disquantity' and reform his train of knights. Certainly her manner and spirit in making this demand are hateful, and probably her accusations against the knights are false; and we should expect from any father in Lear's position passionate distress and indignation. But surely the famous words which form Lear's immediate reply were meant to be nothing short of frightful:

> Hear, nature, hear; dear goddess, hear!
> Suspend thy purpose, if thou didst intend
> To make this creature fruitful!
> Into her womb convey sterility!
> Dry up in her the organs of increase;
> And from her derogate body never spring
> A babe to honour her! If she must teem,
> Create her child of spleen; that it may live,
> And be a thwart disnatured torment to her!
> Let it stamp wrinkles in her brow of youth;
> With cadent tears fret channels in her cheeks;
> Turn all her mother's pains and benefits
> To laughter and contempt; that she may feel
> How sharper than a serpent's tooth it is
> To have a thankless child!

The question is not whether Goneril deserves these appalling imprecations, but what they tell us about Lear. They show that, although he has already recognised his injustice towards Cordelia, is secretly blaming himself, and is endeavouring to do better, the disposition from which his first error sprang is still unchanged. And it is precisely the disposition to give rise, in evil surroundings, to calamities dreadful but at the same time tragic, because due in some measure to the person who endures them.

The perception of this connection, if it is not lost as the play advances, does not at all diminish our pity for Lear, but it makes it impossible for us permanently to regard the world displayed in this tragedy as subject to a mere arbitrary or malicious power. It makes us feel that this world is so far at least a rational and a moral order, that there holds in it the law, not of proportionate requital, but of strict connection between act and consequence. It is, so far, the world of all Shakespeare's tragedies.

But there is another aspect of Lear's story, the influence of which modifies, in a way quite different and more peculiar to this tragedy, the impressions called pessimistic and even this impression of law. There is nothing more noble and beautiful in literature than Shakespeare's exposition of the effect of suffering in reviving the greatness and eliciting the sweetness of Lear's nature. The occasional recurrence, during his madness, of autocratic impatience or of desire for revenge serves only to heighten this effect, and the moments when his insanity becomes merely infinitely piteous do not weaken it. The old King who in pleading with his daughters feels so intensely his own humiliation and their horrible ingratitude, and who yet, at fourscore and upward, constrains himself to practise a self-control and patience so many years disused; who out of old affection for his Fool, and in repentance for his injustice to the Fool's beloved mistress, tolerates incessant and cutting reminders of his own folly and wrong; in whom the rage of the storm awakes a power and a poetic grandeur surpassing even that of Othello's anguish ; who comes in his affliction to think of others first, and to seek, in tender solicitude for his poor boy, the shelter he scorns for his own bare head; who learnes to feel and to pray for the miserable and houseless poor, to discern the falseness of flattery and the brutality of authority, and to pierce below the differences of rank and raiment to the common humanity beneath; whose sight is so purged by scalding tears that it sees at last how power and place and all things in the world are vanity except love; who tastes in his last hours the extremes both of love's rapture and of its agony, but could never, if he lived on or lived again, care a jot for aught beside—there is no figure, surely, in the world of poetry at once so grand, so pathetic, and so beautiful as his. Well, but Lear owes the whole of this to those sufferings which made us doubt whether life were not simply evil, and men like the flies which wanton boys torture for their sport. Should we not be at least as near the truth if we called this poem *The Redemption of King Lear,* and declared that the business of 'the gods' with him was neither to torment him, nor to teach him a 'noble anger,' but to lead him to attain through apparently hopeless failure the very end and aim of life ? One can believe that Shakespeare had been tempted at times to feel misanthropy and despair, but it is quite impossible that he can have been mastered by such feelings at the time when he produced this conception.

To dwell on the stages of this process of purification (the word is Professor Dowden's) is impossible here; and there are scenes, such as that of the meeting of Lear and Cordelia, which it seems almost a profanity to touch.[2] But I will refer to two scenes which may remind us more in detail of some of the points just mentioned. The third and fourth scenes of Act III. present one of those contrasts which speak as eloquently even as Shakespeare's words, and which were made possible in his theatre by the absence of scenery and the consequent absence of intervals between the scenes. First, in a scene of twenty-three lines, mostly in prose, Gloster is shown, telling his son Edmund how Goneril and Regan have forbidden him on pain of death to succour the houseless King; how a secret letter has reached him, announcing the arrival of a French force; and how, whatever the consequences may be, he is determined to relieve his old master. Edmund, left alone, soliloquises in words which seem to freeze one's blood:

> This courtesy, forbid thee, shall the duke
> Instantly know; and of that letter too:
> This seems a fair deserving, and must draw me

That which my father loses; no less than all:
The younger rises when the old doth fall.

He goes out; and the next moment, as the fourth scene opens, we find ourselves in the icy storm with Lear, Kent, and the Fool, and yet in the inmost shrine of love. I am not speaking of the devotion of the others to Lear, but of Lear himself. He had consented, merely for the Fool's sake, to seek shelter in the hovel:

> Come, your hovel.
> Poor fool and knave, I have one part in my heart
> That's sorry yet for thee.

But on the way he has broken down and has been weeping (III. iv. 17), and now he resists Kent's efforts to persuade him to enter. He does not feel the storm:

> When the mind's free
> The body's delicate: the tempest in my mind
> Doth from my senses take all feeling else
> Save what beats there:

and the thoughts that will drive him mad are burning in his brain:

> Filial ingratitude!
> Is it not as this mouth should tear this hand
> For lifting food to't? But I will punish home.
> No, I will weep no more. In such a night
> To shut me out! Pour on; I will endure.
> In such a night as this! O Regan, Goneril!
> Your old kind father, whose frank heart gave all,—
> O, that way madness lies; let me shun that;
> No more of that.

And then suddenly, as he controls himself, the blessed spirit of kindness breathes on him 'like a meadow gale of spring,' and he turns gently to Kent:

> Prithee, go in thyself; seek thine own ease:
> This tempest will not give me leave to ponder
> On things would hurt me more. But I'll go in.
> In, boy; go first. You houseless poverty—
> Nay, get thee in. I'll pray, and then I'll sleep.

But his prayer is not for himself.

> Poor naked wretches, wheresoe'er you are,

it begins, and I need not quote more. This is one of those passages which make one worship Shakespeare.[3]

Much has been written on the representation of insanity in *King Lear*, and I will confine myself to one or two points which may have escaped notice. The most obvious symptom of Lear's insanity, especially in its first stages, is of course the domination of a fixed idea. Whatever presents itself to his senses, is seized on by this idea and compelled to express it; as for example in those words, already quoted, which first show that his mind has actually given way:

> Hast thou given all
> To thy two daughters? And art thou come to this?[4]

But it is remarkable that what we have here is only, in an exaggerated and perverted form, the very same action of imagination that, just before the breakdown of reason, produced those sublime appeals:

> O heavens,
> If you do love old men, if your sweet sway
> Allow obedience, if yourselves are old,
> Make it your cause;

and:

> Rumble thy bellyful! Spit, fire! spout rain!
> Nor rain, wind, thunder, fire, are my daughters:
> I tax not you, you elements, with unkindness;
> I never gave you kingdom, call'd you children,
> You owe me no subscription: then let fall
> Your horrible pleasure; here I stand, your slave,
> A poor, infirm, weak, and despised old man:
> But yet I call you servile ministers,
> That have with two pernicious daughters join'd
> Your high engender'd battles 'gainst a head
> So old and white as this. O! O! 'tis foul!

Shakespeare, long before this, in the *Midsummer Night's Dream,* had noticed the resemblance between the lunatic, the lover, and the poet; and the partial truth that genius is allied to insanity was quite familiar to him. But he presents here the supplementary half-truth that insanity is allied to genius.

He does not, however, put into the mouth of the insane Lear any such sublime passages as those just quoted. Lear's insanity, which destroys the coherence, also reduces the poetry of his imagination. What it stimulates is that power of moral perception and reflection which had already been quickened by his sufferings. This, however partial and however disconnectedly used, first appears, quite soon after the insanity has declared itself, in the idea that the naked beggar represents truth and reality, in contrast with those conventions, flatteries, and corruptions of the great world, by which Lear has so long been deceived and will never be deceived again:

> Is man no more than this? Consider him well. Thou owest the worm no silk, the beast no hide, the sheep no wool, the cat no perfume. Ha! here's three on's are sophisticated: thou art the thing itself.

Lear regards the beggar therefore with reverence and delight, as a person who is in the secret of things, and he longs to question him about their causes. It is this same strain of thought which much later (IV. vi.), gaining far greater force, though the insanity has otherwise advanced, issues in those famous Timon-like speeches which make us realise the original strength of the old King's mind. And when this strain, on his recovery, unites with the streams of repentance and love, it produces that serene renunciation of the world, with its power and glory and resentments and revenges, which is expressed in the speech (V. iii.):

> No, no, no, no! Come, let's away to prison:
> We two alone will sing like birds i' the cage:
> When thou dost ask me blessing, I'll kneel down,
> And ask of thee forgiveness: so we'll live,
> And pray, and sing, and tell old tales, and laugh
> At gilded butterflies, and hear poor rogues
> Talk of court news; and we'll talk with them too.
> Who loses, and who wins; who's in, who's out;
> And take upon's the mystery of things,
> As if we were God's spies: and we'll wear out,
> In a wall'd prison, packs and sects of great ones,
> That ebb and flow by the moon.

This is that renunciation which is at the same time a sacrifice offered to the gods, and on which the gods themselves throw incense; and, it may be, it would never have been offered but for the knowledge that came to Lear in his madness.

I spoke of Lear's ' recovery,' but the word is too strong. The Lear of the Fifth Act is not indeed insane, but his mind is greatly enfeebled. The speech just quoted is followed by a sudden flash of the old passionate nature, reminding us most pathetically of Lear's efforts, just before his madness, to restrain his tears:

> Wipe thine eyes:
> The good-years shall devour them, flesh and fell,
> Ere they shall make us weep: we'll see 'em starve first.

And this weakness is still more pathetically shown in the blindness of the old King to his position now that he and Cordelia are made prisoners. It is evident that Cordelia knows well what mercy her father is likely to receive from her sisters; that is the reason of her weeping. But he does not understand her tears; it never crosses his mind that they have anything more than imprisonment to fear. And what is that to them? They have made that sacrifice, and all is well:

> Have I caught thee?
> He that parts us shall bring a brand from heaven,
> And fire us hence like foxes.

This blindness is most affecting to us, who know in what manner they will be parted; but it is also comforting. And we find the same mingling of effects in the overwhelming conclusion of the story. If to the reader, as to the bystanders, that scene brings one unbroken pain, it is not so with Lear himself. His shattered mind passes from the first transports of hope and despair, as he bends over Cordelia's body and holds the feather to her lips, into an absolute forgetfulness of the cause of these transports. This continues so long as he can converse with Kent; becomes an almost complete vacancy; and is disturbed only to yield, as his eyes suddenly fall again on his child's corpse, to an agony which at once breaks his heart. And, finally, though he is killed by an agony of pain, the agony in which he actually dies is one not of pain but of ecstasy. Suddenly, with a cry represented in the oldest text by a four-times repeated 'O,' he exclaims:

> Do you see this? Look on her, look, her lips,
> Look there, look there!

These are the last words of Lear. He is sure, at last that she *lives:* and what had he said when he was still in doubt?

> She lives! if it be so,
> It is a chance which does redeem all sorrows
> That ever I have felt!

To us, perhaps, the knowledge that he is deceived may bring a culmination of pain: but, if it brings *only* that, I believe we are false to Shakespeare, and it seems almost beyond question that any actor is false to the text who does not attempt to express, in Lear's last accents and gestures and look, an unbearable *joy.*[5]

To dwell on the pathos of Lear's last speech would be an impertinence, but I may add a remark on the speech from the literary point of view. In the simplicity of its language, which consists almost wholly of monosyllables of native origin, composed in very brief sentences of the plainest structure, it presents an extraordinary contrast to the dying speech of Hamlet and the last words of Othello to the bystanders. The fact that Lear speaks in passion is one cause of the difference, but not the sole cause. The language is more than simple, it is familiar. And this familiarity is characteristic of Lear (except at certain moments, already referred to) from the time of his madness onwards, and is the source of the peculiarly poignant effect of some of his sentences (such as ' The little dogs and all . . .'). We feel in them the loss of power to sustain his royal dignity; we feel also that everything external has become nothingness to him, and that what remains is 'the thing itself,' the soul in its bare greatness. Hence also it is that two lines in this last speech show, better perhaps than any other passage of poetry, one of the qualities we have in mind when we distinguish poetry as 'romantic.' Nothing like Hamlet's mysterious sigh 'The rest is silence,' nothing like Othello's memories of his life of marvel and achievement, was possible to Lear. Those last thoughts are romantic in their strangeness : Lear's five-times repeated 'Never,' in which the simplest and most unanswerable cry of anguish rises note by note till the heart breaks, is romantic in its naturalism; and to make a verse out of this one word required the boldness as well as the inspiration which came infallibly to Shakespeare at the greatest moments. But the familiarity, boldness, and inspiration are surpassed (if that can be) by the next line, which shows the bodily oppression asking for bodily relief. The imagination that produced Lear's curse or his defiance of the storm may be paralleled in its kind, but where else are we to seek the imagination that could venture to follow that cry of 'Never' with such a phrase as 'undo this button,' and yet could leave us on the topmost peaks of poetry?[6]

NOTES

[1] Of course I do not mean that he is beginning to be insane, and still less that he *is* insane (as some medical critics suggest).

[2] I must however point out that the modern stage-directions are most unfortunate in concealing the fact that here Cordelia sees her father again *for the first time*.

[3] What immediately follows is as striking an illustration of quite another quality, and of the effects which make us think of Lear as pursued by a relentless fate. If he could go in and sleep after his prayer, as he intends, his mind, one feels, might be saved: so far there has been only the menace of madness. But from within the hovel Edgar—the last man who would willingly have injured Lear—cries, 'Fathom and half, fathom and half! Poor Tom!'; the Fool runs out terrified; Edgar, summoned by Kent, follows him; and, at sight of Edgar, in a moment something gives way in Lear's brain, and he exclaims:

> Hast thou given all
> To thy two daughters ? And art thou come to this?

Henceforth he is mad. And they remain out in the storm.

I have not seen it noticed that this stroke of fate is repeated—surely intentionally—in the sixth scene. Gloster has succeeded in persuading Lear to come into the 'house'; he then leaves, and Kent after much difficulty induces Lear to lie down and rest upon the cushions. Sleep begins to come to him again, and he murmurs, 'Make no noise, make no noise; draw the curtains; so, so, so. We'll go to supper i' the morning. So, so, so.' At that moment Gloster enters with the news that he has discovered a plot to kill the King; the rest that 'might yet have balm'd his broken senses' is again interrupted; and he is hurried away on a litter towards Dover. (His recovery, it will be remembered, is due to a long sleep artificially induced.)

[4] III. iv. 49. This is printed as prose in the Globe edition, but is surely verse. Lear has not yet spoken prose in this scene, and his next three speeches are in verse. The next is in prose, and, ending in his tearing off his clothes, shows the advance of insanity.

[5] [Lear's death is thus, I am reminded, like *père* Goriot's.] This interpretation may be condemned as fantastic, but the text, it appears to me, will bear no other. This is the whole speech (in the Globe text):

> And my poor fool is hang'd! No, no, no life!
> Why should a dog, a horse, a rat, have life,
> And thou no breath at all? Thou'lt come no more,
> Never, never, never, never, never!
> Pray you, undo this button: thank you, sir.
> Do you see this? Look on her, look, her lips,
> Look there, look there!

The transition at 'Do you see this?' from despair to something more than hope is exactly the same as in the preceding passage at the word 'Ha!':

> A plague upon you, murderers, traitors all!
> I might have saved her; now she's gone for ever!
> Cordelia, Cordelia, stay a little.
> Ha!
> What is't thou say'st? Her voice was ever soft,
> Gentle, and low, an excellent thing in woman.

As to my other remarks, I will ask the reader to notice that the passage from Lear's entrance with the body of Cordelia to the stage-direction *He dies* (which probably comes a few lines too soon) is 54 lines in length, and that 30 of them represent the interval during which he has absolutely forgotten Cordelia. (It begins when he looked up at the Captain's words, line 275.) To make Lear during this interval turn continually in anguish to the corpse, is to act the passage in a manner irreconcilable with the text, and insufferable in its effect. I speak from experience. I have seen the passage acted thus, and my sympathies were so exhausted long before Lear's death that his last speech, the most pathetic speech ever written, left me disappointed and weary.

[6] The Quartos give the 'Never' only thrice (surely wrongly), and all the actors I have heard have preferred this easier task. I ought perhaps to add that the Quartos give the words 'Break, heart; I prithee, break!' to Lear, not Kent. They and the Folio are at odds throughout the last sixty lines of *King Lear*, and all good modern texts are eclectic.

Harold C. Goddard
KING LEAR

IV

He who masters his passions is king over them. Here the psychological theme of the play has its political implications. This metaphor of the emotions as a mob bound to dethrone its ruler if he loses control over them goes nobody knows how far back toward the beginnings of human thought. This comparison of the kingdom within to the kingdom without, of the microcosm to the macrocosm, is one of the immemorial and universal figures of speech. Plato founded his Republic on it. Jesus erected his Kingdom of Heaven on an extension and sublimation of it. Shakespeare evinced the keenest interest in it from the beginning.

In Henry VI the young poet found a king who, whatever his failures, had the almost unique success of retaining his individuality as a man in spite of his title, the beginning at least of a synthesis of the two kingdoms. The deposed Henry is in a situation not wholly unlike that of the deposed Lear, and the conversation in *III Henry VI* between him and Two Keepers on this very theme of man and king, with its talk of a spiritual crown that kings seldom attain, seems like a far-off gleam of the poet's supreme tragedy, as in another way does Henry's soliloquy on the Simple Life. In *King John* Shakespeare devoted a whole play to a demonstration that a man may be kinglier than a king. Henry IV's soliloquy on Sleep is a variation on the same theme, with its envy of the wet sea-boy to whom sleep comes on the giddy mast in the storm while it is denied to the king in his bed. The relation of king and subject is the explicit topic of debate between Henry V and the soldiers among whom he wanders disguised as one of them, the night before Agincourt. "I think the king is but a man, as I am," says Henry to Bates, ". . . his ceremonies laid by, in his nakedness he appears but a man." He would never have dared tell that truth but for the double protection of disguise and night. And the ensuing soliloquy on Ceremony

From *The Meaning of Shakespeare* (Chicago: University of Chicago Press, 1951), pp. 526–29, 533–35, 541–47.

follows out the same thought. Indeed, this entire group of plays is founded on the double personality of Henry: Henry as Hal, the man and pal of Falstaff, and Henry as Prince Henry, heir to Henry IV and later King Henry V. *Hamlet*, as its full title, *Hamlet, Prince of Denmark*, shows, rests on the same distinction between man and prince. Only in this perspective can we catch the significance of Hamlet's reply to Horatio when the latter says of his father:

> I saw him once; he was a goodly king.

> He was a man,

Hamlet retorts. He knows which title is more honorable.

> And not a man, for being simply man,
> Hath any honour, but honour for those honours
> That are without him, as place, riches, and favour,
> Prizes of accident as oft as merit.

In these words of Achilles in *Troilus and Cressida* we have the more generalized form of the theme, the contrast between the role a man plays before the world and the man himself. It is one of the most persistent ideas in Shakespeare. It is the subject of Isabella's great tirade on the abuse of power in *Measure for Measure* and of the King's long disquisition in *All's Well* on the indistinguishableness of various bloods. It is behind Hamlet's "insolence of office." It is the "captive good attending captain ill" of the 66th sonnet and in innumerable other passages. But none of them quite reach the pitch of the mad Lear's revulsion against the very thing that he has been:

> LEAR: Thou has seen a farmer's dog bark at a beggar?
> GLOUCESTER: Ay, sir.
> LEAR: And the creature run from the cur? There thou mightst behold the great
>   image of authority: a dog's obeyed in office.

With the standing exception of Henry VI (and Malcolm, whom we do not see on the throne), all Shakespeare's kings in both history and tragedy up to this point are weaklings, worldlings, or villains, sometimes two of the three or all three at once. "What is a king?" I once asked a little girl out of pure curiosity to see what she would say. Looking up at me with shining eyes, she replied without a moment's hesitation: "A king is a beautiful man." She was in her fairy-tale stage. Shakespeare would have understood her—for *King Lear* is the story of how a king in the worldly sense became a king in the fairy-tale sense, of how a bad king became a beautiful man. *Henry V* is an account of how a man became a king. *King Lear* is an account of how a king became a man. Until you have read *King Lear*, you have never read *Henry V*.

Nor is Shakespeare content with weaving this theme into his plot and rendering it explicit in almost every scene of the play. He makes it, both literally and symbolically, visible to the eye. We see Lear in the first act with crown and robe

and all the other marks of authority and accoutrements of office, exercising, as in the banishment of Kent, an extreme form of absolute power. We see him in the fourth act, after his buffeting by night and tempest, crowned and robed with common flowers and wayside weeds, his authority exchanged for an emerging humility, his egotism for the sympathy and wisdom of an incoherent mind, his court for loneliness or the society of beggars and the blind. What inversions of everything!

> The trick of that voice I do well remember,

says the blinded Gloucester, hearing the tragedy in lieu of seeing it,

> Is't not the king?
>> Ay, every inch a king!

replies Lear. We agree. It is now, not at the beginning, that he is every inch a king, for he has taken the first steps toward self-conquest: he has questioned his own infallibility; he has recognized the sufferings of others. From this it is but a step to mercy.

> When I do stare, see how the subject quakes,

the Old King, flaring up, cries to the phantasmal vassals of his insanity. But the New King quickly extinguishes him in the next line:

> I pardon that man's life. What was thy cause?

words which, I think, are generally mistaken. On the stage, as I remember, the implication always is that Lear first pardons one of the imaginary culprits who stand before him, and then, turning to a second, asks him *his* cause. But surely a single culprit is involved. The whole point is the fact that Lear offers pardon first and only afterward asks what the offense is that he has pardoned. When one is possessed of a spirit of universal forgiveness, of what moment is it to know the nature of the crime? It is like the Duke's

> I pardon thee thy life before thou ask it,

to Shylock, or the Duchess's

> "Pardon" should be the first word of thy speech,

in *Richard II*. Mercy, Shakespeare is saying, is the mark of the man who is every inch a king. It might have been from *King Lear* that Abraham Lincoln, one of the few rulers who ever practiced it, learned that truth.

It ought to be plain by now why the play is called *King Lear*. Macbeth was a king, Hamlet was a prince, Othello was a general, yet the plays in which they figure are simply *Macbeth*, *Hamlet*,[1] and *Othello*. But it is *KING* Lear. Unless we are merely labeling it, we should never refer to it, as so many do, as *Lear*. Shakespeare knew what he was about when he named his greatest play. ⟨. . .⟩

V I

Lear, at the beginning of the play, possesses physical eyesight, so far as we know, as perfect as Gloucester's. But morally he is even blinder. He is a victim, to the point of incipient madness, of his arrogance, his anger, his vanity, and his pride. A choleric temperament, a position of absolute authority, and old age have combined to make him what he is. The night and the storm into which he is thrust out on the heath are Shakespeare's symbols for the truth that blindness and passion go hand in hand. The darkness that descends on Lear's mind in its impotent fury is the counterpart of the blackness in which the tempest rages. But, like the flashes of lightning that momentarily illuminate the landscape for the lost traveler, there is a spiritual lightning that illuminates the lost soul.

No, I will be the pattern of all patience; I will say nothing.

Nothing! Cordelia's very word at the beginning when Lear sought to test her affection. However far behind, the father has at least caught sight of the daughter. "Nothing will come of nothing," he had warned her in that opening scene. But something "enskyed" and starry was to come of that "nothing," if no more than Lear's capacity to say "I will say nothing." The lightning has struck in his soul, and it is at the very moment when he cries "my wits begin to turn" that he thinks for the first time of someone else's suffering before his own.

Come on, my boy. How dost, my boy? Art cold?

he cries to Poor Tom. More and more from that moment, the tempest in Lear's mind makes him insensible to the tempest without. Increasingly, he sees that madness lies in dwelling on his own wrongs, salvation in thinking of the sufferings of others:

Poor naked wretches, wheresoe'er you are,
That bide the pelting of this pitiless storm,
How shall your houseless heads and unfed sides,
Your loop'd and window'd raggedness, defend you
From seasons such as these? O, I have ta'en
Too little care of this! Take physic, pomp;
Expose thyself to feel what wretches feel,
That thou mayst shake the superflux to them,
And show the heavens more just.

Exactly Gloucester's conclusion! Agony leads the two men to one mind. But compare the passages, and it will be seen how much more concrete, moving, and tragic Lear's is. And besides, he had been king.

All through these three tremendous scenes, on the heath, before the hovel, and in the farmhouse, the night of madness grows blacker and blacker, the flashes of spiritual insight more and more vivid. It is imagination at grips with chaos. Vision with blindness. Light with eternal night. Here is a microcosm of the macrocosm.

Here is War. Here, too, then, there should be a clue to what, if anything, can subdue that ancient and most inveterate enemy of man. Embryonic patience or ancestral passion: which will win? Even up to the terrific arraignment of the two recreant daughters in the chambers of Lear's imagination in which these scenes culminate, we do not know. Hatred and rage are in the ascendant when the phantasmal Regan dashes from the phantasmal courtroom and Lear cries:

> Stop her there!
> Arms, arms, sword, fire!

Here is revealed how entangled with the imagery of war are both the personal emotion of revenge and the hidden temper of those supposed instruments of social justice that are too often only judicial vengeance in disguise. And yet but a moment and the wind-struck vane has whirled through a hundred and eighty degrees and a diametrically opposite treatment of the same daughter is prescribed: "Then let them anatomize Regan; see what breeds about her heart. *Is there any cause in nature that makes these hard hearts?*" Here is another universe. Hell has given place to Heaven. The tolerance, one might almost say the scientific detachment, of that "anatomize," and the humility of

> The little dogs and all,
> Tray, Blanch, and Sweetheart, see, they bark at me,

tell us which side is winning. If there was War, here is Peace. And the gods seem to confirm it when the blessing of sleep finally descends on the exhausted old man. In his History Plays, Shakespeare had explored at length the feudal conception of the royal prerogative. In a few scenes in this play, of which this is one, he reveals the genuine divine right of kings—and of men. The angels that come to the aid of this stricken monarch are unrelated to those in whom Richard II had such confidence in virtue of his mere title, but who failed him so ignominiously at the crisis of his career.

But Shakespeare does not so much say it as make us see it. When we next behold the King, immediately after the attempted suicide of Gloucester, he enters fantastically robed and crowned with flowers. The symbolism of that, even without the echo of Ophelia, is unmistakable. The simple costless jewels of the fields and meadows have replaced the courtly pomp of gold and purple. Here is not merely Nature's king, but Heaven's. Before speaking further of that, however, we must return for a moment to Gloucester.

Surely a main reason why Shakespeare contrived the meeting of the two old men just when he did was to emphasize the fact that Lear, whatever his sufferings, unlike Gloucester, never for one instant dallied with the idea of self-destruction as a way out. Life: though nature, man, and apparently the gods conspired to make it an endless agony of crucifixion, even at fourscore and upward it never even occurred to Lear to question whether it was better than death. No more can we while we are under his spell.

> O, our lives' sweetness!
> That we the pain of death would hourly die
> Rather than die at once!

And then this play is called pessimistic! How inferior anyone who uses that word to describe it proves himself to its own glorious old hero! It may seem like a grotesque juxtaposition and the two may have little else in common, but King Lear and Falstaff embrace in their unbounded and unquenchable love of life for its own sake. ⟨. . .⟩

IX

⟨. . .⟩ we must say a word about Cordelia. The extraordinary vividness of her portrayal, considering the brevity of her role, has often been commented on. The beauty of her nature—its sincerity and its combined strength and tenderness—goes far toward explaining the clarity of impression. But it is the fact that never for an instant do we forget her that compensates for the infrequency of her physical presence. Shakespeare sees to this in several ways. The antithesis with her sisters, to begin with, brings her to mind whenever they are on the stage. His sense of guilt with regard to her keeps her perpetually in Lear's memory—and so in ours. And the Fool's love for her, both on its own account and because he is forever insinuating thoughts of her into the King's mind, works the same way. Kent, too, makes his contribution. The best verbal embodiment I can think of for what Shakespeare's magic gradually turns Cordelia into in our imaginations is that starry phrase of Emily Dickinson's: Bright Absentee. *Bright Absentee:* that is exactly what Cordelia is during most of the play, and the phrase is doubly appropriate when we remember that the Cordelia-like New England poetess employed it to express a not less spiritual love than Cordelia's of a younger woman for an older man.

Now the fact and the success of this method of characterizing Cordelia are generally felt, I believe, but what is not recognized is that Shakespeare used it not just because it fitted the plot and was effective, but for a minutely specific reason. The last scene of this fourth act, the most tenderly pathetic in the play, begins to apprise us of what that reason is.

The place is a tent in the French camp. Lear is brought in asleep, and we hear and see administered the two of all the medicines in the world that in addition to sleep itself can bring back his sanity, if any can: music and Cordelia's kiss. The King gives signs of returning consciousness. "He wakes," says Cordelia to the Doctor, "speak to him." But like most of Shakespeare's physicians, this one has psychological insight as well as physiological skill, as his use of music as a healer has already hinted. "Madam, do you; 'tis fittest," he replies to Cordelia. Whereupon, with a wisdom equal to his, she addresses her father by his former title, seeking thereby to preserve his mental continuity:

> How does my royal lord? How fares your majesty?

But Lear believes he has awakened in hell and is gazing across a great gulf toward one in heaven:

LEAR: You do me wrong to take me out o' the grave:
Thou art a soul in bliss; but I am bound
Upon a wheel of fire, that mine own tears
Do scald like molten lead.
COR.:   Sir, do you know me?
LEAR: You are a spirit, I know. When did you die?

Lear is "still, still, far wide!" as Cordelia expresses it under her breath. Yet in another sense, as it befits Cordelia alone not to know, Lear was never before so near the mark. Cordelia, we know, *is* a spirit, and, in that shining line, Shakespeare harvests the promise of four full acts which have been subtly contrived to convince us of the same truth. That which without being apprehensible to the senses is nevertheless undeniably present is a spirit—and that Cordelia has been through most of the play. Now she becomes *visibly* that to Lear, and we, as readers or spectators, must be able to enter into the old man's vision, or the effect is lost. Shakespeare has abundantly seen to it that we shall be able. Here is that unknown something that is indeed "dearer than eyesight"—something that is related to eyesight as eyesight is to blindness.

It is a pity to skip even one line of this transcendent scene. But we must. What a descent from king and warrior to this very foolish fond old man, fourscore and upward, who senses that he is not in his perfect mind! But what an ascent—what a perfect mind in comparison! He begins to realize vaguely that he is still on earth:

LEAR: Do not laugh at me;
For, as I am a man, I think this lady
To be my child Cordelia.
COR.:   And so I am, I am.
LEAR: Be your tears wet? Yes, faith. I pray, weep not.
If you have poison for me, I will drink it.
I know you do not love me; for your sisters
Have, as I do remember, done me wrong:
You have some cause, they have not.

"No cause, no cause," replies Cordelia: a divine lie that will shine forever beside the one Desdemona uttered with her last breath. "Am I in France?" Lear asks at last, coming back to earth. "In your own kingdom, sir," Kent replies, meaning England, of course; but we know that Shakespeare means also that Lear is now in a kingdom not of this earth. And in a moment more the scene closes—and the act. It would seem as if poetry could go no further, and yet it is scarcely an exaggeration to say that this scene is nothing in comparison with what Shakespeare still has in store for us in the scene to which this one specifically leads up.

X

The event which determines everything else in the last act is the battle between the British and the French. But what a battle! Except for the quick passage of the French forces over the stage, with an alarum and a retreat, it all takes place behind the scenes and exactly one line of the text is devoted to the account of it:

King Lear hath lost, he and his daughter ta'en.

The brevity of it is a measure of how insignificant the mere clash of arms becomes in comparison with the moral convulsion that is its cause, and the strife between and within the human beings who are its agents. Shakespeare is here tracking Force into its inmost lair. To have stressed the merely military would have thrown his whole drama out of focus. Cordelia, for all her heroic strength, is no Joan of Arc, and it would have blotted our image of her to have spotted it with blood. Instead, we remember the final lines of *King John*, and, forgetting entirely that France is invading England, think only of the battle between love and treason. Even Albany, in effect, fights on the other side. His hand is compelled to defend his land against the invader, but his heart is with the King:

Where I could not be honest
I never yet was valiant.

Ubi honestas, ibi patria.

Lear and Cordelia are led in captive. But for him, she would be ready to "out-frown false Fortune's frown," and, as it is, she is willing to confront her captors. But all that he begs is to spend the rest of his life with her in prison. That will be paradise enough, and the words in which he tastes that joy in imagination are one of the crests of all poetry. Shakespeare in the course of his life had many times paid his ironic respects to worldly greatness and temporal power, but it may be doubted whether he ever did it more crushingly than in the last lines of this daydream of a broken old king who had himself so recently been one of "the great." Lear's words are elicited by Cordelia's glorious challenge to Fortune, which exhibits her at the opposite pole from Hamlet with his weak attempt to rationalize Fate into the "divinity that shapes our ends." Cordelia will be fooled by no such verbal self-deception. "For if the trumpet give an uncertain sound, who shall prepare himself to the battle?" Cordelia's ringing sentences are the very stuff into which the pugnacity of the race ought to be sublimated:

COR.:   We are not the first
Who with best meaning have incurr'd the worst.
For thee, oppressed king, am I cast down;
Myself could else out-frown false Fortune's frown.
Shall we not see these daughters and these sisters?
LEAR: No, no, no, no! Come, let's away to prison;
We two alone will sing like birds i' the cage.
When thou dost ask me blessing, I'll kneel down,

And ask of thee forgiveness. So we'll live,
And pray, and sing, and tell old tales, and laugh
At gilded butterflies, and hear poor rogues
Talk of court news; and we'll talk with them too,
Who loses and who wins; who's in, who's out;
And take upon 's the mystery of things,
As if we were God's spies: and *we'll wear out,*
In a wall'd prison, packs and sects of great ones,
That ebb and flow by the moon.

Even Shakespeare seldom concentrated thought as he did in those last lines. "That ebb and flow by the moon": what indeed is the rise and fall of the mighty but just that, the meaningless coming in and going out of a tide, never registering any gain, forever canceling itself out to all eternity? And who are these mighty? "Packs and sects of great ones." Into those half-dozen words the poet condenses his condemnation of three of the forces he most detests: (1) the mob, which is nothing but the human counterpart of the pack; (2) that spirit which, in opposition to the one that makes the whole world kin, puts its own sect or party above humanity; and (3) "greatness," or worldly place and power. Under each or any of these dispensations the harmony man dreams of is denied. The mob is its destroyer. The sects or party is its defier. Power is its counterfeiter. And the extremes meet, for power rests on the conquest and subservience of the mob. In the face of such might, what can the imprisoned spirits of tenderness and beauty do? "We'll wear out...." And it does indeed sometimes seem as if all they can do is to wear it out with patience, even as the weak ancestors of man outwore, by outlasting, the dynasties of now extinct "great ones," the mastodons and saber-toothed tigers that dominated the earth in an earlier geologic age.

But Shakespeare, however profound his reverence for patience, does not leave it at that. His phrase, in this scene, for the opposite of packs and sects and great ones is "the common bosom," and Edmund does not intend—any more than Claudius did in Hamlet's case—that pity for the old King shall be able

To pluck the common bosom on his side,

or that the general love for Cordelia shall have a like effect.

Her very silence and her patience
Speak to the people, and they pity her.

It might still be Edmund speaking of Cordelia. Actually the words are uttered of Rosalind by her envious uncle. As they show, a turn of Fortune's wheel could easily have converted the play of which she is the heroine into tragedy, and Rosalind herself into a Cordelia. She would have met the test, too! Meanwhile, Edmund is as relentless as the usurping Duke in *As You Like It.* His retort to Lear's mental picture of his final days with Cordelia is an abrupt

Take them away,

and a moment later we are given a typical glimpse of one of Lear's "great ones" in action, as Edmund promises advancement to a captain if he will carry out his bloody purpose.

> EDM.:   Know thou this, that men
> Are as the time is; to be tender-minded
> Does not become a sword. Thy great employment
> Will not bear question; either say thou'lt do 't,
> Or thrive by other means.
> CAPT.:   I'll do 't, my lord . . .
> I cannot draw a cart, nor eat dried oats;
> If it be man's work, I'll do 't.

XI

The dying Edmund, mortally wounded by Edgar in their duel, changes his mind too late. Edgar's account of their father's death of mingled grief and joy obviously touches him. It is as if the incipient prompting to goodness that may for just a moment be detected in Iago in the presence of Desdemona had survived into another life and come to bud in Edmund. When the deaths of Goneril and Regan are announced, deeply moved again, he exclaims:

> I was contracted to them both. All three
> Now marry in an instant,

and when the bodies of the two sisters—one poisoned by the other, the other self-slain—are brought in, the balance is finally tipped:

> I pant for life. Some good I mean to do,
> Despite of mine own nature.

He attempts to rescind his fatal order.[2] But in vain, as we see a moment later when Lear enters with the dead Cordelia in his arms. "Dead as earth," he pronounces her. And yet the next second he is willing to believe that she may still be revived. He calls for a looking glass to see if her breath will mist it, and Kent, gazing at the pathetic picture, cries: "Is this the promis'd end?" "Or image of that horror?" echoes Edgar, while Albany begs the heavens to "fall, and cease!" All three utterances converge to prove that this is indeed Shakespeare's version of the Last Judgment.

Failing a mirror, Lear holds a feather to Cordelia's lips:

> This feather stirs; she lives! If it be so,
> It is a chance which does redeem all sorrows
> That ever I have felt

(words that must on no account be forgotten). Kent, and then Edgar, bend above the old man, but Lear, intent on his work of resuscitation, waves them away. They have jostled him at the critical moment, he thinks:

A plague upon you, murderers, traitors all!
I might have sav'd her; now she's gone for ever!

The test of breath, of touch, has failed. But there still remains the test of hearing:

Cordelia, Cordelia! stay a little. Ha!
What is't thou say'st? Her voice was ever soft,
Gentle, and low; an excellent thing in woman.
I kill'd the slave that was a-hanging thee.

And an officer standing by confirms him:

'Tis true, my lords, he did.

The officer's word causes Lear to look up, and he gazes with groping vision at Kent. "See better, Lear," Kent had bade his master, we recall, when he rejected Cordelia. Lear has followed that injunction: he recognizes his friend and servant. (But of that we have already spoken.) "Your eldest daughters," Kent goes on,

    have fordone themselves,
And desperately are dead.

And Lear, as though he had known it for a thousand years, replies with an indifference as sublime as if a granite cliff were told that an insect had dashed itself to death against its base:

Ay, so I think.

"He knows not what he says," Albany observes, and while Edmund's death is announced, Shakespeare, as if perceiving that the scene should inspire anyone who participates in it in the theater, leaves to the actor the immense freedom of devising business for Lear that shall bridge the dozen lines that the others speak. Albany, by right of succession, is now entitled to the throne. Seeking to make what amends he can, he steps aside:

          For us, we will resign,
During the life of this old majesty,
To him our absolute power.

Lear is again to be king! His reign, however, as Albany does not know, is to be a matter of seconds. But what is time except for what it contains? and into those seconds is to be crowded such a wonder as never occurred in the longest reign ever chronicled of the most venerable of earth's kings.

What Lear has been doing while Albany is speaking is left, as I said, to the imagination, but that it is something profoundly moving is indicated by the sudden, "O, see, see!" with which Albany interrupts the train of his thought. And thereupon Lear begins what is possibly the most poetically pathetic speech existing in the English, if not in any, language:

And my poor fool is hang'd!

are his first words. . . . Hundreds of other words have been written about those six. Do they refer to the Fool, or to Cordelia?

Why did Shakespeare create one of the most beautiful and appealing of his characters—perhaps his masterpiece in the amalgamation of the tragic and the comic—only to drop him completely out a little past the middle of the play? To those who think Lear remembers his faithful jester at the end, those six words are the answer: he dropped him out precisely in order to stress this parting allusion to him. But why was the Fool hanged? And why, at this supreme moment, should Lear have a thought for anything but what is in his arms? No—another school of interpreters, a vast majority, tells us—"poor fool" is a colloquial term of endearment, and it is Cordelia to whom it is applied. Yet I challenge anyone in his heart of heart to deny that, so taken, *at such a moment* the phrase jars. Furthermore, Shakespeare is not in the habit of sending us to our glossaries at such emotional pinnacles: he has too sure a sense of what is permanent in language.

The solution of the enigma is simple. Remember the Third Murderer in *Macbeth.* Surely the whole point of the phrase is that Lear is referring to both Cordelia and the Fool. His wandering mind has confused them, if you will. But what a divine confusion! Has *wedded* them would be the better word. Think how the Fool loved his master! Think how he adored Cordelia and pined away after she went to France! Surely this is the main reason for Shakespeare's banishing the Fool from his play—that he might reappear united to Cordelia on his dear master's lips:

Where dead men meet, on lips of living men.

In what other Heaven would the Fool have preferred to meet those other two? "Let me not to the marriage of true minds admit impediments."

All three
Now marry in an instant.

Goneril, Regan, Edmund. Cordelia, Lear, the Fool. (And the supererogatory Nahum Tate thought this drama lacked a love story, and proceeded to concoct one between Edgar and Cordelia!)

But the union of Cordelia and the Fool is but the first act of King Lear's reign. The restored King goes on speaking, holding his child's body closer as it grows colder. The tests of touch and hearing have failed.

No, no, no life!
Why should a dog, a horse, a rat, have life,
And thou no breath at all? Thou'lt come no more,
Never, never, never, never, never!

—a last line that fathoms the nadir of annihilation as utterly as that earlier

kill, kill, kill, kill, kill, kill,

had touched the nadir of revenge. . . . But the uprush of emotion has been too much for the old man:

Pray you, undo this button. Thank you, sir.

Lear has lifted his head while the service was performed. Now he looks down again at what is in his arms. And on the instant, like a bolt of divine lightning—that "lightning before death" of which Romeo told—the Truth descends:

Do you see this? Look on her, look, her lips,
Look there, look there!

Cordelia lives! The Third Test—of vision—has not failed, and those earlier words echo through our minds:

She lives! If it be so,
It is a chance which does redeem all sorrows
That ever I have felt.

And Lear, clasping his restored child to his heart, falls "dead" of joy.[3] For all its sound and fury, this story at least is not a tale told by an idiot, signifying nothing. And here the rest is not silence.

XII

On the contrary, it will be said, Lear's delusion only makes the blackness blacker, another night fallen on mid-night. For *we* know that Cordelia *is* dead.

We do? How do we? And if we do, we know more than Shakespeare. For like a shower of golden arrows flying from every angle and every distance to a single target, every line of the play—almost—has been cunningly devised to answer our skepticism, to demonstrate that Lear is right and we are wrong. Why but to make the old King's dying assertion incontrovertible does Shakespeare so permeate his play with the theme of vision?

Only consider for a moment the grounds the poet has given—pre-eminently in this play, but also in all he had written from the beginning—for having faith in the testimony of Lear's imagination.

First—though least important and not indispensable to the point—Lear is an old old man, and Shakespeare has over and over indicated his adherence to the world-old view that age, which is a synonym for experience, coupled with a good life, brings insight and truth. Adam, in *As You Like It* (a part that Shakespeare himself may have played), Priam in *Troilus and Cressida*, Belarius in *Cymbeline*, or the Old Tenant who aids Gloucester in this very play are good examples. Lear has had long experience; and if he was tardy in attaining the good life, he has at least packed enough virtue into its last days to compensate for its previous failure. Here we have at least a foundation for a faith in Lear's power to see the truth. The wisdom of experience. The wisdom of old age.

But there is something more cogent than that.

Second, Shakespeare believes that suffering and affliction, to those at least who will give ear, bring power to see things as they are. To prove that in detail would be to pass his Tragedies in review. With what clairvoyance Othello, for example, sees the truth at the moment when he begs to be washed in steep-down gulfs of liquid fire. With what prophetic power Queen Margaret foresees the doom of the House of York. "Nothing almost sees miracles but misery," says Kent, at night, in the stocks, confident of sunrise. By which rule, laid down in this very play, Lear at the moment of supreme misery might be expected to see the supreme miracle. He does. To the vision and wisdom of old age are added the vision and wisdom of misery.

But Lear, if he is an old and a miserable, is also a dying, man; and if there is any ancient belief that Shakespeare credits, it is that "truth sits upon the lips of dying men." Over and over he has said it: "Holy men at their death have good inspirations";

> The tongues of dying men
> Enforce attention like deep harmony;

and over and over he has illustrated it in the death scenes, whether in bed or on the battlefield, of his plays:

> The setting sun, and music at the close,
> As the last taste of sweets, is sweetest last.

There is a human counterpart of the legend of the dying swan, or that legend, rather, is a symbol of this human truth. Even worldly men and women, like Warwick or Henry IV, if they regret or repent, may see their lives at last in something like true perspective, and evil ones, like Cardinal Beaufort, Lady Macbeth, or Edmund in this play, may confess, or may face the truth in nightmare or terror. The vision of death is a *third* form of inspired seeing.

And a fourth is the vision of insanity. Primitives, instead of degrading them as we do, worship the insane, holding that madness is in touch with the gods.

> Some madness is divinest sense,

says Emily Dickinson. *Some* madness. The fact that there is plenty of insanity of the infernal brand has not blinded poets to the same truth that primitives accept too indiscriminately. As with crime, so with mental abnormality, it is certain species of it only that are of tragic interest: the madness of Orestes, of Cassandra, of Don Quixote, of Kirillov and Ivan Karamazov. Lear, sane, is exiled from the truth. His egotism is intolerable. He is devoid of sympathy. It is Lear of so-called sound mind who disinherits Cordelia, banishes Kent, and curses Goneril. But as his mind begins to break, truth begins to break in on it. Indeed, Shakespeare chooses Lear's shattered brain as the vehicle of not a few of his own profoundest convictions, mixed, it is true, with wild ravings, as lightning is with wind and night. After the restoration to him of Cordelia, he is never again incoherent, and he never utters a word that does not enforce attention either by its truth or its pathos. But his mind is not in normal condition, and, just before his dying speech, Shakespeare is careful, for our guidance, to have Albany remark,

He knows not what he says.

His last flash of insight is the perception of a supernormal mind.

Or better, it may be, of a *childlike* mind. For Lear, after the return of sanity, is in his second childhood, not in the ordinary sense of being afflicted with stupidity and dulness, but in the rarer sense of being gifted with a second innocence and ingenuousness, as if he had indeed been born again.[4] And so at the end it is more strictly the wisdom of simplicity than the wisdom of insanity with which he is crowned. The artlessness—not to say monosyllabic bareness, considering the tragic intensity effected—of his last speeches, especially the last of all, has often been the subject of comment. Shakespeare has already familiarized us with the insight of simplicity in scores of humorous and humble characters from Launce to Desdemona, always differentiating it sharply from commonness or uncouthness. In the present play, Edgar and the Fool are strikingly simply but penetratingly wise.

And so on that last line and a half of Lear's role are concentrated, like sunbeams by a burning glass, the inspired visions of old age, of misery, of death, of insanity and simplicity, to put beyond the possibility of challenge the truth of what Lear at this extremest moment *sees*.

> Death but our rapt attention
>   To immortality.

It might have been this last scene of *King Lear*, with the father intent on nothing but what he saw on his daughter's lips, that elicited those astounding seven words of Emily Dickinson's.

> Prove true, imagination, O, prove true!

prayed Viola. So prayed Shakespeare, and, by writing *King Lear*, helped answer his own prayer. This is Keats's "truth of Imagination." Like Cordelia's, its voice is ever soft, gentle, and low, and the din of the world easily makes it inaudible. But in the end, Shakespeare seems to say, it is the only voice worth listening to. How many other wise men have said the same thing! "Power to appreciate faint, fainter, and infinitely faintest voices and visions," says Emerson, "is what distinguishes man from man." And Thoreau, improving even upon Emerson, exclaims: "I will attend the faintest sound, and then declare to man what God hath meant." This is the "genuine" way of knowing which Democritus differentiates from the "obscure" way. "Whenever the obscure way has reached the minimum sensible of hearing, smell, taste, and touch," Democritus asserts, "and when the investigation must be carried farther into that which is still finer, then arises the genuine way of knowing, which has a finer organ of thought." *King Lear* might have been written to make that distinction clear.

Such a piling-up of persuasions as we have been reviewing might seem sufficient. But it is not for Shakespeare. For him, there is still the obverse side of the coin. The objective must supplement the subjective. Not content with showing that Lear is capable at death of spiritual vision, Shakespeare must also show that there is spirit *there* to be seen.

But here we have forestalled the demonstration—for precisely this is what we have already abundantly seen. Why, all through the play, has Shakespeare exercised the last resources of his art to make us conscious of Cordelia's presence even when she is invisible, except in preparation for the end?

You are a spirit, I know.

So we too say, and if we did not at that moment add to Lear's assertion his question, "When did you die?" it is only because the restoration scene is but a rehearsal of the death scene. In *it* all the poetical forces that verify Lear's first vision of Cordelia as a spirit come back with compound interest to verify his last one. Cordelia lived in the Fool's imagination, and in her father's before death; the Fool is united with Cordelia in his master's imagination at death; Cordelia still lives in Lear's imagination after death. And she lives in ours. In all these ways, Shakespeare confers upon her existence in the Imagination itself, which, as William Blake saw, is only our human word for Eternity. "Love without Imagination is eternal death." From *Julius Caesar* on, Shakespeare's faith in the existence of spiritual entities beyond the range of ordinary consciousness, and hence objective to it, increases in steady crescendo. Of his belief in the reality of infernal spirits, he has long left us in no doubt. In the storm scene of *Othello*, and in the "divine" Desdemona, we can sense the coming of the last scene of *King Lear*. But in *King Lear* more unequivocally even than in *Othello*—however embryonically from the merely human point of view—he asserts the reality of a celestial spirit. The debased current use of the word "imagination" must not be permitted to confuse us. The imagination is not a faculty for the creation of illusion; it is the faculty by which alone man apprehends reality. The "illusion" turns out to be the truth. "Let faith oust fact," as Starbuck says in *Moby-Dick*. It is only our absurd "scientific" prejudice that reality must be physical and rational that blinds us to the truth.

And right here lies the reason for the numerous references to the lower animals in *King Lear*. They are so used as to suggest that the evil characters of the play have slipped back from the human kingdom to the kingdom of beasts and brutes. Goneril, for instance, shows whither Henry V's injunction to imitate the action of the tiger ultimately leads. She has become a tiger. Hyenas, wolves, serpents—men under slavery to passion pass back into them by atavism; yet it is an insult to these subrational creatures to compare human abortions like Regan and Cornwall to them, and Shakespeare seems to be asking himself, as Bradley so admirably expresses it,

> whether that which he loathes in man may not be due to some strange wrenching of this frame of things, through which the lower animal souls have found a lodgment in human forms, and there found—to the horror and confusion of the thinking mind—brains to forge, tongues to speak, and hands to act, enormities which no mere brute can conceive or execute.

> *Er nennt's Vernunft und braucht's allein,*
> *Nur tierischer als jedes Tier zu sein,*

says Goethe of man. For this monstrous state of affairs words stronger than brutal or bestial, infernal words, are demanded. Albany feels this when he calls his own wife a devil:

ALB.:   See thyself, devil!
Proper deformity seems not in the fiend
So horrid as in woman.
GON.:   O vain fool!
ALB: Thou changed and self-cover'd thing, for shame!
Be-monster not thy feature. Were 't my fitness
To let these hands obey my blood,
They are apt enough to dislocate and tear
Thy flesh and bones. Howe'er thou art a fiend,
A woman's shape doth shield thee.

If this is not the doctrine of "possession," what is it? To Albany, Goneril is not a woman in the shape of a fiend, but a fiend in the shape of a woman. The distinction may seem slight or merely verbal: actually it involves two opposite views of the universe.

And so the play takes on what may be called an evolutionary or hierarchical character—but more in a transmigratory than in a Darwinian sense—with the dramatic persons on an ascending and descending scale, from the evil sisters and their accomplices at the bottom up through Albany and Edgar and Kent to the Fool, the transformed Lear, and Cordelia at the top. "O! the difference of man and man!" The effect is indeed Cosmic, as if the real battle were being fought over men's heads by devils and angels, and as if man's freedom (yet how could he crave more?) consisted, as in *Macbeth*, not in any power to affect the issue by his "own" strength, but rather in the right to stand, as he wills, in the light or in the shadow, to be possessed, as he chooses, by spirits dark or bright.

XIII

Spirits! The word sends us back to the Ghost in *Hamlet*. What a contrast! The son kneeling to the spirit of his father; the father kneeling to the spirit of his child. The warrior demanding vengeance in stentorian tones that every man and woman in the theater can hear and understand; the daughter breathing reconciliation in a voice so low that no one in the theater can hear—the only evidence to auditor or reader of its existence being its reflection in the voice and face and gestures of him who bends over her, when, though he cannot hear, he sees the movement of Life on her lips.

In this scene is finally registered the immense advance that Shakespeare's own vision had taken since *Hamlet*. From *Romeo and Juliet,* or earlier, to *Hamlet,* and perhaps beyond, Shakespeare held, so far as we can tell, that the human ideal, as Hamlet said, lay in a proper commingling of blood and judgment. But he grew wiser as he grew older. Blood is life itself. It is heat, intensity, passion, driving force: it is our inheritance from an indefinitely long animal and human past with all its vast capacity—for good, yes, but especially for rapacity and destruction. And that enormous energy is to be ruled by judgment! Judgment: what a colorless abstraction beside red blood!—as if a charging stallion were to be turned aside not by a bit but by politely calling his attention to the danger of his speed and fury. It just will not do. Hamlet himself discovered too late the terrible inadequacy of "reason" in this sense. And so did Shakespeare—but not too late. The infinite can be controlled only by the infinite—by something of its own order. In *Othello, Macbeth,* and *King Lear* invisible and superhuman spiritual agencies have taken the place of judgment as the hoped-for curb of blood. Love, tenderness, patience, forgiveness are our too too human names for the manifestations within human life of something which comes as incontrovertibly from what is beyond and above it as the appetites do from what is beyond and below. Because these rare words are tarnished with hypocrisy and soiled by daily misuse, they lose their power—until a Shakespeare comes along to bring them to life in a Desdemona or a Cordelia.

But it would be wrong to the point of grotesqueness to suggest that he implies that reason has no place. It has, he seems to be saying, but it is a secondary one. Reason is what we have to fall back on when imagination fails—as we have to fall back on touch when eyesight fails. Or, in another figure, reason is the bush that saves us from plunging down the declivity, not the wings that enable us to soar in safety above it. Such wings only some brighter spirit, like Dante's Beatrice, can bestow. Cordelia is one—of the first magnitude. *King Lear* is Hell, Earth, and Heaven in one. It is Shakespeare's reconciliation of blood and spirit, his union of the Red Rose and the White.

XIV

From *Henry VI* onward, Shakespeare never ceased to be concerned with the problem of chaos, or, as we would be more likely to say today, of disintegration. Sometimes it may be no more than a hint of chaos in an outburst of individual passion or social disorder. Often it is chaos under its extreme aspects of insanity or war. Always the easy and obvious remedy for chaos is force. But the best force can do is to impose order, not to elicit harmony, and Shakespeare spurns such a superficial and temporizing solution. "How with this rage," he perpetually asks,

> How with this rage shall beauty hold a plea,
> Whose action is no stronger than a flower?

In play after play he pits some seemingly fragile representative of beauty against the forces of inertia and destruction: a dream, the spirit of innocence or play, love, art—whether as poetry, drama, or music especially. Force and Imagination: they are the ultimate foes. Force or Imagination: that is the ultimate choice. But always up to *King Lear* the conflict seemed to fall short of finality. It remained for Shakespeare's supreme play to oppose physical force with imagination in its quintessential form of metaphysical Vision. Not only does the poet incarnate that struggle in the action of the drama; he has the Duke of Albany state it in so many words.

Anyone who reads those words, if he notices them at all, thinks he understands them. But it may be questioned whether he can understand them unless he reads them in the light of those other words, the last utterance of King Lear, to which, as I have tried to show, the entire tragedy in a sense leads up.

In this, his version of The Last Judgment, Shakespeare has demonstrated that hatred and revenge are a plucking-out of the human imagination as fatal to man's power to find his way in the universe as Cornwall's plucking out of Gloucester's eyes was to the guidance of his body on earth. The exhibition, in fearful detail, of this self-devouring process is what makes *King Lear* to many readers the most hopeless of Shakespeare's plays. But *King Lear* also exhibits and demonstrates something else. It shows that there is a mode of seeing as much higher than physical eyesight as physical eyesight is than touch, an insight that bestows power to see "things invisible to mortal sight" as certainly as Lear saw that Cordelia lives after her death.

What is the relation between these two aspects of Shakespeare's Last Judgment?

He states it with the utmost exactitude in the words of Albany to which I have referred. The last three of the five lines that make up this passage I have already quoted. The first two, as those familiar with the text may have noted, I omitted at that time. I suppressed them intentionally. Albany says:

If that the heavens do not their visible spirits
Send quickly down to tame these vile offences,
It will come,
Humanity must perforce prey on itself,
Like monsters of the deep.

Such is the predestined end of humanity, if the heavens do not send down their spirits and if those to whom they are sent down do not achieve the power to see them. If the heavens do not.... But the heavens did—and King Lear did not fail them.

You are a spirit, I know. When did you die?...
Do you see this? Look on her, look, her lips,
Look there, look there!

And so, in *King Lear* at least, humanity did not devour itself, and King Lear and his child were lifted up into the realm of the gods.

King Lear takes us captive. That is what it ought to do and what we ought to let it do, for only as we give ourselves up to it will it give itself up to us. "Enthusiastic admiration," says Blake, "is the first principle of knowledge, and its last." And it is right too that we should wish to share our wonder. "O! See, see!" cries Albany over the dying Lear. "Look there, look there!" cries the dying Lear over the dead

Cordelia. This play draws those same exclamations about itself from everyone who feels its power. But that does not mean that anyone has the right to insist that his way of taking it is the only possible one. I hope that I have myself given no impression of speaking "the truth" about *King Lear* in this sense. All I have wanted to do is to point out the figures I see moving in this fiery furnace of Shakespeare's imagination, in the hope, naturally, that others may see them too. But if others do not see them, for them they are not there. Far be it from me in that case to assert that I am right and they are wrong. If, as the old King bends over his child and sees that she still lives, he is deluded and those who know that she is dead are right, then indeed is *King Lear,* as many believe, the darkest document in the supreme poetry of the world. And perhaps it is. There come moods in which anyone is inclined to take it in that sense. But they are not our best moods. And the chief reason, next to the compulsion of my own imagination, why I believe I have at least done no violence to Shakespeare's text is that I have so often witnessed the effect on youth of this reading of the final scene of his tragic masterpiece. I have already quoted the words of one such young person on first coming under its spell. They are worth repeating:

"*King Lear* is a miracle. There is nothing in the whole world that is not in this play. It says everything, and if this is the last and final judgment on this world we live in, then it is a miraculous world. This is a miracle play."

NOTES

[1] *Hamlet, Prince of Denmark* is of course the full title, and the subtitle should be coupled with the title oftener than it is to emphasize both Hamlet's princely qualities and his disdain of royalty. Cf. *Prince Myshkin* in Dostoevsky's *The Idiot.*

[2] Bradley and Stoll both think the delay of Edmund is a sacrifice of reality to stage effect. I should say, on the contrary, that it is motivated with the very nicest gradations.

[3] Note how the death of Gloucester, whose heart "burst smilingly," prepares for Lear's.

It was Bradley, I think, who first pointed out that Lear dies of joy, not grief. A rare insight. But to leave it at that is to leave the harvest of that insight ungarnered.

[4] Emerson, in his last days, was "broken" in this beautiful sense.

Barbara Everett

THE NEW KING LEAR

It is generally acknowledged that *King Lear* is not only a much better play than its principal source, *King Leir and His Three Daughters,* but also a quite different one. It is not a pious chronicle-history, but a tragedy in a pagan setting. Yet the orthodox approach to *King Lear* has, in recent years, so much stressed the "Christian" content and method of the play, that it is sometimes a little difficult to know which of the two plays is in question. It seems, at any rate, a very far cry from the days when Johnson could object that "Shakespeare has suffered the virtue of Cordelia to perish in a just cause, contrary to the natural ideas of justice, to the hope of the reader, and, what is yet more strange, to the faith of chronicles ..."[1]. Though the pressure of human feeling, and a particular belief in the moral responsibility of the arts, could make Johnson accept with relief the public's decision to allow Cordelia to retire "with victory and felicity", his own "sensations" allowed him no doubt as to the real ending of Shakespeare's play: "I was many years ago so shocked by Cordelia's death, that I know not whether I ever endured to read again the last scenes of the play till I undertook to revise them as an editor." And it must, surely, be principally of this play that Johnson was thinking when he made the grave charge against Shakespeare that "he sacrifices virtue to convenience, and is so much more careful to please than instruct, that he seems to write without any moral purpose ... he makes no just distribution of good and evil ...".

Johnson is making here a firm judgment on Shakespeare as an artist: that, despite all his great gifts, he failed to satisfy the moral sense in any but the most elementary way ("he that thinks reasonably must think morally"). If one compares this with, for instance, the Introduction to the New Arden *King Lear,* then it is clear that an equally firm judgment is being made, which is precisely opposite to Johnson in its conclusions: "... the symbolic significance of the trial of the two daughters by a mad beggar, a dying Fool, and a serving-man is perfectly clear. *He hath put down the mighty from their seats, and hath exalted the humble and meek*... The old Lear died in the storm. The new Lear is born in the scene in which he is reunited

From *Critical Quarterly* 2, No. 4 (Winter 1960): 325–39.

with Cordelia. His madness marked the end of the wilful, egotistical monarch. He is resurrected as a fully human being. We can tell from his protest—

> You do me wrong to take me out of the grave

that the awakening into life is a painful process. After the reconciliation, Lear makes only two more appearances. In the scene in which he is being led off to prison he has apparently overcome his desire for vengeance; he has left behind him all those attributes of kingship which had prevented him from attaining his full stature as a man; he has even passed beyond his own pride. At the beginning of the play he is incapable of disinterested love, for he uses the love of others to minister to his own egotism. His prolonged agony and his utter loss of everything free his heart from the bondage of the selfhood. He unlearns hatred, and learns love and humility. He loses the world and gains his own soul.... The play is not, as some of our grand-fathers believed, pessimistic and pagan; it is rather an attempt to provide an answer to the undermining of traditional ideas by the new philosophy that called all in doubt." Even so long a quotation as this cannot do justice to Professor Muir's fullness and variety of approach in the Introduction; but it can suggest his ideas on what he calls Shakespeare's "religious attitude" and on the nature of the work of art he is discussing. Shakespeare, for him, is obviously *not* merely content with "the real state of sublunary nature", but has imposed upon it something approaching a transcendental design, didactic in intention; and this is (so, I think, the stress of such criticism suggests) the greatest of his great gifts. That a work of art can carry such widely divergent interpretations is a sign of its vitality. But when two such inter-pretations can seem to be mutually exclusive, it is perhaps worth while to wonder on what bases the propositions rest; so that, if they cannot be reconciled, they may, at least, be clarified.

To suggest that Johnson was not taking the play "seriously", or was not "responding" to it fully, would of course be quite misleading. He feels "a perpetual tumult of indignation, pity, and hope ... So powerful is the current of the poet's imagination, that the mind, which once ventures within it, is hurried irresistibly along". He is, rather, disturbed by that very intensity with which he feels a piece in which "the virtuous miscarry". The quality in the play which seems to dominate his mind and impress him so deeply is its logic of action and character, whereby "villainy is never at a stop ... crimes lead to crimes, and at last terminate in ruin". In his discussion of the play, the words which recur are "events ... story ... action"; his reactions are caused by the "plot", which presents a spectacle of motivated actions culminating in almost intolerable suffering.

Those critics who find in the play either a partial, or a total Christian allegory, are alike in one thing, however different their respective approaches may be: this is an interest in such parts of the play as seem to make a statement which is differentiated from the "plot" (that is, the story as it would stand as a prose tale.) They are interested in the kind of "poetic" statements which the play seems to make, in contradistinction from what actually happens. Thus Professor Muir quotes the famous lines beginning "We two alone will sing like birds i' th' cage ..." and quotes approvingly from another critic: "A life of sins forgiven, of reciprocal charity, of clear vision, and of joyous song—what is this but the traditional heaven transferred to earth?" And Professor Knight, stressing the "purgatorial" aspect of *King Lear*, finds much of the play's meaning in the lines uttered by Lear on his awakening—"Thou art a soul in bliss ...": "The naturalism of King Lear pales before this blinding shaft of transcendent light. This is the justification of the agony, the sufferance, the gloom".[2] Curiously, in the word "justification", we come close not only to the world of distinctively Christian experience, but to the world of "poetic justice", which Johnson looked for in the play, and could not find.

Such a stress on the "poetry" of the play is of course a Romantic one, in the sense that one finds the beginnings of such criticism—the "plot" being poetry, rather than what happens to characters-in-action—in the great Romantic critics. The sense that Shakespeare is creating a great spiritual adventure, to which the outer world—whether of "what actually happens", or of stage representation— merely offers expendable symbols, is first found in Lamb's famous attack on stage performances of *King Lear:* "The greatness of Lear is not in corporal dimension, but in intellectual ... On the stage we see nothing but corporal infirmities and weakness, the impotence of rage; while we read it, we see not Lear, but we are Lear; we are in his mind ... ".[3] Hazlitt quotes this passage in writing on *King Lear,* and supports Lamb's contention that the poet's work is to "personate passion, and the turns of passion" with his own: "the greatest strength of genius is shown in describing the strongest passions ... our sympathy with actual suffering is lost in the strong impulse given to our natural affections, and carried away with the swelling tide of passion, that gushes from and relieves the heart."[4] Coleridge, a greater and subtler critic than either Lamb or Hazlitt, stresses, like them, the "independence of the interest on the story as the ground work of the plot."[5] It is Lear's "character, passions, and suffering" which are "the main subject-matter of the play." *"Lear* is the most tremendous effort of Shakespeare as a *poet." King Lear* has become King Lear: the play moves us by sympathy for Lear: and that sympathy is created by poetry. We enter, as it were, the poetic element which is Lear's world, and whatever happens is dominated by what is felt (which is principally what Lear feels) and what is felt is found in the poetry. Since "poetry" used in the Romantic sense is, I think, plot-less—Being, so to speak, rather than Becoming—the stress on the "unhappy ending" of *Lear,* that Johnson could scarcely "endure", grows less and less: what is valuable in the play has no "ending".

Though these critics stress "feeling" in *King Lear,* their treatment of the play could scarcely be called transcendental. The first critic of whom the word might be used is, of course, Bradley; though he himself acknowledges his debt to Dowden, who stresses the sovereignty of the "moral world" in the play. Bradley's profound study of the play is remarkable, both for the way in which he feels a Romantic sympathy for, or participation in, the central character, to an extreme degree, and also for the way in which he soberly refuses to take it any further. If he directs the reader to a more "transcendental" interpretation of the play, he does so hesitantly, hedging his observations round with careful reservations. Thus, when he suggests that we should call "this poem *The Redemption of King Lear*"[6] (what happens to Lear's soul outweighing what happens to his body) he does so only in answer to such criticism as Swinburne's, that stresses the "pessimism" of the play, and himself affirms the power and partial verity of such criticism; and the narrowing reference, too, to the play as "this poem", is counteracted by the constant analysis of character and dramatic effect. Again, he closes his essay on the play with the affirmation that at least a part of its beauty, and at least a part of its meaning, depend on the feelings aroused by the death of Cordelia: "If only we could see things as they are, we should see that the outward is nothing and the inward is all . . . Let us renounce the world, hate it, and lose it gladly. The only real thing in it is the soul, with its courage, patience, and devotion. And nothing outward can touch that". But this very affirmation he balances by saying that "this strain of thought . . . pursued further and allowed to dominate . . . would destroy the tragedy; for it is necessary to tragedy that we should feel that suffering and death do matter greatly, and that happiness and life are not to be renounced as worthless." Cordelia's death may arouse a sense of unworldly values, but Cordelia herself is far from perfect, and fully involved in the tragedy: "At the moment where terrible issues join, fate makes on her the one demand which she is unable to meet".

Thus, though Bradley is the first to make an impressive appeal for a more "mystical" interpretation of *King Lear,* he insists again and again that it is a "mystery we cannot fathom", and that no explicitly religious interpretation will serve: "Any theological interpretation of the world on the author's part is excluded from [the tragedies], and their effect would be disordered or destroyed equally by the ideas of righteous or unrighteous omnipotence . . . If we ask why the world should generate that which convulses and wastes it, the tragedy gives no answer, and we are trying to go beyond tragedy in seeking one". His feeling for the intense actuality of Shakespearian characterisation (and the ability to see a dramatic character as a cluster of images is not, perhaps, one that comes without some peculiar habituation) makes him resist any theoretical design overriding such characterisation: "Perhaps, in view of some interpretation of Shakespeare's plays, it may be as well to add that I do not dream of suggesting that in any of his dramas Shakespeare imagined two abstract principles or passions conflicting, and incorporated them in persons". For him, the plays stand rather at the point where intensity of experience becomes religious potentiality: but that potentiality finds no fit expression in the world that is the necessary stage for tragedy, and becomes rather aspiration, suffering, moral responsibility. It might perhaps be said that this sense of unfulfilled potentiality is a part of his vision of Shakespearian tragedy.

To turn from Bradley to the criticism of *King Lear* that has appeared over the last twenty or thirty years is to realise to what a startling extent it is indebted to him—startling, in that he has hardly been popular among critics for a very long time. Obviously the "new" approach to *King Lear* cannot wholly be explained by Bradley's influence. A greater knowledge, both of Elizabethan rhetoric and poetic technique, and of what has been called "the Elizabethan world picture" in its debt to mediaeval thought, has made readers see the play as a poetic work, whose imagery has as great an effect on the mind as the plot and characters, and also as a work that has a strong strain of the allegorical and even of the didactic. But it is interesting to see so many of Bradley's cautious hints and suggestions purified of their accompanying reservations and now seen as dominating the play. The famous suggestion, for instance, that Lear dies "in an agony of ecstasy" is now accepted almost universally: what is interesting is its appearance in critics as different as Professor Empson ("He dies of a passion of joy at the false belief that Cordelia has recovered"[7]), Professor Wilson Knight ("what smiling destiny is this he sees at the last instant of racked mortality?"[8]), and Professor Muir ("His actual death-blow is not his bereavement but his joy when he imagines that Cordelia is not dead after all. That joy was based on an illusion. The earlier joy of reconciliation, however shortlived, was not an illusion: it was the goal of Lear's pilgrimage. His actual death was comparatively unimportant"). The mere borrowing of what is certainly a fine, and may be a true, interpretation of Lear's last words is less important than the hypothesis, or suggestion, that accompanies this reading in two of the three: the "smiling destiny" ("their effect would be disordered or destroyed equally by the ideas of righteous or unrighteous omnipotence") and "his actual death was comparatively unimportant" ("suffering and death do matter greatly").

What is most remarkable is the predominance of the idea of the feeling of "reconciliation" at the end of the tragedy, which is Bradley's attempt to answer the question of "tragic pleasure": since one finds this quite as strong in those who would probably deny keenly any affiliation to Bradley, or even any desire to see the play as a Christian allegory; the sense of a "happy ending" takes the form of what is called variously the Restoration of Order, or of the Family Bond, or of Reason. In reading such studies, one is impressed by their inner coherence and their cogent force; yet one remembers, perhaps, Bradley's own introduction of such a thesis of "moral order", and his doubtful conclusion: "Nor does the idea of a moral order asserting itself against attack or want of conformity answer in full to our feelings regarding the tragic character ... When, to save its life and regain peace from this intestinal struggle, it casts [the tragic heroes] out, it has lost a part of its own substance—a part more dangerous and unquiet, but far more valuable and nearer to its heart, than that which remains ... That this idea, though very different from the idea of a blank fate, is no solution to the riddle of life is obvious; but why should we expect it to be such a solution? Shakespeare was not attempting to justify the ways of God to men, or to show the universe as a Divine Comedy."

Bradley's *Redemption of King Lear* is tempered by such considerations. The modern King Lear is certainly redeemed: what has disappeared is Bradley's "honest doubt". "Shakespeare makes [*King Lear*] end, not in the final victory of evil, but in the final victory of good ... *King Lear* is, like the *Paradiso*, a vast poem on the victory of true love."[9] "[*King Lear*] is at least as Christian as the Divine Comedy."[10] If *King Lear* is to be a Christian allegory, then search must be made for a Christ-figure; Lear, in that he is the *persona patiens*, is given some such characteristics, but he is too completely individualised to serve. Thus stress falls on Cordelia, as both the most beautiful, and the most lightly sketched-in of the characters. "Divine love, symbolised by Cordelia, enters a kingdom already divided against itself, which is the Christian definition of hell... If Bradley be right, it is not the chance, but the certainty that she does indeed so live [in resurrection] which causes Lear's hitherto indomitable heart to break, and the great sufferer dies at last, not of sorrow, but in an ecstasy of joy."[11] Perhaps one ought to remember precisely what Bradley *did* say: "To us, perhaps, the knowledge that he is deceived may bring a culmination of pain: but if it brings *only* that, I believe we are false to Shakespeare... All that matters is what she is. How this can be when, for anything the tragedy tells us, she has ceased to exist, we do not ask; but the tragedy itself makes us feel that somehow it is so." A similar statement of Cordelia's allegorical function can be found elsewhere: "Cordelia, in that she represents the principle of love, is idealised[12]..." "... Cordelia cannot stand for individual sanity without at the same time standing for rightness in the relation of man to man—social sanity ... Cordelia for Shakespeare is virtue ... [she] stands for wholeness ... Cordelia is Shakespeare's version of singleness and integration ... She constitutes the apex of the pyramid ... She is the norm itself ..."[13] Again, one returns by contrast to Bradley's patient attempts to trace *all* the strands of characterisation he finds in Cordelia, however much less simple this may make the final effect: "Yes, 'heavenly true.' But truth is not the only good in the world, nor is the obligation to tell truth the only obligation. The matter here was to keep it inviolate, but also to preserve a father. And even if truth *were* the one and only obligation, to tell much less than truth is not to tell it."

Such recent studies have enriched the reading of *King Lear* to such a degree, by illuminating the strange blend of feelings and attitudes, of theology and philosophy that the play contains, that one would be far from wishing to "prove", in any way, their inferiority to Bradley, or to Coleridge, or to Johnson. A study of the genealogy, or growth, of such an interpretation may simply help to show how a play that must still seem, to the naïf consciousness, appalling in its content and terrible in its conclusions, can be described as almost a Divine Comedy: "He unlearns hatred, and learns love and humility. He loses the world and gains his own soul". It is a truism that every age of criticism finds in Shakespeare precisely what it is looking for: and perhaps what it looks for is really there, in a potential form. An image, or a human character, are both potentials, and may be interpreted *ad infinitum*. And yet, for all the pleasures of electicism in criticism, it is always possible to have reservations about any theory, or attitude, that is both extreme and exclusive; and criticism that sees a Shakespearian tragedy as at least tending toward didactic allegory of a peculiar kind, is surely even more doctrinal in its assertions than is a "judging" critic like Johnson, who has a resourceful habit of giving back with one hand, so to speak, what he has taken away with the other. Johnson's conclusions on *King Lear* bear out his contention that "there is always an appeal open from criticism to nature", and throw open the argument to the reason of the common reader: "A play in which the wicked prosper, and the virtuous miscarry, may doubtless be good, because it is a just representation of the common events of human life: but since all reasonable beings naturally love justice, I cannot easily be persuaded, that the observation of justice makes a play worse ..." These words are rather hesitant and perplexed, than bombastic; whereas the reader is, perhaps, a little provoked to dissent by the very doctrinaire quality evinced in such phrases as "the *certainty* that she does indeed so live . . ." "the symbolic significance of the trial of the two daughters . . . is *perfectly clear.*"

It is obviously impossible to decide, simply, whether or not *King Lear* is a "Christian" play. To set it beside a play that uses even so great a degree of Christian context, as *Dr. Faustus,* is to realise what one means by the phrase "a mind naturally Christian"; *King Lear* is not only profoundly concerned with the moral repercussions of desires and actions, nor does it simply present an area of imaginative experience that constantly moves from philosophical into moral and metaphysical speculation, but it also presents these words, "moral" and "metaphysical", in a peculiarly Christian way. The splendours of pride, passion, aspiration, are constantly mutating, as it were, into the virtues of humility, gentleness, and endurance. Yet, when all this is said, there remains the fact that there are many kinds of art, and many kinds of statement, that a "mind naturally Christian" might make. Montaigne also seems, from his writing, to have loved gentleness and courage; yet it would be difficult to make a case for him as a Christian allegorist. The question is not open to solution either way, nor is it, strictly speaking, the critic's business to answer it. All that might be argued is rather the *kind* of statement which Shakespeare is making in *King Lear;* whether or not it is as doctrinal, and as didactic, as it seems, in, for instance, Professor Muir's version of the play.

Much of the poetry in the play that is quoted as evidence of Lear's apprehension of "Heavenly" things—such as, for instance, the two passages mentioned above: "We two alone will sing like birds i' th' cage . . ." and "Thou art a soul in bliss . . ." seems to me to be peculiarly conditioned by the way it is used in the play. These passages are of such great beauty that one realises the degree of imaginative potency that they have. And yet Shakespeare often reserves his most "beautiful" passages, in the tragedies, for a peculiar purpose: to suggest, that is, an imaginative state in ironical opposition to the actual, or to create an atmosphere or a scene that is in some ways irrelevant to the central issues, and heightens them by contrast. One may quote the lyrical phantasies of the mad Ophelia, or the exquisite pastoral of her death, occurring in a play of darkness, corruption, and sophistication; or the elaborate splendour of Othello's "It is the cause, it is the cause, my soul"—surely the most "beautiful" speech in the play—which is based on the completely unfounded assumption that Desdemona is unfaithful; or Duncan's and Banquo's praise of the serene calm of the castle that is to hold the blood of one, and the ghost of the other. In both the *King Lear* passages, imagination is "still, still far wide". The beautiful and curiously civilised vision of a purgatorial wheel, or the dream of a shared life in a hermit's cell, are both, with their exquisite rhythm and lucid images, in some way apart from what one thinks of as the "poetic language" of the play, and—to one reader at least—less impressive and moving than this language at its height, as in Lear's and the other characters' speeches in the storm, and Lear's at Cordelia's death. Nor is the poetic vision embodied in such speeches as "We two alone . . ." of such a power as to outweigh, so to speak, the truth of the action in which they occur. The issue at hand is the battle which, being lost, must result eventually in the death of both Lear and Cordelia. In relation to that issue, Lear's speeches have the nature of decorative art, integral perhaps only in the sense that they contribute to the tragedy of a man in love with "our lives' sweetness" in a world that refuses to be sweet. The deliberately child-like tone that enters the second of these speeches especially ("And pray, and sing, and tell old tales, and laugh") certainly can be said to have a divine innocence, but it can also be said to reduce the world of the play to something like a child's playground; to be "God's spies" and to see the flux of human life turn to a game of cards ("wear out packs" may perhaps stand this interpretation) may be a true vision of the "little world of man", but it is very little indeed, compared to the rest of the play.

The scenes which are most full of explicitly "Christian" phrasing, or suggestion, or feeling, are confined, on the whole, to one particular part of the play; that is, to the period between the storm-scenes and the last long scene that contains the meeting of Edgar and Edmund and Lear's entry with Cordelia dead in his arms. It is, perhaps, possible that the mood and tone of these scenes may be caused as much by artistic reasons as by moral design. The storm-scenes form the first climax of the play, to which the whole of the first part proceeds with a speed, violence, and—despite the sense of confusion of time and place—an emotional logic that brings a feeling of complete inevitability: one action of violence generates another with compulsive force. In the storm-scenes Lear is at his most powerful and, despite moral considerations, at his noblest; the image of a man hopelessly confronting a hostile universe and withstanding it only by his inherent powers of rage, endurance, and perpetual questioning, is perhaps the most purely "tragic" in Shakespeare. The last scene of all returns to this mood, and forms a second climax, but the tragic mood is altered by the addition of understanding to Lear's character. The presence of purely tragic pain—the desire to "crack heaven's vault" and deny inevitability by a powerful outcry of feeling—is rarified, as it were, by a more precise knowledge of the source of that pain: the universal issues are intensified and clarified to the form of a single dead body. It is these parts of the play that provide the dominant tragic effect. The quieter scenes on Dover cliff (with the intellectualised memory or echo of violence in Gloster's 'suicide'), the moment of Lear's awakening and first meeting with Cordelia, and the scene in which they are taken away to prison, form a necessary bridge between the more tragic scenes, designed both to rest and to prepare the mind, and to accumulate a sense of the knowledge or understanding necessary to the second climax of the play—that of Lear's death. Hence they will stress not so much what happens, what is seen and felt, but rather what is intellectually understood; and their tone will become necessarily more contemplative and philosophical. The characters, too, of both Lear and Gloster will suffer a diminishment, absorbed, as it were, into the "background"—

As mad as the vex'd sea, singing aloud,
Crown'd with rank fumiter and furrow weeds. . . .

It remains possible that even if one does not lay stress on these particular scenes, and concentrates, rather, on the scenes which show Lear suffering from intense evil, one might make, out of his history, the kind of Christian morality that shows a man "losing the world and gaining his own soul"; and this remains a permanent possibility, in that any picture of good and evil actions must contain suggestions of Christian experience, especially where the good suffer. One can, perhaps, merely remember the strength of Bradley's argument—that in the world of Shakespearian tragedy, one single "nature" generates both good and evil. *King Lear* surely begins, at least, on an assumption that the world of "life" itself—the world, perhaps, of *Twelfth Night* and *Henry IV*—is rich, powerful, beautiful, and important. That the faculties of the mind and body, and the strength and significance of the individual, should be impaired and lost in the course of a play, remains in itself a tragedy, if not *the* tragedy. A concept that can include the suggestion that a hero's death is "comparatively unimportant", is at least a little dangerous—however "metaphysically" it is taken—in that one of the vital functions of tragedy is, surely, to ennoble and illuminate the moment of death. Whatever the structural climax of a Shakespearian tragedy may be, its emotional climax must remain the moment of its hero's death. And the lesser forms of death in a tragedy come with only a slightly smaller impact—loss of profession, loss of love, loss of friends. The worst performance of *King Lear*—and those seen by Lamb were presumably far from good—can at any rate present "an old man tottering about the stage with a walking-stick", and, with this, at least a part of the tragedy. That Lear should be forced, by the evil of two of his daughters, to kneel and plead ironically

> Dear daughter, I confess that I am old:
> Age is unnecessary: on my knees I beg
> That you'll vouchsafe me raiment, bed, and food . . .

is terrible, and the moral impact of the moment is great; but that Lear should choose, because of the goodness of his third daughter, to kneel and confess seriously

> I am a very foolish fond old man
> Fourscore and upward, not an hour more nor less;
> And, to deal plainly,
> I fear I am not in my perfect mind . . .

has also something of the terrible in it, and the impact is not, perhaps, what could be called precisely a "moral" one. Shakespearian tragedy often acts, so to speak, under the level of moral responsibility. Lear's "compensation" is said to be that at least he learns from his sufferings: he "loses the world, and gains his soul". But *what* he learns is that he is "not ague-proof", that he is "old and foolish"; and this in itself contains further ranges of common suffering. No moralistic outline that blurs this can be fully satisfying. Such an outline must also, to some degree, blur the character of Lear. A phrase like "he loses the world" suggests a context of peculiarly Christian experience; that is, it suggests a man (like, for instance, Polyeucte) who makes a conscious and responsible choice, and is aware of at least some of the unhappiness he is willing to suffer. Lear's character is surely scarcely comparable. His greatness lies not in the choice of "the good", but in the transformation, into something vital and strong, of the suffering that is forced upon him, partly as a result of his own foolishness; and this transformation is a part of that love of the "pride of life" that is involved in his first mistake, and that never leaves him up to his death. He fights passionately, at his noblest, against the form of death that the Lear of Professor Muir's revised version of the play would accept willingly—the death of self; his last speeches are as much devoted to an infinitely pathetic threnody for his own waning powers, as they are to the dead Cordelia.

That Lear is represented as a character making perpetual discoveries is certainly true, even if it is hard to accept that the moral weight of these discoveries presents some kind of counterpoint to the sufferings he undergoes; since, if he merely "learns humility", then humility is represented in such a physical way that it contains in itself further active suffering. But perhaps Lear in fact "learns" something rather different from this, or in a rather different way. That society may be corrupt, that justice may become meaningless in the light of this corruption, that both private and public loyalties may be broken and an old order turned into chaos, that humanity is "not ague-proof"—none of these is a particularly new or exciting statement. The interest lies, rather, in the light in which these discoveries show themselves to a certain peculiar character. Lear is divested of that degree of civilised intelligence, subtlety, and rationality that Hamlet and Macbeth, and perhaps even Othello, possess: that he shows, often, the consciousness of a child, with immense power and will, is a truism of criticism. The one gift that he possesses is a colossal power of life itself: "We that are young / Shall never see so much, nor live so long". He is represented as feeling—and not only feeling, but living through, enduring, and becoming consciously and responsibly aware of—actions of profound evil; he feels, with a child's intensity, a range of suffering that a child could never meet. All these forms of evil—the weakness of age, the denial of power, the cruelty of his servants and subjects, social corruption and injustice—present themselves to him as a denial of life, at its profoundest and most simply physical; not, as with the other heroes, as a denial of purity, or of honour, or of imagination, or of the spirit. One recalls Berenson's insistence on the quality of what he calls "life enhancement" by stimulating the sense of "tactile values" to creativity, in Italian Renaissance painting; similarly Lear commands attention continually by the degree to which the simplest discoveries become, through him, a matter of immediate physical experience, felt both intensely and comprehensively.

This faculty to be found in the play, of an imaginative recreation of a physical awareness both intense and wide-ranging, from "I feel this pin prick" to "this great world shall so wear out to nought", is accompanied by something that is in one sense its diametric opposite, and in one sense an extension of itself: which is an apprehension of nothingness. There is a sense in which this apprehension of absolute cessation of being, appearing whenever the word "nothing" drops into the dialogue, is a worse evil than any of the forms of moral evil that Lear meets.

Ironically, the Midas touch of the poet converts even what appals the moral sense into something, if not beautiful, at least intensely interesting, and intensely alive; it is surely not possible to argue that Goneril, who is, in one of Albany's few magnificent phrases

> not worth the dust
> That the rude wind blows in your face—

is less *interesting* than the just and dull Albany himself. The only way, perhaps, in which Renaissance art can convey a sense of evil, or death, is by an antithesis of itself. Thus Lear, whose one heroic quality is a habit of totality of experience, demanding absolutes of love, of power and of truth itself ("who is it who can tell me who I am?" ... "Thou art the thing itself ...") is "rewarded" by an apprehension of the one absolute that the tragic world can offer—the absolute of silence and cessation; and even this apprehension is hedged about by a paradoxical and painful vitality: "Why should a dog, a rat, a horse have life / And thou no life at all?" The silence of the dead Cordelia is a final summary of the presence of what Donne calls "absence, darkness, death; things which are not," throughout the play, wherever a question is asked and not answered, or a command is not obeyed. That this silence *may* contain, strangely enough, as much potentiality of good as of evil, is suggested by the degree of intense life generated by Cordelia's first "Nothing"; but one thing, at least, it finishes—the idea of the overriding power of heroic and individual experience. The hero is only a hero insofar as he is able to envisage the limits of the heroic world.

It is perhaps in this way that one could make out a case for a "metaphysical" *King Lear;* that it shows a world of extreme power and vitality embracing its antithesis. This sense of startling disparities contained within one imaginative world is much more reminiscent of a mind like Pascal's than of the symbolic clarity of a Morality or the simplicity of a mystery play. Intellectual reflection on the play is more likely to need to quote, as it were, phrase after phrase of Pascal's, than to refine from the play itself a pious summary. "On n'est pas misérable sans sentiment. Une maison ruinée ne l'est pas. Il n'y a que l'homme de misérable. *Ego vir videns* ... La grandeur de l'homme est grande en ce qu'il se connaît misérable. Un arbre ne se connaît pas misérable. C'est donc être misérable que de se connaître misé-rable; mais c'est être grand que de connaître qu'on est misérable ... Toutes ces misères-là prouvent sa grandeur. Ce sont misères de grand seigneur, misères d'un roi dépossédé." "Quand l'univers l'écraserait, l'homme serait encore plus noble que ce qui le tue, parce qu'il sait qu'il meurt; et l'avantage que l'univers a sur lui, l'univers n'en sait rien."[14] One feels a sense of recognition in such phrases be-cause, though Pascal was a man almost certainly wholly unlike Shakespeare in mind, temperament, and way of life, his writing postulates a world in which it is still possible to think both seriously and ironically of "La grandeur de l'homme", and to see that the conditions on which such grandeur is based are close to those of tragic experience. One of these conditions is a profound doubt—"une impuissance de prouver"—which perpetually accompanies "une idée de la verité";

the only entire certainty is death: "Le dernier acte est sanglant, quelque belle que soit la comédie en tout le reste." Pascal's image of man—perhaps one learned from Montaigne—is of a creature bewilderingly made "un milieu entre rien et tout", perpetually conditioned and limited by his senses, and yet able to comprehend "all and nothing".

It is such an image that Lear presents in the closing scene of the play. Whether or not Lear's "Look there" does, as Bradley interprets it, suggest a belief that Cordelia is still alive, the last half-dozen lines as a whole condense the poetic experience of the play, whereby the physical and the non-physical are shown in their mysterious relationship.

> Thou'lt come no more,
> Never, never, never, never, never!
> Pray you, undo this button. Thank you sir.
> Do you see this? Look on her, look, her lips,
> Look there, look there!

It is natural enough that the central character of a poetic tragedy should finish by directing the attention, as it were, finally to the closed mouth of a dead human being, an image which presents most of what can be said about the physical limitations to an aspiring mind. Each of the great tragedies ends similarly with a momentary directing of the attention to the full effect of the tragic action:

> What is it you would see?
> If aught of woe or wonder, cease your search ...
> give order that these bodies
> High on a stage be placed to the view ...

> Look on the tragic loading of this bed.
> This is thy work.

> Behold where stands
> Th' usurper's cursed head ...

That Lear should himself turn chorus—("Look on her, look ...") and himself endure "the new acquist / Of true experience from this great event" even while still alive, is consonant with his rôle throughout the play: his own death is the one thing that cannot be presented through the heroic consciousness.

Perhaps the chief reason, then, why one feels doubt about an extremely allegorical interpretation of the play is not that such an interpretation can be said to be "wrong", but simply that the play succeeds so well in another way. Rather than setting up an absolute dichotomy between "the world" and "the soul", between concretes and abstracts, it shows a continual relation between the two that strengthens and enriches both; so that a sense of extreme evil can be conveyed in a phrase of casual malice—("What need one?" "And all night, too") and a sense of extreme good in the commonest expression of a woman's kindness:

> Mine enemy's dog,
> Though he had bit me, should have stood that night
> Against the fire; and wast thou fain, poor father,
> To hovel thee with swine and rogues forlorn
> In short and musty straw? Alack, alack!

It also fulfils that function by which tragedy makes the unendurable endurable by bringing it within an artistic design, while retaining its essential truth; the forms of suffering in the play are transformed not so much by being seen *"sub specie aeternitatis"*, but rather by being seen as forms of intense life. If the play exhilarates, it is less because "Cordelia, from the time of Tate, has always retired with victory and felicity", whether temporal or spiritual, than because it exhibits a poetic power in the writing of the play itself, in the consciousness given to its central character, and in the responsive awareness of audience or reader, that can understand and endure imaginatively actions of great suffering, and by understanding can master them: . . . "L'homme serait encore plus noble que ce qui le tue, parce qu'il sait qu'il meurt." If "Hamlet and Lear are gay", and if tragedy does exist to "give a great kick at human misery," then this is perhaps more because of the gaiety of mastery inherent in the creative act than because of any cheerful propositions made by tragedy itself. The more terrible the propositions, the greater is the mastery; the greater the degree of the "un-tragic", the "un-sublime", contained—the ugly, the humiliating, the petty, the chaotic, the ridiculous, the mad, the gross, the casual, and the carnal—then the greater is the act that can turn these into "the good, the beautiful, and the true", and yet retain the nature of the things themselves. Whether this is, in itself, a highly moral act is a question too difficult to answer; but it is, perhaps, not best answered by turning *King Lear* into a morality play.

NOTES

[1] Johnson: *Preface and Notes to Shakespeare.*
[2] G. Wilson Knight: *The Wheel of Fire.*
[3] Lamb: "On the Tragedies of Shakespeare".
[4] Hazlitt: *Characters of Shakespeare's Plays.*
[5] Coleridge: *Shakespearian Criticism* (ed. Raysor).
[6] Bradley: *Shakespearean Tragedy.*
[7] Empson: *Structure of Complex Words.*
[8] G. Wilson Knight: op. cit.
[9] R. W. Chambers: *King Lear.*
[10] J. F. Danby: *Shakespeare's Doctrine of Nature.*
[11] G. Beckersteth: *The Golden World of King Lear.* B. A. Lecture 1936.
[12] G. Wilson Knight: op. cit.
[13] J. F. Danby: op. cit.
[14] Pascal: *Pensées.*

William Rosen

KING LEAR

Apart from action, there are two major devices that delineate character on the stage: direct self-characterization—what the hero says of himself—and the characterization of the hero by others. Often Shakespeare anticipates and prefigures the entrance of the tragic hero by having characters talk about him before he actually comes onto the stage; and such a technique is used notably in *Romeo and Juliet, Julius Caesar, Othello, Antony and Cleopatra,* and *Coriolanus.* By prefiguring the hero the dramatist imposes upon the audience a certain angle of vision: the playwright provides the audience with a dramatic attitude towards the central figure by having others preview his traits or impart value judgments on him. Thus we actively entertain certain emotions towards the hero before meeting him; and when he does appear, his words and actions are inevitably compared to the brief portrait already sketched for us.

In *King Lear,* though the king's character is not sketched before he appears on stage, he nevertheless comes immediately into a certain frame of reference, not through the technique of prefiguring, but through his own exalted status. For an Elizabethan audience particularly, his figure would expand in minds to encompass a whole context of values. The person of Lear is from the very beginning associated with great honor, for he can be viewed as the highest human embodiment of all the elements which give order and dignity to society: he is king of his nation, father of his family, and he is an old man. Hence the respect which he should command is triply compounded. Now it is not absolutely necessary to turn to Elizabethan concepts of kingship or order to understand the respect and honor due to one who is king, who is father, and who is old. Such ideas have not disappeared with the passing of some three hundred and fifty years. However, a brief reference to Elizabethan attitudes is appropriate here because the respect due to Lear is central to the play.

Certainly "kingship" had an evocative power for Elizabethans. There is divinity

From *Shakespeare and the Craft of Tragedy* (Cambridge, MA: Harvard University Press, 1960), pp. 1–51.

that hedges a king—we find this idea reiterated in much of the writing of the age.[1] Furthermore, the correspondence between the power of the king and that of the father was an Elizabethan commonplace illustrating the order of a universe in which, as God governed all, so kings ruled states, and fathers, families.[2] In *The French Academie*, whose popularity is attested by its many English editions from 1586 to 1614, La Primaudaye makes an observation that might serve as a commentary on *King Lear*:

> Everie house must be ruled by the eldest, as by a king, who by nature commandeth over everie part of the house, and they obey him for the good preservation thereof.... This commandement over children, is called roiall, bicause he that begetteth, commandeth by love, and by the prerogative of age, which is a kind of kingly commanding.... The father is the true image of the great & soveraign God, the universal father of al things.[3]

Thus the ordered family, the private life of a nation, is a mirroring in miniature of the ordered hierarchy of public society; and analogies between the king and his subjects and the father and his children prevailed.

It is within such a context that we first see King Lear: his figure activates in the minds of an audience patterns of value of which he is the embodiment. His formal entrance highlights all the dignity and authority associated with kingship. The set of notes sounded, the "sennet," ushers in the concrete symbol of royalty, "enter one bearing a coronet"; and the stage directions give the precise order of entrance which accords with the prerogatives of rank: "King Lear, Cornwall, Albany, Goneril, Regan, Cordelia, and Attendants." On the Elizabethan stage this would be a stately procession of splendor, Lear the central figure in a crowded scene. All are Lear's subjects, dependent on him.

Lear's stature is even further magnified in his first extended pronouncement in which he tells of his intentions to divest himself of "rule, / Interest of territory, cares of state" (I.i.50), for we see him in the role of public and private figure at one and the same time. Because he is king, his actions in dividing the realm have public consequences affecting the density of the state; as benefactor to his children in this division, his actions affect the private life of the family as well. And yet, though the figure of the king bodies forth the ideal, the highest good of family and nation, it is important to see that in this scene Shakespeare presents his central character as an ironist would; and in this way: that the audience does not fully engage its sympathies with Lear or those who oppose him since the dramatist supports the values which Lear represents while revealing the king's misguided position.

Lear's character is objectively dramatized at the beginning. And in situations that are dramatized rather than narrated, the task of projecting states of mind devolves upon the language itself. In Lear's first lengthy speech, which is balanced and regally formal, Shakespeare has the king dramatically reveal himself as proud, authoritative, at the height of his power, wishing to hear not truth, but flattery:

> Tell me, my daughters,—
> Since now we will divest us both of rule,
> Interest of territory, cares of state,—
> Which of you shall we say doth love us most,
> That we are largest bounty may extend
> Where nature doth with merit challenge? Goneril,
> Our eldest-born, speak first.   (I.i.49)

Lear's abdication is thus the occasion for a pageant of flattery: each daughter is to vie with the other in a public display of love. Goneril fulfills his expectations:

> Sir, I love you more than word can wield the matter;
> Dearer than eye-sight, space, and liberty;
> Beyond what can be values, rich or rare;
> No less than life, with grace, health, beauty, honour;
> As much as child e'er lov'd, or father found;
> A love that makes breath poor, and speech unable:
> Beyond all manner of so much I love you.   (I.i.56)

Shakespeare makes it obvious that Lear already has in mind the kind of answer he expects from his daughters. It is significant that after Goneril's fulsome protestations of love Lear does not evaluate or praise her remarks. He makes no comment at all on her speech. He has heard what he has wanted to hear, and he immediately bestows upon her a share of the kingdom. It is interesting to note that in *The True Chronicle History of King Leir,* when Goneril proclaims her love for him, Leir comments, "O, how thy words revive my dying soul" (I.iii.54).

Shakespeare reinforces this imperious characteristic of Lear. Again, after Regan's testimony of love, Lear makes no reference to her speech; in *The Chronicle History* he says, "Did never Philomel sing so sweet a note" (I.iii.74). He allots her portion and calls on Cordelia to "Speak." And it is important to observe that in the three instances where Lear asks the daughters to proclaim the extent of their love, he imperiously concludes with the curt, monosyllabic, "Speak." (The Folio omits the concluding "Speak" addressed to Regan.)

Thus, when Cordelia refuses to follow her sisters in answering with 'glib and oily art,' the stage has been dramatically set for Lear's wrathful indignation.

> LEAR: what can you say to draw
> A third more opulent than your sisters? Speak.
> CORDELIA: Nothing, my lord.
> LEAR: Nothing!
> CORDELIA: Nothing.
> LEAR: Nothing will come of nothing. Speak again.
> CORDELIA: Unhappy that I am, I cannot heave
> My heart into my mouth. I love your Majesty
> According to my bond; no more nor less.   (I.i.87)

Lear's real attitude comes out when in thwarted rage he revealingly says to Cordelia: "Better thou/Hadst not been born than not t' have pleas'd me better" (l.i.237).

The situation presented here is the problem of any human relationship: shall we attempt to understand another, really understand another person, or will we accept him only on our own terms? Shakespeare presents Lear as a powerful king, wilful and unyielding, a man who has no desire to understand others or communicate with them. He has not here the humanity of thinking beyond himself. He hears only what he wants to hear, tinting everything with the color of his own mind. When Cordelia speaks these words:

> Good my lord,
> You have begot me, bred me, lov'd me: I
> Return those duties back as are right fit;
> Obey you, love you, and most honour you.
> Why have my sisters husbands, if they say
> They love you all? Haply, when I shall wed,
> That lord whose hand must take my plight shall carry
> Half my love with him, half my care and duty.
> Sure, I shall never marry like my sisters,
> To love thy father all.

Lear, expecting an entirely different answer, the kind of satisfying flattery given by the politic Goneril and Regan, makes no attempt to understand what Cordelia is really trying to say, and casts off the person dearest to him.

Though Lear acts in wrathful haste and blindness, his actions are analyzed, his motivation unfolded, that the audience may see and understand his character fully and unambiguously. Lear even explains himself, like an onlooker unfolding the psychology of action. When he shouts to Cordelia, "Better thou/Hadst not been born than not t' have pleas'd me better" (l.i.237), he is, in a way, impartially describing himself as one who values love only as a means of adding to his own vanity. And in Kent's banishment there is the same self-revelation. In violent outburst Lears says that Kent must be banished because he sought to make the king break his vow and reverse his sentence which "nor our nature nor our place can bear" (l.i.174). Yet such statements cannot be taken as indications of a high degree of self-awareness on the part of the protagonist. They are best viewed as a mode of partial narrative which S. L. Bethell has described as "appropriate to poetic drama, since it renders the psychological situation clear without transferring attention from the verse to the process of naturalistic induction."[4]

One can say that in the beginning Lear equates "nature" with his own "conception" of himself; that for Lear the natural rights inherent in majesty, fatherhood, and age demand—or, rather, take for granted—the unquestioning and undivided love of children for parent, benefactor and king; the respect of youth for age; and the complete obedience of subject to ruler. Thus, when Cordelia refuses to conform to Lear's own conception of what is natural, the king arbitrarily casts her off as unnatural, disclaiming all "paternal care,/Propinquity and property of blood" (I.i.115). He banishes Kent because his "nature" allows not the breaking of vows. For Lear, then, nature is not the external world, or reason, but his own image; and he looks out onto a world which must mirror back his own conceptions of loyalty, love, justice, perfection. Proudly independent in the omnipotence of self, he is detached from all, and in his isolation feels no responsibility and kinship towards others. Lear's folly, like that of Oedipus, is one of blindness, the overweening belief in the infallibility of one's own being, the failure to recognize the limitations of mortality.

To characterize Lear's folly as anything but the result of misguided intellect is to reduce his stature and worth, and turn him into a pathetic figure, as Lamb's version of a "painful and disgusting" spectacle, "an old man tottering about the stage with a walking-stick turned out of doors by his daughters in a rainy night";[5] or Lily B. Campbell's version of Lear as "the slave of habitual wrath";[6] or the very extreme view of G. W. Knight who pictured Lear as the supreme pathetic figure of literature because of his "puerile intellect."[7]

That Lear has no true insight into himself, his actions, and those about him can, on analysis, be seen as the leitmotif of the opening scene. The loyal Kent draws attention to the problem of appearance versus reality when he says to Lear:

Thy youngest daughter does not love thee least:
Nor are those empty-hearted whose low sounds
Reverb no hollowness.   (I.i.154)

Certainly hollowness is Kent's judgment of Goneril and Regan, a pointed reference to their earlier professions of love. Notice the abstractions that Goneril used when she affirmed her love to be dearer than space, liberty, life, grace, health, beauty, honor. In his blind pride Lear has been deceived by the world of appearances; he mistakes the outward appearance of Goneril and Regan, their veneer of words which cover the evil within them, for the real, sincere and speechless love of Cordelia. As has often been noticed, a similar situation exists in Sophocles' *Oedipus Rex* where Oedipus is at first blind to the realities of the world in which he lives. The prophet who was blind, Tiresias, saw; and the king who saw was blind.

When the bluntly speaking Kent, who sees true relations and is not deceived by appearances, is banished with Lear's words echoing, "Out of my sight," he replies, "See better, Lear,"—an exhortation which is given further significance at the end of the scene when Regan tells Goneril that the king "hath ever but slenderly known himself" (I.i.296). And when Lear's explosive, "now, by Apollo,—" is picked up by Kent, "Now, by Apollo, king,/Thou swear'st thy gods in vain" (I.i.162), it is an ironic comment on the king's inability to distinguish true value, the faithful Cordelia and Kent, from mere appearance, the seemingly dutiful Goneril and Regan. It is to be remembered that Apollo was the god of light, and that inscribed on the temple of Apollo at Delphi was the famous "Know Thyself." Also inscribed there was the injunction "Nothing in Excess."

The first scene presents us with the basic facts of the play: the division of kingdom, the scorning of the faithful Cordelia and Kent. Shakespeare gives the audience a point of view towards the hero of the play: through Lear's own speech and actions we see him as proudly blind and regal; and this view is substantiated for us by Lear's friend, Kent, and by his future antagonists, Goneril and Regan. These three appraise him and reach the same conclusions. Kent slightingly calls him "old man," characterizes his actions as "folly" and "hideous rashness." At the end of the scene, when Goneril and Regan review the happenings in businesslike prose, their final judgment of the king, shrewd and incisive, has already been dramatized as truth:

> GONERIL: You see how full of changes his age is; the observation we have made of it hath not been little. He always lov'd our sister most; and with what poor judgement he hath now cast her off appears too grossly.
> REGAN: 'Tis the infirmity of his age; yet he hath ever but slenderly known himself.
> GONERIL: The best and soundest of his time hath been but rash; then must we look from his age to receive not alone the imperfections of long-engraffed condition, but there-withal the unruly waywardness that infirm and choleric years bring with them.   (l.i.291)

The speeches of Goneril and Regan at the end of this exposition scene attune us to their later treatment of Lear by arousing a state of expectation, of speculation as to how they will curb their father and king, who has given up his power and yet would, as Goneril fears, still "manage those authorities / That he hath given away!" (l.iii.17)

In analyzing the way in which Shakespeare portrays Lear at the beginning of the play it becomes evident that the audience sees and understands events not primarily through Lear's eyes, thus becoming one with him, sympathizing with his actions, but through the eyes of Kent and Goneril and Regan who interpret him for us. Friend and foes, by agreeing on the folly which impels Lear, formulate a dramatic attitude towards the character.

II

When next we encounter Lear there begins a shift in the audience's point of view because there is an attendant change of focus. Certainly the ideal of Lear is the world which precedes the division of kingdom: a world of his own order, of undivided loyalty, of absolute respect for king and father and age. These values were not attacked as values in the opening scene of the play. Shakespeare portrayed Lear's great stature and dignity while at the same time incisively criticizing his misguided intellect. When Lear acted, he acted blindly, unwisely, and with morally shocking consequences. Now, Lear suddenly moves precipitously from an old world of his own conception into a tough new world which stretches him upon its rack. In this new world Lear finds himself a stranger, rejected, and his is a continual battle to maintain self-respect, to hold desperately to the vision of the man he once was. His values—true values—are no longer recognized; and it is this sudden shift into a new world that drastically changes the dramatic point of view towards Lear.

In Lear's act of dividing the kingdom we saw him at the height of his power. From this high point begins a fall which culminates in the stripping of Lear to the very bone in the storm scene on the heath, a stripping of the respect and honor due him as king, father, and old man. And it is this profound respect which he should command, which is his natural and inherent right, that comprises the informing context of values and determines the audience's point of view towards Lear.

There are several direct references to "stripping" in the play. France, questioning Lear's treatment of Cordelia, stresses the idea of dismantling:

> This is most strange,
> That she, whom even but now was your best object,
> The argument of your praise, balm of your age,
> The best, the dearest, should in this trice of time
> Commit a thing so monstrous, to dismantle
> So many folds of favour.   (I.i.216)

Goneril, commenting on Lear's treatment of Cordelia, tells "with what poor judgement he hath now cast her off" (I.i.294); Lear sees himself as a "discarded" father (III.iv.74); Kent, discussing Lear's remorse over his treatment of Cordelia, says that Lear is overwhelmed with the shame of "His own unkindness, / That stripp'd her from his benediction" (IV.iii.44). Indeed, R. B. Heilman has gone to extremes in abstracting from the play what he has termed "The Clothes Pattern" to show that "the poor naked wretches of the play, the victims of the world, will survive in spirit. The gorgeous are doomed. In proud array, Lear failed; uncrowned, half-naked, he is saved. This is a central paradox of the play."[8]

That Lear's stripping is a preparation for his regeneration has been noted by all who discuss this play. What has not been noticed is the integral part that this concept of stripping has in the dramatic design of the play, reminiscent of *Everyman*, where the hero is stripped of all save Good Deeds. An analysis of *Lear's* dramatic line of development shows that up to the point of the actual tearing off of clothes on the heath, in every scene in which Lear appears he undergoes relentless stripping—of honor, of dignity.

The stripping process is the major movement of the first part of *King Lear*. It begins when Lear disinherits himself. With a pointing of a finger to the map before him he divests himself of his lands and retains only the name and honor of king without responsibility or power. Next Lear strips from himself Cordelia, then Kent. We note the further fall of the king and his further dismantling in the colloquy between Goneril and Oswald. When Goneril learns that Lear struck her gentleman for chiding his fool, she tells Oswald that when the king returns from hunting she will not speak to him; Oswald is to tell the king that she is sick. Furthermore, she even instructs the servant to show disrespect to her father and king:

> Put on what weary negligence you please,
> You and your fellows; I'd have it come to question.
> If he distaste it, let him to my sister,
> Whose mind and mine, I know, in that are one,
> Not to be over-rul'd. Idle old man,
> That still would manage those authorities
> That he hath given away!   (I.iii.12)

Goneril, evincing this attitude to Oswald, triply compounds her felony: she is disrespectful to kingship, fatherhood and old age.

The relentless stripping of the king continues. When Lear asks Oswald where Goneril is, Oswald does not answer; he merely departs. And when Lear asks his knight why Oswald did not return when called, the knight reports, "he would not" (I.iv.59). Such an answer is given to the king, and we must remember that he still commands the respect owing to a king, and that here a servant has given him insult. The knight feels impelled to speak out: "to my judgement, your Highness is not entertain'd with that ceremonious affection as you were wont. There's a great abatement of kindness appears as well in the general dependants as in the Duke himself also and your daughter" (I.iv.61). Lear's reply, "Thou but rememb'rest me of mine own conception," is a poignant recognition of what is beginning to take place. And immediately after this, when Lear and Oswald meet, and Lear commandingly asks Oswald, "Who am I, sir?" (I.iv.85), Oswald replies with what can only be considered a deliberate insult: "My lady's father." Here the superiority of degrees so central to the Elizabethan conception of an ordered hierarchic society is completely overthrown and the position of king is subverted.

In this same scene the Fool, acting as chorus, focuses attention on these aspects of overturned degree. It is the Fool who gives the king a lesson in government, pointing out his folly in dividing the kingdom: "When thou clovest thy crown i' th' middle, and gav'st away both parts, thou bor'st thine ass on thy back o'er the dirt. Thou hadst little wit in thy bald crown when thou gav'st thy golden one away" (I.iv.175). "Thou art an O without a figure," the Fool tells Lear, "I am better than thou art now; I am a Fool, thou art nothing" (I.iv.212). It is natural that a king should rule a kingdom; it is unnatural for him to give it away. It is natural that a man should ride an ass; it is unnatural that he should carry the ass on his back. This is the complete overturning of what is natural. As in *Gorboduc,* an undivided kingdom symbolized order and due subordination in the realm; with the division of kingdom comes the breaking of all natural bonds, and chaos ensues.

The Fool holds up before Lear the mirror of his follies that he might clearly see his actions and their consequences. In the beginning of the play Kent, Goneril and Regan framed Lear's figure by objectively analyzing him. Now the Fool's utterances help frame the king, and the audience, seeing Lear in terms of the Fool's remarks, quickly perceives the relations between the two. While the Fool is certainly the disinterested truthteller, the "punctum indifferens" of the play, as Enid Welsford tells us in her social and literary history *The Fool,*[9] his truth narrows upon the folly of a king who would give away his titles; of a father who would allow the child to rule him; of a man who deserves to be beaten for being old before his time. The Fool is, as it were, a mirror for magistrates and fathers. But it is to be noticed that Lear does not seem to recognize his own figure in the Fool's mirror. It is we, the audience, who see it far more clearly than Lear. Thus, the audience is drawn into sympathetic participation with Lear because it can see, Lear cannot; it shares the Fool's superior knowledge, unintelligible to Lear for the most part, and recognizes in Lear the collision of opposites: a man who would still cling to the conception of proper place, the values taken for granted before; yet now, in a new world, put in his improper place. And once having entered into Lear's perspective we are forced to look on the world with his eyes.

Though Kent has said to Lear concerning the Fool, "This is not altogether fool, my lord" (I.iv.165), Lear will not recognize the significance of the Fool's wisdom until later, and it will be a self-recognition, not the result of another's explanation, but gained through his own suffering. In Act I, scene iv, Lear does not realize the significance of the Fool's statement: "thou mad'st thy daughters thy mothers; for when thou gav'st them the rod, and puttest down thine own breeches...." No sooner does the Fool say this than his statement is demonstrated: Goneril, the daughter, comes in and reproves the king for what she considers to be his insolent retinue. Here we have an example of the daughter instructing the father. Again we see the stripping of Lear—in this instance, of the dignity and respect which a daughter owes him. Again, the Fool acts as chorus: "May not an ass know when the cart draws the horse?" (I.iv.244)—another reference to the inversion of order: the cart drawing the horse; the daughter applying the rod to the father.

And when the daughter, Goneril, wants to diminish the king further, when she suggests that he reduce the number of his retinue, he breaks forth in impassioned anguish, calling her degenerate bastard, and goes off to his other daughter, Regan, who he thinks will not, could not, be so unkind.

The whittling away of the king's stature continues unabated. When the disguised Kent becomes a messenger for the king and is put into the stocks by Cornwall for striking Oswald, it is a further insult to Lear, and this is pointed out by both Kent and Gloucester. To Cornwall, Kent exclaims:

> I serve the King,
> On whose employment I was sent to you.
> You shall do small respect, show too bold malice
> Against the grace and person of my master,
> Stocking his messenger.   (II.ii.135)

while Gloucester protests to Cornwall, "The King must take it ill / That he, so slightly valued in his messenger, / Should have him thus restrain'd" (II.ii.152). And when Lear sees his messenger in the stocks, this insult against kingship is the first thing to come to mind: "What's he that hath so much thy place mistook / To set thee here?" "Thy durst not do't," he cries out. "They could not, would not do't. 'Tis worse than murder / To do upon respect such violent outrage"(II.iv.12).

But the outrage proceeds. Lear now learns that Cornwall and Regan refuse to speak with him. He still has not attuned himself to the realities of his new world where the inversion of which the Fool speaks has become the norm; and he tries to rationalize and minimize the affront; and still he cannot do so:

> Deny to speak with me? They are sick? They are weary?
> They have travell'd all the night? Mere fetches;
> The images of revolt and flying off.
> Fetch me a better answer. (II.iv.89)

Gloucester by speaking of "the fiery quality of the Duke," his "fix'd" nature (II.iv.93) only heightens the contrast between the respect due to Lear and the ignominious situation into which Lear is continually being pushed. Lear is torn between a conception of his elevated position and dignity, what should be, and an awareness, now growing more intense, of how that pattern of hierarchal values is being violated. These clashing views and Lear's struggle within himself are caught up and juxtaposed in a single speech:

> The King would speak with Cornwall; the dear father
> Would with his daughter speak, commands her service.
> Are they "inform'd" of this?   My breath and blood!
> "Fiery"? The fiery duke? Tell the hot duke that—
> No, but not yet; may be he is not well.
> Infirmity doth still neglect all office
> Whereto our health is bound; we are not ourselves
> When nature, being oppress'd, commands the mind
> To suffer with the body. I'll forbear;
> And am fall'n out with my more headier will,
> To take the indispos'd and sickly fit
> For the sound man. (II.iv.102)

Here the verse is flexibly mimetic, immediately conveying the curve of Lear's emotions. In the beginning, authority communicated in determined commands; the stressing of kingship, of fatherhood. With Lear's shift from the indicative mood in "would speak" to the imperative "commands her service" there is an indication of a rage that grows within him, as if Lear at that moment recognizes that he is losing his authority as king and father. And with his words, "Tell the hot duke that—" there is a sudden breaking off, reflecting a will to disbelieve the calculated affront to his person, a reluctance to accept the indignity as truth, and an attempt to reason himself into calmness. But when he looks upon Kent in the stocks there can be no doubt of the insult being done himself; and he passionately commands that his servant be released and that Cornwall and Regan be immediately summoned.

In this scene Lear is further degraded. After Regan finally comes, she says to Lear:

                                    I pray you
          That to our sister you do make return;
          Say you have wrong'd her, sir.   (II.iv.152)

And Lear replies:

                                    Ask her forgiveness?
          Do you but mark how this becomes the house:
          "Dear daughter, I confess that I am old;
          Age is unnecessary. On my knees I beg
          That you'll vouchsafe me raiment, bed, and food."   (II.iv.154)

The king actually kneels before Regan in enacting the shame that would be his were he to return to Goneril, forced to beg her forgiveness and favors. Here we have a picture of the grandeur that was king, now plundered of dignity, bent at the knees.

A further reminder of his ignominy comes when the trumpet heralds not a person of eminence, but, ironically, Oswald, who brought galling shame upon him. The indignities against Lear are compellingly, mordantly dramatized when, in a stylized manner, the king is forced to turn from one daughter to the other as they relentlessly reduce the number of his followers. What began as a retinue of one hundred for the king is halved to fifty by Goneril; halved to twenty-five by Regan (here Lear cries out, "I gave you all"). And when Lear turns to Goneril with the words:

                                    I'll go with thee.
          Thy fifty yet doth double five and twenty,
          And thou art twice her love.   (II.iv.261)

the number is further reduced, until Regan divests him of all—"What need one?"

The daughters have finally stripped him of everything: honor, respect, filial devotion, retainers. The dismantling of the king is almost completed; its culmination is to come in the scene on the heath. When Regan says to Lear, "What need one?" he replies in words which show a turning point in his characterization:

          O, reason not the need! Our basest beggars
          Are in the poorest thing superfluous.
          Allow not nature more than nature needs,
          Man's life is cheap as beast's. Thou art a lady;
          If only to go warm were gorgeous,
          Why, nature needs not what thou gorgeous wear'st,
          Which scarcely keep thee warm. But, for true need,—   (II.iv.267)

If man is stripped of that which gives him dignity—his true need, if he is judged solely by his basic needs, he is no more than an animal? Is it only clothes which make a man, which separate him from the beast? Deprived of the last vestige of outward dignity, Lear asks questions about the status of human values. His speech is an address not only to Regan, but to the world,[10] an agonizing attempt to find universal meaning, universal justice. His particular fate therefore becomes the fate of mankind, and the audience can no longer take an objective view of Lear. To see a man fall from greatness and be reduced to nothingness is an awful spectacle. But when Lear universalizes his particular experience in his address to the world the dignity of all men is at stake: "not the dignity of kings and robes," as Melville was to write of the anguish at the undraped spectacle of Starbuck, his valor-ruined man, "but that abounding dignity which has no robed investiture."[11] Sympathizing with Lear's values and his precarious position, through his speech we move into his consciousness; we see the world with his eyes, we are committed to his point of view. Commenting on Yeats' poetry, C. M. Bowra explained an analogous experience in this way: "In the highest moments of all great poetical drama the personality of the character does not count so much as his situation, which is typical of a tragic human destiny, and . . . at such moments individuality is merged in poetry."[12]

The particular experience of Lear achieves its universality when in his speech to Regan he attempts to pierce through superficialities to the realities they disguise, to expose the real as it should be; for in this he presents the universal human desire to find in the world meaning and order. Waging a heroic battle to preserve his self-control and dignity in the face of the abuses which his daughters have heaped upon him, Lear, in his great agony, turns to address the heavens themselves:

> You heavens, give me that patience, patience I need!
> You see me here, you gods, a poor old man,
> As full of grief as age; wretched in both!
> If it be you that stirs these daughters' hearts
> Against their father, fool me not so much
> To bear it tamely; touch me with noble anger,
> And let not women's weapons, water-drops,
> Stain my man's cheeks!   (II.iv.274)

Isolated, forsaken, despairing of men on earth, Lear can only call upon cosmic powers for help. This sense of isolation, of alienation from society, is characteristic of the tragic hero. Lear, like Job, has had his values and beliefs shaken, and finding no comfort or understanding in men of his own society, turns to the heavens. So Job, understood neither by his wife nor the comforters, had only one recourse: he carried on a monologue directed not so much to the comforters as to the heavens above, pleading to see and reason with God.

In this climactic speech Lear's thoughts focus upon the respect due to age and fatherhood. In a previous speech he poignantly summarized all the respect and honor which should have been his by right: " 'Tis not in thee," he told Regan,

> To grudge my pleasures, to cut off my train,
> To bandy hasty words, to scant my sizes,
> And in conclusion to oppose the bolt
> Against my coming in. Thou better know'st
> The offices of nature, bond of childhood,
> Effects of courtesy, dues of gratitude.

> Thy half o' th' kingdom hast thou not forgot,
> Wherein I thee endow'd.   (II.iv.176)

Lear therefore bodies forth the traditional values which give order and cohesion to society: the offices of nature, bond of childhood, effects of courtesy, dues of gratitude. No longer, as in the opening scene of the play, is a balanced point of view maintained towards Lear, where the audience is put in the position of his opponents, seeing the events primarily through their eyes. All the former tensions and conflicts are viewed in a new light because they are seen in a new intellectual and emotional perspective: the ideal of objective values, the order and civilized decency which Lear represents. When Goneril and Regan degrade their father, more than an individual is threatened; the civilized values of humanity are imperilled.

The gulf between the real and the ideal, between what Goneril and Regan actually do and what they should do, is so enormous that it tears Lear's reason to shreds, pitching him into insanity. Lear has come to recognize fully what his daughters are doing to him; and after appealing to the gods, he turns upon his daughters in bitterness. Stripped of his authority to command respect, his appeal to natural courtesies unheeded, the broken rhythms and thoughts of his speech reflect his impotency and aching bewilderment:

> No, you unnatural hags,
> I will have such revenges on you both
> That all the world shall—I will do such things,—
> What they are, yet I know not; but they shall be
> The terrors of the earth. You think I'll weep:
> No, I'll not weep.
> I have full cause of weeping; but this heart
> > (*Storm and tempest.*)
> Shall break into a hundred thousand flaws,
> Or ere I'll weep. O, Fool! I shall go mad!   (II.iv.281)

The oncoming storm in the macrocosm, indicated by the Folio stage direction, "*Storm and tempest,*" coincides with the storm which is beginning in the microcosm, the seething conflict within Lear's own mind. Driven to the edge of madness, Lear flees to an inhuman nature which is on the very edge of the civilized world. This nature to which he flees is a nature of chaos corresponding to the chaos in himself. Both the macrocosm and the microcosm are rent and in discord, no longer an expression of cosmic harmony and reason.

III

Serving as a skeletal framing device for *King Lear* is the contrast between the values of an old and a new world, which can also be viewed as the conflict between generations, one of the archetypal themes suggested by the Jungian psychologist Maud Bodkin.[13] Lear himself calls attention to this contrast early in the play when he announces his intent "to shake all cares and business from our age, / Conferring them on younger strengths" (I.i.40)—a marked change from the religious motivation of the older play of *Leir* where the king says:

> The world of me, I of the world am weary,
> And I would fain resign these earthly cares,
> And think upon the welfare of my soul:
> Which by no better means may be effected,
> Than by resigning up the crown from me,
> In equal dowry to my daughters three.[14] (I.i.24)

The young and the strong are to inherit the earth—"The younger rises when the old doth fall" (III.iii.26) is how Edmund pithily expresses the matter. The leading representatives of the new regime are Goneril and Regan in the main plot of the play, and Edmund in the subplot.

With varying emphases, critics have repeatedly noted basic similarities in the characters of Goneril, Regan and Edmund.[15] While all three share certain traits, they are most closely related by a common philosophical outlook: representatives of a new world, they hold values radically different from Lear's. Their world is one in which nature is not fundamentally good, and evil is not a mere aberration, the result of misguided reason. Nor is the new moral and political order built upon the natural and divine law expounded by Hooker, in whose orthodox Elizabethan world view the will continually seeks the good: "evil as evil cannot be desired: if that be desired which is evil, the cause is the goodness which is or seemeth to be joined with it."[16] Rather, the desire for power and sexual pleasure—natural emotional drives—are the dominant urges of those who represent the new world. The bastard Edmund would top his legitimate brother and expropriate his land, disclaiming "the plague of custom" (I.ii.3); to gain all the property he betrays his father to Regan and Cornwall. The daughters, Goneril and Regan, strip their father of all; both lust after Edmund. Goneril would even have Edmund murder her husband, thus freeing her to marry him.

For Elizabethans this naturalistic aspect of human life was above all associated with the name Machiavelli—in Marston's description, "deepe, deepe observing, sound brain'd Macheveil."[17] Machiavelli provided in his writings, particularly in *The Prince*, a rational appraisal of the human condition, man as he is, rather than man as he ideally should be.[18] His emphasis was on the here and now, his concern was not with moral considerations but analytic observation and practical action whose end was the security and well-being of the ruler.[19]

To call the new world in *King Lear* Machiavellian is not to say categorically that Shakespeare patterned his characters exclusively on Machiavelli's writings. It is merely to affirm that Machiavellianism was part of a prevailing mode of thought which undermined established beliefs and hierarchic values. One might also cite many other figures who contributed to this movement, and point to philosophies which were as challenging to orthodoxy as Machiavelli's realism and materialism: epicureanism, naturalism, skepticism.[20] What is important is to see the fundamental differences which put the two conflicting societies of *King Lear* in sharp dramatic opposition.

The representatives of the new society look at the world in the same way. They advance their fortunes by scrutinizing men and events to gain mastery over them. They have a rational account of everything; they live in the realm of fact where only the things that are seen have worth because these can be pragmatically evaluated. That Goneril repeatedly refers to Lear's condition as "dotage" (I.iv.315; I.iv.349; II.iv.200) is revealing, an indication that hers is a reason that works from the visible world. She would not recognize that duty and honor befit old age, for these are of the unseen, known only to the spirit. The same can also be said of Regan and Edmund.[21]

Regarding as negligible such values as love, loyalty, respect, the things that are unseen and of the spirit, the leaders of this new society would hold in contempt the traditional humanistic concern for "right reason" and "virtue," for these would be considered but the shadows of reality, mere customs, having no foundation in the nature of things, Cicero can be taken as representative of the humanistic point of view when he writes that "Law is the highest reason, implanted in Nature, which commands what ought to be done and forbids the opposite...."[22] Machiavelli would substitute the vision of the fox and the lion for a transcendent reason shared with gods and beyond transient occasions. He would maintain that for nations and individuals to survive successfully, force and policy are necessary to combat human savagery. But, warned the humanists insistently, without transcendent reason to guide and reprove man, the sacred is profaned, man turns into a beast, all the bonds of nature fly asunder, and chaos and bestiality reign. This upheaval of everything traditional patterns the whole new order of *King Lear*. We are projected into a world where everything turns upside-down: the daughters become rulers of the father; the father and the king becomes their subject. "Sons at perfect age and fathers declin'd, the father should be as ward to the son" (I.ii.77) is a conviction which Edmund himself holds, but ascribes to Edgar. The cart draws the horse; the fool who should be mad is wise; and the king who should be wise is a fool and actually becomes mad. Those who are really good, Cordelia, Kent and Edgar, are rejected. The good even have to hide in this paradoxical world: both Kent and Edgar are forced to go into disguise.

Everything is topsy-turvy. And this reversal of what is natural comes out most overpoweringly in the imagery of bestiality used to depict the leaders of the new society. Of all the characters in the play, only Edmund, Goneril and Regan are pointedly likened to beasts.[23] Though Gloucester calls Edgar "Unnatural, detested, brutish villain! worse than brutish!" (I.ii.81) when told that Edgar has often maintained that "fathers declin'd, the father should be as ward to the son" (I.ii.78), the sentiments are Edmund's, not Edgar's, and Gloucester's imprecations rightly apply to his bastard son. Lear recurringly sees his daughters as unnatural and loathsome; he pictures them as animals and diseases. Goneril is called "degenerate bastard" (I.iv.275), "detested kite" (I.iv.284); she is seen as "wolvish" (I.iv.330), as a "vulture" (II.iv.137), a "serpent" (II.iv.163). Regan is called a "disease" (II.iv.2325), a "boil"

(II.iv.226), a "plague-sore" (II.iv.227). Both Goneril and Regan are referred to as "pelican daughters" (III.iv.77) and "she foxes" (III.vi.24). Albany calls both daughters "tigers" (IV.ii.40). "Most barbarous, most degenerate" (IV.ii.43), and likens them to "monsters of the deep" (IV.ii.50).

These recurring references to the bestial in *Lear* call to mind the brute tooth-and-claw nature of Machiavelli's world. The actions of Edmund, Goneril and Regan are patently Machiavellian. However, it is important to recognize that the bestial imagery also relates to an equally significant association: the unnaturalness of ingratitude. Certainly one source of Lear's great torment is the shock of discovering that those whom he loves most are his worst enemies and unworthy of his love. His mind is torn apart because he cannot believe that the apparent falseness of Goneril and Regan is reality, and that what is reality can be so hideously monstrous. At the same time thoughts of ingratitude and unkindness also combine to force Lear into madness. Goneril and Regan owe their kingdoms to Lear; he is their benefactor, as well as their father and king. But once they gain their lands and authority they so fail in their corresponding duty to remain grateful that thoughts of filial ingratitude continually sear Lear's mind. He calls Goneril "thankless child" (I.iv.311), designates her actions as "sharp-tooth'd unkindness" (II.iv.137). He rails against "ingratitude, thou marble-hearted fiend" (I.iv.281). The corrosive thought of "monster ingratitude" (I.v.43) forces from him the first agonizing mention of madness as he exclaims:

> O, let me not be mad, not mad, sweet heaven!
> Keep me in temper; I would not be mad! (I.v.49)

"Unkindness" and "ingratitude" are often used synonymously in the sixteenth century, and are invariably called "unnatural." The basic meaning of "unkindness" being "unnatural conduct,"[24] "ingratitude," a form of unnatural conduct, came to be linked with it. Together they form the most reprehensible qualities to be found in man, against which Elizabethan writers constantly inveigh.[25] Ingratitude in *Lear* becomes so monstrous that its intensity is expressed in language that conveys immense physical pain. Lear exclaims in anguish:

> Filial ingratitude!
> Is it not as this mouth should tear this hand
> For lifting food to 't? (III.iv.14)

The image of the intimate natural bond which should exist between father and child is here transformed into a vision of the unnatural and bestial tearing of one part of a human body by another. Lear can only believe that "nothing could have subdu'd nature / To such a lowness but his unkind daughters" (III.iv.72). And his knotted, internal frustration is so urgent and pressing that at times he sadistically explodes into a fitful verbal attack on all nature—

> Crack nature's moulds, all germens spill at once
> That makes ingrateful man! (III.ii.8)

—while at other times he tortures himself:

> I tax not you, you elements' with unkindness;
> I never gave you kingdom, call'd you children;
> You owe me no subscription. Then let fall
> Your horrible pleasure.
>
> (III.ii.16)

Job and Lear face similar torments. Both are isolated because they can no longer understand their worlds; both impose upon life a kind of contract: Job, by being an eminently virtuous man, expects God to reward him; and Lear, by giving his daughters all, expects them, in a like manner, to fulfill their contractual obligation. Both Job and Lear confront a world which is indifferent to their demands.

Thoughts of ingratitude, of obligations unfulfilled, so tear at Lear's mind that he must either purge himself of them or else go mad:

> O Regan, Goneril!
> Your old kind father, whose frank heart gave all,—
> O, that way madness lies; let me shun that;
> No more of that.
>
> (III.iv.19)

But the idea of filial ingratitude, and the accompanying frustration of being in a world which refuses to conform to his conception of what it should be, continually overwhelms him. The first time he sees the begrimed Edgar who is reduced to animal existence, Lear can only think of one cause for such misery: "Did'st thou give all to thy daughters, and art thou come to this?" (III.iv.49) and again, when he hears Edgar's mad gibberish, he can only think of one explanation for such derangement: "Has his daughters brought him to this pass?/Couldst thou save nothing? Wouldst thou give 'em all?" (III.iv.64) Shakespeare, in projecting Lear into a new order of things, a world which makes no provision for the old ways of life, concentrates keen attention on the dramatic clash of values and on a human being who is forced to undergo the ultimate of all tests: to see the world anew; to re-examine himself and his past.

IV

Having described the conflicting values of the old and new world in *Lear*, we return to an analysis of Shakespeare's dramatic technique in establishing a certain point of view towards Lear. Much has been written of Lear's personality, of the flaw that leads to his downfall, of his regeneration, and even of his salvation. However, there is, in connection with Lear's personality, an important point to be considered: is it the king's character that accounts for his greatness? Can the greatness of any tragic hero be established solely in terms of a definite personality? Or does Melville's declaration, "To produce a mighty book, you must choose a mighty theme,"[26] demand equal consideration? The matter can be answered best through an analysis of structure and dramatic technique, for these, after all, shape the work, and elicit particular emotions and attitudes from an audience.

Beginning with Act III, Shakespeare puts at the center of the stage not the personality of Lear, a particular king, but a moral problem which transcends a particular personality. Not character, but values, becomes most important; not personality, but a situation typical of tragic human destiny. Several considerations of structural emphasis lead to this judgment. An investigation of the shifting of scenes in Act III, the calculated playing off of the subplot against the main plot for definite effects, will point to the main dramatic preoccupation of the act. An analysis of what *dramatis personae* say of the hero and what the hero says of himself will reveal the central concern of the action. And finally, by seeing the change that takes place in Lear's personality in connection with the dramatic context, we gain full perspective.

Before proceeding to an analysis of the interplay between the main plot and subplot in Act III, it would first be best to set forth the general pattern of interrelationships in the play. Many critics of Shakespeare have commented on the parallelism of characters and events in *Lear,* and we shall review these only briefly. Pervading the realms of the cosmos, society, and the individual is a breakdown of order, testimony to all the natural bonds which are broken in the play: the natural bonds of kingdom are broken with its division; the natural ties of family are broken when Lear casts off Cordelia, when Goneril and Regan degrade and persecute their father and even seek his death, when sister turns against sister, when Edmund turns against his brother Edgar, and against his father Gloucester. And on the individual level, Lear's madness is the wrenching of human order; and the storm in the macrocosm becomes a projection of the storm in the microcosm.[27]

In respect to plot, the story of Gloucester and his two sons Edgar and Edmund parallels the story of Lear and his daughters. Resembling many of the morality plays which bring forth their good and bad characters in two separate presentations, *King Lear* has a double opening, the subplot initiated by Edmund who, from the beginning, nakedly reveals his role as villain. The two plots of *Lear* finally merge in Act IV. There are also many other parallels in the play. The plain-speaking of Cordelia is re-enforced by the bluntness of Kent and contrasted with the flattery of Goneril and Regan. Lear's mock court (III.vi.18–59—omitted in the Folio) metes out justice in fantasy; Cornwall's kangaroo court (III.vii) imposes injustice in reality. Gloucester first learns to see the truth about Edmund and Edgar when he is physically blind; Lear fully penetrates the world of appearances and sees reality when he is mad.

Turning to Act III, we find that the subplot has very important functions. That it mirrors and reinforces the main plot has been duly noted by all. But the subplot provides more than intensification. We are made to see that the filial ingratitude and treachery which Lear endured is no isolated occurrence; it has happened in the past and it will happen again. In Act III, Gloucester experiences what Lear had previously undergone. We have a merging of past and present, and the force and depth of evil are brought upon us. Drama becomes the chronicle and brief abstract of the time, revealing how the reality of evil is not a mere passing phenomenon, but rooted in the spiritual structure of an era.

Let us briefly consider the interplay of plots in Act III. Scene iii, placed in Gloucester's castle, is the first shift from main to subplot; and it shows how history repeats itself. Here Gloucester reveals how Lear's daughters "took from me the use of mine own house" (III.iii.3). Though Edmund calls this "most savage and unnatural" (III.iii.26). The two plots become more intimately connected when Gloucester's efforts to mitigate Lear's suffering bring about his own misery. This is developed in the next change from main to subplot (scene v) where we also see history further repeat itself: the unnaturalness of Lear's daughters is paralleled when Edmund betrays his father to Cornwall. Finally, in the last scene of Act III we have Lear's situation paralleled in detail. Gloucester, like Lear, has furnished Regan and Cornwall with all. They reside in his castle, yet they scant his courtesies. "You are my guests" (III.vii.31) . . ., "I am your host" (III.vii.39), Gloucester would vainly remind them, just as Lear vainly repeated to his daughters, "I gave you all." Moreover, Cornwall and Regan again show little regard for the respect that is due old age; Regan even shamelessly plucks Gloucester's white beard. At the end of the scene Gloucester is thrust out at the gates to "smell / His way to Dover" (III.vii.93), just as at the end of Act II the castle doors slammed shut against Lear. And blind Gloucester groping his way to Dover in the opening scenes of Act IV parallels Lear's mad wanderings in Act III.

In its contrast with the main plot, the subplot intensifies and enlarges the theme of filial ingratitude and the depravity of man. This is to see the events objectively, from the outside. Something of equal—perhaps greater—significance must be taken into account. And that is the cry of Gloucester, "Give me some help!—O cruel! O you gods!" (III.vii.70)—a cry for justice which corresponds to Lear's cry to the heavens for understanding and justice at the end of Act II. Both Lear and Gloucester are pushed into outer chaos and solitude, forced to question the rightness of things. When these two events occur we have a decided shift in the play's angle of vision; we move from character which looks on the world objectively, to character which suffers. Lear and Gloucester can no longer act as though they still believed in the justice of the world about them. And in their intense suffering, in their appeal to the heavens, they actually address the conscience of the world. We, the audience, are that conscience.

We have therefore an important shift in vision: we move from the plight of individual man to the terrors of everyman. The personalities of Lear and Gloucester are also transformed. In their deepest loneliness they must blindly wander in a wilderness to find truth. Action becomes a quest for truth and certainty, and transcends mere personality. The opening of Act III points to this shift in emphasis. At the end of Act II the powerful members of the new order retreated "out o' th' storm" and the "wild night" and the doors of the castle were shut behind Lear. At the beginning of Act III, when the action moves to the heath, we feel that we have reached the end of the human world. Nature's bounds are broken. When Kent asks, "Where's the king?" a gentleman paints in words the picture for the audience:

Contending with the fretful elements;
Bids the wind blow the earth into the sea,
Or swell the curled waters 'bove the main,
That things might change or cease; tears his white hair,
Which the impetuous blasts with eyeless rage
Catch in their fury, and make nothing of;
Strives in his little world of man to out-scorn
The to-and-fro-conflicting wind and rain.
This night, wherein the cub-drawn bear would couch,
The lion and the belly-pinched wolf
Keep their fur dry, unbonneted he runs,
And bids what will take all.   (III.i.4)

In the absence of scenery and lighting on the Elizabethan stage, words alone establish atmosphere and description. Through the eyes of the gentleman we see the king on the wild heath, the rain pouring down upon his bare head, the wind lashing him mercilessly. Shakespeare often sets up two points of contrast, Egypt and Rome in *Antony and Cleopatra,* for one example, or court and country, which is frequent in the comedies, and by switching from one to the other, heightens a situation or an emotion. Here we have a sudden contrast between castle and moor. If one visualizes the play as acted on the Elizabethan stage, where action is often unbroken, unhampered by changing scenery and sets, the impact of the contrast between castle and moor is heightened. We get the impression that just outside the walls of a castle is the world of animals and brute nature. Perhaps the only things that divide men from the beasts are clothes and the comforts of a hearth.

It is with the gentleman's speech that we begin our investigation of what the *dramatis personae* say about Lear. Such analysis, we suggest, will illuminate the central concern of the action. What does the gentleman's speech, which prefigures Lear, stress? We see all civilization a place of storm, with Lear at the center, raging thundering defiance. The king, once regally confident in his own conception of what constituted nature, now is a prey to the elements. Lear—the gentleman emphasizes—would impose upon nature his puny will; but nature is indifferent. Lear contends with the elements. "That things might change or cease." And the extremes of these two demands—change or complete destruction—give a most revealing insight into the king's condition. His present situation is so intolerable that it must either be temporary or give way to the end of the world.

We are concerned, then, with personality in conflict with the existing universe. Because of this monumental struggle, Lear's spiritual stature is greatly magnified; and because he represents civilized values which are threatened, all men are endangered. If we concentrate on the remarks made about Lear, we see that these form a significant pattern. Kent talks of the "hard rein" which Albany and Cornwall have "borne / Against the old kind king" (III.i.27); of "how unnatural and bemadding sorrow / The King hath cause to plain" (III.i.38). Gloucester predicts to Edmund that

"These injuries the King now bears will be revenged home" (III.iii.12). To Regan's demand to know why Gloucester sent the king to Dover, he replies, "Because I would not see thy cruel nails / Pluck out his poor old eyes; nor thy fierce sister / In his anointed flesh stick boarish fangs" (III.vii.56). Going beyond Act III, we find Albany indicting Goneril:

> Tigers, not daughters, what have you perform'd?
> A father, and a gracious aged man,
> Whose reverence even the head-lugg'd bear would lick,
> Most barbarous, most degenerate! have you madded.
> Could my good brother suffer you to do it?
> A man, a prince, by him so benefited!
> If that the heavens do not their visible spirits
> Send quickly down to tame these vile offences,
> It will come,
> Humanity must perforce prey on itself,
> Like monsters of the deep.   (IV.ii.40)

Cordelia explains her military expedition in this way:

>   O dear father,
> It is thy business that I go about;
> Therefore great France
> My mourning and importun'd tears hath pitied.
> No blown ambition doth our arms incite,
> But love, dear love, and our ag'd father's right.   (IV.iv.23)

And later, in the French camp, Cordelia speaks these impassioned words in reviewing Lear's experience on the heath:

> Had you not been their father, these white flakes
> Did challenge pity of them. Was this a face
> To be oppos'd against the warring winds?
> To stand against the deep dread-bolted thunder?
> In the most terrible and nimble stroke
> Of quick, cross lightning? to watch—poor perdu!—
> With this thin helm? Mine enemy's dog,
> Though he had bit me, should have stood that night
> Against my fire; and wast thou fain, poor father,
> To hovel thee with swine and rogues forlorn
> In short and musty straw? Alack, alack!
> 'Tis wonder that thy life and wits at once
> Had not concluded all.   (IV.vii.30)

All the comments on Lear, except for Regan's reference to the "lunatic king" (III.vii.46), have a single focus: they serve as collective chorus and conscience, pointing to the dignity of fatherhood, age and kingship, the values that inhere in Lear's person. Even Edmund reveals this in his report to Albany:

> Sir, I thought it fit
> To send the old and miserable king
> To some retention and appointed guard;
> Whose age had charms in it, whose title more,
> To pluck the common bosom on his side,
> And turn our impress'd lances in our eyes
> Which do command them. (V.iii.45)

With Troilus it might be asked, "Weigh you the worth and honour of a king ... in a scale / Of common ounces?"[28]

We see that all references to Lear's misfortune direct our attention to the king's value, and this value remains constant; it does not shift according to the point of view of the onlooker. The accidents of personality recede, and we confront not particular man or ideal man, but the image of Lear embodying institutions and obligations necessary to the continuance of a moral society. The opposition between moral systems has brought about this plight of values. While the conscienceless fail to remember obligations, Lear and Gloucester vainly invoke that memory. Instead of holding to the bonds of gratitude, the leaders of the new amoral world greedily batten on others, their abuse finally turning into horrors. And this clash of opposing worlds brings into focus the overriding concern of players and audience alike: once man is free from memory and responsibility, can there be any limits to presumption? At stake is the most pertinent question of all: from this conflict what mode of life will finally prevail? Albany objectifies this concern when he appeals for retributive justice to set things right:

> If that the heavens do not their visible spirits
> Send quickly down to tame these vile offences,
> It will come,
> Humanity must perforce prey on itself,
> Like monsters of the deep. (IV.ii.46)

And in the situation paralleling the injustice done to Lear, the Second and Third Servants in Gloucester's castle also universalize the particular when, after the gouging out of Gloucester's eyes, they too question the meaning of their world:

> 2. SERVANT: I'll never care what wickedness I do,
> If this man come to good.
> 3. SERVANT: If she live long,
> and in the end meet the old course of death,
> Women will all turn monsters. (III.vii.99)

Shakespeare, in every dramatic technique he employs, concentrates our vision on world order and the predicament of everyman. This results in a rapport between Lear and audience, which is explained by Aristotle, who reminds us of the intimate relationship between fear and pity when he defines fear as pity lest the undeserving misfortune of another overtake us.[29]

Lear's own speeches also point to the concern for values and justice. Arthur Sewell has provided a very stimulating comment on exposition of character: there are two kinds, he says, one in which "the character is presented or presents himself in general relation to the world and to society, and the other in which the character is presented or presents himself merely in terms of the facts and feelings of the particular situation."[30] Almost all of Lear's speeches on the heath are directed to the world and society, only incidentally to the particular situation. When he refers to his immediate predicament, invariably it is to relate it to a larger context, universal justice. His first utterance on the heath is an apostrophe to the heavens; it is a lament; it is a wish for annihilation:

> Blow, winds, and crack your cheeks! Rage! Blow!
> You cataracts and hurricanoes, spout
> Till you have drench'd our steeples, drown'd the cocks!
> You sulph'rous and thought-executing fires,
> Vaunt-couriers of oak-cleaving thunderbolts,
> Singe my white head! And thou, all-shaking thunder,
> Strike flat the thick rotundity o' th' world!
> Crack nature's moulds, all germens spill at once
> That makes ingrateful man!   (III.ii.1)

Wolfgang Clemen has traced the development in pre-Shakespearian drama of this type of speech, the "Klagerede," as he terms it.[31] From rhetorical formulas, unintegrated in the structure of earlier dramas, this type of speech developed in Shakespeare's mature work into an integral part of the play's structure.

How much a part of the play's structure these rhetorical formulas are, we see when we consider the meaning of Lear's plight. From the start of Act III Lear is an exile on the wild heath; and though he is accompanied in his wanderings by the Fool, Kent, Edgar, Gloucester—spiritually he is utterly alone as he searches for a meaning to his existence. Before the division of kingdom, we are led to believe, Lear was able to extend his own conception of reality to the external world. He rewarded Goneril and Regan because they conformed to his idea of what was natural. He banished Cordelia and Kent because they would not match their actions to his expectations. Now, on the heath, his individual will is of no avail. Cut away from his former world, he has lost his identity. If there is to be any order and meaning in life he must search for it, or create it anew, or perish in despair.

In his wanderings he searches and aches for recognition, needing almost to clutch in his hand the "why" of his misery. His soliloquies, addressed to the heavens, become addresses to the world, and since we, the audience, are that world, he speaks to our moral conscience. A world devoid of contractual obligations makes no sense to him; it is a world where nature's bonds are broken, just as they are on the heath. Hence he exclaims:

Rumble thy bellyful! Spit, fire! Spout, rain!
Nor rain, wind, thunder, fire are my daughters.
I tax not you, you elements, with unkindness;
I never gave you kingdom, call'd you children;
You owe me no subscription. Then let fall
Your horrible pleasure. Here I stand your slave,
A poor, infirm, weak, and despis'd old man;
But yet I call you servile ministers,
That will with two pernicious daughters join
Your high-engender'd battles 'gainst a head
So old and white as this. Oh! Oh! 'tis foul!   (III.ii.14)

Shakespeare, we can see, has woven the formulaic and rhetorical patterns of the lament, the complaint, the wish for annihilation into the texture of the play. Lear's speech here and elsewhere is detached neither from the physical setting nor the dramatic concern of the moment.

In his speeches Lear continually refers his own situation to the problem of universal justice. The particular repeatedly gives way to the universal. At one moment he would seek personal recognition from nature's forces, calling upon them to obliterate the world. In this he would find satisfying retributive justice. At another moment he would find the seat of justice, search out the meaning of the universe—but in this too he is thwarted: he can only envision corruption festering everywhere, for his degradation is testimony of a lawless universe:

Let the great gods,
That keep this dreadful pudder o'er our heads,
Find out their enemies now. Tremble, thou wretch
That hast within thee undivulged crimes,
Unwhipp'd of justice! Hide thee, thou bloody hand;
Thou perjur'd, and thou simular of virtue
That are incestuous! Caitiff, to pieces shake,
That under covert and convenient seeming
Has practis'd on man's life! Close pent-up guilts,
Rive your concealing continents, and cry
These dreadful summoners grace. I am a man
More sinn'd against than sinning.   (III.ii.49)

Whenever Lear calls attention to the concern of the moment, it is only briefly; he is continually seeing in the particular a higher meaning. Even when he thinks of simple things, when he asks the Fool, "Where is this straw?" he proceeds to translate the immediate concern into a recognition of values: "The art of our necessities is strange / And can make vile things precious" (III.ii.70). On the heath Lear continually pushes his thoughts beyond his present moment to universal questions. He is concerned with the reason, the justice of an event. His terror, for example, is for that which is out of time:

Thou think'st 'tis much that this contentious storm
Invades us to the skin—

he tells Kent;

                                                        so 'tis to thee;
But where the greater malady is fix'd,
The lesser is scarce felt.
. . . .

                                    the tempest in my mind
Doth from my senses take all feeling else
Save what beats there. Filial ingratitude!
Is it not as this mouth should tear this hand
For lifting food to 't?   (III.iv.6)

Serving as a perfect contrast to Lear is the Fool, for the Fool feels terror for that
which is in time, for the immediate occasion:

O nuncle, court holy-water in a dry house is better than this rain water
out o' door. Good nuncle, in; ask thy daughters' blessing. Here's a night pities
neither wise men nor fools.   (III.ii.10)

For Lear the storm and his own physical hardship are significant only because they
reveal the spiritual chaos of the time. The Fool, ever practical, sees only the bare
facts.

That Lear now sees more meaning in things than the Fool is a significant
reversal of what had previously taken place. Before the heath scene the Fool served
as *raisonneur*, continually pointing out the significance of happenings of which Lear
was hopelessly unaware. Before, the Fool asked questions of Lear; now it is Lear
who asks many questions. He wants to know whether Edgar's daughters have
reduced him to the level of a beast. He would talk with the disguised Edgar, calling
him "philosopher," "learned Theban," "good Athenian" (III.iv). He asks Edgar, "What
is the cause of thunder?" (III.iv.160) and "What is your study?" (III.iv.163) And when
the Fool sings out the moral of an occasion:

"He that has and a little tiny wit,—
    With heigh-ho, the wind and the rain,—
Must make content with his fortunes fit,
    For the rain it raineth every day."   (III.ii.74)

Lear replies, "True, boy"—a remarkable change from his previous reactions to the
Fool's utterances. Before the heath scene Lear never recognized the Fool's pointed
moralizing. He either threatened to whip the Fool for his words or paid them no
heed.

All this points to the significance, in dramatic terms, of Lear's wanderings on
the heath. His is a quest for knowledge and certainty, a journey to find, somehow,
a way back to order and civilization. While many critics have treated Lear as the

study of the unstoical man,[32] Lear's unstoical conduct must be related to the dramatic movement of the play—his search for justice. Lear repeatedly tries to reconcile himself to the rending occasions. He strives for stoic endurance, for this would lead to freedom from pain and suffering. "You heavens, give me that patience, patience I need!" (II.iv.274) he cries out when his daughters would deprive him of all his retainers. "No, I'll not weep" (II.iv.286) he steadfastly maintains. On the heath, overwhelmed with grief and on the edge of self-pity, he steels himself with these sentiments: "No, I will be the pattern of all patience; I will say nothing" (III.ii.37). "I will endure" (III.iv.18) is his continual resolve.

That Lear does not unalterably continue in these stoic thoughts is to be explained in terms of the dramatic concern of the action: his main preoccupation is with justice, not his physical condition. To accept a stoic morality would involve a hardening to suffering, an attainment of peace through withdrawal and indifference. It would mean the acceptance of Marcus Aurelius' counsel: "When you are grieved about anything external it is not the thing itself which afflicts you, but your judgment about it. This judgment it is in your power to efface."[33] Lear can not do this, for Shakespeare has focused all attention on the problem of man who seeks justice in a world that has no justice. And this is the basis of the dramatic conflict. To argue that Lear is completely unstoical is to give the impression that Shakespeare is advocating in the play a support for stoic conduct: that Lear brings on his misfortunes because he has not the discernment of a stoic. Such analysis neglects dramatic structure and technique and turns drama into moral and philosophical formulas.

Lear's search for values and justice on the heath is also an attempt to regain his identity and once again recognize his former figure. "Who am I?" Lear insistently repeats this question in various ways, endeavoring to clutch at the shadow of his former being. Does this not explain his repeated references to himself as king even in his most desperate moments of madness? When, completely deranged, he makes his appearance late in Act IV, his first words are: "No, they cannot touch me for coming; / I am the King himself" (IV.vi.83). The blind Gloucester recognizes him by his voice, "The trick of that voice I do well remember. / Is't not the King?" And Lear replies with great majesty in his madness:

> Ay, every inch a king!
> When I do stare, see how the subject quakes.
> I pardon that man's life. What was thy cause?
> Adultery?
> Thou shalt not die. Die for adultery! No;
> The wren goes to't, and the small gilded fly
> Does lecher in my sight.   (IV.vi.109)

Completely isolated, alone with himself, speaking to himself, Lear creates his own world where none are guilty, for all are guilty. Yet he must have justice; and in Act III, scene vi, he sits as judge of all humanity. Before the Fool, Edgar, and Kent he arraigns Goneril and Regan in a mad judgment day where he can still demand justice and assert the prerogatives of kingship. Finally, his pathetic statement, "Come, come, I am a king, / My masters, know you that?" (IV.vi.203) is a desperate attempt to hold on to his identity.

Since the audience looks at the world through Lear's eyes, it shares his agony and his view; the more intense his suffering, the more heightened the experience of the audience. Through Lear's address to the world our vision is directed to the quest for justice. In searching for his own identity in the midst of chaos, he does so for all mankind. A bewildered Lear, who has lost his proper place, must set himself against a hostile world, while the pragmatic Edmund invokes its aid. Is the tragic view, then, the depiction of a man of great stature and value who is helpless against an indifferent or malevolent nature? Is "the key to it all" what Herman Melville has termed the "ungraspable phantom of life" when he alluded to the story of Narcissus, "who because he could not grasp the tormenting, mild image he saw in the fountain, plunged into it and was drowned. But that same image, we ourselves see in all rivers and oceans. It is the image of the ungraspable phantom of life; and this is the key to it all."[34] The answer is to be found in the much discussed transformation that Lear undergoes on the heath.

At the beginning of the play Shakespeare portrays Lear as a proud man who lacks the humanity of thinking beyond himself; he even values love only as a means of adding to his own vanity. On the heath there comes to Lear an emotion which has not shown itself in him before: a concern for others. We first see this in Lear's words to the Fool:

> My wits begin to turn.
> Come on, my boy. How dost, my boy? Art cold?
> I am cold myself. Where is this straw, my fellow?
> The art of our necessities is strange
> And can make vile things precious. Come, your hovel.
> Poor Fool and knave, I have one part in my heart
> That's sorry yet for thee.   (III.ii.67)

For the first time Lear reaches out to touch another human being. Seeing the Fool's suffering, he makes a sympathetic connection, "I am cold myself." He notices the Fool's adversity first; and through sympathetic identification he comes to recognize his own condition. In spite of innumerable outward differences, in one respect Lear and the Fool are equals: they share a common fate; and in their humanity they are kin. No longer do we see Lear as proud and vain. He recognizes other human beings and shows compassion for them. When Kent bids him seek refuge in the hovel, Lear would torture himself further by remaining out in the storm; but he shows concern for Kent, counselling him, "Prithee, go in thyself; seek thine own ease" (III.iv.23). And when he does decide to go into the hovel, he bids the Fool enter first. "In, boy; go first." There follow significant statements which show his concern for the sufferings of "poor naked wretches" everywhere:

Poor naked wretches, wheresoe'er you are,
That bide the pelting of this pitiless storm,
How shall your houseless heads and unfed sides,
Your loop'd and window'd raggedness, defend you
From seasons such as these? O, I have ta'en
Too little care of this! Take physic, pomp;
Expose thyself to feel what wretches feel,
That thou mayst shake the superflux to them,
And show the heavens more just.   (III.iv.28)

Lear's whole personality undergoes a complete transformation. From a desire to find personal vindication and personal recognition, his thoughts turn to sympathy for each individual being. He approaches the view that a moral society depends on the recognition of each man's value. This stress on the responsibility of one man for all makes Lear one with all humanity and binds all humanity into oneness. In his speech he strips away all thoughts of comforts and superficialities to lay bare basic truth, the human condition which underlies the world of fleeting appearances. In an unforgettable moment on the heath Lear translates his verbalization of this necessity for bare truth into a physical act as he asks the tormenting question:

Is man no more than this? Consider him well. Thou ow'st the worm no silk, the beast no hide, the sheep no wool, the cat no perfume. Ha! here's three on's are sophisticated! Thou art the thing itself; unaccommodated man is no more but such a poor, bare, forked animal as thou art. Off, off, you lendings! come, unbutton here.   (III.iv.107)

And he tears off his clothes.
    Two interpretations may be offered for Lear's action. First, consider Lear's statement to Regan when she argued that he had no need of any retainers:

O, reason not the need! Our basest beggars
Are in the poorest thing superfluous.
Allow not nature more than nature needs,
Man's life is cheap as beast's. Thou art a lady;
If only to go warm were gorgeous,
Why, nature needs not what thou gorgeous wear'st,
Which scarcely keeps thee warm. But, for true need,—   (II.iv.267)

If man's life is as cheap as beast's, if it is only clothes which make a man, which separate him from the beast, then it is unnecessary for man to borrow from animals the clothes which cover his nakedness. Thus, one can say that in stripping off his clothes Lear dramatically acts out his words to Regan. Casting off his lendings, he makes a radical return to nature, becoming one with the beasts. And we can only ask: is this the bare truth about man? Is this reality, naked man, man as beast?
    One can also view Lear's tearing off his clothes as the stripping away of all the

superfluous values by which he has lived. One can say that he is acting out his words.

> O, I have ta'en
> Too little care of this! Take physic, pomp;
> Expose thyself to feel what wretches feel,
> That thou mayst shake the superflux to them,
> And show the heavens more just.   (III.iv.32)

If one views this act of the stripping of clothes as an act of purgation, a return to essential man, then a new Lear will emerge from such torments.

These two interpretations have equal validity, for one is part of the other. What we are concerned with now, it is quite obvious, is more than the personality of a particular king; it is a confronting of the universe, and in that crisis, a questioning and a recasting of one's vision of reality. Previous to the division of kingdom, reality for Lear consisted of the values in his mind, and these he imposed upon the external world. As long as he had power to control nature, he could project his expectations and, with a high degree of success, have them realized. But the will to believe does not constitute reality. Power is accidental and temporary; things can appear to be what they are not; man can seek more justice in the world than there is. Consequently, the most urgent problem—the concern of the greatest works of art—is to learn to see reality as it is. In tearing off his clothes Lear divests himself of the husks of appearance, the accidents of power and rank. The reduction to unaccommodated man puts him on an equal basis with all men; he is, therefore, akin to all men. This act looks forward to a theme which preoccupied Dostoevski: the idea that each man is responsible for all men. As Markel says in *The Brothers Karamazov,* "Every one is really responsible to all men for all men and for everything."[35] When man sees that he is like all men, neither better nor worse, he begins to feel a bond with all humanity. The opposite—isolation—results from proud independence and selfish aloofness.

Lear's recognition of his kinship with all men makes him see more sympathy and understanding in the world than before. Through sympathy he discovers himself. We have a moral reorientation, a shift from individual power to the principle of universal justice. We have a different vision of society, which is now seen as organic. Each individual is so intimately united to another that the misery of all is the misery of one. And we approach a recognition that the most important bonds of society are inner and spiritual, not merely the external and the formal.

The stripping of Lear suggests even more levels of significance. It is the culmination of his daughters' stripping him of honor and dignity, the final dismantling of the king. It suggests that man by himself, against nature's forces, is insignificant; that he is not, as Protagoras maintained, the measure of all things; that he derives his strength from his dependence on his fellow men. It is a suggestion that all men, at one time or another, are outcasts and wanderers. It is a recognition that man's worth is independent of rank and power. It is a test of man's true strength, for, as William Segar wrote in his Elizabethan treatise *The Booke of Honor and Armes,*

"Seneca saith, that who so will trulie judge what worthines is in man, must consider of him naked, laying aside his livings and titles of honor . . . and then weigh of what value or excellencie he is in minde, because nobilitie is placed in the minde."[36]

In *Lear* the mind confronts the universe to discover if there is any relationship between the world and man. Such action partakes of the religious experience, for as Alfred North Whitehead has observed, "Religion is what the individual does with his own solitariness."[37] Lear is not the only one who undergoes an experience which forces him to face his world alone, see himself anew, and make what settlement he can with the world. The numerous other addresses to the world— by Gloucester (IV.vi.34), Edgar (IV.i.10), Albany (IV.ii.46), Cordelia (IV.vii.14)— show the play's recurring preoccupation with man's quest for values. From personal suffering each learns something; and whatever we call the individual's experience in confronting the universe or invoking its aid—whether *anagnorisis*, self-recognition, or epiphany—the very number of addresses to the world reveals the concern with the question, "What is man?" or in individual terms, "Who am I?" For many of the characters it is necessary that they first lose their way before they can find themselves; and this action also partakes of the religious experience, for it deals with the problem, "What must man do to be saved?"

Our concern is with Lear and what he learns from his experience on the heath. When the rain came to wet him and the wind made him chatter, when nature would not conform to his wishes, when, as Lear says in his madness, "the thunder would not peace at my bidding" (IV.vi.103), he learns that he is not everything, that he can not control nature, and in his madness he clearly sees the true character of Goneril and Regan:

> They flatter'd me like a dog, and told me I had the white hairs in my beard ere the black ones were there. To say "ay" and "no" to everything that I said! "Ay" and "no" too was no good divinity. . . . they told me I was every-thing; 'tis a lie, I am not ague-proof.   (IV.vi.97)

Lear discovers that there are no special laws in the universe for man. Dostoevski's treatment of an analogous episode illuminates Lear's situation at this point. When, in *The Brothers Karamazov*, the saintly monk Zossima dies, Alyosha expects that nature would show signs of glorifying death. That the monk's body prematurely stank, that the saint should be so dishonored, agonizes Alyosha and momentarily destroys his faith in the universe. It was not miracles he looked for in this instance, "it was justice, justice, he thirsted for."[38] Just as Lear sought, in time of great crisis, personal recognition from nature and the gods, so Alyosha looked for nature's special laws: "Where is the finger of Providence? Why did Providence hide its face 'at the most critical moment' (so Alyosha thought it), as though voluntarily submitting to the blind, dumb, pitiless laws of nature?"[39] While Alyosha had been taught to love everyone and everything, he had concentrated his love on one man, one ideal, and Dostoevski stresses the significant consequences. On the day that Zossima dies and there occurs the scandal of the stinking body, Alyosha forgets everyone and everything: he forgets about Dimitri's vexing problems; he forgets to take two hundred roubles to Ilusha's father, though he had firmly resolved to do so the previous evening. When nature will not fulfill Alyosha's expectations of justice, he sets himself apart from creation in judgment, refuses to accept the world and objectifies his rebellion by spitefully doing things he would never have done before. He asks for sausage, vodka; and finally, to complete his degradation and fall from saints to sinners, would go to Grushenka. In this spiritual crisis there comes to Alyosha the recognition that the elf can be fulfilled only through communication with others. Where Alyosha goes to Grushenka to find a companion in degradation, he finds, instead, sympathy and loving pity, and because of her he is saved from despair. In turn, because Alyosha does not judge or condemn Grushenka, she is saved. Only when we see that all are equally guilty and equally worthwhile, Dostoevski stresses, can we live a meaningful life, for then we do not withdraw from sinful creation in horror and self-righteous judgment, but participate fully in the world, acknowledging individual responsibility for all and for everything. In this greatest of all recognitions for Dostoevski, man goes through a psychological and moral reorganization of personality; but even more: man makes a meaningful discovery about the world.

Lear's transformation on the heath is strikingly similar to the experience of Alyosha and other characters of Dostoevski. Lear also seeks personal recognition from nature and gods, and would have special laws recognize the justice of his cause. Frustrated, he too finally finds that the abnegation of self is prerequisite to communion with all men; and further—that a person achieves true identity when his humanity is recognized by others. While these ideas control the development of Dostoevski's characters and give structure to his work, they operate less rigidly in *Lear*. Edgar's development, to take but one example as contrast to Lear, is towards stoic withdrawal. Finding nature a blank wall, he does not seek for a justice immanent in nature, nor does he strive to impose his will on nature. He is, nevertheless, a man of action; he rights personal wrongs in combat. He acts where he has power to act, not against the universe, but against evil embodied in men. His lament and address to the world in Act IV serves as contrast to Lear's situation:

> Yet better thus, and known to be contemn'd,
> Than, still contemn'd and flatter'd, to be worst.
> The lowest and most dejected thing of fortune
> Stands still in esperance, lives not in fear.
> The lamentable change is from the best;
> The worst returns to laughter. Welcome, then,
> Thou unsubstantial air that I embrace!
> The wretch that thou hast blown unto the worst
> Owes nothing to thy blasts.   (IV.i.1)

Lear, like Edgar, comes to know that it is better to be contemned than still contemned and flattered. But their final visions of the world differ. Lear, like many of Dostoevski's characters, loses himself to find himself part of all humanity. In terms of dramatic action, Lear is first stripped of all; then he strips himself of all; and finally, his madness is the complete loss of self. In terms of personality, Lear intermittently progresses to a denial and surrender of the individual will which finally enables him to kneel before Cordelia and beg her forgiveness.

V

Is there an explanation for the greatness of Lear? Is Lear's stature to be wholly explained by pointing to the fact that he is a king, a father, an old man? If such were the case the Lear of the opening scene, garbed in splendor and authority, would fulfill the essentials of true greatness. Is Lear's topmost grief his topmost greatness? A Hieronimo may rant and rave and still be a small figure; Gloucester and Edgar undergo equally painful torments, yet never achieve Lear's greatness. There is no simple answer, of course; we can only offer observations which provide, at best, partial explanations.

First, we can say that contributing to make Lear's stature greater than that of any other character in the play is the fact that we, as audience, know more about him than about any of the others. In a letter of Keats we find this statement: "There may be intelligences or sparks of the divinity in millions—but they are not Souls till they acquire identities, till each one is personally itself."[40] In drama the character shapes his identity in speech far more than in deeds. Though Lear, for most of the play, is acted upon, "more sinned against than sinning," he is the most vigorously eloquent of all. To be convinced of this we need only compare the moment when the main and subplot merge, when the mad Lear and the blind Gloucester meet on the heath. Gloucester speaks prosaically, though at times his trenchant conciseness is most effective, as when Lear tells him, "You see how this world goes" (IV.vi.151), and the blind Gloucester replies, "I see it feelingly." Lear, on the other hand, continually speaks imaginatively and expansively. Throughout the play he reveals himself fully in his speeches.

"You should know, Sancho," said Don Quixote, "that one man is no more than another unless he does more than another." Lear does more than any other person in the play. Too often critics overemphasize the point that Lear is mainly acted upon; Mark Van Doren goes so far as to say that "the deeds of the tragedy are suffered rather than done; the relation of events is lyrical instead of logical, musical instead of moral."[41] Though most of Lear's struggle is inward, that conflict is externalized imaginatively in words, and we come to know that Lear wages the most heroic battles of all: against the cosmos, and the new society, and finally, against his own hardened self. He is glorified in his suffering because, for one thing, he represents a striving for justice and civilized values. There is another point. His situation is much like that of King Richard the Second; both are humbled to nothingness because of their own actions. But Richard does not grow spiritually, as Lear does. That is the most important distinction. Lear reaches the very lowest state of existence, unaccommodated man, he loses that which distinguishes man from animal, his reason, but from nothingness he progresses to Truth, about himself and others. He sees beyond the world of pomp, state, contractual obligations. His vision is of truth or perfection or blessedness, not the center of a flower or blinding light, but a secular vision of love and the community of mankind. Hell, Dostoevski continually reminds us, is "the suffering of being unable to love."[42]

In essential agreement with many of thee points is Arthur Miller, himself a playwright trying to mold tragedy out of contemporary life, but faced with a difficulty which did not exist for Shakespeare, the "split between the private life of man and his social life."[43] Miller has written that all plays we call great are ultimately concerned with some aspect of a single problem: "How may a man make of the outside world a home? How and in what ways must he struggle, what must he strive to change and overcome within himself and outside himself if he is to find the safety, the surroundings of love, the ease of soul, the sense of identity and honor which evidently, all men have connected in their memories with the idea of family?"[44] In this statement Miller succinctly reviews considerations we have found to be so central to *King Lear*. Our analysis of the point of view established toward Lear has revealed how Shakespeare, through the dramatic clash of two worlds, has concentrated attention on the survival of civilized values; how, in the structure of the play, the individual's quest for truth and certainty and identity is so important; how, finally, Lear's plight is more than one of individual personality, but is typical of tragic human destiny. While Miller maintains that the memory of family is man's most abiding value, his ultimate truth, such a context is to be associated more with drama since Ibsen; it is not so valid for Greek or Shakespearian tragedy where the vision is more cosmic. Lear finds his greatest happiness in Cordelia's unselfish love; but in preparation for this his view of the world has extended beyond, to a recognition for this his view of the world has extended beyond, to a recognition of the community of men.

Nevertheless, Lear's insight into truth and happiness is not negotiable in this tough world. He cannot convert his experience into saving advantages. To give the play a Christian interpretation and make of it a divine comedy is to distort the work. By the end of the play Lear's world has narrowed to Cordelia, but she is dead in his arms. "Is this the promis'd end?" (V.iii.263) Kent cries out in anguish; and Edgar joins in, "Or image of that horror?" "Fall, and cease!" is Albany's tortured utterance. Evil is the world and there is no escape. It is much better, says Kent, that Lear die:

> Vex not his ghost; O, let him pass! He hates him
> That would upon the rack of this tough world
> Stretch him out longer.   (V.iii.313)

In *King Lear* Shakespeare takes us to the edge of the human world to front the terrors of life and the viciousness of man's brutality. He offers no solution to the ungraspable phantom of life. However, in the midst of terror we see the nobility and greatness of man's spirit. Keats gives us one of the most illuminating insights into the nature of tragedy: "The excellence of every art is its intensity, capable of making all disagreeables evaporate, from their being in close relationship with Beauty and Truth. Examine 'King Lear,' and you will find this exemplified throughout...."[45]

From the time of Aristotle, men have maintained that great art has a civilizing function: it tells us, like history or science, what is; but even more, it can tell us what ought to be. Lear's suffering, his search for justice and identity, is a facing of the fearful elements of the world. His vision of truth and his complete change of character give us a sense of the nobility of spirit which can transcend the confinements of man's condition. "There lies within the dramatic form," Arthur Miller tells us with great conviction, "the ultimate possibility of raising the truth-consciousness of mankind to a level of such intensity as to transform those who observe it."[46]

NOTES

[1] M. Steeven Guazzo, in *The Civile Conversation*, trans. George Pettie (London, 1581), II, 47, exhorts the courtier that Princes are "Gods on earth," and to "call into question their dooinges, is nothing else, but with the Gyants, to lay siege to heaven." Hence the courtier is called upon to give the Prince "the love, fidelitie, diligence, and reverence, whiche is due to Princes"; the Prince being "a God on earth, it behoveth him to doe him honoure as a sacred thing" (III, 55–56).

William Baldwin, in his dedication "To the nobilitye and all other in office" in *The Mirror for Magistrates*, ed. Lily B. Campbell (Cambridge, England, 1938), p. 65, asserted a view that had widespread acceptance; that a king governs "Gods owne office" and "therefore hath God established it with the chiefest name, honoring & calling Kinges, & all officers vnder them by his owne name, Gods."

King James, indeed, vigorously espoused such doctrines, boldly asserting the divine right of kings: that no subject had the right to question the justice of any royal act "for Kings are not only God's Lieutenants vpon earth, and sit vpon Gods throne, but euen by God himselfe they are called Gods. ...That as to dispute what God may doe is Blasphemie... So is it sedition in Subiects, to dispute what a King may do in height of his power" (*Political Works of James I*, ed. Charles H. McIlwain, Cambridge, Mass., 1918, pp. 307, 310). Bacon, in his fragmentary "Essay of a King," also voiced the idea that "A King is a mortal God on Earth, unto whom the living God hath lent his own name as a great honour" (*Works of Francis Bacon*, ed. James Spedding, Robert L. Ellis, Douglas D. Heath, London, 1861, VI, 595).

For a detailed presentation of the divine right of kings in England as well as France, see J. W. Allen, *A History of Political Thought in the Sixteenth Century* (London, 1941). See also, Ruth L. Anderson, "Kingship in Renaissance Drama," *Studies in Philology*, 41:136–155 (1944).

[2] For discussions of Elizabethan order, see Alfred Harbage, *Shakespeare and the Rival Traditions* (New York, 1952), pp. 133–185; Theodore Spencer, *Shakespeare and the Nature of Man* (New York, 1955), pp. 1–92; E. M. W. Tillyard, *The Elizabethan World Picture* (New York, 1944).

[3] Pierre de La Primaudaye, *The French Academie*, trans. T. B[owes] (London, 1602), pp. 494, 501, 507.

[4] *Shakespeare and the Popular Dramatic Tradition* (London, 1944), p. 71.

[5] Charles Lamb, "On the Tragedies of Shakespeare," in *Shakespeare Criticism: A Selection*, ed. D. Nichol Smith (London, 1949), pp. 204–205.

[6] *Shakespeare's Tragic Heroes: Slaves of Passion* (New York, 1952), p. 189.

[7] *The Wheel of Fire* (London, 1954), pp. 172, 162.

[8] *This Great Stage: Image and Structure in* King Lear (Baton Rouge, 1948), p. 86. Such pattern abstractions, while at times illuminating, often neglect dramatic interrelations of character and distort the structure of the work. One can see this tendency in Heilman, whose major tenet is that from the plot of the play we can discern only "partial outlines of tragic form" which must be "amplified or corrected by the evidences of the symbolic language" (p. 32). For a penetrating analysis of the excesses of Heilman's technique, see W. R. Keast, "Imagery and Meaning in the Interpretation of *King Lear,*" *Modern Philology*, 47:45–64 (1949).

[9] *The Fool: His Social and Literary History* (New York, 1935), p. 267.

[10] Arthur Sewell has formulated this extremely useful concept of the character's "address to the world" in his book *Character and Society in Shakespeare* (Oxford, 1951).

[11] Herman Melville, *Moby-Dick* (Modern Library ed., New York, 1930), p. 166.

[12] *The Heritage of Symbolism* (London, 1943), p. 197.

[13] *Archetypal Patterns in Poetry* (London, 1934), pp. 15–17.

[14] *The Chronicle History of King Leir*, ed. Sidney Lee (London, 1909).

[15] A. C. Bradley has characterized the figures of Goneril, Regan, Edmund, Cornwall, and Oswald as

"hard self-seeking," while suggesting that Cordelia, Kent, Edgar, and the Fool represent "unselfish and devoted love." The two forces, Bradley maintained, "are set in conflict, almost as if Shakespeare. like Empedocles, were regarding Love and Hate as the two ultimate forces of the universe" (*Shakespearean Tragedy*, London, 1904, p. 263).

Enid Welsford has portrayed the two groups in a similar manner. On the one hand are those who are "erring men, warm-hearted but self-willed," having in common the capacity for "fellow-feeling"; and in sharp contrast, those who are calculating, who could never be considered "candidates for the cap and bells" (*The Fool*, p. 257).

Harley Granville-Barker pictured Goneril and Regan as "realists. Their father wants smooth speech of them and they give it...." (*Prefaces to Shakespeare*, Princeton, 1952, I, 301). This characterization was also arrived at by W. H. Clemen in his analysis of the imagery of their speech: "They speak rationally; they address their words to their partner, and converse in a deliberate and conscious manner. They have a goal which they seek to attain and everything they have to say is bent upon this. Their language does not betray to us what is taking place within them—in the form of 'imaginative visions'; it reveals to us solely their aims and attitudes, and how they intend to put these into practice" (*Development of Shakespeare's Imagery*, London, 1951, p. 135).

Edwin Muir (*The Politics of* King Lear, Glasgow, 1947, p. 24) has characterized the world of Edmund and Goneril and Regan as one where "the man of policy in the latest style ... regards the sacred order of society as his prey, and recognizes only two realities, interest and force, the gods of the new age."

In an extensive investigation of Shakespeare's doctrine of nature in *King Lear*, John F. Danby found that "Edmund and the sisters see society as a competition" (*Shakespeare's Doctrine of Nature: A study of* King Lear, London, 1949, p. 108), while R. B. Heilman, in a study of metaphorical patterns in the play, concluded that they are pragmatists who see in "nature no intensified claim of Nature but only an aspect of the physical world to be properly estimated and used"; that they represent "a new order which is coolly calculating, on the make, quick to take advantage of flaws which sharp minds detect in the old men whose roots are in the past" (*This Great Stage*, pp. 141, 279).

For D. A. Traversi, Goneril, Regan, Edmund, and their cohorts exemplify the "ruthless exercise of the acquisitive instinct in its determination to break the bonds of 'nature' and custom in the free following of its own unlimited desire for power" ("*King Lear*, II," *Scrutiny*, 19:137, 1953).

Hiram Haydn (*The Counter-Renaissance*, New York, 1950, p. 638) views the whole play as "unmistakably concerned with a dying order, in which the protagonists of Nature and Stoicism fight for supremacy."

[16] Richard Hooker, *Ecclesiastical Polity*, in *Works*, ed. John Keble (Oxford, 1885), I, 223.

[17] *Antonios Revenge*, in *Plays of John Marston*, ed. H. Harvey Wood (London, 1934), I, 109.

[18] *The Prince*, ch. xv, trans. W. K. Marriott (Everyman ed., London, n.d.), pp. 121–122: "But, it being my intention to write a thing which shall be useful to him who apprehends it, it appears to me more appropriate to follow up the real truth of a matter than the imagination of it ... because how one lives is so far distant from how one ought to live, that he who neglects what is done for what ought to be done, sooner effects his ruin than his preservation; for a man who wishes to act entirely up to his professions of virtue soon meets with what destroys him among so much that is evil.

"Hence it is necessary for a prince wishing to hold his own to know how to do wrong, and to make use of it or not according to necessity."

[19] Ibid., p. 123: "And again, he [the prince] need not make himself uneasy at incurring a reproach for those vices without which the state can only be saved with difficulty, for if everything is considered carefully, it will be found that something which looks like virtue, if followed, would be his ruin; whilst something else, which looks like vice, yet followed brings him security and prosperity."

[20] See George T. Buckley, *Rationalism in Sixteenth Century Literature* (Chicago, 1933); Hiram Haydn, *The Counter-Renaissance*. For Montaigne's influence on Shakespeare, now accounted as negligible, see Alice Harmon, "How Great Was Shakespeare's Debt to Montaigne?" *PMLA*, 57:988–1008 (1942).

[21] See Heilman, *This Great Stage*, p. 141.

[22] *Laws*, I.vi, in *Cicero: De Republica, De Legibus*, trans. Clinton W. Keyes (Loeb Library ed., London, 1928), p. 317.

[23] Regan calls Gloucester "ingrateful fox" (III.vii.28) and "dog" (III.vii.75) in a tense and dramatic situation. But this is an isolated case, and Gloucester is not otherwise depicted in such language.

[24] *New English Dictionary*, X (Part II), 250.

[25] See E. Catherine Dunn, *The Concept of Ingratitude in Renaissance English Moral Philosophy* (Washington, D.C., 1946).

[26] *Moby-Dick*, p. 655.

[27] While almost every writer on *Lear* elaborates on some of these parallels, George R. Kernodle has devoted an entire article to them: "The Symphonic Form of *King Lear*" in *Elizabethan Studies and Other Essays in Honor of George F. Reynolds* (Boulder, Colorado, 1945), pp. 185–191. For an early (and most thorough) study of Natural Law in *Lear*, see Hardin Craig, "The Ethics of *King Lear*," *Philological Quarterly*, 4:97–109 (1925).

[28] *Troilus and Cressida*, II.ii.26.

[29] *Aristotle on the Art of Poetry*, ed., trans. Ingram Bywater (Oxford, 1909), xiii, p. 35. For ideas on Shakespeare's appeal to the audience I am greatly indebted to Harry Levin, "An Explication of the Player's Speech," *Kenyon Review*, 12:273–296 (1950), and to Arthur Sewell, *Character and Society in Shakespeare*.

[30] *Character and Society in Shakespeare*, p. 21.

[31] *Die Tragödie vor Shakespeare* (Heidelberg, 1955).

[32] In "The Salvation of Lear," *Journal of English Literary History*, 15:93–109 (1948), Oscar J. Campbell, after presenting an incisive account of Elizabethan Stoic thought, interprets Lear as a completely unstoical man. Hiram Haydn, in *The Counter-Renaissance*, pp. 642–651, sees the entire drama as a "Stoic play," and characterizes Kent, Cordelia, and Edgar as stoics, and Lear as unstoical.

[33] *Meditations*, Bk. VIII, ch. 47, trans. George W. Chrystal (Edinburgh, n.d.), p. 150.

[34] *Moby-Dick*, p. 4.

[35] Trans. Constance Garnett (Modern Library ed., New York, 1950), p. 344.

[36] (London, 1950), p. 35.

[37] *Religion in the Making* (New York, 1926), p. 16.

[38] *Brothers Karamazov*, p. 408.

[39] Ibid.

[40] Letter 123: "To George and Georgiana Keats," in *The Letters of John Keats*, ed. Maurice B. Forman (Oxford, 1948), p. 336.

[41] *Shakespeare* (New York, 1953), p. 204.

[42] *Brothers Karamazov*, p. 387.

[43] "The Family in Modern Drama," *Atlantic Monthly*, 197:40 (1956).

[44] Ibid., pp. 36–37.

[45] Letter 32: "To George and Thomas Keats," in Forman, p. 71.

[46] "The Family in Modern Drama," p. 41.

Russell A. Fraser

REDEMPTION IN *KING LEAR*

Evil, which is yoke fellow to ignorance, stems from a failure rightly to distinguish the good. *Lear* documents amply the result of that failure. Its decisive manifestation is in the opening lines of the play. Thus one may speak of all that follows as a long denouement. The action wanes as it waxes. But the play describes a second curve, antithetical to the first. The action waxes as it wanes. The new moon is cradled in the arms of the old. This is to say that the delineating of the greatest evil is made that of the greatest good. Where you find Goneril, there do you find Cordelia. Edmund's cruelty is the occasion of Edgar's compassion, Lear's decline the condition of Lear's rejuvenescence.

> There is some soul of goodness in things evil,
> Would men observingly distil it out.   (*Henry V*, 4.1.4f.)

The rising action of the play, the suspense it engenders, is, not in the adversity with which the characters are visited, but in their discovery of the uses of adversity. When Lear's daughters drive him out in the storm, there is in his banishment no discovery, or peripeteia. The wicked daughters confirm, it is true, their evil design. It is, however, a design that has been long maturing, long patent. Only Lear is oblivious of it.

> I know you what you are.

The exciting discovery he makes on the heath.

He had thought himself a king, in his lexicon a rare (an impossible) being, fenced off from the ills that flesh is heir to. He discovers that the king and the outcast are one, that but for idle ceremony the slave has the forehand and vantage of the king. Ceremony, a king's prerogative, is not proof against the fever. (4.6.107) Divest a king of his robes, undeck the pompous body, and you find him a cipher (1.4.212, 251), just such a forked animal as any other. (3.4.110f.)

From *Shakespeare's Poetics in Relation to* King Lear (London: Routledge & Kegan Paul, 1962), pp. 119–37.

But now a king, now thus.   (*King John*, 5.7.66)

Who, from the skull of a king or a peasant, can distinguish the king or the peasant?[1] In this sense the garment determines the man. King Cophetua and the beggar maid are not so much different as the same.

The king's a beggar, now the play is done.   (*All's Well*, Epilogue)

One event happens to all. What is more: if man is kin to the angels, he is also, however you clothe him, kin to the worm. (4.1.33)

Discovering so much, Lear makes the unshunnable inference. Men are players merely, chimeras who pursue the chimerical. 'We are both on the stage,' writes the Parliamentary general Sir William Waller to the royalist friend whose defeat and wounding he brought about at the battle of Lansdown. 'We are both on the stage, and we must act the parts that are assigned to us in this tragedy.'[2] But the universal theatre presents more woeful pageants than the scene in which Waller and his adversary play. (*As You Like It*, 2.7.137–9) All the world's a stage to feed contention in a lingering act. (*2 Henry IV*, 1.1.155f.) You great men take the centre, says the Bastard in *King John*; lesser men stand around you

> As in a theatre, whence they gape and point
> At your industrious scenes and acts of death.   (2.1.375f.)

The hurly, by definition, is only a simulacrum of the genuine drama. In that manner Nashe, in *Summer's Last Will and Testament*, describes it:

> Heaven is our heritage,
> Earth but a player's stage.

Totus mundus agit histrionem. All the world plays the actor.[3] All sweat without purpose, contend for a hollow applause. But you cannot feed capons so. It follows that man's life is a great stage of fools. (4.6.185) But the actor, as he plays his part there, is played upon also. And so the further inference: man's life, even at its zenith, is a theatre of all miseries. (Plate XLVI) His tormentors are fleshly lust, sin, and death.[4] His insistent business is sorrow, in all his entrances and exits. (4.6.180–5)

> For sorrow holds man's life to be her own,
> His thoughts her stage where tragedies she plays.[5]

If man is no more than this,[6] who should be mindful of him, or of the puerilities with which he wears out a life? True wisdom will hold the world but as the world.[7] To Herbert of Cherbury, delivering his 'Elegy over a Tomb', the wise man is one who

> did delight no more to stay
> Upon this low and earthly stage
> But rather chose an endless heritage.

Lear comes to concur in the wisdom of Antonio, the Merchant of Venice. He holds the world but as the world. He laughs at gilded butterflies (5.3.12f.) who attend on the flame that consumes them.[8]

Thus hath the candle singed the moth.
Oh, these deliberate fools! (*Merchant of Venice*, 2.9.79f.)

But he does not find out their folly with his eyes. He is able to see truly only when he can see feelingly. Like Timon, 'He will not hear, till feel'. (2.2.7) He who feels nothing knows nothing. (4.1.71f.) The eyes and ears are inadequate reporters. Gloucester stumbled when he saw. (4.1.21) Bereft of sight, he ceases to stumble. (3.7.91f.)

His overthrow heaped happiness upon him,
For then, and not till then, he felt himself. (*Henry VIII*, 4.2.64f.)

Given, Edgar once more in his *touch*, he'd say he had *eyes* again. (4.1.25f.)

I see it feelingly. (4.6.152)

Lear, humiliated and unheard before Cornwall's castle, and later, goaded from that castle, grows an adept in the art of feeling sorrows. (4.6.223)

I am not ague proof. (4.6.107)

Wind and cold are councillors that feelingly persuade him what he is. (*As You Like It*, 2.1.10f.)
But to taste my own misery is common, is casual. Mere existence entails it.

We came crying hither. (4.6.182)

To sorrow for my neighbour, to make my misery mine, is the uncommon case, and the harder. That is to shake the holy water from one's eyes. (4.3.31f.) Lear, like Cordelia, is vouchsafed that kind of pity. It is the chief leaven of his schooling.

In, boy, go first. (3.4.26)

Charity solicits him; like Edgar, he gives it room. (5.3.166)

I'll forbear.[9] (2.4.110)

None is without fleck. He declines, in consequence, to cast the first stone. But none is without merit. He learns to feel for the pariah, to assimilate him. The lash that falls on the prostitute is laid on his own back as well. (4.6.165–70) He learns, as Kent has learned, that self-love lacks in magnitude and savour, that a man knows no greater love than to hold his life but as a pawn for his friend.[10] (1.1.157)

But charity, if an attribute of Heaven, is not endemic in men but achieved. Charity is not gratuitous. One must be brought to thrust his fingers in the wounds, and not for ocular proof but, to change the sense of the story, to confirm on one's own pulses the misery of another. Lear, like Didymus called Thomas, is made to bear witness. Only then does he grow pregnant to good pity. (4.6.224) He feels necessity's pinch. (2.4.213)

But what I am want teaches me to think on.   (*Pericles*, 2.1.76)

It is at once his expiation and his schooling, a requital for wrong, a changing of vile things to precious, of precious things—the sign and flag of temporal power— to vile. (3.2.70f.) 'Like as Golde and Siluer is tried in the fire: euen so are acceptable men, in the fornace of aduersitie.'[11] The horror *Lear* treats of is causal in its origin, and thus one can endure the play. But the horror is also instrumental: it leads on to perceiving; and for that reason the play is not depressing but inspiriting.[12]

But suffering alone does not quit the king, nor make him wise. Antonio and Sebastian seek the lives of Prospero and Alonso; they suffer in consequence, but they are not schooled. They end as they began, confirmed in evil.

But one fiend at a time,
I'll fight their legions o'er.   (*Tempest*, 3.3.102f.)

As well as suffering, one must know repentance.

Oh, my follies!
Kind gods, forgive me that.   (3.7.91f.)

Lear is elbowed by a sovereign shame: humanity renascent. (4.3.44, 47–49) It brings him to beg forgetting and forgiving. (4.7.84) But even more is incumbent on him. The god servant in *Pericles* advises his master

To bear with patience
Such griefs as you do lay upon yourself.   (1.2.65f.)

Lear also must possess his soul in patience.[13] He must endure.[14] The progress he goes is the wonted progress of Shakespearean tragedy, which descends, through chaos, to harmony at the close. The way up and the way down are depicted in an unpublished commonplace book dating from about the year of the first quarto of the play (1608), and ascribed to one Thomas Trevelyon. The cycle of Peace and War, as Trevelyon represents it, turns downward on the entrance of Pride, whom you know by her peacock-feathered head-dress, and the fan of peacock feathers in her hand. In her wake come Self Indulgence or Pleasure, and Envy gnawing at her heart, and War brandishing the torch and sword. But as the lowest point is reached, a return to the highest is predicted: enter Poverty in rags; and after Poverty, Humility; and then Patience with clasped hands and eyes raised to Heaven. The final figure in the sequence, whose way these others have been preparing, is Peace.[15] So Lear, as he is patient, proceeds from misfortune to reconciliation.

And not only Lear. Edgar, made tame to Fortune's blows (4.6.222), enjoins patience. (4.6.80) Edgar endures. (5.3.211) Kent, at the worst, is equable still. (2.2.180) Cordelia is the pattern of all patience. (4.3.17f.) Gloucester, who would shake off his affliction (4.6.35–38), who, in a real sense, is tempted by the Fiend to throw himself down (4.6.219f.), resolves at last to bear affliction until affliction dies.[16] (4.6.75–77) But Lear himself is the great exemplar.

> Thou must be patient.[17]   (4.6.180)

A man's office is too bear a cheek for blows,[18] to take the weight of the time (5.3.323), to abide it. (5.2.9f.) Ripeness is all. Charity, which saves because it instructs, rises from suffering and repentance and endurance. These, in Shelley's phrase, are the seals which bar the pit.

Now the humble, whom the world calls the foolish, are made to suffer most, in the nature of things. They ought in logic to enjoy a better chance, not to heap up the good things of Heaven—the crass promise of crude religions—but rather to live the good life, one founded in sophistication, in right reading. Poverty, says Primaudaye, 'is the mistress of manners ... a schoole of vertue'. Philosophy finds her best scholars among the poor.[19] Not to be foolish, or wicked: if you beat a man enough, you make him insensible, no longer a man but a beast. But, in the ideal case (which is, I take it, the concern of the play, any play), the suffering man, who is likely to be one of the lowly, is more sensible to feeling than another, and so more acute in perceiving.

> Nothing almost sees miracles
> But misery.   (2.2.172f.)

The world, alive only to his beggarly status, dismisses the fruit of that status. Thus the acuity of the humble man becomes, in popular estimation, the muddied vision of the fool. Kent, who has more man that wit about him, who takes one's part that's out of favour, had best put on the coxcomb. (2.4.42;1.4.109–12) Kent is a fool; and Cordelia a greater, who pays contempt with kindness and ends in prison for her pains.

> And my poor fool is hang'd!   (5.3.305)

But Kent, for all that he is merely a retainer, is wiser than the king, in real fact the true blank of his eye. (1.1.159) The king is a fool. Lear's wicked daughters, who rejoice at the banishment laid on Cordelia, when all is said discriminate but poorly. It is they who are all-licensed fools. (1.4.220) Lear's Fool, who pines for Cordelia (1.4.79f.), is the better able to assay.

> This is not altogether fool.   (1.4.165)

The Dutch patriots, who wore a coarse grey livery distinguished only by the cap and bells, were not so foolish as their well-attired oppressors, who had not the wit to understand that a Brutus might be found beneath the costume of a fool,

> Covering discretion with a coat of folly.   (Henry V, 2.4.38)

The besotted are wise; they see whose eyes are dazzled.[20]

Much madness is divinest sense
To a discerning eye;
Much sense the starkest madness.

Gloucester, thrust out at gates to smell his way to Dover (3.7.93f.), is succoured by a bedlam beggar. Madmen lead the blind. (4.1.46) Gloucester's title does not exalt him a step above his fellows. Partly it is otherwise: as he ascends, he may be said to descend. But the words themselves are beguiling.

> If we consider how our common mother the earth, being prodigall in giuing vnto us all things necessary for the life of man, hath notwithstanding cast all of vs naked out of her bowels, and must receiue us so againe into her wombe, I see no great reason wee haue to call some rich, and others poore; seeing the beginning, being, and ende of the temporall life of all men are vnlike in nothing, but that some during this little moment of life haue that in abundance and superfluitie, which others haue only according to their necessitie.[21]

Hierarchy, in first and last things, is a nonce word. To acknowledge the puissance of the lion—or king—is to be cognizant also of the claims of the hare:

> Those members ... which we think to be less honourable, upon these we bestow more abundant honour ... [for] God hath tempered the body together, having given more abundant honour to that part which lacked.[22]

The greater puissance is a fiction. The humble are exalted, and the mighty put down.

Lear, like Gloucester, must learn of the humble. His tutors are the Fool and Poor Tom. He calls them philosophers, learned justicers, sapient sirs. And the jest is not that he errs, but that he is right.

> The wise man's folly is anatomized
> Even by the squandering glances of the fool.   (*As You Like It*, 2.7.56f.)

Foolishness is wisdom; and poverty, riches. Things hid from the wise and the prudent are revealed to the babe. The saying of the Evangelist (Matthew, xi.25) is tested and confirmed by the playwright, who

> in babes hath judgement shown
> When judges have been babes.   (*All's Well*, 2.1.141f.)

As Lear's wits begin to leave him, he is lessoned, he grows wise. A fantastic, crowned with wild flowers, he figures as Christ, who is the king of fantastics.

> O thou side-piercing sight!   (4.6.85)

But if the innocence of the infant is wisdom, the wisdom of the world is great folly. The knave turns fool that runs away. (2.4.85) Machiavelli is wrong. The shrewd choice is the stupid choice. Goneril and Regan, who think it shrewd to take a sister's portion, are not so well endowed as the sister who has lost it. Burgundy, shrewdly rejecting the dowerless Cordelia, is not a tithe so perceptive as France, who takes her up. To see nothing where everything is patent ought, you would think, to require a faith that reason without miracle could never implant. (1.1.221–3) It does not fall out so:

> Fathers that wear rags
>   Do make their children blind,   (2.4.48f.)

and so the gods discover when they walk among men. But the affluent, who bar their doors against a stranger, poorly led, are not so sophisticated as the humble, who take them in. *Pii sunt cura diis.*[23] Baucis and Philemon find their reward.

Peter, deserting Christ when the great wheel begins to run down hill, is not so sophisticated as Veronica, who tenders Christ her veil. One must be a fool for Christ's sake. He who would save his life must lose it. The last shall be first. Edgar, the son and heir of his father, is scanted.

> Edgar I nothing am.   (2.3.21)

Become so little, he is fulfilled. A rich man shall hardly enter into the kingdom of Heaven. The bedlam and the pauper occupy his room.

>   Willing misery
> Outlives incertain pomp, is crown'd before.   (*Timon*, 4.3.244f.)

Justice, which weighs poverty in the scale against temporal power, gives you to see how light and how weak is that power.

> The latter quick up flew, and kicked the beam.   (*Paradise Lost*, IV.1004)

Nothing comes of nothing: power is nugatory: it displaces no air.[24] Edmund, who looks always to power, knows his mounted scale aloft: his eyes are bent, as he tells you, on nothing. (1.2.31)

Riches, power, sapience as the world describes it, do not denote real riches, power, sapience. The Beatitudes are apposite here. Motley may be the garb of the wise man, a material fool (*As You Like It*, 3.3.32), rich apparel the garb of the genuine fool, he who wears motley in his brain. For those honours laid upon him,

> He shall but bear them as the ass bears gold,
> To groan and sweat under the business.   (*Julius Caesar*, 4.1.21f.)

His pride of accoutrement marks him the servitor, and gull.[25]

>   If thou art rich, thou'rt poor,
> For, like an ass whose back with ingots bows,
> Thou bear'st thy heavy riches but a journey,
> And death unloads thee.   (*Measure for Measure*, 3.1.25–28)

But the genuine fool is not simply a beast of burden but the servant of his servant: like Lear, he bears his ass on his back. (1.4.176f.) (Plato XLIX) It is the efficient cause of his destruction. It pulls him under. Thus the faithful steward to Timon of Athens:

> thy great fortunes
>
> Are made thy chief afflictions.   (4.2.43f.)

The wretch—Edgar, at the worse, the lowest and most dejected thing of fortune (4.1.2f.)—as he is stripped naked by fortune, finds his burden lightened.[26] He is the better able to throw aside the torrent. His defects prove commodities. (4.1.22f.) Like Crates of Thebes, as Tom Nashe describes him, he gives what he has to the waters: his appetites are ungracious: it is better that they should drown than he himself.[27] In that sense, it is the naked who survive. Or, another metaphor: the wretch, who is blown to the worst, embraces the storm, yields and bends as it directs him (4.1.6f.) But the great man, who is given to command, little given to defer, seeks to outstare it. He is shattered.[28] His means secure him.

> Merciful Heaven,
>
> Thou rather with thy sharp and sulphurous bolt
>
> Split'st the unwedgeable and gnarlèd oak
>
> Than the soft myrtle.   (*Measure for Measure*, 2.2.114–17)

And so the injunction: 'Take no thought for your life, what ye shall eat, or what ye shall drink; nor yet for your body, what ye shall put on.'

The poor and the oppressed are the salt of the earth to the degree that they inherit, not its riches but its wisdom. Poverty, says the homilist, 'hath beene the onely and principall cause of enriching many with ... [the treasures of wisedome and vertue]'.[29] If, unhappily, much of his eulogy is the conventional humbug: money is the root of all evil—still, the initial assertion may stand. The play is its surety. Prisoners, idiots, beggars, pedlars, slaves: all those whom the world, cozened by show, duped by appearance, calls nothing, those to whom the world denies substance, are invested with substance by Shakespeare. His mind beats on them constantly: they afford him the stuff of nearly half of the images he draws from classes and kinds of humanity.[30] Lear's redemption is signallized by the unwonted care he bestows on those poor naked wretches of whom, hitherto, he had taken little care. (3.4.28, 32f.) Like Gloucester, whose case exactly parallels his own, he would shake them the superflux:

> So distribution should undo excess,
>
> And each man have enough.   (4.1.70f.)

Heaven collaborates in the charity of Gloucester and Lear. To the poor man, God holds out fullness; to the rich man, nothing at all.[31] Not to spy out the point of that final apportioning, to shut one's mind against it, to believe that the poor are intrinsically poor, that Cordelia, say, who utters nothing, means in fact nothing is to be reduced infallibly to nothing oneself. So Lear is reduced.

But not for ever. The play is a kind of *Commedia*. Life peers through the hollow eyes of death.[32] The dry bones are made fruitful.[33] Lear, forgetting

> Aged contusions and all brush of time
>
> ... like a gallant in the brow of youth,
>
> Repairs him with occasion.   (*2 Henry VI*, 5.3.3–5)

As he ages, he grows young: the lost sheep is restored, the man who perishes is reborn.[34] But rebirth is founded on destruction. *Mors vitae initium.* The beginning of life is death.

> For nothing can be sole or whole
> That has not been rent.

Lear verifies the paradox. Like the phoenix, to be reborn he must consume his heart away.[35] Like the eagle, he must cast his plumes before he can renew them.[36] *Lux ex tenebris:*[37] light treads on the limping heel of darkness. A captive, Lear is given his freedom; a sick man, he is given his health; a blind man, he is given his eyes again; a tatterdemalion, he is newly arrayed. The looped and windowed garments are forgotten, in which his worser hours were clothed.

> In the heaviness of his sleep
> We put fresh garments on him.   (4.7.21f.)

He is made by the dramatist to remark his change of raiment (4.7.66f.): it is not simply a physical change. Neither is it adventitious, but rather a consequence of the discovery he makes on the heath. His new learning begets compassion: he grows pregnant to pity. That is to put off the old man, to put on the new. (Ephesians, iv.22–24) Age, because it is corrupted, is wasted. (Colossians, iii.8) 'Come, my old son,' says the Duchess of York to Aumerle, the repentant rebel of *Richard II,* 'I pray God make thee new.' (5.3.146) Age dies a felon's death: 'our old man is crucified'. (Romans, vi.6) Youth gapes to be his heir.

But youth, who is the scion, is also the parent of age. The working out of that riddle is the essential business of Shakespeare's last plays. Thus Pericles to his daughter Marina:

> Thou that beget'st him that did thee beget.   (5.1.197)

In a curious and very tentative way, it is also the business of Shakespeare's earliest comedies.

> Would you create me new?   (*Comedy of Errors,* 3.2.39)

But, whereas in a play like *The Comedy of Errors,* the recreating or renewal turns pretty much on sleight of hand, in the late romances and in a tragedy like *King Lear* it is made a matter of organic change in the protagonist. A prince is bereft of all his fortunes (*Pericles,* 2.1.9)—Lear, Pericles, or Prospero. In his adversity he makes himself over, puts on the whole armour (Ephesians, vi.11), the beaver, the brace, the coat of mail, that formerly he had neglected to wear. In comedy, even in the late comedies, though the protagonist suffers and changes, still the armour is given him by the god from the machine: in *Pericles,* it is washed up from the sea. In tragedy, in *Lear,* though—as in the romances—it is not his except he be born again, still he is seen and felt to deserve it, even to seize and fashion it himself. But the result of the metamorphosis in each case is the same. That old Adam is put off. The new man succeeds him, whose marks are forbearing and forgiving (4.7.84), and charity above all these others. (Colossians, iii.12–14)

Lear puts on the new man. It is right to insist that he earns his renewal. There is about Shakespearean tragedy, at least the appearance of logic and sequence. No suggestion of the miraculous intrudes in *King Lear,* as it does in *Pericles* and *Cymbeline, The Winter's Tale* and *The Tempest.* But if Lear earns or merits regeneration, it is also tendered him, not obviously, sensationally, as in comedy, but none the less gratuitously, if you like graciously. Really, it is independent of his willing. Shakespeare's comedies and tragedies, though superficially very different, are at bottom, in that particular, the same. The comedies emphasize intrinsic weakness, made good by the convolutions of the plot. Protagonists in comedy are felt to be moved.

> O Time, thou must untangle this, not I!
> It is too hard a knot for me to untie!   (*Twelfth Night,* 2.2.41f.)

The tragedies have to do with strength. The tragic protagonist succumbs, it is true, but of his own volition: strength turning back on itself. He is, initially, one who moves.

> I dare do all that may become a man.
> Who dares do more is none.

The inference is clearly that Macbeth, a man sufficiently strong, unmans himself. It can hardly be otherwise in tragedy, which is fraught with suspense to the degree that it seems to admit of alternatives. Tragedy rests, formally, on conflict and choice. Where everything is fated, nothing is dramatic. But when Macbeth, resisting all this while the importunities of his wife, declares suddenly, 'I am settled' (1.7.79), and commits himself to the murder of Duncan, it is hard, however closely you scrutinize it, to rationalize his choice. Why does he alter?

Macbeth, as he is innocent, is in the state of grace, to use the appropriate metaphor. But the perpetuating of his innocence seems a condition of the perpetual dispensing of grace.

> For every man with his affects is born,
> Not by might mastered, but by special grace.

The best of intentions, if you endorse Berowne's counsel in *Love's Labour's Lost* (1.1.152f.), cannot stand against wilful inclination. The plot of that play seems to offer corroboration. In *Henry V,* it is the cool and temperate wind of grace that overblows the clouds of evil behaviour. (3.3.30–32) Failing grace, they would rain down contagion. The king's passion is subjected to grace, as are the wretches fettered in his prisons. (1.2.242f.) But it is, at least a question, how much credit is owing to the king. For a man cannot enlist the aid of grace, as he can compel to his support the aid of reason. Grace is not within his giving; and yet it is indispensable. Withhold it, and the wretches burst their fetters. In the Fray of Cupid and Apollo, lust and reason, an engraving described by Vasari and dated

1545, it is necessary for the Mind, a beautiful woman poised on the clouds above the battle, to illuminate and so to succour reason by the flame of divine wisdom. Without that intervention, reason would falter.[38] 'Our dull workings', of themselves inadequate, function only as they are informed by 'the grace, the sanctities of Heaven'. (2 Henry IV, 4.2.21f.)

Innocence, then, as it turns on the accession of grace, is kindred to good fortune. It is as fragile as fortune and as dependent for its life on caprice. 'You are in the state of grace,' says an impudent servant to Pandarus, in Troilus and Cressida. (3.1.15) He means, You are fortunate, in favour. On the other hand, a frustrated lover, in As You Like It, is necessarily content with scraps of favour, because he is 'in such a poverty of grace' (3.5.100), because, that is to say, he is so little lucky. Helena, in All's Well, will cure the king of his sickness, 'The great'st Grace lending grace'. (2.1.163) The proviso is crucial. It is always crucial, though Shakespeare rarely adverts to it, and for the very good reason that its felt presence is inimical to real drama.

Grace is the condition of survival. Man does not have the bestowing of grace. But perhaps the indispensable gratuity, on the face of it antipathetic to the spirit of drama, may be assimilated and made dramatic, at least in part. For the offering of grace is not niggardly but magnanimous; grace is open to all men. But how does it happen that only some men receive it? What does it mean, to be 'past grace'? Imogen, in Cymbeline (1.1.137), offers an explanation: 'Past hope, and in despair; that way, past grace'[39]. Apemantus, in Timon, sneers at a page who 'outruns't grace'. (2.2.91) Richard III, affecting the philosopher, is sententious: 'All unavoided is the doom of destiny.' He is answered by Queen Elizabeth: 'True, when avoided grace makes destiny.' (4.4.217f.) Survival is the accepting, destruction the eschewing of grace. Man is weak, but grace buttresses his weakness. And grace is his if he will have it. Therefore man, potentially, is strong. He falls, not of necessity, but as he turns from the help that is offered him. To retrieve or to maintain his innocence, he has only to cry grace.

But after all the argument, the attempt to bring what is whimsical within the limits of the play, is not altogether successful. Richard falls—and after him, Edmund—because he avoids what he ought to receive. What occasions the avoiding? How account for the folly that runs away from grace? And if the receiving of grace is interdicted by despair, how account for the despair? Lear adjures the wicked to cry grace. (3.2.58f.) He is one of the wicked himself. And grace is bestowed on him. But his antagonists never taste it. You may say that they do not want to. But that is to argue in a circle: why are they indifferent, or hostile? Albany turns back, and Cornwall goes forward: grace is given to the former, or accepted by him; it is withheld from the latter, or repudiated by him. But the giving and withholding, the accepting and repudiating, are equally capricious. No man of himself can justify himself. The common measure is not strength but debility.

None does offend, none, I say, none.[40]   (4.6.172)

That is why, in the emblem, the halt conduct the blind (as, in the play, the bedlam beggar has the leading of old Gloucester); why, in the fable, the lowly rat must enfranchise the lion.[41] All are blind, all are crippled.

> Their malady convinces
> The great assay of art.   (*Macbeth*, 4.3.142f.)

But 'the things which are impossible with men are possible with God' (Luke, xxviii.27) who, in His infinite whimsy, separates the elect from those who are devoted to death. It does not matter whether, disputing the current fashion, which makes Shakespeare a scholar of St. Thomas, you put away grace and choose another word in its room. The metaphor from theology has at least the merits of defining the random nature of those decisions on which the play turns. Who does not feel Angelo to be as guilty as Claudius? The attempt of each at repentance is essentially the same.

> —Heaven hath my empty words,
> Whilst my invention, hearing not my tongue,
> Anchors on Isabel. Heaven in my mouth,
> As if I did but only chew His name,
> And in my heart the strong and swelling evil
> Of my conception.   (*Measure for Measure*, 2.4.2–7)

Claudius is only more terse:

> My words fly up, my thought remain below.
> Words without thoughts never to Heaven go.   (*Hamlet*, 3.3.97f.)

But Claudius dies, presumably unregenerate. Angelo is redeemed. The decision, what to do with either, is the dramatist's alone, who plays Calvin's God. He looks down, as it were, and observes of the one:

> This my long sufferance and my day of grace
> They who neglect and scorn shall never taste;
> But hard be hardened, blind be blinded more,
> That they may stumble on, and deeper fall.

And, inscrutably, of the other:

> Once more I will renew
> His lapsèd powers, though forfeit and enthralled
> By sin to foul exorbitant desires.   (*Paradise Lost*, III.198–201, 175–7)

Lear's powers are renewed. The renewal, it is true, does not save his life, as it saves the life of Angelo. But the difference, and it is the great observable difference between comedy and tragedy, is not so crucial as it looks. The clearest gods, who make them honours of men's impossibilities, are said to have preserved Gloucester in his supposed fall from the cliffs. (4.6.73f.) They do not care, as it happens, ultimately to preserve him, or his master the king, as they do—to choose at random—Prospero and his daughter, who put to sea in the rotten carcass of a butt, and who are, for a wonder, transported safe to land. But they do bring Lear and Gloucester out of the darkness, where Edmund and the wicked sisters remain, and that, *sub specie aeternitatis,* is intervention enough, an act as merciful, or whimsical, as the staying of a tempest, the saving of a life. This is in it more than nature was ever conduct of. (*Tempest,* 5.1.243f.) Arbitrariness remains at the heart of the play.

NOTES

[1] Gabriele Rollenhagio, *Nucleus Emblematum Selectissimorum,* Cologne, 1611, Sig. C1v, glosses the emblem of skull, sceptre, and farm tool: 'Mors sceptra ligonibus aequat. Le sceptre E le hoyau sont en leur fin semblables, Payants egal tribut aux Parques redoutables; Car qui pourra dire, que ce crane hideux, Ait esté d'un paisan, ou d'un Roy genereux?'

[2] Quoted in Patrick Cruttwell, *The Shakespearean Movement,* New York, 1960, p. 123.

[3] J. A. K. Thomson, *Shakespeare and the Classics,* London, 1952, p. 113, drawing on T. W. Baldwin, traces the saying to Palingenius, whose astronomical text, *Zodiacus Vitae,* was the most popular treatise of its kind in the Renaissance. The idea is a commonplace. It occurs in Juan Vives and, ultimately, in the *Satyricon* of Petronius.

[4] *Lasciva caro, peccatum, morsque.*

[5] Fulke Greville, *Caelica,* sonnet 86. See also Wisdom, vii.3,5; Florio's Montaigne (*Essayes,* London, 1603), i.107; Holland's Pliny, vii, Proem, edn. 1601, p. 152, cited in Kenneth Muir's Arden edition of *King Lear* (1957), p. 181n.

[6] With 3.4.105, cf. Hebrews, ii.6.

[7] *The Merchant of Venice,* 1.1.77. Jaques' famous speech in *As You Like It,* 2.7.139–65, is a parallel utterance.

[8] Rollenhagio, Sigs. B4r–v, glosses his emblem of the fly and the candle: 'Cosi vivo piacer conduce a morte. La douce volupté peste de nostre vie, Est de mille peinnes E mille maux suyvie, Car un poure amoureux semblable a un flabeau, Se consume soy mesme, E se mene au tombeau.' Daniel Heinsius, *Emblemata Aliquot Amartoria,* ?1613, Sig. F1r, p. 32, gives a similar emblem.

[9] Prospero, in *The Tempest,* 5.1.25–27, is the comparable case.

[10] Camillo's office and understanding, in *The Winter's Tale,* 4.2.8f., parallels Kent's.

[11] Sig. F2 f7v in Thomas Palfreyman, *The Treatise of Heauenly Philosophie,* London, 1578.

[12] R. W. Chambers, *King Lear,* Glasgow, 1940, p. 48, in a fine phrase, sees Gloucester as climbing the Mountain of Purgatory, and—levying on Keats—the play itself as a Vale of Soul-Making.

[13] In an emblem by Rollenhagio, no. 28: 'Vixtrix patientia duri'), a tree grows despite the board that blocks its progress. The gloss, Sig. B2r: 'De mesme que tu vois une palme umbrageuse, Contre le pesant faix se dresser genereause: Ainsi par patience, on dompte le malheur, Et de luy triomphant, on en reste vainqueur.'

[14] *Vincit qui patitur.* So Geoffrey Whitney, *A Choice of Emblemes, and Other Devices,* Leyden, 1586, Sig. e2v, p. 220, moralizes the fable of the oak and the weeds, bent before the storm. See also Philippe Desprez, *Le Theatre des animaux,* Paris, 1620, p. 92: 'Endurer, quand on ne peut mieux'; and Rollenhagio emblem 23, 'Patior, vt potiar'. The gloss, Sig. B1v: 'Qui veut donc recevoir quelque contentement, Il faut premier le mal porter patiemment.' Heinsius, *Amateoria,* Sig. C3r, p. 21, uses the same legend for an emblem of Cupid (who replaces the bear in Rollenhagio's emblem) taking honey from a tree.

[15] Samuel C. Chew, *The Virtues Reconciled: An Iconographic Study,* Toronto, 1947, pp. 126–8.

[16] Isabella's prayer, *Measure for Measure,* 5.1.115f., anticipates Gloucester's: 'Then, O you blessed ministers above, Keep me in patience.'

[17] See also 3.2.37f.

[18] With 4.2.51, cf. Matthew, v.39.

[19] *The French Academie,* p. 149

[20] The story of Egmont's retainers and their taunting of Cardinal Granvelle is given in John Lothrop Motley, *The Rise of the Dutch Republic,* London, 3 vols., n.d., I, 387. See also Florio's Montaigne, iii.284, 298, iv.19, quoted Muir, p. 252. Erasmus, in *The Praise of Folly,* plays on the ambiguity of the word, *fool.*

Enid Welsford, *The Fool: His Social and Literary History*, London, 1935? New York, n.d., treats of it exhaustively.

[21] *The French Academie*, p. 148.

[22] I Corinthians, xii.23–24. And see 'Tous peuvent servir au besoin' in Desprez, Sig. B2v, p. 12, for the fable of the lion and the hare, in which the passage from Corinthians is applied.

[23] Ovid, *Metamorphoses*, Lib. viii, Fab. iv.97. And see Matthew, xxv.34–36.

[24] *Ex nihilo nihil fit.* See 1.1.90, and Muir, p. 9n.

[25] In Titian's 'Sacred and Profane Love' (*c.* 1515, Galleria Borghese), the nakedness of 'Felicità Eterna' (Ficino's *Venere Celeste* or eternal beauty) denotes her contempt for perishable earthly things. The handsome and costly dress of 'Felicità Breve' (Ficino's *Venere Volgare* or evanescent beauty) is emblematic of the ephemerality of mundane things. See Erwin Panofsky, *Studies in Iconology*, New York, 1939, fig. 108. and p. 150.

[26] *Levitas secura.* See Rollenhagio, emblem 74, glossed Sig. Dlr: 'Omnia mea mecum porto.'

[27] Thomas Nashe, *Anatomie of Absurditie*, *Works*, ed. McKerrow, I, 34; cited E. Taylor, 'Lear's Philosopher', *Shakespeare Quarterly*, VI, 1955, 364.

[28] See also William Strachey's sonnet, 'Oh Sejanus': 'How high a Poore man showes in low estate Whose Base is firme, and whole Frame competent, That sees this *Cedar*, made the Shrub of Fate, Th' on's little, lasting; Th' others confluence spent'; quoted Muir, p. xxiii. In Marlow's *Edward II*, Mortimer, just before his fall, likens himself to '*Ioues* huge tree', to whom all others are shrubs, II. 2579f. Mario Praz, *Studies in Seventeenth-Century Imagery*, 2. vols., London, 1939, I, 201, cites Horace, *Odes*, II, x, 11, 12; and Ovid, *Rem. Am.*, 370.

[29] *The French Academie*, p. 150.

[30] Caroline F. E. Spurgeon, *Shakespeare's Imagery and What It Tells Us*, New York, 1935, p. 33.

[31] The apposite illustration is in Furmer, *The Use and Abuse of Wealth*, first pub. in Latin, 1575, and trans. into Dutch by Coornhert, 1585, p. 6; given in Henry Green, *Shakespeare and the Emblem Writers*, London, 1870, p. 489. *Timon of Athens*, in its constant exalting of the poor above the rich, is a long gloss on the sense of the emblem.

[32] *Richard II*, 2.1.270. Rollenhagio, Sig. Blv, glosses his emblem of grain growing from a skull: 'Mors vitae initium. Come un grain de froument, dans la terre mourant, En renaissant produict maint espi blondissant; Ainsi l-homme iuste par sa mort naturelle, Commence a vivre heureux une vie eternella.'

[33] See J. J. Boissard, *Emblematum Liber*, Metz, 1588, Sig. E4r, p. 39: 'In morte vita'; and *Spes Altera Vitae*, in Camerarius, edn. 1595, emblem 100, pt. I, p. 102; given in Green, p. 184.

[34] See also Willard Farnham, *The Medieval Heritage of Elizabethan Tragedy*, Berkeley, 1936, p. 452: 'Lear loses the world only to save his soul'; and Matthew, xvi.25. Rollenhagio, Sig. C14, glosses emblem 45 of a child and skull with the words: 'Ce qui perit renaist.' In Titian's 'Sacred and Profane Love', Cupid, who is placed near the figure of Venus Volgare, the generative goddess, stirs a fountain that is really an ancient sarcophagus. Once it held a corpse; now it is the spring of life. See *Stud. in Icon.*, p. 152, fig. 108. And so to T. S. Eliot.

[35] Freitag appends to his emblem of the phoenix the quotation from Ephesians, iv.22. See *Mythologica Ethica*, 1579; and Green, p. 381. The phoenix is reborn in Desprez, *Le Theatre*, p. 103; Boissard, *Emblematum Liber*, Metz, 1588, Sig. F4r, p. 47; Whitney, *Emblemes*, Sig. Z1r, p. 177 (in Green, p. 387); and on the t.p. and again on the verso of the colophon, in each case with the motto 'Semper Eadem', in *La Pittvra di Leonbattista Alberti Tradotta per M. Lodovico Domenichi*, Venice, 1547. The t.p. moralizes the emblem with the phrase, 'De la mia morte Eterna Vita I Vivo'. Green, pp. 380–90, lists references to the phoenix as an emblem of redemption in Shakespeare, in his contemporaries, and in older writers.

[36] The eagle illustrates the legend, 'Renovata Iuventus', in Camerarius, emblem 34, 'ex Volatilibus', in Green, p. 369. And see Psalms, ciii.5.

[37] Jacob de '[Angermundt] Bruck, *Emblemata Moralia & Bellica*, 1615, emblem 12.

[38] The engraving, after Baccio Bandinelli, is reproduced in *Stud. in Icon.*, fig. 107. The Florentine neo-Platonism of Ficino is adduced as a gloss: 'For reason can conquer the flames of man's lower nature only by turning to a higher authority for enlightenment.'

[39] J. M. Nosworthy, editing the New Arden *Cymbeline*, notes that commentators have detected in this passage an allusion to Calvin's doctrine of election. 'It is unlikely that these bear any relation to Shakespeare's own religious convictions.' (Pp. 10f.n.) But surely the attempt here is to get clear of Calvin's doctrine, and to make explicable the dispensing or withholding of grace.

[40] See Romans, iii.23.

[41] See (for the halt and the blind) *Emblemes d'Alciat*, Sig. N2r, p. 195; Whitney, *Emblemes*, sig. I1r, p. 65; and (for the fable of the rat and the lion) Desprez, Sig. A3v, p. 6.

Rosalie L. Colie

LIMITS OF THE PASTORAL
PATTERN IN *KING LEAR*

As Maynard Mack has said in his provocative book on the play,[1] *King Lear* is an enormous anti-pastoral, a reversal of the usual pastoral correspondence between the shepherd and his peaceful environment. Yes and no: it is, certainly, in its unpastoral, even anti-pastoral, stress on violence and savagery, a reversal of the pastoral tone, an inversion of many traditions within the pastoral modes. But at the same time it maintains many elements of the pastoral pattern: this *is*, as a generation of students has learned from Theodore Spencer and E. M. W. Tillyard and their faithful *epigoni*, a correspondence between Lear's mental state and the meteorological conditions of his world—it is the ideology that is reversed, not the convention of pastoral; the decorum, not the device. Certainly, in Lear's wild nature, we are not led to expect reformation or recovery: precisely its *lack* of nurturing capacity distinguishes the nature of *King Lear* from the pastoral norm.

In true pastoral, however disordered nature might appear, nonetheless if a shepherd died or a shepherdess rejected his love, seasonal regeneration is consistently invoked to promise redress of present imbalance. Not so here: chaos is come, and nature gives no indication of future reconstitution, even promise of the seasonal round. All the same, there is a sense in which the storm gives comfort to the desperate King, even in its denial to him of a comforting antidote to his condition: in just its wildness and intractability, nature seems to Lear indifferent throughout to human fate, but sympathetic in providing him with a dramatic background tonally appropriate to his mood and his mental state. Like Lear, to whom he is often likened, Prospero was extruded from his sovereignty, though, we must note, that deed was done in secret; by means of his art, Prospero entered into intimacies with nature which enabled him to promote total restoration of the human and social disorders of his environment. Prospero's sojourn in nature involved an *otium* very active indeed: Lear's self-chosen abandonment of kingly duty and royal *negotium* left him (literally) without resources. In *King Lear*, too, there is no such inscrutable, backdoor solution to the exile's critical condition: his daughters

From *Shakespeare's Living Art* (Princeton: Princeton University Press, 1974), pp. 303–16.

are open in their persecution, he is open in his flight from the persecuting, peripatetic court. And nature is correspondingly open in this play. The storm proclaims extremity over the whole region: Regan sees it coming, and men publicly recognize its bitter significance for the old King. Though he runs out into the terrible night clad in his regalia, Lear has none of the protection offered by Prospero's cloak; he meets nature undefended and resourceless.

The nature which receives King Lear, which receives the reduced Edgar, is even more niggardly than the rocky wilderness to which Belarius fled with his charges. In *Cymbeline*, wild creatures may have threatened the boys, but they learned to hunt them for food. In *King Lear*, the wild creatures, as Albany says, are all human, and they do the hunting until it seems to Albany that "Mankind preys upon itself." In contrast to its mysterious, unlocated, pursuing court, *King Lear* offers a nature bare, hard, unpeopled, unresponsive, a nature as reduced as are the human beings it entertains, a nature pared down to its most abstract qualities, an ecology indifferent to its inhabitants. Nonetheless, it is a nature appropriately arranged to correspond to human beings concerned exclusively with extremity: it is an absolute, a stoic landscape.[2] We cannot even frame questions about life on this heath, so abstracted it is: did Edgar actually eat newt and toad, like Macbeth's witches? How was Lear nourished, if at all, Lear, who in the old world cried for his dinner the moment he came in from hunting? This heath is too stark for such workaday considerations; this heath is, simply, the minimal ground for existence, the plainest possible area on which men may work out such justifications as they can for their bare existence.

But even in this, Shakespeare has covertly offered us one comfort inherent in the thematics of pastoral: such nature as we have in this play is invoked in relation to Lear and the Lear party. The storm is an unmetaphored metaphor for *Lear's* state of mind—no natural parallel is offered, for the equally turbulent and far crueler minds of his daughters. However askew the "natures" in question, external and human, it is only to Lear and his friends that even an adumbrated suggestion is vouchsafed of the contact possible between man and nature. Thus, on the heath, where the playwright makes no effort to delineate a specific natural landscape (such as was provided in the harsh cave of *Cymbeline*), he does offer a fit landscape all the same for a debate so crucial and so abstract as that on the nature of man. All the pastoral words are critical in this play: "nature," "natural," "unnatural," "kind," "kindness," "unkind," "unkindness," "generous" and "ungenerous" recur, as each scene reveals more evidence for the question's consideration. But rarely are these words used in connection with landscape, and never in connection with a possible pastoral nurturing scene. It is with human nature that the play concerns itself, and the metaphoric, supportive thematic possibilities of "nature" are correspondingly reduced.

Nonetheless, as Maynard Mack has said, the pastoral pattern *is* in this play, which also investigates, at a level far deeper than the customary, more overt pastoral debate, the problems of nature and nurture, of court and country, of human kind, kindness, and unkindness, which are classically themes of the pastoral mode. First of all, in *King Lear* civilization itself is called into question, far more radically than in Leontes' Sicily or Cymbeline's Britain. In *King Lear,* neither nature nor nurture turns out to have much to do with kindness: family offers no guarantees, nor is there a recognizable generic gentility either. Edmund had been "out" nine years—that is, his father, like Oliver's brother, had not proffered him a nobleman's training. We might on these grounds incline to excuse his parody of courtly behavior, but no such excuse can be found for Goneril and Regan, to say nothing of Cornwall and even of the Duke of Burgundy, all bred to their station. If they "should" have performed better in a world of gentility, why then, so "should" Lear have done; in terms of protocol, even his good daughter is rude (though her silence makes her seem polite, in contrast to her father's response to that silence).[3]

"Nature" means different things to different people in this play, as fine commentators have taught us. Edmund invokes nature as his authority for the dog-eat-dog life upon which he sets out; Lear invokes an equally heartless nature when he curses Goneril with the sterility he, too late, wished he had had himself; later, he invokes the Lucretian version of Epicurean nature in his remarks upon universal generation. Kent and the nameless Gentleman note that the natural tempest is too great for human "nature" to bear; Gloucester takes nature to be simply fate, a cryptic determiner of man's destiny. No one in this play thinks of appealing to a generous, nourishing, supportive nature; only in the play's *structure* can we see a remnant of this philosophical view of nature's relation to mankind.[4] We hear and see much of what is both natural and unnatural, kind and unkind; again and again, characters consider birth and breeding. The bond of kind is variously recognized: by Gloucester in the play's opening exchange; by Cordelia in her stiff, limited, but absolute answer to Gloucester in II.i; in Lear's appeal to his second daughter's "kindness," the "bonds of childhood" due him now. "Breeding" is both the biological begetting of a child (as Gloucester speaks of Edmund, and Cordelia of her father's having bred her) and the bringing-up, the nurture and education, of that child. In Edmund's case, for instance, Gloucester was responsible for "breeding" in the first sense and utterly failed his responsibilities in the second. The same may have been true of Lear, although all we know from the play is that his elder daughters were not brought up to be what he had wished. The First Servant, loyal to an order of nature higher than Cornwall's, speaks of his service to the Duke "since I was a child," and was spoken of as having been "bred" or brought up by Cornwall—but all the same, in spite of that environment, the Servant has roots in kind and kindness which Cornwall clearly never put down. A narrower view of things (such as Regan's) responds with shock to the Servant's treatment of Cornwall, but we, with our attention drawn to the deeper implications of breeding, may well wonder how the Servant's sense of values was as true as it was. Kent marvels at Lear's get, that "one self mate and make" could "beget such different issues"; and Lear marvels, too, even to considering the possibility, only dimly fantasized, that he had been cuckolded by his wife. Rather a cuckold, then, than to have fathered from his own loins such unkindness.

Class and caste are in this play no warranties of courtesy, kindness, or gentleness, whatever the derivations of these words may suggest: the Fool asks if a madman be a gentleman or a yeoman, implying insanity's democracy; from Tom we hear, and in Edmund we perceive, that the Prince of Darkness is a gentleman. Certainly this would appear true enough, as we watch the blinding of an earl by a duke, his guest, hear Edmund claiming so brutally his "rank" against an unknown challenger, see Goneril and Regan harry their father into despair like the wolfish sheepdogs they are. In the world of rank and privilege, the world by tradition called "gentle," there is considerable reassurance in hearing Kent assert to a stranger-gentleman his own gentle birth and breeding, his actions so clearly corroborating the point. As a gentleman, through a gentleman, he sends his message offstage to that symbol for truth and gentleness, the lady Cordelia.

No wonder, then, that amidst all this whirligig of custom, behavior, and ideas, King Lear becomes obsessed with the idea of "breeding," lawful and unlawful. Tom keeps the notion alive for him in his own talk of Pillicock, and for us in Gloucester's incorporation of "the foul fiend Flibbertigibbet," "a walking fire," as he enters with a lantern as an emblem of his old self, burning in lust. Lear's great speeches later, in iv.vi, on lechery and adultery, reach a thematic crescendo of all this material: everything goes to 't, from the small gilded fly to great ladies. Epicurean nature, unnatural only in its obsessive singleness of purpose, justifies for the moment all that Lear must undergo. Though these are the clichés of Renaissance naturalism, for Lear as for Edgar, behavior so limited to the naturalistic comes to seem, simply, monstrous, below and thus beyond the capacities of human beings. "Down from the waist they are centaurs, / Though women all above" draws one line of that mounting appeal to concepts and images of monstrousness, savagery, and preda-tion so constant through the play. That monstrousness is harbored in the hearts of great ones is irony enough, but that (as in *The Winter's Tale*) such savagery should cluster in the place traditionally at the center of civilization, at court, whence law, courtesy, graciousness traditionally emanate, compounds the bitterness of Lear's situation. Men are beasts; of these beasts, courtiers are particularly savage; of courtiers, the greatest are the most brutal. It is part of Edgar's disguise, not of his fundamental nature, to say of himself that he was (like those left at the court) "hog in sloth, fox in stealth, wolf in greediness, dog in madness, lion in prey." Like Guiderius', Edgar's self-disgust at these animal qualities in him speaks through the lines.

The pattern of predation—the pattern Jaques sentimentalized over and Cym-beline's sons follow as a matter of survival—is reversed in this play, to offer yet another version of the play's anti-pastoralism. At the same time, the nearly un-bearable inhumanity at the center of power reinforces the very myth exemplified in pastoral drama, that civilization brings corruption and cruelties from which the only refuge is nature, a countryside beyond the reach of such uncreatural sophis-tications. In *King Lear*, good men are proclaimed outlaws, and the only "nature" for them to flee to is the last resort of the affliction, exiled, and persecuted, a landscape so inhospitable that no one else will inhabit it, so hard and uncompromising that it can offer solace (if that is what mere "philosophers" are offered) only to the mind.

The self-acknowledged tempest in Lear's mind is such that he does not seem to have missed the roof he has abjured; but both Fool and Kent realize the insufficiency of the shelter they find, prefer it though they do to the "hard house" from which they have been barred. In the hovel the Fool (a natural) and the King (who has acknowledged and will again acknowledge his folly) find an emblem of their own and all human misfortune, a man evidently so reduced in wits, social status, and material condition that to them he appears literally a "naked soul," "the thing itself, unaccommodated man." As we know, Edgar-Tom has deliberately erased in himself all visible characteristics of his early life, has chosen the role and the condition of social outcast, bedlamite and beggar. In the topsy-turvydom in which he is trying simply to survive, to be safe at all Edgar must undertake a condition normally, in the real world, quite unsafe. But such is the situation of this play that only as outcast, only as outlaw, can he find protection against human beings turned beasts of prey. From this figure of Tom, the real Fool flees as from a savage creature or a fiend. The destitute King, however, moves toward him at once, as if recognizing in this new outcast a case of his own kind. The speed with which Lear turns to philosophizing on the nature of man is at once a naturalistic sign of his intelligence, even when under the siege of the madness he so feared. Edgar is the emblematic figure for such discussion, its subject and its illustration. In his scanty costume[5] he actualizes Lear's earlier generalization about "naked wretches" with "homeless heads and unfed sides," with the "loop'd and window'd raggedness." With the guise and garb of madness, Edgar reduces himself by another level, to the "worst" of all social conditions.

Certainly, the heath scenes are of the utmost importance in the play's consideration of "man"—who is, as Lear says, "no more than this." No more than *what?* We know, as Lear does not, who and what Edgar actually is. Whatever he may seem, he is not the unaccommodated man Lear takes him for, but rather is disaccommodated, in much the way Lear himself is. Edgar was *someone,* and though he has had to exchange his identity for a role, he remains throughout someone far more complex and significant than his role characterizes. Emblematically, the question is valid enough: is man no more than this?—than a self-deposed, dispossessed king and rejected father, cut off from his family, his environment, his society, from all the holdfasts he had ever known? than a court Fool, never so foolish and never so great as when choosing to follow his master into the wilderness? a man, then, designated as a "natural" in a specific and limiting sense? or, than a disguised madman, destitute like the King and like the King ejected from a highly privileged position in the deference society into which he was born. All three of these are certainly at the extremity of their experience. And more: we are brought to feel that their extremity is the limit of human suffering as well—and yet not one of these figures is unambiguously what he seems, no one is the reduced human being hypothesized in Lear's speech about the poor naked wretches. The pastoral conventions of disguise work even here, in this extraordinarily hard-pastoral scene. These men are not what they seem, to the audience or to each other—what they *are* beyond their appearances is what is important, valuable, even great about "human nature."

Just this very ambiguity, unstressed and unforced, points to the deeply problematical in human nature—in a man's relation to himself, and in his relations to anyone else in his world. The reduction of any man to "the thing itself" forces us to consider those systems, institutions, and habits which keep any man from being simply human: as in the frankly pastoral plays with which these chapters are concerned, As You Like It, The Winter's Tale, Cymbeline, The Tempest, we must draw on our ideas of the relations between nature and nurture, between man and his environment, his culture, his civilization. In King Lear, the naturals before our eyes, those extreme figures of basic if stripped and warped humanity, cast and self-cast as moral emblems of necessity and destitution, are exposed as the absolute human minimum and displayed against a background of minimum nature as well. We are forced to think not only of the relation to humankind of external nature, but of the importance (at court, in the country, anywhere at all) of human kindness, the only quality distinguishing man from beast. We see it, startlingly, working even in the perverted court, as Gloucester's servants seek homely remedies for their master's eye-sockets; we see it in the country, as the tenant helps his landlord and the frightening "naked one" with him; we see it on the heath, in Lear's "In, boy, in." Much later, at the other end of the social scale from servant, peasant, and outcast, we see it in Cordelia's remarkable charity[6] and unquestioning forgiveness, for a moment sufficient counterbalance to the planned ferocity of her court-bound sisters.

Between these charities, themselves set within a frame of shocking savagery spontaneous and premeditated, is set the animate debate on the nature of man, on human nakedness, and naked humanity. Is man no more than this? In his rags, self-mutilated,[7]Edgar-Tom stands for "this," nearly an animal and yet, as Lear sees, independent of the creatures as well ("Thou ow'st the sheep no wool, the cat no perfume"). At the bottom of the human scale, isolated, aloof, Edgar-Tom is nonetheless human—he stands out like a man from his stark environment. So reduced, Edgar bears a wry, comforting message underneath his horrifying report on human degradation. After all the earlier talk of gorgeousness and garments, the handy-dandy with garb and attribute already displayed on the stage with Edgar, Kent, Lear, and the Fool, the two-facedness of the powerful and the seekers after power, it comes as a relief to think, if only for a moment, of man irreducible, or man as "poor, bare, forked animal," "no more than this."

Extremity forces Lear to philosophy, and he then attributes philosophy to his speculative stimulus, Tom, his figure for extremity, "this philosopher," "good Athenian," "this same learned Theban." Not only has the association of madness with philosophy to do with the long tradition, exemplified in both the Fool and in Lear himself, of docta ignorantia, idiotes, and holy folly, but it derives as well from the stoical and cynical defenses of man as properly naked and poor, properly delivered from "accommodation."[8] Lear's recognition of Tom as a man is symbolic of his recognition of kind: men had argued for centuries that a minimal humanity be recognized as equally human as the greatest urbanite. In the pseudo-Lucianic dialogue The Cynic, as Edgar-figure debates the merits of an extremely hard pastoral morality against an agora-type, Lycinus, a representative of urbs, civitas, and negotium. Lycinus opens the dialogue by asking,[9]

You there, why in heaven's name have you the beard and the long hair, but no shirt? Why do you expose your body to view, and go barefooted, adopting by choice this nomadic anti-social and bestial life? Why unlike all others do you abuse your body by ever inflicting on it what it likes least, wandering around and prepared to sleep anywhere at all on the hard ground, so that your old cloak carries about a plentiful supply of filth, though it was never fine or soft or gay?

The figure so garbed is the Cynic, who as Lycinus says, is "no better than the paupers who beg for their daily bread."[10] The Cynic invites his interlocutor to enter with him upon what is essentially a debate on reason and deed. "What need one?" Regan had asked, about Lear's servants. The Cynic would have been, for quite different reasons from hers, on Regan's side: his feet are more suited to their function, he says, than the average man's, likewise the rest of his body, made stronger by his diet (this is "the food that comes first to hand"—Edgar's "swimming frog, the toad, the todpole, the wall-newt, and the water"). Lycinus complains of the Cynic's habits: like a dog, or like Tom, he eats whatever he finds and sleeps on straw. The Cynic then demonstrates that the clothes Lycinus wears scarce keep him warm, that his rich food and fine house merely publish his greed.[11] The Cynic goes on to say, as if providing an epigraph for this play,[12]

> Gold and silver may I not need, neither I nor any of my friends. For from the desire for these grow up all men's ills—civic strife, wars, conspiracies, and murders. All these have as their fountainhead the desire for more. But may this desire be far from us, and never may I reach out for more than my share, but be able to put up with less than my share.

The paradigm of sufficiency, material and moral, lies behind another element fully exploited in this play, the working-out in the play's action of those Renaissance restatements of the stoic paradoxes designed to question the material requirements of civilized society. The Cynic offers another point of reference for the connection of physical endurance with moral strength, a question debated, illustrated, and counter-illustrated throughout King Lear. Considering the background to all this talk of stripping, we must acknowledge anew that the pastoral skeleton of this play has indeed been stripped of its Arcadian lendings. As in the prose epic from which he took such a significant part of this play's fiction, Shakespeare has used the notion of Arcadia allusively, to force the memory and the meaning of pastoral nature as a norm against which, our awareness tripped of its presence here, we can measure the barbarity of the play's dominant predatory culture. The bare bones of the pastoral paradigm and of pastoral ideology support the many other intellectual and literary elements given voice in King Lear: without apology, and without customary generic cryptic coloration, the pattern and its themes are developed throughout. Perhaps the pastoral ideas are the stronger here for their very reticence. Another decorum, a nature either so uncompromising or so un-compromised as to be anti-pastoral, offers the ground—the scene, the costume, the language—for this ultimate confrontation of men with a nature so harsh that most men choose never to acknowledge its existence.

But "kindness" is not simply the recognition of humanity so schematically presented on the heath; it is also the acknowledgment of humanity's needs, such as the "naked fellow's" kindness to Gloucester in seeming at once to do the old man's will and at the same time preventing the self-destruction he sought. Edgar shifts, even here, from role to role,[13] the more easily for his father's blindness; but his symbolic affirmation of humanity's kindness is the greater because of his anonymity to his father onstage and his specific identity of disavowed son, known to the audience watching. In the scene at Dover cliffs, the dramaturgy expresses with wonderful economy the generosity exchanged which, in Sidney's prose version, had all to be described and explained in a long, rhetorical narrative by the Paphlagonian king. In keeping with his technique elsewhere, here too the playwright has condensed radically, called on his whole technical vocabulary of poetics and stagecraft to enrich his model. As with Cordelia's behavior to her father, Edgar's relation to Gloucester expresses both the enormous complexity and the basic simplicity of human connections. Through these specific characters, in this specific situation, we know general human needs and how they can be coped with; we see that in human beings, such recognition draws forth specific, appropriate responses of human support.

In Gloucester's suicide-attempt, we have the emblematic enactment of what we have earlier sensed in the heath-scene, with its debate of kind. The old man seeks his (unstoical) death, but learns—a surprise to him, a surprise to us—stoicism after all. As in the case of Antaeus, Gloucester's gesture of self-abandonment to natural forces, to nature itself, restores his strength. He rises from his grotesque contact with the earth capable of endurance, capable of life, and (how unlikely this is!) capable even of further moral growth and insight. His gesture, flinging himself down upon the earth,[14] makes graphic the symbolic content of the earlier, differently visual debate: however unyielding and unresponsive, nature in this play nonetheless offers to human beings a rigorous, severe, but reliable support.

His suicide thwarted, Gloucester is shortly brought to face, in the King running mad, another man's resolution to the same predicament that had brought him to the edge of suicide. Blind man and madman must somehow recognize in each other their own and each other's human extremity and, through their mutilated perception, somehow communicate that recognition of common humanity. Gloucester must, as Lear says, "look with [his] ears"; and, though he cannot see the King's mad parody of Whitsun pastoral festivity ("fantastically dressed with weeds"), Gloucester knows soon enough who it is that speaks so. Lear too has run back again into "nature"—to a natural scene, though, very different from the barren heath on which he met unaccommodated man. Now, as we learn from Cordelia, the weeds are tall, and "our sustaining corn" is highgrown for the harvest—so high that it is easy to lose the King in the fields. Lear himself speaks in this scene in pastoral terms, and Gloucester refers to his "nature." "No, they cannot touch me for coining," Lear says cunningly; "I am the King himself"—that is, whatever artificial kings may have sprung up in Britain, only he is irrevocably royal, by birth and breeding, whose right it is to sanction mintage. Then, by a verbal leap which nonetheless demonstrates that "reason in madness" his hearers recognize, he adds the classical judgement of the pastoral *paragone:* "Nature's above art in that respect." He is, then, intrinsically the King. No counterfeit, of coinage or of kingship, will do. The arts and crafts of those who usurp his position are no more than those artifices held up to criticism and for rejection in the pastoral rivalry of nature with art—mere imitation, mere fancy, mere illusion.

Gloucester's response to the King's words—"O ruin'd piece of nature!"—presses us past the proud assumptions of Lear's assertion of nature's supremacy to art: nature decays, after all. Whatever else has happened in this play, the King powerful in kindness and in wrath has vanished, leaving only this ridiculous, farcical figure, singing through the fields to recall in disjointed phrases the force, for good and for ill, once characteristic of Lear. Natural king he is still, but in a sense other than the one he chooses to honor: he is now a natural fool of fortune. Gloucester is equally a ruined piece of nature (as Lear cruelly perceives), restored by his faith-keeping son only to perish in mixed joy and sorrow when he learns that his guide has been, after all, that dutiful child. The two old men are emblematic too: standing, manifestly at the depth of their lives, in the open fields, and all the same the better for their exposure to the elements, the storm, the heath, and the Dover cliffs, the better for their confrontation with each other in the wheatfield. It is true that Lear is now finally mad, but relieved thereby of some of his worst anguish and about to be rewarded by the fantastic forgiveness of his kind daughter. Like Lear in the storm and on the heath, Gloucester too has touched the bottom of his nature at the imagined cliffside; Edgar like his elders has emerged from the philosophical demonstration on the heath to resume, by degrees, his function and his identity. He works through his remaining family obligations, reordering his disordered kin as he rescues his father and punishes his brother, ready at last to undertake the social responsibilities laid on him at the play's end. Lear, Gloucester, Edgar: all three touch natural reality at its farthest remove from their normal lives, and build back from that contact to a renewed, if painfully qualified, understanding of their own humanity and the nature of humankind. The hard pastoral of this play, with its rigid version of irreducible nature, serves them as the pastoral interlude serves Rosalind and her father, as his pastoral interlude serves Prospero, his daughter, and the others, or as theirs serves Perdita, Florizel, and Sicily and Bohemia as well. From such contact with nature, men gain strength to re-enter the world of their inheritance. *King Lear's* nature is geologically and emotionally hard, like the rocky space that serves its pastoral function in *Cymbeline,* where the landscape supports death as readily as life, and is designed to train men for exceptional undertakings. Nature in *King Lear* is far harsher and more inhospitable than Belarius' cave-nature, however: in *King Lear,* the characters find nature no less hard than the "hard house" which Lear fled and where Gloucester lost his eyes, but its reliable neutrality and consistency offer support to exiles nonetheless. This nature, unlike the human beings in their lives, does not persecute men, even in their extremity; indeed, for all its forbidding severity, this nature, like the conventional pastoral vacation, offers men pressed to the utmost another chance to recover their sense of reality and their sense of themselves.

Lear is right, of course. The elements are not organized along familial lines:

Nor rain, wind, thunder, fire, are my daughters:
I tax you not, you elements, with unkindness;
I never gave you kingdom, call'd you children,
You owe me no subscription.   (III.ii.15–18)

Mad as the speech sounds, it says something very important about the play's underlying schemes. Nature affords man a sufficiency, his life—no more than that, but that. Whatever else a man have, achieve, receive, or acquire, he must get from human beings, from himself and from others, must build from his social awareness. The last eclipses of the sun and moon have nothing whatever to do with generational conflicts or with a man's dealing with his friends; the harvest of this play is not of the sustaining corn through which the mad Lear runs, but of great figures dead of violence and heartbreak. Nature is not the "opportunity" with which Edmund's invocation equates her, as we watch the opportunists go down with the generous. Cornwall, Oswald, Regan, Goneril, Edmund, all die with their moral betters, and die in ways fitting their contempt of law, of custom, and of emotional claim. Nature simply *is*, as the stoics conceived of the matter, offering the support only of her stringent simplicity. And yet the play is paradoxical, in this as in so much else: from contacts with this inhospitable, inhuman, remote nature, maimed men are able to reassert their humanity and their kindness in the face of nearly insuperable emotional odds, and to draw (even in madness) on their own persistent human-kindness. To those who have the wit to risk themselves to nature's handling, this hard-pastoral nature offers the benefits of hardness—uncomfortable, barren, and unyielding support to those who can recognize it for what it is, and can take it.

NOTES

[1] Mack, King Lear *in Our Time* (Berkeley, 1965); and Nancy R. Lindheim, *"King Lear* as Pastoral Tragedy," *Some Facets of* King Lear, ed. Rosalie L. Colie and F. T. Flahiff (Toronto, 1974).

[2] For Lear's stoicism, see William Elton, King Lear *and the Gods* (San Marino, 1966), pp. 97–107, 272–76, and the literature cited. Cf. Seneca, *Medea*, 426–28 ("Sola est quies, /mecum ruina cuncta si video obruta; / mecum omnia abeant"), for an analogue to Lear's relation to nature.

[3] For Cordelia's speech, see Sheldon P. Zitner, *"King Lear* and Its Language," *Some Facets;* and Emily W. Leider, "Plainness of Style in *King Lear," Shakespeare Quarterly,* xxi (1970), 45–53.

[4] Paul J. Alper's *"King Lear* and the Theory of the 'Sight Pattern,' " *In Defense of Reading,* ed. Reuben A. Brower and Richard Poirier (New York, 1963), pp. 133–52, deals with the primacy of feeling over understanding, as does Lindheim, op. cit.

[5] Maurice Charney, "Nakedness in King Lear," *Some Facets.*

[6] Cf. Sears R. Jayne, "Charity in King Lear," *Shakespeare 400,* ed. James G. McManaway (New York, 1964), pp. 277–88.

[7] Cf. Zitner, *"King Lear* and Its Language."

[8] For material on holy folly, see Walter Kaiser, *Praisers of Folly* (Cambridge, Mass., 1963), chapter 1; and Rosalie L. Colie, *Paradoxia Epidemica* (Princeton, 1966), Introduction, and chapter 15.

[9] Lucian, "The Cynic" (*Works,* Loeb Classical Library), viii, 381.

[10] Lucian, vIII, 383.

[11] Lucian, vIII, 397–99; and Lucretius, v, 1423–29.

[12] Lucian, vIII, 405.

[13] Cf. Zitner, "Language"; and Thomas F. Van Laan, "Acting and Action in *King Lear,*" *Some Facets.*

[14] For a full interpretation of the poetics of the morality-function in this scene, see Bridget G. Lyons, "The Subplot as Simplification," *Some Facets;* as well as Harry Levin, "The Heights and the Depths," *More Talking of Shakespeare,* ed. John Garrett (New York, 1959); Alvin B. Kernan, "Formalism and Realism in Elizabethan Drama: The Miracles in *King Lear,*" *Renaissance Drama,* IX (1966).

Leslie Smith
EDWARD BOND'S *LEAR*

Imagine, if you will, a mixture of the plays of Brecht and Strindberg, Brecht's social and political purposiveness allied to Strindberg's tormented vision of man's self-destructiveness, and you will get some idea of the double vision that informs Edward Bond's dramatic world. It is a world in which a sombre sense of man's inhumanity to man co-exists with hopefulness and a strong socio-political awareness. Bond has a great playwright's ability to express this double vision in dramatic images, in dialogue and action that have extraordinary force and power. In the earlier plays of contemporary working-class life, *The Pope's Wedding* and *Saved,* the tension between perverse, destructive energies and constructive ones was expressed in naturalistic terms: in *Saved,* the gang stoning the baby in a South London park, Len mending the chair in his girl-friend's house. In later plays, Bond experiments with surrealism and the grotesque: the tug of war between rival armies on Beachy Head in *Early Morning,* the Balmoral Picnic in Heaven in the same play, in which Queen Victoria, her ministers and her subjects, governors and governed alike, devour each other; and Florence Nightingale hides the head of her loved one in her voluminous skirts. The later plays in general make more use of fable and fantasy and are set in places and periods remote from present day England: Japan in the seventeenth, eighteenth, and nineteenth centuries (*Narrow Road to the Deep North*), Shakespeare's England (*Bingo*), a Victorian fantasy world (*Early Morning*), a Britain that is a timeless mix of the primitive and the contemporary (*Lear*). But there is a clear line of development between the earlier, more naturalistic plays, and the later ones. "I think quite often," Bond has said, "one feels the need to see something at a bit of a distance just to see its relationship to oneself better."[1] Fable and fantasy are ways of exploring, not of escaping from, contemporary reality: "I can't think that *Early Morning* is set in a limbo in a way that *Saved* isn't. In order to express reality, the simplest and best and most direct way isn't necessarily to say, well, the time is now six fifteen and it's the third of March. . . . The plays I am told are based on social realism very often seem to me the wildest

From *Comparative Drama* 13, No. 1 (Spring 1979): 65–85.

fairy stories ..." (TQ, 8). I would suggest, in fact, that in Bond's *Lear* (1972) there is a coming together of the matter-of-fact realism of the earlier plays, and the mythical, fantasy elements of *Early Morning* and *Narrow Road to the Deep North*. It is the culmination of Bond's work up to 1972. And it has particular interest for a modern audience because of the relationship in which it stands to Shakespeare's great original.

When T. S. Eliot sought to create a distinctive poetic drama between 1934 and 1958, he felt the overpowering necessity of escaping from the shadow of Shakespeare, whose genius had queered the pitch for subsequent poetic dramatists. But Eliot's efforts were doomed to failure. Putting his poetry on too thin a diet, he often rendered it indistinguishable from prose; rejecting Shakespeare, he tried for a mixture of classical myth and drawing room comedy that never quite gelled. Bond suffers from no such inhibitions. His poetry of the theatre is not dependent on verse: it functions through the concrete action and the physical images of the drama. "What I begin from," he has said, "is a series of small visual images ... when I write, the rhythm—the whole concentration of the writing—requires action. Finally somebody has to get up and do something" (TQ, 6). And because he is secure in his own technique and moves confidently in the medium of drama as Eliot never did, Bond has always felt free to respond to and use aspects of Shakespeare's dramatic world in his own plays.

It was indeed a performance by Wolfit of Shakespeare's *Macbeth* that gave him his first impulse to become a writer:

> My education really consisted of one evening, which was organised by the school (Crouch End Secondary Modern). They took us along to a play at the old Bedford Theatre in Camden Town. We saw Donald Wolfit in *Macbeth*, and for the very first time in my life—I remember this quite distinctly—I met somebody who was actually talking about my problems.... I *knew* all these people, they were there in the street or in the newspapers—this in fact was my world. And also out of the play I got a feeling of resolution—that there were certain standards. My reactions were absolutely naive, but I knew that if one could maintain these standards they could work in social situations and produce certain results. So that after seeing that play I could say, well, yes, now I know what I have to do, what it means to be alive.... And also what came across from Wolfit's performance—and that play suited him very well—was a sense of dignity about people.... And so I got from that play a sense of human dignity—of the value of human beings. (TQ, 5–6)

Bond's subsequent career as a dramatist can be seen as stemming from that first realisation of the power of the theatre and its potential for enlarging our sensibilities.

But his approach to Shakespeare was never merely reverential. Bond has pondered deeply the question of the artist's relationship to society. To be an artist, a dedicated "being apart," is not enough; for Bond the artist is a man among men, and he must be a functioning part of the moral structure of society. In *Narrow Road to the Deep North*, the play that preceded *Lear*, Bond had written a bitter

Brechtian parable about the seventeenth-century Japanese poet, Basho, who in his personal pursuit of wisdom and enlightenment, passes by opportunities to help his fellow citizens and, in so doing, brings terrible suffering upon his country. "What particularly incensed me about Basho," writes Bond, "was that everybody says oh, what a marvellous poet. But I really am only talking about his actions."[2] And in the play that follows Lear, Bingo (1973), Bond audaciously turns an equally disenchanted eye on Shakespeare in retirement at Stratford. We know that at the time of Shakespeare's retirement, the livelihood of farm-labourers and small-holders was being threatened by the wealthier landowners, with their policy of enclosing common land. We know further, as Bond puts it, that "a large part of [Shakespeare's] income came from rents [or tithes] paid on common fields at Welcombe near Stratford. Some important landowners wanted to enclose these fields and there was a risk that the enclosure would affect Shakespeare's rents ... [Shakespeare] sided with the landowners." Bond is keenly interested in the resulting paradox, between the art and the life. For art, he affirms, "is always sane."

> It always insists on the truth, and tries to express the justice and order that are necessary to sanity, but are usually destroyed by society. All imagination is political. It has the urgency of passion, the force of appetite, the self-authenticity of pain or happiness. . . . Shakespeare's plays show this need for sanity, and its political expression, justice. But how did he live? His behaviour as a property owner made him closer to Goneril than Lear. He supported and benefitted from the Goneril society, with its prisons, workhouses, whipping, starvation, mutilation, pulpit-hysteria, and all the rest of it.[3]

To some extent Bond resolves the paradox in his play by having Shakespeare expiate the moral neutrality into which he has retreated, by committing suicide. But Bond is a more complex playwright than his prefatory statements sometimes indicate. (He is in this respect comparable with Shaw.) He may have intended a sardonic portrait of a great artist failing as a human being and pronouncing his own self-condemnation in suicide. But what in fact comes over as the strong feeling of the play is the pain and bewilderment of a man who understands more profoundly and sees further than his fellow citizens, and is—perhaps precisely because of that vision—somehow powerless to act. Not least of the ironies of this fascinating play is that Shakespeare, the great word-magician, is for large parts of the action left speechless, stunned into silence by the confusion and violence he sees around him. Consumed by the suffering he witnesses, and wandering, the worse for drink, in the snowbound Stratford landscape past a gallows tree from which a corpse is hanging, Shakespeare becomes his own tormented Lear, adrift among the elements, with only a mad old gardener for companion. And when he does speak it is to affirm that writer's responsibility to his society that is central to Bond's own vision:

> Every writer writes in other men's blood. . . . Even when I sat at my table, when I put on my clothes, I was a hangman's assistant, a gaoler's errand boy. If children go in rags, we make the wind. If the table's empty we blight the

harvest. If the roof leaks we send the storm. God made the elements but we inflict them on each other.

Bond, far from distancing himself critically from Shakespeare, seems here to identify with him.

When Bond conceived the idea of doing his own version of *King Lear,* he did so with a very real sense of its disturbing power as a play: "I can only say that Lear was standing in my path and I had to get him out of the way. I couldn't get beyond him to do other things that I also wanted, so I had to come to terms with him" (TQ, 8). But he also approached the play in a questioning and sceptical spirit directed particularly at traditional responses to it:

> I very much object to the worshipping of that play by the academic theatre . . . because it is a totally dishonest experience. "Oh, yes, you know, this marvel-lous man suffering, and all the rest of it." I think that at the time it would have been a completely, totally different experience to see Lear reacting in the Tudor set up. . . . Now, I think it's an invitation to be artistically lazy, to say, "Oh, how . . . sensitive we are and this marvelous artistic experience we're having, understanding this play," and all the rest of it. . . . He's a Renaissance figure and he doesn't impinge on our society as much as he should. So that I would like to rewrite the play to try and make it more relevant. (G. 24)

One can develop Bond's point a little by saying that what an audience gets from a traditional production of the play is the sense of a man ennobled by suffering, who initially brings that suffering upon himself. Lear's progress through the play is a kind of purgatorial pilgrimage in which his arrogance, moral blindness and inhumanity are stripped away, and a fundamental humanity is left. The deaths of Cordelia and Lear are cathartic in the extreme, arousing deep pity and fear in the audience, the more so since they come so quickly upon the almost paradisal awakening into new life that the old king experiences in the brief reunion with his daughter. Goneril and Regan, in a traditional production, are types of ultimate evil and total inhumanity. In the world of the play that evil is finally expelled, but at a terrible cost in human suffering. In the subdued final passages of the play there is a sense of order in the kingdom reasserting itself. If perhaps any lines can be quoted as central to this traditional view, which Bond rejects, they might be the lines of Sophoclean resig-nation spoken by Edgar: "Men must endure / Their going hence, even as their coming hither. / Ripeness is all." But, if Bond rejects the traditional view certain directors take of the play, I do not think Peter Brook's very untraditional and contemporary view of the play, in his production for the RSC, with Paul Scofield as Lear, would altogether have satisfied him. For this production, the bitter despair of Gloucester, "As flies to wanton boys, are we to the gods; / They kill us for their sport," was more the keynote. Brook, influenced to some extent by Jan Kott's essay on *Lear* in *Shakespeare Our Contemporary,* saw Shakespeare's play in terms of Beckett's *Endgame.* The scenes on Dover Cliff between the mad Lear and the blind Gloucester seemed to echo some of the exchanges between Hamm and Clov in

Beckett's play: man's existential despair in a world of minimal meaning. Brook refused to distance his audience in any way from the action. He wished to involve them totally, as with a play of contemporary life.

To this end, Scofield's Lear was no absolute monarch, set apart by Divine Right; instead he was an impossibly difficult, unpredictable and choleric old man, whose knights were indeed as turbulent and bad-mannered as his daughters alleged: an elderly relative who would be an embarrassment in any household. Goneril and Regan, in this production, were no types of absolute evil: unpleasant and vicious certainly, but with some justification, given Lear's behaviour. Brook made us feel the kinship between the father and the evil daughters. He humanised and scaled down the situation, removing from it some of the awesome, ritualistic, larger-than-life quality that a traditional production can give us. One of the small, but significant touches in Brook's production, symptomatic of his handling of the play, occurred with the scene of Gloucester's blinding. The sadistic violence of Cornwall and Regan is visited on the helpless old man, whose eyes are gouged out on stage in full view of the audience. At the end of the scene, two of the servants are left on stage with the blind and bleeding Gloucester. In the script, they express concern and sympathy, horror at what has happened.

> If she live long
> And in the end, meet the old course of death,
> Women will all turn monsters.
> ....
> Go thou, I'll fetch some flax and whites of eggs,
> To apply to his bleeding face. Now heaven help him.

Shakespeare places the horrific deed in a context of normal and kindly human behaviour, and to some extent guides our response to it, through these comments. Peter Brook cut the servants' brief conversation at the end of the scene, and brought the house lights up for the interval as the blinded Gloucester attempted to grope his way off stage, bumped into furniture, was jostled by indifferent servants— all this while some members of the audience, encouraged by the house lights, were already on their way to the bar. Brook was most certainly not inviting our mockery of a blind old man, or adding an extra sadistic turn of the screw to the cruelty of the scene. What he was doing was to give us a powerful image of our potentially dangerous indifference to violence and cruelty. He brought this home to us directly, by bringing up the house lights as the scene ended, enabling a majority of the audience to see a minority of their fellows hurrying off at once to the bar, showing an indifference to Gloucester's fate similar to that evidenced among the servants on stage.

Brook evidently felt that the expressed indignation of the servants in the original script too easily let the audience off the hook, allowing them to feel that condemnation had been expressed, guilt apportioned. He wished to bring the uncomfortable facts more directly home to us. How would we respond, undistanced by the historical perspective and moral framework that may come between us and the play? Brook returns to this problem of violence and our reaction to it in a section of his book *The Empty Space,* which could almost be a comment on his own staging of the blinding scene, and which I quote because his views are very relevant to Bond's use of violence in the theatre. In real life, he asserts, the shocking atrocity stories, or the photograph of the napalmed child,

> are the roughest of experiences—but they open the spectator's eyes to the need for an action which in the event they somehow sap. It is as though the fact of experiencing a need vividly quickens the need and quenches it in the same breath. What then can be done? I know of one acid test in the theatre. And it is literally an acid test. When a performance is over, what remains? Fun can be forgotten, but powerful emotion also disappears and good arguments lose their thread. When emotion and argument are harnessed to a wish from the audience to see more clearly into itself—then something in the mind burns. The event scorches on to the memory an outline, a taste, a trace, a smell, a picture. It is the play's central image that remains, its silhouette, and if the elements are highly blended, this silhouette will be its meaning, this shape will be the essence of what it has to say. When years later I think of a striking theatrical experience I find a kernel engraved in my memory: two tramps under a tree, an old woman dragging a cart, a sergeant dancing, three people on a sofa in hell—or occasionally a trace deeper than any imagery. I haven't a hope of remembering the meanings precisely, but from the kernel I can reconstruct a set of meanings. Then a purpose will have been served. A few hours could amend my thinking for life. This is almost, but not quite impossible to achieve.[4]

Perhaps, of the two kinds of *Lear* production I have been describing, Bond would prefer Peter Brook's untraditional and contemporary view of the play. Brook's views on the problem of violence and how the theatre may deal with it are close to his own. He is equally concerned to see the relevance of the play to our own age. Yet as a dramatist bent on writing his own version of *Lear,* the Beckett-like existential despair of Brook's version serves his purpose no better than the Sopho-clean resignation of traditional Lears.

Bond's is a more radical, a more revolutionary concept of art: "Art has to be the equivalent of hooliganism in the streets. It has to be disruptive and questioning, also at the same time to give a rational explanation of the circumstances in which it is occurring" (G, 5). His Preface to *Lear* describes the moralised aggression of our social and political institutions, "as if an animal was locked in a cage—and then fed with the key. It shakes the bars but can never get out." Yet the description of our "diseased culture," our "institutionalised and legitimised tyranny," is given less from a Marxist than a Blakean humanist-anarchist viewpoint. Bond has a healthy disrespect for power-politics, whether of the left or right: "It is so easy to subordinate justice to power ... when this happens power takes on the dynamics and dialectics of aggression, and then nothing is really changed. Marx did not know about this problem, and Lenin discovered it when it was too late." He has no wish to put forward a blueprint of the future: "If your plan of the future is too rigid you start to coerce people to fit into it. We do not need a plan of the future. We need a method of change." If his art is to have a function, it is to contribute "to a general consciousness of the sort of dangers that society is now in." So, if he sometimes prompts comparison with Brecht, it is not because he is overtly didactic as Brecht can be, but because of a purposiveness in his drama, an impulse towards "a method of change," and because, like Brecht, he is too good a dramatist not to give full value to irony, complexity, and ambiguity in his plays. What he has said of Brecht he could have said of himself: "His naivety covers painful knowledge."

Bond's *Lear* has a three-act structure, which Bond characterises thus: "Act I shows a world dominated by myth. Act II shows the clash between myth and reality, between superstitious men and the autonomous world. Act III shows a resolution of this in the world we prove real by dying in it." In discussing the play I will try to suggest how the Shakespearean original functions as stimulus and point of departure for Bond's contemporary version.

In Act I of Bond's play, Lear does not abandon his authority as in Shakespeare's play. Bond wishes to get away from the Renaissance concept of a betrayal of kingly responsibility which releases powers of evil and anarchy in the land, and instead to focus on an old man, an authority figure, overtaken by revolutionary violence, who becomes as a child again, and learns, ultimately at the cost of our own life, the true nature of his society (which could be our own) and of the folly of its power structure. So, says Bond, "I begin at the Revolution."[5] Lear's great enterprise in Bond's play, his lifetime's work, has been the building of a great wall, to keep his enemies out and his allies in. The play begins and ends with the killing of a man working on the wall. It is one of the great central images of oppression and confinement in the play, and it brilliantly evokes both an ancient landscape and a modern one: we think at one and the same time of the Berlin wall and the Cold War; and of the massive earthworks near Bond's home called Devil's Dyke and Fleam Dyke thrown up by the East Anglians after the departure of the Romans to protect themselves from marauders. Lear, on the tour of inspection that starts the play, could be any contemporary field marshal or bellicose politician claiming to defend the peace by preparing for war, and calling self-imprisonment freedom:

> I started this wall when I was young. I stopped my enemies in the field, but there were always more of them. How could we ever be free? So I built this wall to keep our enemies out. My people will live behind this wall when I'm dead. You may be governed by fools but you'll always live in peace. My wall will make you free.

The dramatic irony of the scene is given an additional savage twist as Lear, in the same breath as he proclaims his love for his people, shoots one of the workers, wrongly suspected of sabotage.

With a number of swift, bold strokes, and using various forms of theatrical foreshortening and simplification, Bond gives us, in the remainder of Act I, the revolution that overthrows Lear, the irresponsible cruelty and violence it brings with it, Lear's madness, and the temporary pastoral refuge he secures with only a "fool" (the Gravedigger's boy) and a "wild man" (his tortured general, Warrington) for company. The Shakespearean echoes are strong and insistent: Goneril and Regan, renamed Bodice and Fontanelle, exist in a kind of parodic relation to their formidable and venomous prototypes. They are, for Bond, figures of black farce, figures out of Jarry's *Ubu Roi*, childishly indulging their cruelties and sexual appetites. They initiate the revolution by contracting marriages with Lear's enemies, the Dukes of North and Cornwall, and then complain in bitter asides to the audience of their husbands' sexual incompetence. "When he gets on top of me," says Fontanelle, "I'm so angry I have to count to ten. That's long enough. Then I wait till he's asleep and work myself off. I'm not making do with that for long." "Virility," says Bodice, "it'd be easier to get blood out of a stone, and far more probable. I've bribed a major on his staff to shoot him in the battle." Bond's variation on the blinding of Gloucester has Warrington subjected, like a puppet figure in an evil Punch and Judy show, to every kind of monstrous cruelty. His tongue already cut out, he is methodically beaten up, while Bodice calmly knits and Fontanelle jumps up and down with perverse, infantile glee:

> FONTANELLE: Christ, why did I cut his tongue out? I want to hear him scream . . . smash his hands; . . . kill his feet! . . . kill him inside! Make him dead! Father, Father! I want to sit on his lungs!
>
> BODICE (knits): Plain, pearl, plain. She was just the same at school.

We have to remember that Bond's purpose in Act I is to create a world dominated by myth. These caricature figures belong well enough to this mythical world, albeit that world has its contemporary reference, and we can glimpse something of twentieth-century cruelties and obscenities in the distorting mirror of farce and grand guignol. The horrible fun that Bond gets from these grotesque figures also serves some very useful dramatic purposes. Bond knows many in the audience will be familiar with the *Lear* original. He wants in Act I to confront directly and in caricature form the extremities of cruelty and violence in *King Lear*, and, as it were, to exorcise some Shakespearean ghosts. In so doing he prepares the ground for his own exploration of violence and oppression in Acts II and III. And it is not only a matter of the *King Lear* original. Bond has written: "I write about violence as naturally as Jane Austen wrote about manners. Violence shapes and obsesses our society, and if we do not stop being violent we have no future. People who do not want writers to write about violence want to stop them writing about us and our time. . . ."[6] For such a writer it is very important to create the right context for the subject. In introducing the theme on a farcical level before returning to it at a deeper and more serious level, Bond prepares the audience psychologically. He does the same thing in *Early Morning*, where the theme of cannibalism is first introduced farcically—Len and Joyce stand trial for eating a man while queuing outside the Kilburn Empire to see a film called "Policeman in Black Nylons"—and cannibalism then becomes more and more the central image for men devouring and destroying each other. It is of course a technique that goes as far back in British drama as the medieval miracle plays, where in the Towneley *Secunda Pastorum* the farcical sheep-stealing and mock nativity precede and strengthen the serious and real nativity.

Lear, overthrown by his daughters, seeks refuge with the Gravedigger's boy, who is a pig-farmer, and his wife, Cordelia (not, as in Shakespeare, one of Lear's daughters). Both are figures of crucial importance in the later action of the play. Suffice here to note that the gravedigger's boy, like Shakespeare's fool, criticises the king, but offers him counsel and friendship; and that echoes of Shakespeare's storm scenes on the heath are never far away. There is Lear's constant obsession with filial ingratitude: "Have you any daughters?" he asks the boy. "No." "Then I'll come. No daughters! Where he lives the rain can't be wet or the wind cold, and the holes cry out when you're going to tread in them." There is the macabre animal imagery that runs through Lear's speeches: "My daughters empty their prisons and feed the men to the dead in their graveyards. The wolf crawls away in terror and hides with the rats. Hup, Prince! Hup, Rebel! Do tricks for human flesh! When the dead have eaten they go home to their pits and sleep." And there is the presence of a Mad Tom figure in the crazed and tortured figure of Warrington hiding in the well. At the same time the house of the gravedigger's boy is a real, if temporary pastoral refuge for Lear; no thunder, lightning, and tempestuous rain show us disorder in the universe, reflecting disorder in the body politic. Here is no great chain of being in the Elizabethan manner. Bond's world is a world without God or the gods. And it is at the end of Act I, when the brief pastoral dream turns to nightmare, that Bond's strong individual presence asserts itself and the very different direction of his play begins to become clear. The pillaging soldiers hunting for the escaped king arrive on the scene. They capture Lear, slaughter the pigs, kill the boy, and rape his wife. The violence here is not in any way caricatured. It is grimly matter-of-fact. And Bond drives home the cruelty most powerfully by two very striking dramatic effects. One is an auditory effect: the off-stage squealing of the pigs as they are slaughtered, a sound which is to return, quite spine-chillingly, near the end of the play. The second is an extraordinary and most powerfully contrived visual effect on the death of the gravedigger's boy. His wife's washing is on the line, and, as he is shot, he clutches at one of the sheets which folds round him. The stage direction reads: "For a second he stands in silence with the white sheet draped round him. Only his head is seen. It is pushed back in shock and his eyes and mouth are open. He stands rigid. Suddenly a huge red stain spreads on the sheet." This is not simply a shock effect. Although it does, undeniably, shock. It is a strange, fantastic image of a living man turning into a ghost before our eyes, preparing the way for the continuing presence of the boy as a ghost accompanying Lear for much of Acts II and III, rather as the skeleton of Arthur's Siamese twin George is fixed to him for much of *Early Morning*. The red stain is a fine image of the creeping and spreading violence consuming the world of the play: and in the strange paradox it also suggests of a bleeding ghost, it evokes a kind of death-in-life, a feeling of something sinister and unhealthy which we shall increasingly come to associate with the ghost of the gravedigger's boy.

In Act II Bond opens up his own contemporary world of dream and nightmare, of purgatorial suffering, through which Lear must pass to achieve sanity and understanding. In a succession of strange and haunting scenes he creates a dramatic poetry of action, speech, and image no less powerful than some of Shakespeare's scenes.

Thus, Lear, put on trial, refuses to recognise either his daughter Bodice or his own reflection in a mirror that is handed to him:

> How ugly that voice is! That's not my daughter's voice. It sounds like chains on a prison wall. And she walks like something struggling in a sack (Lear glances down briefly at the mirror). No, that's not the king. . . . This is a little cage of bars with an animal in it. No, no, that's not the king! Who shut that animal in that cage? Let it out. Have you seen its face behind the bars? There's a poor animal with blood on its head and tears running down its face.

Bond may be recalling the abdication scene in *Richard II* where Richard calls for a mirror and eventually shatters it; if so the echo is apt, for Lear demonstrates a similar self-pity and self-dramatisation here. But Bond's vivid imagery and terse command of colloquial idiom is very much his own; and the image of man as a caged animal reverberates beyond the immediate context, and is as central to the meaning of Bond's play as the imagery of storm and tempest is to *Lear*. It relates to the governed as much as the governors, people and rulers alike, imprisoned within a social and political structure that does not answer to their real needs.

The trial is followed by a succession of prison scenes, quite extraordinary in their blend of realism and fantasy, the timeless and the contemporary, pathos and terror. In the first of these scenes (scene 2), it is a little as if Bond had taken the speech of Lear to Cordelia as point of departure for his own dramatic invention:

> Come, let's away to prison;
> We two alone will sing like birds i'the cage.
> When thou dost ask me blessing, I'll kneel down
> And ask of thee forgiveness.

The modern soldiers acting as prison orderlies bring Lear to his cell. He is just another number to be ticked off the list; it's a job they prefer to front-line duty. Then, as it might be in *Macbeth* or *Hamlet*, "The ghost of the gravedigger's boy appears. His skin and clothes are faded. There's old dry blood on them." Lear's appalled sense of the world's cruelty and destructiveness strangely now impels him to reach out towards his evil daughters. "What I wanted Lear to do," says Bond, "was to recognise that they *were* his daughters—they had been formed by his activity, they were children of his state, and he was totally responsible for them" (TQ, 8). The gravedigger's boy, as in some strange folk ballad, whistles up the ghostly presences of Bodice and Fontanelle as the children they once were. The scene of mutual comfort and tenderness that results as Lear cradles the heads of his daughters in his lap and strokes their hair is in no way mawkish. It is important dramatically in a number of ways. It shows Lear reaching out beyond his immediate anguish to a vision of a world that might be:

We won't chain ourselves to the dead, or send our children to school in the graveyard. The torturers and ministers and priests will lose their office. And we'll pass each other in the street without shuddering at what we've done to each other.... The animal will step out of its cage, and lie in the fields, and run by the river, and groom itself in the sun, and sleep in its hole from night to morning.

Here is a dramatic poetry not dependent on verse which captures something of the same restorative peace as is found in Shakespeare's "We two alone will sing like birds i'the cage." It is important too in humanising the daughters after the grand guignol horror of the earlier scenes. But, above all, it establishes, in the re-enacted terror of Lear's daughters as little children, the responsibility of environment and family for shaping or misshaping its sons and daughters. Bond invents a striking and effective piece of stage business for this. Bodice, as a child, struggles frantically to get into the dress of her dead mother, and comes to Lear for his approval. "Take it off!" says Lear. Bodice refuses. And Lear replies: "Yes, or you will always wear it! (He pulls her to him) Bodice! My poor child, you might as well have worn her shroud." Nothing could better suggest the child's development, distorted or misshaped by parental pressures, and Lear's tardy realisation of his responsibility in this direction. We are brought back to "everyday" reality from this strange dream world, with its visual suggestion of Blake's engraving of *Job and His Daughters,* by the soldier's cell-inspection routine, and by the old orderly coming to fetch Lear's untouched food. The orderly, like the porter in *Macbeth,* lists all those lost souls including himself who have been consigned to oblivion in this place of suffering and death:

> I come in 'ere thousands of years back, 'undreds a thousands. I don't know what I come in for. I forgot. I 'eard so many tell what they come in for it's all mixed up in me 'ead. I've 'eard every crime in the book confessed t' me. Must be a record. Don't know which was mine now. Murder? Robbery? Violence? I'd like to know. Just t'put me mind t'rest. Satisfy me conscience. But no-one knows now. It's all gone. Long ago. The records is lost. 'Undreds of years back.

This is, if you like, Shakespearean in its down-to-earth comic relief; but it also evokes a very contemporary, Kafka-esque world, of the KGB, the midnight knock on the door; the unspecified crime for which you are put away for ever. The scene ends with the ghost's frightened plea to remain with Lear:

> GHOST: Let me stay with you Lear.... Look at my hands, they're like an old man's. They're withered, I'm young but my stomach's shrivelled up, and the hairs turned white. Look, my arms! Feel how thin I am. Are you afraid to touch me?...
>
> LEAR: ... Yes, yes. Poor boy. Lie down by me. Here, I'll hold you. We'll help each other. Cry while I sleep, and I'll cry and watch you while you sleep. We'll take turns. The sound of the human voice will comfort us.

There are echoes here of Shakespeare's Lear and the fool on the heath:

> LEAR: Poor fool and knave. I have one part in my heart
> That's sorry yet for thee
>
> ....
>
> In boy, go first. Your houseless poverty
> Nay get thee in. I'll pray and then I'll sleep.

Lear's human concern for the boy in the Bond scene is moving; but there is also a sense that Lear, in embracing the ghost, is nursing his own grief too much, and withdrawing into an unreal world. Particularly is this so, as the ghost himself is a strange, equivocal figure who is already wasting away and clinging parasite-like to the living Lear. When he whispers ingratiatingly, "Let me stay with you Lear.... Are you afraid to touch me?" there is already the suggestion, which is to become stronger, of the ghost representing something in Lear (as George does for Arthur in *Early Morning*), which has to die before Lear can find his true strength. After two brief scenes, set in the rival army camps, of revolution and counter-revolution (Cordelia is now leading the "freedom-fighter" forces of counter-revolution), the counter-revolutionaries carry the day; and Bond returns us, for the conclusion of the Act, to the prison and the caged animals within it. A chain of prisoners moves along a country road, with heavy gunfire in the distance. Lear is one of the chain gang, and to it the defeated Fontanelle, in her turn, is manacled. Bond's great gift for vivid theatrical metaphor, for images that act out the meaning of the play, is here again in evidence: one of the central themes of the play—the vicious circle of violence and oppression, in which governors and governed, tyrants and victims end up chained to each other, is simply and memorably expressed. Then, back in the prison, Bond brings the act to its audacious climax. Katherine Worth has said that often with Bond "it is in the most grotesque areas of the play that his technique is seen at its most boldly inventive, and—strange paradox—the mystery of human feeling is given most delicate expression."[7] The paintings of Francis Bacon, or the Goya engravings of the *Disasters of War*, might provide comparable examples in the world of art. In Shakespeare's original we have the mad Lear crying out in the hovel: "Then let them anatomise Regan, see what breeds about her heart. Is there any cause in nature that makes these hard hearts?" Bond, as it were, accepts the challenge of that despairing question, and uses the idea literally. Fontanelle is executed, and the prison officer conducts an autopsy in cool scientific fashion. He "anatomises" Fontanelle, and Lear, tormented by his sense of the cruelty of mankind, looks on to "see what breeds about her heart."

> LEAR: So much blood and bits and pieces packed in with all that care. Where is the ... Where? ... Where is the beast? The blood is as still as a lake. ... Where? Where? ...
> 4TH PRISONER: What's the man asking?
> LEAR: She sleeps inside like a lion and a lamb and a child. The things are so beautiful. I am astonished. I have never seen anything so beautiful. If I had

known she was so beautiful . . . how I would have loved her . . . Did I
make this—and destroy it? . . . I knew nothing, saw nothing, learned nothing! Fool! Fool! Worse than I knew. (He puts his hands into Fontanelle
and brings them out with organs and viscera. The soldiers react awk-
wardly and ineffectually). Look at my dead daughter! . . . I killed her! Her
blood is on my hands! Destroyer! Murderer! And now I must begin again.
I must walk through my life, step after step, I must walk in weariness and
bitterness, I must become a child, hungry and stripped and shivering in
blood. I must open my eyes and see!

Harry Andrews, who played Lear in Bill Gaskill's production at the Royal Court,
was worried about whether this scene would produce the wrong reactions in the
audience; and Gaskill told him: "The author has made a big gesture. If it doesn't
work, it doesn't work, but you have to have the courage to play it."[8] In the event,
the scene did work, and very powerfully, as Katherine Worth testifies: "[It] could so
easily have been either ludicrous or overpoweringly offensive. But it worked. There
was no laughter of the wrong kind. . . . We were too deep in feeling, too affected
by the solemn and complex movements of events."[9] Lear, then, at this moment,
finds his answer to the question posed in Shakespeare's play. There is no cause in
nature, that makes these hard hearts. The speech, with its Blakean and Biblical
overtones (cf. "Dare he laugh his work to see? Dare he who made the lamb make
thee?"—"The Tyger"; "the wolf shall dwell with the lamb . . . and the calf and the
young lion together; and a little child shall lead them"—Isaiah 2) expresses Lear's
astonished reverence for the mystery and beauty of creation and for the natural
innocence of man, uncorrupted by environment. The cause is in man, not nature.
And Lear takes upon himself a total, almost Christ-like responsibility for man's
destructiveness: "I must become a child . . . I must open my eyes and see. . . ."
    Ironically, but aptly enough, it is at this moment, in the crowning act of violence
in Act II, that he is blinded. The blinding continues the use of Shakespeare's text for
Bond's own purposes. As in Shakespeare, it is a dramatic metaphor for insight. "I
stumbled when I saw," says the blinded Gloucester: that Lear is blinded immediately
after the revelation he experiences at the autopsy suggests how much that he has
needed to learn he has now learnt. What he will choose to do with this wisdom will
be the theme of Act III. The blinding also continues and extends the image of power
imprisoning and hurting those who wield it. For Lear's "crown" in this scene, which
"turns him into a king again," is in fact the square, box-like device fitted over his
head to extract his eyes. It is a kind of savage, theatrical conceit, in which Bond
forces together the idea of power and the idea of a cruel blindness, a self-
imprisonment associated with authority. And it also continues the deliberate and
very effective use of anachronisms—the mixing of contemporary and historic
detail—in the play. Bond, in a postcard to Gaskill during the rehearsals of the
production, spoke of the need to preserve this mixture: "The anachronisms are for
the horrible moments in a dream when you know it's a dream but can't help being
afraid. The anachronisms must increase, and not lessen the seriousness. . . . They

are like desperate facts."[10] So here this latest scientific gadget which hygienically "decants" the eyes into a "soothing solution of formaldehyde crystals" and sprays the sockets with an aerosol reminds us of modern torture techniques and pseudo-scientific concentration camp experiments practised on victims of the Nazi terror.

The final act of Bond's play differs in three crucial respects from Shakespeare's. For Bond's Lear, ripeness is not all; and though he is tempted towards an "easeful death" by the Gravedigger's boy and his own moments of despair, he finds the courage to resist this mood, to realise that, far from enduring his "going hence" even as his "coming hither," he still has work to do. This Lear's death is a heroic death that comes about as a result of a political act—a small and seemingly ineffectual act, but none the less one of great symbolic importance. Pathos and pity, overpower-ingly present in Shakespeare's last act, are associated, in Bond's last act, with the increasingly spectral and parasitical figure of the Gravedigger's boy and are seen as debilitating and harmful emotions. Finally, instead of a reconciliation with Cordelia, there is a confrontation between her, as the new head of a people's government, and the old autocratic ruler, in which Lear decisively rejects her.

Consider first the gravedigger's boy. "I can stay with you now you need me," murmurs the ghost insidiously when Lear has been blinded; and his sinister pres-ence remains with Lear for much of Act III encouraging him to despairing and destructive acts: "Get rid of the lot of them, then we'll be safe. . . . Let me poison the well. . . ." At the same time, the ghost is a figure of genuine pathos, wasting away, frightened of dying a second time, haunting the scenes of his happy early life. The beauty of that pastoral existence that Lear briefly glimpsed has its persuasive appeal, and the ghost is there to remind him of it. Through the gravedigger's boy, he has seen a vision of a golden age which his own political activities have helped to destroy. But, as Bond puts it, "he has also to recognise that its loss is irrevocable . . . there are great dangers in romanticising." And so, "it's very important for Lear that he should get rid of this other figure; he has to disown something of himself, this instinctive thing he calls the Gravedigger's boy. . . . Some things are dead—but they die with difficulty" (TQ, 8). That difficult death Bond accomplishes in another striking "coup de théâtre," which eerily brings the wheel full circle, linking past to present. At the moment Lear formulates his plan of action and rejects Cordelia, there is heard off-stage "the distant squealing of angry pigs, further off than at the end of Act One, scene seven." "The ghost stumbles in. It is covered with blood. The pig squeals slowly die out." The ghost, gored and trampled by the pigs, makes a final, anguished appeal to Lear: "Help me! Help me! . . . Lear! Hold me!" But Lear can say nothing but: "No, too late! It's far too late! . . . You were killed long ago! . . . Die, for your own sake, die." As the boy drops dead at Lear's feet, the pig squealing finally stops. And Lear's brief and moving valediction is full of the imagery of light, of clear vision, and of an understanding that goes beyond grief:

I see my life, a black tree by a pool. The branches are covered with tears. The tears are shining with light. The wind blows the tears in the sky. And my tears fall down on me.

Cordelia, in Shakespeare's play, aroused a strong and hostile reaction in Bond: "One of the very important things in the play was to re-define the relationship between Cordelia and Lear. I don't want to make this seem easy or slick, but Cordelia in Shakespeare's play is an absolute menace. I mean she's a very dangerous type of person..." (TQ, 8). Bond's Cordelia is, of course, not one of Lear's daughters. But, like Shakespeare's Cordelia, she is an idealist; she puts her ideals (in Bond's play, political ones) above human needs (condemning a would-be recruit to death because "we can't trust a man unless he hates," and prepared to have Lear killed if he will not cease from preaching to the disaffected); and, just as Cordelia in Shakespeare's play is perhaps most like Lear in a certain uncompromising forth-rightness, reckless of consequences, so Bond's Cordelia becomes most like the Lear of Act I. She insists, as he once did, that building the wall is an essential part of the power game; she has the same conviction that she is the saviour of her people. And though Bond is careful to give her respectable liberal arguments in Scene 3, as befits her more enlightened government, those arguments, as Lear recognises, perpetu-ate violence and the suppression of truth:

> You sacrifice truth to destroy lies, and you sacrifice life to destroy death.... Your Law always does more harm than crime, and your morality is a form of violence.

This confrontation with Cordelia is for Lear the crucial turning point. We have seen him in the early scenes of Act III as a Tiresias-like figure, an elderly blind sage, preaching in parables to the crowds who come to hear him. But it is a form of withdrawal from the world that he is practising. No leadership is offered, no action suggested: there is simply the detached wisdom of a man at the end of his life, waiting for death. But now Lear knows that this phase of resignation, of ripe wisdom, is over. He has a journey to go on, and an act to perform. In a brief ending, but one splendidly dramatic in its gathering together of the play's meaning into a final symbolic action, Lear sets to work with bare hands and a shovel to tear down the wall that it has been his life's work to build, the wall that Cordelia wishes to perpetuate. The wall has from the beginning imposed its dark shadow over the action. But Bond reserves its actual physical presence for the last scene. When it looms up, filling the stage, it is a moment of great dramatic effect. And the struggle of the frail old man to demolish it is the inevitable climactic moment towards which everything in the play has been leading. It is a heroic gesture. It is also a tragic gesture, for it costs Lear his life. He is shot by one of the junior officers in charge of operations. But it is not a futile gesture. Bond, in a final stage-direction that reveals his understanding of how dramatic action can sometimes speak louder than words, specifies that, as the workers on the wall move away from the body, at their officer's command, "one of them looks back." In that looking back with its sugges-tion that the lesson of Lear's death will not be forgotten, lies a frail but real and important hope for the future.

Thus Bond completes a play which, I would argue, does not suffer by com-parison with Shakespeare's great original. In the romantic and post-romantic period, critics and writers placed too much stress on the artist's originality. Latterly we have been more willing to concede the artist's right to use another man's themes and subjects as the springboard for his own invention. A writer's originality is often best seen in his individual variation on a traditional theme. One must, of course, discriminate. Nahum Tate, when he decided to "improve" Shakespeare for Restoration taste by giving Lear a happy ending and arranging a marriage between Cordelia and Edgar, merely showed how deep his incomprehension of the original was. By contrast, Bond sets up in his play a real, creative dialogue with the original, out of which comes a theatrical experience of impressive power, a *Lear* as seen by one of the most original and versatile dramatists of our time.

NOTES

[1] Edward Bond, as quoted by Roger Hudson, Catherine Itzin, and Simon Trussler, in "Drama and the Dialectics of Violence," *Theatre Quarterly*, 2 (January–March 1972), 8. Hereafter, TQ.

[2] Irving Wardle, "A Discussion with Edward Bond," *Gambit*, 5, No. 17 (1970), 9. Hereafter, G.

[3] Edward Bond, Preface to *Bingo* (London: Eyre Methuen, 1972), p. ix.

[4] Peter Brook, *The Empty Space* (New York: Pelican, 1973), p. 152.

[5] Edward Bond, "An Interview with Tony Coult," *Plays and Players* (December 1975), p. 13.

[6] Edward Bond, Preface to *Lear* (New York: Hill and Wang, 1972), p. v.

[7] Katharine Worth, *Revolutions in Modern British Drama* (London: G. Bell, 1972), p. 183.

[8] Gregory Dark, "Production Casebook, No. 5: Edward Bond's *Lear* at the Royal Court," *Theatre Quarterly*, 2 (January–March 1972), 28.

[9] Worth, *Revolutions in Modern British Drama*, p. 180.

[10] Dark, "Production Casebook, No. 5," p. 22.

Michael Goldman

HISTRIONIC IMAGERY IN *KING LEAR*

In this essay, I want to approach *King Lear* by focussing on the tools Shakespeare gives his leading player for solving some especially daunting problems in the title role. To do this, I shall look extensively at the role in terms of what might be called its histrionic imagery. What I have in mind when I use this phrase are various motifs of enactment Shakespeare has built into the part: mental, physical, and emotional movements the actor is called upon to make that are particularly related to his basic work of sustaining the part in performance.

Let me give an example of what I mean. The first problem that confronts an actor who wants to play Lear is gross and obvious. The part makes staggering emotional demands on the performer. The actor is required to portray a quick-tempered, eighty-year-old, absolute tyrant, who five minutes into his first scene bursts into the greatest rage of his life at Cordelia. Two brief scenes later he bursts into a greater rage at Goneril and carries on with increasing intensity for nearly a hundred lines. Next he gets *really* angry at Regan; while he is raging at her, Goneril appears and he gets angrier. His fury and outrage mount wildly until the end of the scene, at which point he goes mad. This of course is only the beginning. Three long scenes of madness still lie ahead during which, among other things, the actor has to outshout a storm. After these scenes on the heath come alternations of hallucination and murderous rage in the scene with Gloucester, the ecstatic joy of reunion with Cordelia, yet another reversal of fortune when the old king and his daughter are captured by their enemies, and finally the anguish of Cordelia's death, a scene in which the actor is required to enter literally howling and to go on from there. "The wonder is," as Kent says, "he hath endured so long," and most actors don't.

The actor who plays Lear must appear to reach an emotional extreme at the start, and then go on to greater and greater extremes. The danger is that he will soon have nothing left—not so much that he will run out of voice or physical energy, but that he will lose the capacity for discriminating his emotional response,

From *Acting and Action in Shakespearean Tragedy* (Princeton: Princeton University Press, 1985), pp. 71–93.

that he will be unable to render the emotions truthfully, with freshness and particularity, and will fall into shouting or scenery chewing or playing what actors call generalized emotion, that is, some sort of all-purpose posturing. If this happens, the actor will not only be doing a great injustice to the text, he will also in a matter of moments bore his audience irremediably. Does Shakespeare do anything to help the actor with this problem?

Trained actors usually learn a variety of techniques for sustaining exact and vivid emotion in scenes of demanding intensity. One technique is to focus on a particular object. If the actor feels in danger of losing an emotion or falsifying it, he may single out a button, say, or a chair, or an eyebrow and make it the recipient or evoker of his feeling. He may direct his emotion toward the object, or find his emotion by reacting to it. In *King Lear* Shakespeare has written this technique into the title role. Repeatedly, at moments of emotional intensity, Lear will focus closely on a specific point—on an area of the body and its sensation or on a small object that produces a bodily sensation. He takes a pin and pricks himself with it; he feels the pressure of a button at his throat; he pinches himself; he holds a feather to Cordelia's mouth; he peers at Gloucester's blinded eyes; he touches Cordelia's cheek to feel the wetness of her tears; he glares at Regan's and Goneril's clasped hands; he smells and wipes his own hand; he imagines two little flies copulating; he stares at Cordelia's lips. These are all highly specific points of focus, and by playing to them and *off* them the actor is able to keep his feeling fresh. They help him to keep the performance alive, to keep the pain Lear feels coming and growing, and to keep the audience's perception of that pain vivid and exact.

These recurring gestures or movements of focus are an example of what I call histrionic images. If we were simply to consider the objects Lear focuses on by themselves, we might treat them as what are usually called poetic or dramatic images. But I am concerned with a unit of *enactment,* something Shakespeare has prescribed for the character to do, by means of which the actor projects the part. Hence, it is this repeated focussing on an area of bodily sensation that constitutes one pattern of histrionic imagery in *Lear.*

How do these images contribute to our larger experience of the play? Clearly, one of the issues *King Lear* raises is the problem of human suffering. Why do we suffer? Is there anything to be gained from it? What values can be conserved in the face of monstrous pain? These are questions the characters keep posing or addressing. And the action is designed so that we frequently find ourselves, like Edgar, believing that things cannot get any worse, only to have something happen that is more awful than anything else that has happened so far. The play's interest in suffering and endurance is plainly echoed in the problem of playing Lear and in our reaction to the performance of the role. How much more can the actor take? we ask—and the question implies, how much more can we take? A good production of *Lear* is not easy on its audience.

Now, the sequence of repeated focussings I have just described may be seen as part of the play's subtle and growing insistence on *feeling* as a source of enduring value in the chaos of cruelty and pain that threatens to overwhelm the characters, the actors, and the audience. The function of these histrionic images is, not to insist on a theme, but to engage the audience in an experience. That is, through the action of the principal actor we share the experience of discovering new precisions of feeling—moments of sympathy, tenderness, insight, or horror, for example—in spite of and indeed because of being forced to undergo scenes that strike us as unendurable and that threaten to wipe us out. They give us the sensation of advancing deeper into pain than we thought we could take, and of advancing, not into profounder awareness, finer sensitivity, which could only be achieved by going this far, by having these many stages of exact response to increasing pain. And this I think is a not insignificant part of the art and vision of *King Lear.*

II

I would like now to look at some other patterns of histrionic imagery, in which the actor is called upon to address himself to other characters, to the words he speaks, and above all to his own emotions.[1] I want especially to draw attention to the emotional and intellectual activity that all these motifs require of the actor and communicate to the audience. For, by means of these devices, Shakespeare provides the gifted actor with a set of habits and methods that allow him to relate to his own emotions, to build them, vary them, wield them, and, as we have seen, to keep them from turning imprecise or numb. This is particularly important in *Lear* because Lear's own relation to his emotional life is one of the great issues of the play.

We tend to think of *Lear* as a play about human suffering, and no doubt we are right to do so. The play deliberately overwhelms us with examples of suffering that arouse our own most vivid fears of vulnerability to pain. How easy it is for our eyes to be put out, how easy it would be for the ones we trust most to betray us, how easily nature or the appetites of others can destroy us, how true it is that things can always get worse. But in spite of all the malice and cruelty directed at Lear, his greatest source of suffering remains internal. The play is less concerned with the assault upon the King from outside than with his vulnerability to the play of his own emotions.

Indeed, it is through Lear's early emotional outbursts that the play first involves us in the kind of analytic awareness of action we have noticed—with different emphasis—in *Hamlet* and *Othello,* that is, with a problematic sense of the way inner and outer events may be related. In the play's early scenes, Lear seems peculiarly agitated by the connections between the self and its acts. Like most of Shakespeare's tragic heroes, he is inclined to work out a personal, abnormal variation on the process that links thinking and feeling with saying and doing. For Hamlet and Brutus, this variation takes the form of a desire to separate the two components, to divide one's inner life from its external manifestations—to insist with Brutus on separating what he calls the "genius" from the "mortal instruments" (II, i, 66), or with Hamlet that whatever one's acts may be, one has something within which passeth show. Lear on the other hand insists on intention and action as monolithically connected and on defining his own nature as powerfully and dangerously joining the two. He denounces Kent for attempting to break the connection when Kent tries to persuade him to revoke his decision to disinherit Cordelia, and he uses language that insists on the leap from self to action as something violent, powerful, instantaneous, and irresistible:

Come not between the dragon and his wrath.   (I. i., 122)

The bow is bent and drawn; make from the shaft.   (143)

Lear seems unwilling or afraid to slow down the rhythm by which he moves from intention to act. In this he resembles Macbeth, who frequently wishes to act quickly in order to escape from the pressure of his imagination. Macbeth would like to act the things in his head before he can scan them; he wants the firstlings of his heart to be the firstlings of his hand. Action for him is a way to blot out reflection and feeling. And the question of feeling, in particular, is important for both *Macbeth* and *King Lear*. In both plays, a false notion of manhood seems to struggle with the claims of feeling. The point is more easily seen in *Macbeth*. There the hero's desire to leap forward unreflectingly into action is highlighted by contrast with Macduff. After Macduff has heard that his wife and children have been murdered, he pauses before calling for revenge. He does so because, as he explains, in order to dispute it like a man, he first must feel it as a man. Macduff insists on the importance of feeling in a man's life, while Macbeth, concerned with doing all that may become a man, acts to keep from feeling. Similarly Lear, up to the storm scene, clings like Macbeth to an idea of a manly way of acting that seals one off from feeling. Confronting Regan and Goneril before Gloucester's palace, Lear, fighting against tears, calls on the gods to visit him instead with what he calls noble anger, a feeling he thinks of as more masculine:

> Touch me with noble anger,
> And let not women's weapons, water drops,
> Stain my man's cheeks.   (II, iv, 273–75)

I imagine that the kind of anger he wants here is the type he displayed in the first scene. He is struggling to summon once more his old power to discharge violent emotional energy without suffering the full range of feeling from which his emotion springs.

Indeed, almost from the beginning of the play, Lear is fighting his feelings. Shakespeare's method of allowing the actor to play against his feelings, by repeatedly insisting, for example, that he will not weep, allows us to experience the movement of feeling toward expression as a terrifying, destructive surge. We feel it as Lear's speeches swiftly shift focus in his fight against rising sorrow:

> O, how this mother swells up toward my heart!
> Hysterica passio, down, thou climbing sorrow,
> Thy element's below. Where is this daughter?   (II, iv, 55–57)

With this last line, he switches attention to Regan, trying to direct action and anger outward, as he has done in the first scene.

Significantly, Lear is aware in this struggle of something unnatural, but he projects it onto his daughters as he flounders in a feeling so violent and unregulated that he cannot think clearly enough even to curse or invent a revenge:

> No, you unnatural hags!
> I will have such revenges on you both
> That all the world shall—I will do such things—
> What they are, yet I know not; but they shall be
> The terrors of the earth.   (275–79)

The power of this speech goes quite beyond its pathos, its picture of a poor old man dissolving in misery yet, like a small boy, refusing to show tears. For, in a kind of prelude to the battle with the storm that comes in the next act, Lear in battling against the mounting tears reaches into himself for a terrifying violence with which to combat them. The long-delayed onslaught of tears, the surrender to his feelings, comes on with the first noise of the storm, and it is so strong that it feels as if he were breaking into a hundred thousand pieces:

> You think I'll weep.
> No, I'll not weep.
> *Storm and Tempest.*
> I have full cause of weeping, but this heart
> Shall break into a hundred thousand flaws
> Or ere I'll weep.   (279–83)

The actor's emotional springboard for this outburst must be found in his fight against tears, while the image of the heart breaking into a hundred thousand flaws gives him his cue for how immense the pressure of the choked-back tears must be. And now comes a dramatic stroke, very helpful to the actor, that is also an important development in the part. Unable to beat back the surge of his emotions, Lear suddenly turns his attention outside again, not to curse and rage, but to confess: "O Fool, I shall go mad!" (283). At the moment of his strongest feeling and his deepest fear, he addresses the Fool. The Fool has already become associated with the kind of feeling Lear has been resisting, that is, with acknowledged suffering. His main role has been to urge the shaming truth that Lear has made a terrible mistake about his daughters. And to Lear, someone who weeps is a fool: "Fool me not so much," he has said in this scene, "to bear it tamely" (272–73), that is, to weep. At this moment, the sudden focus on the Fool allows the actor to let Lear's suppressed feelings flash out for an instant, and the pattern of emotional release through a sudden external focus of attention will grow in importance as the play goes on. A few minutes later, out in the storm, it will be to the Fool that Lear will turn when, for the first time in the play, he acknowledges that someone else can suffer. It is thus through Lear's relation to the Fool that we first begin to feel how the experience of his own pain is being converted into keener awareness of the life around him.

III

For the actor who plays Lear, the problem of handling Lear's emotions is inseparable from the problem of speaking the play's verse. A great deal of study has been devoted to the verse of Shakespeare's plays, but very little to verse movement and texture as part of the performance design.[2] I mean that any striking instance of technical virtuosity in a play's verse will, if the actor can master it, inevitably present itself as technical virtuosity in performance. We have already seen this with the action of exoticism in *Othello*. At this point I want to call attention to some features of the verse that Lear must speak in order to examine what actions they require of the actor. Since they are actions of speech, they will of course involve not simply vocal but also mental and emotional movement.

Lear himself has many styles of speech, many voices, more than I can investigate here. There is, for example, the riddling, shadowy voice we hear very briefly at the beginning of the play:

> Meantime we shall express our darker purpose.   (I, i, 36)

>   ... while we
> Unburthened crawl toward death.   (40–41)

or the torrent of monosyllables in

> I will have such revenges on you both
> That all the world shall—I will do such things—
> What they are, yet I know not; but they shall be
> The terrors of the earth.   (II, iv, 276–79)

or the eerie flickering lightness of the aria that begins "We two alone will sing like birds i' th' cage" (V, iii, 9), not to mention the various voices that mingle in the prose of his madness.

Still, all these voices have one element in common: their suggestion of the operation of some dangerous unregulable power, something not quite contained by the procedures that seek to organize it. And this is equally true of a far more prominent stylistic effect that I wish to look at in some detail. This is the presence, both in Lear's part and in others, of words and phrases that appear to be massively resistant to verse articulation, words like "tender-hefted" or "sea-monster" or "sulph'rous," which seem hard to move around in musical lines or paragraphs. What we appreciate in the music of the lines in which they appear is that the lines somehow find an energy capable of floating or swinging these densely recalcitrant chunks of meaning and sound. Of course it is really the relation of such words to the words around them that creates the impression of difficulty, just as it creates the impression of difficulty overcome. Thus, when we hear:

> Thou art a boil,
> A plague-sore, or embossèd carbuncle
> In my corrupted blood.   (II, iv, 220–22)

or "Strike flat the thick rotundity o' th' world" (III, ii, 7), we feel that somehow words hard to move are being moved.

These words often carry a suggestion of—let me call it—monstrosity; that is, they contribute, through sound and sense, to an impression of sizable, distorted, appetitive, struggling bodies, they burgeon against the forward career of the line:

> If thou shouldst not be glad,
> I would divorce me from thy mother's tomb,
> Sepulchring an adultress.   (II, iv, 127–29)

They seem to overflow, like an unexpected wet animal coming out of a river to snap or lap or slaver at you, or to block your path as the line goes by. Sometimes this impression is specifically carried by the sense of the word itself, sometimes by the context, frequently by the gnarled play of consonants:

> The barbarous Scythian,
> Or he that makes his generation messes
> To gorge his appetite, shall to my bosom
> Be as well neighbored, pitied, and relieved,
> As thou my sometime daughter.[3]   (I, i, 116–20)

The movement of this passage is relatively easy, but, even so, the texture is quite unlike, say, that of Othello's equally savage but fast-moving curses or denunciations:

> Blow me about in winds! roast me in sulfur!
> Wash me in steep-down gulfs of liquid fire!   (V, ii, 279–80)

In *Lear*, this characteristic texture is frequently achieved by using series of words linked by clashing consonants:

> If she must teem,
> Create her child of spleen, that it may live
> And be a thwart disnatured torment to her.
> Let it stamp wrinkles in her brow of youth,
> With cadent tears fret channels in her cheeks.   (I, iv, 283–87)

Lear usually sounds remarkably different from other Shakespearean tragic heroes, even in such a simple matter as a brief explosion of rage. Take a line like "Vengeance, Plague, Death, Confusion!" (II, iv, 92.) Othello typically bursts out on a single note of fury or revulsion: "Goats and monkeys!" or "O Devil, devil!" or "Damn her, lewd minx, damn her!" Hamlet, even in his rage, uses language that multiplies distinctions in series of swiftly linked analytical variations:

> Bloody, bawdy villain!
> Remorseless, treacherous, lecherous, kindless villain!   (II, ii, 586–87)

Lear instead breaks out in four successive, sharply separated calls for sweeping violence. Each is different, each involves, as it were, a going back to the beginning and imagining a new, more violent outbreak of destruction: "Vengeance! Plague! Death! Confusion!"

We can now see some of the characteristic action of performance that this verse texture requires of the actor. Put simply, the testing necessity is for the actor to maintain a precision of feeling and an architecture of response that allows him to swing through the line without falling into rant. To some extent this is a quality any actor must achieve in any passage of intense emotion, but here it is the dominant quality, the one on which the greatest demand is made. Different roles stress different demands. Again the comparison with Hamlet is helpful. The problem with the lines from *Hamlet* I quoted a few moments ago is that, by contrast with *Lear*, it is all too easy to make them superficially musical and thus to lose the play of distinctions and contrasts the words imply in the rapid, nicely modulated interplay of their sounds. Here as everywhere in the role of Hamlet, the challenge is to impose a meaningful coherence on materials that are various, changing, subtly differentiated, and quick moving. When Hamlet tells the players they must remain coherent even in the "very torrent, tempest, and (as I may say) whirlwind of your passion" (III, ii, 5–7), the actor must be at pains to do justice to this volley of interesting distinctions, with their mixture of playfulness, urgency, and critical re-flection, while still holding the speech and the scene together and speaking it all trippingly on the tongue. As in *Lear*, the speaking of these passages is part of the fundamental action of the play.

The verse texture I have been talking about in *Lear* makes its greatest de-mands upon the actor when Lear confronts the storm in Act III:

> Blow, winds, and crack your cheeks. Rage, blow!   (III, ii, 1)

These words are resistant. Each threatens to stop the line dead, to exhaust or baffle the actor's power to articulate. There is no easy musical way to link them. The consonants clash, the vowels expand. It is hard to move from "blow" to "winds" and to get up further energy for "crack your cheeks"; then there are two more imperatives to go, and that only completes the first line. For of course the speech continues:

> Blow, winds, and crack your cheeks. Rage, blow!
> You cataracts and hurricanoes, spout
> Till you have drenched our steeples, drowned the cocks.
> You sulph'rous and thought-executing fires,
> Vaunt-couriers of oak-cleaving thunderbolts,
> Singe my white head. And thou, all-shaking thunder,
> Strike flat the thick rotundity o' th' world.   (1–7)

The actor's problem here is to maintain some movement of thought and articu-lation that will carry them through the dead stopping explosions of "rage" and "blow" and on to the other unwielding, massively active words.

It should be noted, too, that the effort of speech required here echoes Lear's complex relation to the storm. Lear fights the storm, but he also uses it as a means of releasing his own feelings. He claims later that the tempest in his mind keeps him from noticing the tempest around him, but this is plainly inaccurate. For it is through Lear's dialogue with the storm that the audience becomes aware of the tempest in his mind, and it is by playing to the storm that Lear confronts his emotions.

In the speech I have just quoted, Lear is once more attempting to establish the connection between himself and the outside world he has desperately tried to maintain throughout the play. That is, under the stress of his own torment and shame, he again tries to thrust any source of emotional disturbance away from him by uttering angry commands. But now the emotion that is wracking him is so great that it can only be uttered, that is, projected outward, as a total destruction of nature, a cracking of nature's molds, and the effort required to project it outward is captured by the actor's effort to address the storm. The vocal effort needed to get from "blow" to "winds" and so on embodies this, for it is like trying to reach up and touch the storm, to become the thunder and the wind. The storm is significantly called "thought-executing," for in it we feel the explosive release of the thoughts Lear can no longer keep down.[4]

Lear's relation to the storm swings rapidly from commanding it to insulting it to holding his tongue again, and then he returns to identifying with the storm—but now no physical effort of emulation is involved. He is no longer acting out the storm but, as it were, imagining it. And he imagines it in terms of its effects on a population of hidden sinners:

> Tremble, thou wretch,
> That hast within thee undivulgèd crimes
> Unwhipped of justice. Hide thee, thou bloody hand,
> Thou perjured, and thou simular of virtue
> That art incestuous. Caitiff, to pieces shake,
> That under covert and convenient seeming
> Has practices on man's life.   (51–57)

Two points are interesting here. First, this is the first time in the play that Lear focuses on other individuals as centers of suffering. Second, Lear connects the active power of the storm with the eruption of hidden evil. The moral point here is less important than the psychological one. Lear suddenly is no longer talking about violence which comes from outside but about violence that bursts from within:

> Close pent-up guilts,
> Rive your concealing continents and cry
> These dreadful summoners grace.   (57–59)

This shift to erupting guilt makes the lines that follow—"I am a man/More sinned against than sinning"—complex indeed. For Lear is moved to protest the injustice of his suffering, not, as one might expect, by thoughts of what he is being subjected to, but by thoughts of guilt bursting out. What he suffers seems bound up in his mind with guilt, guilt associated with sexual crimes and murder. Perhaps he experiences the force of his emotions as murderous and sexually irregular. The actor can find the emotional life that keeps this scene from degenerating into rant only by carefully charting how Lear's rapidly varying attack on the storm follows the surges of that inner suffering he now begins to acknowledge. He rives his own concealing continents to do so.

It is at this point that Lear says his wits are turning, and suddenly directs his attention to yet another center of suffering. This time it is a real person, not an imagined throng of sinners. He becomes aware that the Fool is cold, comforts him, and admits that he is cold himself. Out of this immense, chaotic explosion of long-denied emotion comes a moment of minute, concrete, ordinary feeling, a tenderness we have not seen before, based on an acknowledgment of shared pain:

> My wits begin to turn.
> Come on, my boy. How dost, my boy? Art cold?
> I am cold myself.   (67–69)

These moments of awareness and tenderness become an important motif in the play as Lear directs his new capacity for close attention to the naked wretches in the storm, to Edgar and, later, to Gloucester and Cordelia.

IV

All the various motifs of performance I have been discussing have in common a demand placed on the actor—and a concomitant opportunity given him—to apprehend concrete, sharply defined foci of pain. They require that the actor keep *renewing* his sensations, opening himself to a particularity of suffering. This of course is crucial to our experience of the play. The actor's renewal of sensation, by keeping the part alive, keeps our own sensitivity alive in the face of *King Lear*'s avalanche of pain.

The scene in Act IV during which Lear meets Gloucester and Edgar on the way to Dover is full of such histrionic opportunities for renewal. There are several things on Lear's mind here: sexual loathing, revenge, a hallucinatory, at times satirical, vision of court life and of himself as king, a fool-like insistence on unpleasant truths in his conversations with Gloucester, and at the same time a tenderness toward Gloucester's suffering. But in each case there is a marked movement of scrutiny—Lear presses forward to examine some detail in its full vividness of sensation. Lear focusses at different moments on, among other things, Gloucester's blinded eyes, a mouse, a wren, a small fly, a man accused of adultery, Gloucester's tears, and finally on the hooves of a troop of horses, shod with felt, pattering across the great stage of the Globe theater.

A few examples from this scene will show the histrionic imagery at work. At its beginning, Lear imagines himself as king. His hallucination projects a world whose dimensions are freely changing. The result is that Lear constantly seems to be on the scale of what he encounters, be it a mouse or a flying arrow or a troop of soldiers:

> That fellow handles his bow like a crow-keeper; draw me a clothier's yard. Look, look, a mouse! Peace, peace; this piece of toasted cheese will do't. There's my gauntlet; I'll prove it on a giant. Bring up the brown bills. O, well flown, bird! i' th' clout, i' th' clout: hewgh!   (IV, vi, 87–92)

The mental movement here is in striking contrast to Lear's stance at the beginning of the play, where he insisted on control, on maintaining a scale through which he dominated. His reference to the bow may recall his great image of irresistible authority in the first scene ("The bow is bent and drawn; make from the shaft"), but now he follows the shaft into the target and mimes its whizzing sound. From the grand command to the thing commanded in an instant, from the straining bow to the little mouse, this new ability is a measure of how Lear has changed.

As the scene progresses, the sense of smell is emphasized, competing with touch and sight for prominence. Sharply concrete references to smell and sexuality are mingled. The hand that smells of mortality, the little gilded copulating fly, the soiled horse, and above all the genitalia of women are on Lear's mind, and he responds to them as if they sweated and stank with a combination of sexual abandon and decay. Even a description of virtue is charged with a grotesque prurience:

> Behold yond simp'ring dame,
> Whose face between her forks presages snow.   (118–19)

The effect of the syntax is to displace a visual image of chastity downward so sharply that it emerges as a grossly suggestive image of sexual license, and leads Lear quickly to sensations of burning and stench:

> But to the girdle do the gods inherit,
> Beneath is all the fiend's.
> There's hell, there's darkness, there is the sulphurous pit, burning, scalding, stench, consumption; fie, fie, fie! pah, pah!   (126–30)

Lear's agony is immense. He has not yet emerged from the tempest in his mind, but now he is harrowed by vivid physical sensations, which he links to emotional disturbance, again, as in the third act, connecting them with sexual transgression. The denial of emotion, the association of unmanageable feeling with humiliating taint is still strong. Now, as Gloucester offers to kiss his hand, Lear imagines that Gloucester is squinting, peering at him perhaps lecherously. At any rate he associates Gloucester with the emblem of blind Cupid, which was sometimes hung as a sign above a brothel:

> Dost thou squiny at me? No, do thy worst, blind Cupid; I'll not love.
>   (136–38)

He rejects love. More important, Lear connects love with the idea of painful scrutiny and does this by means of images that carry the force of the sexual revulsion he feels welling up inside him.

At the end of the scene between them, Lear continues to swing from one tack to another, from imagining a spectacle of injustice, full of specific physical images, to a tender awareness of Gloucester weeping, to the vividly imagined tightness of his probably nonexistent boots, and back to Gloucester,

> If thou wilt weep my fortunes, take my eyes.
> I know thee well enough; thy name is Gloucester:
> Thou must be patient; we came crying hither.   (176–78)

and thus to a sense of the entire career of human life as smelling, weeping, and playing the fool:

> Thou know'st, the first time that we smell the air
> We wawl and cry....
>   we cry that we are come
> To this great stage of fools.   (179–83)

Then suddenly he turns to revenge, but it too is conceived in terms of immediate sensation:

> It were a delicate stratagem, to shoe
> A troop of horse with felt....
> And when I have stol'n upon these son-in-laws,
> Then, kill, kill, kill, kill, kill, kill!   (184–87)

This last line provides an example of another memorable feature of the play's verse—the accumulative pattern, the use of intensifying repetition, and it offers a final instance of how the action of the actor shapes the meaning of the play. For what is the histrionic problem set by lines like "kill, kill, kill, kill, kill, kill" and "Now, now, now, now" and "Never, never, never, never, never" and "Howl, howl, howl, howl"? In performance they act out a tension between the desire for absoluteness of response and the need for renewal, between the thrill of letting go, of crying out, and the labor of concentration, of finding a precise image for each exclamation in the series.[5] Such lines long to be only a cry, but they must have a content or they go dead: they threaten to escape, as every audience and every critic longs to escape, from the dreadful particularity of the play. They too demand, and make possible, that regular renewal of sensation crucial to the role.

V

I want to shift perspective now and consider briefly a few of the ways in which Shakespeare locates the small acting patterns I have been talking about in what we experience as the larger world of the play. I will take as examples some features of Shakespeare's treatment of action and space.

In Shakespeare's tragedies we normally feel that the represented action (*praxis*, in my jargon) proceeds from the interplay of some more or less controlled and steadily maintained personal or political schemes, for example, Hamlet versus Claudius, or Macbeth versus those he first displaces and later is overthrown by. Now, though it is equally easy to discern in *King Lear* the movements of warring parties whose fortunes swing up and down and though there is, when one reflects on it, a surprising amount of intrigue, public and private, in the play (the secret conference, scheming, suspicion, and letter writing that have always formed the staple of the drama of intrigue), our *impression* of the action of *King Lear* is likely to be more chaotic. All the scheming is felt to take place on the edge of a much larger disturbance (Kent and a gentleman exchanging secrets in the storm, Regan and Goneril hurriedly conferring after the first scene as the court breaks up in confusion, Oswald carrying letters back and forth while the world goes mad).

At the same time, a major activity in the play is expulsion: Lear expelling Cordelia and Kent; Goneril and Regan forcing Lear out into the storm; Edmund forcing Edgar to run away; Cornwall throwing out the blinded Gloucester. Even assistance is most often seen, not as taking someone in, but as helping someone get away to an unspecified or temporary location. Thus, the intrigue in the play communicates itself to us as a set of fragile strands of intention winding across a large and threatening outdoor space.

For the sense of space in *King Lear* is unique in the Shakespeare canon. Instead of being presented with the usual two or at most three major locales, we are in great part urged to think of the stage as representing a place en route. And these scenes are unlike the en-route scenes of the histories or other plays that, like *Lear*, have battles in them, because in *Lear* they are felt to be not stages of access to a major location (Shrewsbury, Dunsinane), but rather pieces of a vast, unlocalized, transitional space, the large, exposed, generally inhospitable expanse of England. The largeness of Lear's England has been stressed in the early moments of the first scene, when Lear responds to Goneril and Regan's declarations of total love:

> Of all these bounds, even from this line to this,
> With shadowy forests, and with champains riched,
> With plenteous rivers, and wide-skirted meads,
> We make thee lady.   (I, i, 63–66)

But the greenness and richness of this world seem to vanish with Cordelia's refusal and Lear's curse; only the largeness remains. After the initial explosion in the great, ordered presence chamber, the indoors of the play becomes little more than a series of ad hoc auxiliary confines—a hovel, a lodging, an outbuilding, some convenient, borrowed room for torture. The rest is outdoors, on the way, dust-blown, wind-swept and bare, a space crisscrossed by the play's many frail and circuitous threads of intention: groups hurriedly quitting home, search parties, messengers, outlaws. We see letters moving about through curious and uncertain routes. Not only the messengers but the senders and recipients are on the move, and the letters are read not at leisure but under stress—in a storm, in the stocks, after a fight to the death. This sense of large, unorganized space and of errant, improvised movement through it is fundamental to the play, and helps locate Lear's recurrent focus upon minute particulars of sensation.

Here again we are made aware of precision of response by its contrast with undifferentiated hugeness. Lear's small gestures of scrutiny and physical contact stand out against the large, chaotic space of the play. And it is against the same background that we see one of the play's familiar sights—people supporting each other, one leading another by a hand or arm, two supporting one, one touching another. Edgar, Lear, and Gloucester seem to spend much of the play reeducating themselves in feeling through the exercise of touch, and this, too, adds to the impression of a fragile thread of feeling poised against the storm.

V I

When Cordelia wakes Lear, he does not know whether or not he is alive. To see if he is, he pricks his skin with a pin. It is a basic test, whose meaning is central to the play. To be conscious is to be able to feel pain. Where there's life, there's hurt. Next Lear wants to know if Cordelia is real and human instead of a vision or an angel. He decides she is real when he notices her tears are wet. This tender concentration on the facts of pain takes on a special strength when we reach the play's final scene.

Lear's whole last sequence with Cordelia's body is a series of sharp focussings that insist on the unbearable distinction between life and death. Lear attends carefully to the looking glass, the feather, Cordelia's voice, her breath, her mouth. His eyes are not o' the best, but he makes an effort to scrutinize Kent's face. Then he asks someone to undo a button—at his throat, I think—and turns back to stare at Cordelia's lips. His last words combine his three great modes of enactment—the giving of commands, intensification through repetition, scrutiny of particulars:

> Look on her. Look, her lips,
> Look there, look there.   (V, iii, 312–13)

There is also in this gesture a subtle formal link to the beginning of the play, just as the exhausted triumvirate of Albany, Kent, and Edgar echoes Lear's original division of the kingdom. For as the first scene, with its talk of "all" and "nothing" on the part of Goneril, Regan, and Lear, presented us with towering absolutes, standards of affection and rejection that we knew to be false, as compared with the specificity, the sense of limit, in Cordelia's "no more nor less" (93), so the last scene confronts us with the difference between life and death in terms of tiny particular distinctions we know to be truly absolute.

When Gielgud entered in this scene with Cordelia in his arms, his voice suddenly rose on the last word of "Howl, howl, howl, howl," and became a howl itself, an animal wail.[6] He achieved here the kind of emotional renewal, the kind of continuing specificity, that lines of this type demand. He was taking advantage of the fact that the lines are at once a command and a cry. But they are unlike the commands Lear utters in the opening scenes because they *are* a cry, and because what they command is a sharing of feeling. Like so much in the play, they confront the performer, Lear's onstage audience, and the audience in the theater with the need to *keep* feeling just when we might well wish to stop, to distance ourselves form the pain. And my point in this essay has been that the role of Lear, as Shakespeare has written it, is designed to carry the audience forward into a deep exploration of its own relation to pain and to the problems of feeling and not feeling.

When Gloucester tells Lear that he has learned to see the world feelingly, Lear answers, "What, art mad?" (IV, vi, 150.) For his own madness is a struggle in which he comes to acknowledge his feelings and through them to make a connection with the world that brings him instants of shared love and moments of illumination he could have attained no other way. But the play's ending makes certain that we do not sentimentalize these moments, that we continue to experience the kind of openness to feeling Lear achieves as something desperately difficult, charged always with a weight of possible terror. For to see feelingly means to introduce an element of risk into every human exchange, the risk of being incapacitated, driven mad, destroyed by what one feels. It is to remind oneself that one is always vulnerable, because one is not everything. "They told me I was everything; 'tis a lie" Lear says (IV, vi, 104); and when Cordelia first tries to tell him that no one can be everything, his first reaction is to feel that she is nothing. But without that recognition of vulnerability, as the experience of the play reminds us, and as it must remind the actor who attempts the title role, without that constant focus on the dangerous human facts of feeling, we are nothing indeed.

NOTES

[1] "Histrionic imagery," as I use the term, refers to any element in the text of a play which clearly indicates the manner of an actor's attack, particularly to those which suggest a recurring pattern. The image can be an object or part of the body, as in the examples from *Lear* in the previous section, but, as we are about to see, it can also be a part of speech (Lear's reiterated exclamations), another character (the Fool as Lear addresses him), or even an emotion (Lear's sorrow as he fights to keep it down), anything, in short, which carries with it a specific mechanism or gesture of theatrical self-projection on the part of the actor who engages with it. The lists that Hamlet uses to indicate rapid emotional progressions, the exotic references and locutions that Othello incorporates into his speech, are examples of histrionic imagery. The term is inevitably fuzzy at the edges, because finally everything in a play requires histrionic treatment, and so every object and every word in a dramatic text may be considered a histrionic image. But in practice it is useful to limit the concept to items that can be shown to suggest a reasonably plain and recurrent performance attack.

[2] Again, I am using "performance design" in Marvin Rosenberg's technical sense—the architecture of histrionic possibilities built into a single role.

[3] Note in this passage how "relieve," "pity," and "neighbor," words which carry an opposite sense to monstrosity or violence, take on, by management as well as context, a resistant, snarling texture.

[4] Following Dr. Johnson, editors usually gloss "thought-executing" as *acting with the rapidity of thought.* Kenneth Muir also cites Moberly's, "Executing the thought of him who casts you." But there is also a suggestion of capital punishment in "execute," and this sorts well with the aggressive energy of Lear's own thoughts, which will perhaps be punished when his white head is singed. Note that Lear is once more imagining action as proceeding instantaneously and irresistibly from thought.

[5] Like any attempt to explain a complex theatrical moment or indeed any complex instant of feeling, this runs the risk of sounding over-intellectualized, but it is in no sense over-elaborate. In a good performance we unmistakably feel both the expansive release of Lear's cry—and the intensity of renewed pain at each iteration. If we don't, we feel the actor is faking: shouting has replaced feeling, generalization experience.

[6] This may be heard on Gielgud's *Ages of Man* recording, Columbia OL 5390.

Arthur Kirsch

THE EMOTIONAL
LANDSCAPE OF *KING LEAR*

The tragedy of *King Lear* raises large religious, as well as political and social, questions, and there is a disposition in recent scholarship to treat the play as if it were an argument that gives unorthodox, if not revolutionary, answers to them. Prominent critics have contended that *Lear* is locked in combat with Elizabethan conceptions of Providence and order,[1] and one influential Marxist critic has maintained that the play constitutes both a specific criticism of Elizabethan ideology and a denial of what he calls "essentialist humanism," the belief that, with respect to tragedy, assumes "a human essence which by its own nature as well as its relation to the universal order of things, must inevitably suffer."[2]

The current popularity of such views makes it urgent, I think, to reassert the less fashionable position that though Shakespeare is "the soul of [his] age," as Ben Jonson wrote, he is also "not of an age, but for all time," and that, as Dr. Johnson argued, his plays have "pleased many, and pleased long," because they are "just representations of general nature," "faithful mirror[s]" of manners and of life." Shakespeare's tragedies are, above all else, plays of passions and suffering that we eventually recognize as our own, whatever their social, political, or religious contingencies may have been in the Renaissance. However we may interpret the particular ideological questions *King Lear* seems to pose, it is the universal human anguish that gives rise to them upon which Shakespeare primarily focuses and to which audiences have responded for nearly four hundred years.

The experience of feeling—physical as well as emotional feeling—is at the core of *King Lear,* as the enlargement of our own capacity to feel is at the core of any persuasive explanation of why we can take pleasure in such a tragedy. The word "heart" resonates in the play, describing the extremes of the play's characterizations, from the "honest-hearted" Kent (I.iv.19) to the "marble-hearted" ingratitude and "hard-hearts" of Goneril and Regan (I.iv.237; III.vi.36).[3] "Heart" is the metonym for Lear himself in the storm—"poor old heart, he holp the heavens to rain" (III.vii.60)—and it is the primary register of Lear's experience. He rejects

From *Shakespeare Quarterly* 39, No. 2 (Summer 1988): 154–70.

Cordelia because she cannot heave her "heart" into her "mouth" (I.i.92), and he pronounces her banishment as the divorce of her heart from his own: "So be my grave my peace as here I give / Her father's heart from her" (I.i.125–26), an uncanny line that predicates his eventual reunion with her in death. The heart is physically palpable to Lear. He says he is "struck ... upon the very heart" by Goneril's "tongue" (II.ii.333–34), and the same tactile sense of the heart emerges in the synapse between physical and emotional pain that prompts the first movement of fellow-feeling in him:

> My wits begin to turn.
> (*To Fool*) Come on, my boy. How dost, my boy? Art cold?
> I am cold myself....
> Poor fool and knave, I have one part in my heart
> That's sorry yet for thee.   (III.ii.67–69, 72–73)

As Lear moves toward madness, he recognizes that his rage against Cordelia drew from his "heart all love" and "wrenched" his "frame of nature / From the fixed place" (I.iv.247–248); he then repeatedly identifies his incipient madness with his heart: "O, how this mother swells up toward my heart! / *Histerica passio* down, thou climbing sorrow" (II.ii.231–32); "O me, my heart! My rising heart! But down" (II.ii.292); "But this heart shall break into a hundred thousand flaws / Or ere I'll weep" (II.ii.458–59).

The breaking of the heart "into a hundred thousand flaws" defines the point towards which most references to the heart in *King Lear* eventually move, and suggests the extremity of pain and suffering that is the play's peculiar concern. In his most famous soliloquy Hamlet speaks of the "heartache" of human existence. In *King Lear* we hear of and then see hearts "cracked" (II.i.89) and "split" (V.iii.168). Edgar tells us that his father, Gloucester, died when his "flawed heart ... / 'Twixt two extremes of passion, joy and grief, / Burst smilingly" (V.iii.188, 190–91), and at the moment of Lear's death, Kent says, "Break, heart, I prithee break" (V.iii.288), a line that corroborates the truth of what we have just witnessed, whether it refers to Lear's heart or to Kent's own.

The dramatization of the metaphor of a breaking heart and its association with the extremity of dying are central to *King Lear*, for though, again like *Hamlet*, *King Lear* is essentially concerned with the anguish of living in the face of death, it does not look beyond the grave. It focuses instead, and relentlessly, upon the shattering of the heart and upon actual human deterioration—the physical "eyes' anguish" (IV.v.6) of Gloucester's maiming, the emotional "eye of anguish" (IV.iii.15) of Lear's madness. Nor does the Fifth Act of the play bring relief, as it does in *Hamlet*. There is no recovery from sorrow and grief at the end of *Lear*, and there is no suggestion of the "special providence" that Hamlet, in his luminous reference to Matthew, sees in the fall of a sparrow. The agonized question that Lear asks over Cordelia's lifeless body, "Why should a dog, a horse, a rat have life, / And thou no breath at all?" (V.iii.282–83) is not answered in the play, certainly not by his own few succeeding words; and among those words the ones that are most unequivocal and that we most remember are: "Thou'lt come no more. / Never, never, never, never, never!"

(V.iii.283–84). These lines express the immediate, "essential," feeling of all of us in the presence of the death and dying of those we love, but they have an acute and governing power in *King Lear*.[4] They occur at the very end, they occur after protracted suffering, they violate the hopes that appear to be raised by the reunion of Lear and Cordelia, and they occur over the dead body of a character who has seemed to symbolize the heart's undying resources of love in the play. There is no scene in Shakespeare that represents the wrench of death more absolutely or more painfully; and the scene is not merely the conclusion of the action of the play, it is its recapitulation, the moment in which the whole of it is crystallized.

In this regard, as in others, *King Lear* is very reminiscent of Ecclesiastes. The depiction of suffering in *King Lear* has often been compared to the Book of Job,[5] which, of course, focuses upon the suffering of an individual; and the protraction of Job's suffering as well as his protests against it do indeed suggest the magnitude of Lear's heroic characterization. But there is no Satan at the beginning of *King Lear*, nor a whirlwind from which God speaks at the end to make the play's extraordinary sense of heartfelt pain even intellectually explicable. In its overall conception as well as in much of its ironic texture, *King Lear* is closer to Ecclesiastes, the book of the Old Testament that is most nearly pagan in its outlook and that treats human life almost exclusively in terms of the immanence of its ending.

The Preacher in Ecclesiastes speaks over and over again of the heart, occasionally of the "heart of the wise" or "of fooles" (7:6),[6] but most often of his own: "And I haue giuen mine heart to search & finde out wisdome" (1:13); "I thoght in mine heart" (1:16); "And I gaue mine heart" (1:17); "I said in mine heart" (2.1); "I soght in mine heart" (2:3). The Preacher's experience of the heart suggests many of the major motifs as well as the specific language of *King Lear*. His announced theme is "vanity," a word whose principal connotation (and whose translation in the New English Bible) is "emptiness," and he speaks of man's identity in this life as "a shadow" (7:2) and his achievements as "nothing" (5:14; 7:16). He likens men to beasts:

> For the condition of the children of men, and the condition of beastes *are* even *as* one condition vnto them. As the one dyeth, so dyeth the other: for they haue all one breath, and there is no excellencie of man aboue the beast: for all *is* vanitie.   (3:19)

He describes man's nakedness: "As he came forthe of his mothers belly, he shal returne naked to go as he came, & shal beare away nothing of his labour, which he hathe caused to passe by his hand" (5:14). He talks repeatedly of the paradoxes of wisdom and folly and madness:

> And I gaue mine heart to knowe wisdome & knowledge, madnes & foolishnes: I knewe also that this is a vexacion of the spirit.

> For in the multitude of wisdome *is* muche grief: & he that encreaseth knowledge, encreaseth sorowe.   (1:17–18)

He relates such paradoxes to kingship: "Better is a poore and wise childe, then an olde and foolish King, which wil no more be admonished" (4:13), and he relates them as well to eyesight: "For the wise mans eyes *are* in his head, but the foole walketh in darkenes: yet I knowe also that the same condition falleth to them all" (2:14). He also associates "The sight of the eye" with "lustes" (6:9), and he speaks of how men are killed like fishes in a net and birds in a snare (9:12). And he is preoccupied with the paradoxes of justice and injustice:

> I have sene all things in the daies of my vanitie: there is a iuste man that
> perisheth in his iustice, and there is a wicked man that continueth long in his
> malice.   (7:17)

> There is a vanitie, which is done vpon the earth, that there be righteous
> men to whome it cometh according to the worke of the wicked: and there be
> wicked men to whome it cometh according to the worke of the iuste: I thoght
> also that this is vanitie.   (8:14)

The premise as well as the conclusion of all these experiences is that

> All things *come* alike to all: and the same condition *is* to the iuste and to
> the wicked, to the good and to the pure, & to the polluted, & to him that
> sacrificeth, & to him that sacrificeth not: as *is* the good, so *is* the sinner, he that
> sweareth, as he that feareth an othe.   (9:2)

The "olde and foolish King" is perhaps the most inescapable of the resem-blances between these verses and *King Lear,* but many others are equally sugges-tive: the painful paradoxes of folly and wisdom that are the subject of the Fool's speeches and songs; the realization of the metaphors of sight in Gloucester's blinding; the nakedness of birth and death and of man's whole condition that is lamented by Lear and acted out by both Lear and Edgar; the random wantonness of death of which Gloucester complains; the comparisons of men and beasts that suffuse the language of the play and that are especially prominent in Lear's speeches, including his last; the vision of the confluence of the just and the wicked that consumes Lear on the heath and that leads him to conclude, not unlike the Preacher, that "None does offend, none, I say none" (IV.v.164).

  Ecclesiastes, of course, is not the only source from which Shakespeare could have inherited such preoccupations. Most of them are prominent in Montaigne's "Apologie of *Raymond Sebond,*" a work that clearly lies behind the play,[7] and they are present as well in other parts of the Bible itself, especially its depictions of the end of the world.[8] The vision of the Apocalypse in Mark 13, for example, virtually describes the central action of *King Lear:*

> For nacion shal rise against nacion, and kingdome against kingdome, and
> there shalbe earthquakes ... the brother shal deliuer the brother to death,
> and the father the sonne, and the children shal rise against their parents, and
> shal cause them to dye.   (13:8, 12)

But if the Apocalypse suggests the general social and political outline of *Lear*, the large number of evocations of Ecclesiastes (and many more could be cited) give that outline its emotional definition. The Preacher's lament that "he that encreaseth knowledge, encreaseth sorowe" is a line that the Fool could sing: it evokes the cadence as well as the substance of his characterization and its relationship with Lear's. The Preacher's repeated references to the anguish of his own heart suggest the pain of protest as well as of resignation, a combination of feelings that *King Lear* eventually also elicits—in us, if not also, at the last, in Lear himself. And perhaps most important, if most obvious, *vanitas*, the theme that echoes endlessly in Ecclesiastes and that *King Lear* catches up in its preoccupation with the word "nothing," leads not just to the idea of emptiness, but to its paradoxically full feeling, the feeling to which Edgar refers at the end when he says that we should "Speak what we feel, not what we ought to say" (V.iii.300). This feeling has a far greater amplitude and richness in the play than in Ecclesiastes, but its roots are the same.

Subsuming all of these motifs is the focus upon death as the universal event in human existence that not only ends life but calls its whole meaning into question. The Preacher in Ecclesiastes at one point asks, "Who is as the wise man? and who knoweth the interpretacion of a thing?" (8:1), and the burden of the question is that given the transience and mutability of human life, who *can* know? As in *King Lear*, which also poses this question insistently, there is no satisfying answer, and certainly no consoling one. But again like *Lear*, Ecclesiastes does offer a characteristic perception of human existence in the face of death, if not an interpretation of it. For the Preacher's anguished sense of the dissolution of all things in time almost necessarily impels him to think of those things in terms of polarities—the polarities of beginnings and endings especially, but also of their cognates in creativeness and destructiveness—and to think of life itself as a composition of extremes that have individual moral definition, but that are not necessarily morally intelligible as a whole. He suggests this understanding in the passage already quoted in which he says that "All things *come* alike to all," to the just and the wicked, the good and the pure, and that "as *is* the good, so *is* the sinner," and he does so strikingly in the passage for which Ecclesiastes is now best known and which is regularly cited in liturgies for the dead, the passage that speaks of a time to be born and a time to die, a time to slay and a time to heal, to weep and to laugh, to seek and to lose, to keep and to cast away, to be silent and to speak, to love and to hate (3:1–8).

This polarized landscape suggests the most profound of the affinities between Ecclesiastes and *King Lear*, for the kingdom of *Lear* too is defined by the antinomy of "coming hither" and "going hence" (V.ii.10) and by corresponding oppositions of human states of feeling and being. The association of such oppositions with the experience of death is adumbrated earlier in Shakespeare's career in *Richard II*, a play that is also concerned with an abdication that is a prefiguration of death:

What must the King do now? Must he submit?
The King shall do it. Must he be deposed?
The King shall be contented. Must he lose

The name of King? A God's name, let it go.
I'll give my jewels for a set of beads,
My gorgeous palace for a hermitage,
My gay apparel for an almsman's gown,
My figured goblets for a dish of wood,
My sceptre for a palmer's walking staff,
My subjects for a pair of carvèd saints,
And my large kingdom for a little grave,
A little, little grave, an obscure grave....   (*Richard II*, III.iii.142–53)[9]

Richard's itemization of these oppositions is melodramatic, but the contrasts nonetheless do characterize his sensibility, because once his mind is focused on death
there is no middle ground in which he can live. In *King Lear* these meditative
antitheses are not only acted out by Lear himself but also inform every part of the
play's action. For like Ecclesiastes, *King Lear* is composed of oppositions, oppositions
between weeping and laughing, seeking and losing, being silent and speaking, loving
and hating. The characters embody such contrasts: Cordelia is schematically opposed to Goneril and Regan, Edgar to Edmund, Kent to Oswald, Albany to Cornwall.

Some of these oppositions are combined in single characterizations, especially
those of the Fool and Cordelia, but also those of Gloucester and Lear. The Fool's
embodiment of the paradoxes of wisdom and folly that run through Ecclesiastes is
of course obvious. He incarnates these paradoxes in his traditional role, in his dress,
and in his speech; and he does so with the bias toward the broken heart that is
characteristic both of Ecclesiastes and of the play. Enid Welsford remarks that "the
Fool sees that when the match between the good and the evil is played by the
intellect alone it must end in stalemate, but when the heart joins in the game then
the decision is immediate and final. 'I will tarry, the Fool will stay—And let the wise
man fly.'" She adds that this "is the unambiguous wisdom of the madman who sees
the truth," and that it "is decisive" because it reflects the way that normal human
beings see the world feelingly.[10] I think that though this is perhaps true, the Fool's
"whirling ambiguities" carry a burden that is further reminiscent of Ecclesiastes and
less comforting. The Fool tells Lear that when Lear made his daughters his mothers,

Then they for sudden joy did weep,
    And I for sorrow sung,
That sung a king should play bo-peep
    And go the fools among.   (I.iv.156–59)

Besides providing the keynote of his own characterization, this particular condensation of emotions is also eventually associated with the moment of death itself in
the play. The paradoxical fusion of the extremities of joy and sorrow was often
noted in Renaissance commentaries on the passions,[11] but its identification with
death is peculiar to *Lear*. The correspondence between the two is suggested in the
old ballad that the Fool seems to be adapting:

Some men for sodayne ioye do wepe,
　And some in sorrow syng:
When that they lie in daunger depe,
　To put away mournyng.[12]

It is that shadow of mourning in the Fool, the association of the Fool with Death that is always incipient in his traditional role as the teller of the truths of human vanity and mortality, that makes particularly appropriate Lear's conflation of him with Cordelia at the end of the play, when he says, "And my poor fool is hanged" (V.iii.281).

The combination of opposites is especially profound in Cordelia's character-ization, but the play's most manifest combinations of the extremes that are traced in Ecclesiastes occur in the actions as well as characterizations of Lear and Glouces-ter, the two aged and dying protagonists who participate in the being of all their children, the loving and the hateful, the legitimate and the illegitimate. Indeed a large part of the action of the play consists of Lear's and Gloucester's oscillation between extremes that are never ameliorated, that tear at them, and that ultimately break their hearts.

Gloucester's initial arrogance in his talk of Edmund's bastardy yields very quickly to the demoralizing thought that his legitimate son seeks his death; and the "good sport" (I.i.22) of the scene of Edmund's conception is eventually contrasted with the malignant horror of the scene in which Gloucester is blinded. Edgar, who makes the latter contrast explicit, also tries to treat it homiletically: "The dark and vicious place where thee he got / Cost him his eyes" (V.iii.163–64); but the sym-metry of Edgar's formulation does not dispel our own sense of the gross disparity between the two scenes. And the same is true of Gloucester's states of mind on the heath, after his blinding. Edgar's sententious efforts to preserve his father from despair finally only intensify our sense of the alternations between despair and patience that punctuate Gloucester's feelings, alternations that continue to the point of his death, and that actually constitute it. Near the end Gloucester, in his anguish, says to Edgar that "A man may rot even here" (V.ii.8). Edgar's famous response, "Men must endure / Their going hence even as their coming hither. / Ripeness is all" (V.ii.9–11), might well be a verse in Ecclesiastes. (The exhausted tone of Ecclesiastes is generally apposite to the Gloucester plot.) "Ripeness" is a metaphor not for the fullness of life, but for the need to be resigned to the arbitrariness of its ending. As the context itself suggests, Edgar is evoking a traditional image of ripe fruit dropping from a tree and then rotting.[13] "Ripeness is all" is Gloucester's epitaph.

Similar stark contrasts of feeling, on a far more massive scale, inform Lear's movement toward death, and in his case there is not even the patina of moral commentary. The Fool's comments, which are the analogues of Edgar's, are almost always morally equivocal, and they are entirely absorbed with the paradoxical oppositions that compose Lear's condition. In the second childhood of age, Lear is at the same time "every inch a king" (IV.v.107); and though he sometimes enacts these roles simultaneously, he cannot meditate between them: they remain in opposition until the play's end. His sense of humility grows, but it alternates with his wrath, never replaces it. He rages in his last appearance in the play, as he did in his first. His increasing apprehension, early in the play, of the wrong he did Cordelia is balanced by his excoriations of his other daughters and by the fury of his madness, just as later in the play the joy of his recovery of Cordelia is balanced by the desolation of his loss of her. In a wonderful speech, he imagines kneeling and humbling himself as a child before Cordelia:

> Come let's away to prison.
> We two alone will sing like birds i'th' cage.
> When thou dost ask me blessing, I'll kneel down
> And ask of thee forgiveness; so we'll live,
> And pray, and sing, and tell old tales, and laugh
> At gilded butterflies ...   (V.iii.8–13)

But the childlike humility of this speech is a function of its childlike presumption, for Lear also tells Cordelia that they will "take upon" themselves "the mystery of things / As if we were God's spies" (V.i.16–17).[14] And the yoking of such disparities continues until his death, and in the very moment of it. His very last words express the hope—or delusion—that Cordelia is alive. They join with, they do not transform, the knowledge that she will never return.

It is tempting to see in Lear's movement towards death an image of the homiletic journeys of the protagonists of the earlier morality plays, particularly because those plays seem similarly composed of radically contrasting states of feeling and being—virtue and vice, despair and hope, good and evil, angels and devils. But the resemblances only highlight the profound difference. In the moralities, the summons of death is not ultimately an end but a beginning that retrospectively gives meaning to the large contrasts of human existence. In *King Lear*, as in Ecclesiastes, the summons is to an absolute ending whose retrospect of existence is not morally comprehensible. Edgar tries to make it so for his father's death, and there is perhaps a moral, if barbaric, decorum in Gloucester's destruction by his bastard son. But the Gloucester plot is not the primary plot of *King Lear*. That plot is Lear's, and even Edgar cannot moralize Lear's story. He says of the spectacle of Lear's meeting with Gloucester on the heath, "I would not take this from report; it is, / And my heart breaks at it" (IV.v.137–38). The verb *is* in Edgar's comment suggests that Lear's suffering presents us with the world of unmediated existential extremes we find in Ecclesiastes, where "as *is* the good, so *is* the sinner." The growth in Lear's understanding itself suggests this world. Lear does change on the heath. His own suffering allows him to feel, almost literally to touch, the pain of poor Tom and of the Fool and of poor naked wretches everywhere. This compassion is important and deeply moving. The sympathetic experience of pain establishes a human community in a play that otherwise seems to represent its apocalyptic dissolution, and it informs our sense of Lear's heroic stature. But his compassion should also not be misconstrued in a Romantic fashion, for the knowledge of human frailty that his suffering brings him increases his sorrow to the point of madness. Critics sometimes talk of the "privilege" of Lear's madness, but if we examine our own experience of mentally infirm human beings, we will, like Edgar, know better. It is a horror, and an anticipation of "the promised end . . . Or image of that horror" (V.iii.238–39) that we witness in Cordelia's death.[15]

Cordelia's death is, typically, preceded by her reunion with Lear after he awakens from his madness, a scene that has often been treated as if it were the climax of the action and that has frequently been compared with the reunion of Pericles and Marina. The two scenes have many elements in common: both show old and exhausted fathers, discomposed by suffering, reunited with daughters from whom they have long been separated and who seem to bring them back to life. In both, the recognitions are luminous; and both have verse of extraordinary lyric intensity. But the two scenes are also profoundly different in their immediate and eventual effects as well as in their generic contexts. Pericles's recovery of Marina is at once a recovery of his identity and an acknowledgement of its definition in the stream of time. For though, "wild in [his] beholding" (V.i.221),[16] he draws Marina to himself and embraces her, he also immediately dreams of his eventual reunion with his wife and anticipates giving Marina away in marriage. In addition, he hears the music of the spheres, a music that helps give Marina's nurture of him the cosmic sense of the intelligibility, if not miracle, of rebirth: "O, come hither," he tells her, "Thou that beget'st him that did thee beget" (V.i.194–95). The scene invokes the combination of joy and pain that is habitual in *King Lear*, but with a diametrically different accent. As Pericles recognizes Marina, he says:

> O Helicanus, strike me, honour'd sir!
> Give me a gash, put me to present pain,
> Lest this great sea of joys rushing upon me
> O'erbear the shores of my mortality,
> And drown me with their sweetness.   (V.i.190–94)

Pericles's mixture of joy and pain is a guarantee of renewed life rather than an expression of its ending; and he later discriminates the pattern of the fortunate fall in all his suffering, suffering that is the prelude to joy and that heightens it: "You gods, your present kindness / Makes my past miseries sports" (V.iii.40–41).

The pattern, as well as the texture, of Lear's experience is the reverse. Lear tells Kent at the outset of the play that he had "thought to set [his] rest / On [Cordelia's] kind nursery" (I.i.123–24), and it is the peculiar nursing, rather than rebirth, of Lear that we witness in the scene in which he is reunited with Cordelia. For Cordelia ministers not only to an aged father but also to a man transformed by age into a child again. The metaphor of age as second childhood pervades the sources of *King Lear*, and as G. Wilson Knight suggested long ago,[17] Shakespeare himself tends to give it a harsh, if not grotesque, inflection in the play. The Fool speaks of the king putting down his breeches and making his daughters his mothers (I.iv.153–55), a metaphor that is painfully acted out as Lear kneels to Cordelia and says,

> Pray do not mock.
> I am a very foolish, fond old man,
> Fourscore and upward,
> Not an hour more nor less; and to deal plainly,
> I fear I am not in my perfect mind.   (IV.vii.52–56)

That Lear should have to kneel and confess the infirmity of age to his evil daughters is "terrible," but that he should do so to Cordelia as well "has also something of the terrible in it. . . ."[18] The Fool repeatedly rebukes Lear for giving away his power and turning his family relationships upside down, and Lear's behavior in the opening scene would seem to justify those rebukes. But there is a sad irony in the Fool's speeches, for as Montaigne suggested,[19] and as the play itself eventually shows, human beings of "fourscore and upward" usually cannot do otherwise. There is often no choice for us but to become the parents of our parents in their old age and to treat them as children, and it is painful because whether our motives verge toward Cordelia's or toward Goneril and Regan's (and they may do both) the nursing of parents is not nurture for future life but the preparation for death. It is directly so for Lear. The music he hears in his reunion with Cordelia suggests no larger life into which he can be incorporated, and his recovery of her is the immediate prelude to his excruciating loss of her as well as to his own death. In the manner of the whole play, it is a joy that heightens sorrow, that makes it heartbreaking.

As is well known, Dr. Johnson found Cordelia's death both bewildering and unendurable, and like many later critics, he wished to deny it. He protested that "Shakespeare has suffered the virtue of Cordelia to perish in a just cause, contrary to the natural ideas of justice, to the hope of the reader, and, what is yet more strange, to the faith of chronicles." He added, "I was many years ago so shocked by Cordelia's death, that I know not whether I ever endured to read again the last scenes of the play till I undertook to revise them as an editor."[20] As Johnson's commentary suggests, there is an inner logic to adaptations of King Lear, like Nahum Tate's, that left Cordelia and Lear alive and united at the end of the play. All of Shakespeare's own sources—the old play of King Leir, Holinshed, Spenser, and others—end (in the short term, at least) by giving life and victory to Cordelia and Lear.[21] Only Shakespeare does not, and his insistence on Cordelia's death and Lear's final agony, as Northrop Frye remarks, is "too much a part of the play even to be explained as inexplicable."[22] Lear's and Cordelia's union in death is at the heart of Shakespeare's rendition of the Lear story. It is prepared for by every scene in which they appear together, including their earlier reunion, and is the event that not only concludes the tragedy, but wholly informs it. We cannot deny it, however much we wish to and however much the play itself makes us wish to.

A modern understanding of the psychology of dying can help illuminate this phenomenon.[23] Freud's discussion of King Lear is especially pertinent. He argues that the choice among the three daughters with which King Lear begins is the choice of death. Cordelia, in her muteness, he says, is the representation of death and, as in the depiction of such choices in the myths and fairy tales that *King Lear* resembles, her portrayal as the most beautiful and desirable of the three women expresses the inherent, often unconscious, human wish to deny death. "Lear is not only an old man: he is a dying man," and this reality subsumes both "the extraordinary premise of the division of the inheritance" in the opening scene and the overpowering effect of the final scene:

> Lear carries Cordelia's dead body on to the stage. Cordelia is Death. If we reverse the situation it becomes intelligible and familiar to us. She is the Death-goddess who, like the Valkyrie in German mythology, carries away the dead hero from the battlefield. Eternal wisdom, clothed in primaeval myth, bids the old man renounce love, choose death and make friends with the necessity of dying.[24]

Freud's identification of Cordelia with Lear's death suggests the kind of allegorization that often exasperates literary critics, but in this instance, at least, it seems just. Shakespeare's characterization of Cordelia is very luminous, but it is also very sharply focused. She is from first to last a function of Lear's character, a part of him to which we know he must return. She is clearly the person who counts most to him, and in the extremely crowded action of the play it is his relation to her that we most attend to and that most organizes our responses. Their relationship is the emotional as well as structural spine of the play. Cordelia is the absolute focus of Lear's attention, and ours, in the opening scene; it is Lear's rejection of her that initiates the tragic action; and during that ensuing, often diffuse, action neither he nor we can ever forget her. The Fool, who is Cordelia's surrogate, does not allow us to, both because he keeps her constantly in Lear's mind and because the combination of love and sorrow that he brings to Lear prepares us for a similar combination in Cordelia's final role. The collocation of her reunion with Lear and his loss of her is of a piece with all the words of the Fool that weep for joy and sing for sorrow, and it constitutes the same paradox of heartbreak and death.

Lear himself momentarily associates Cordelia and death in the opening scene of the play, when he says, "So be my grave my peace as here I give / Her father's heart from her," and the association is apparent in the scene's literal action as well. Freud contends that Cordelia's silence directly connotes death, as muteness often does in dreams.[25] But Cordelia also speaks in the scene, and what she says indicates clearly enough that Lear's rejection of her is precisely his denial of the impending death that he ostensibly acknowledges in the very act of dividing his kingdom and in his explicit announcement that he wishes "To shake all cares and business from our age," and "Unburdened crawl toward death" (I.i.39, 41). Cordelia tells her father that she loves him "According to [her] bond, no more nor less." She goes on to say, in a speech that is akin to Desdemona's defiance of Brabantio:

> Good my lord,
> You have begot me, bred me, loved me. I
> Return those duties back as are right fit—
> Obey you, love you, and most honour you.
> Why have my sisters husbands if they say
> They love you all? Haply when I shall wed
> That lord whose hand must take my plight shall carry
> Half my love with him, half my care and duty.
> Sure, I shall never marry like my sisters.   (I.i.93, 95–103)

Cordelia exhibits not a little of Lear's own stubbornness in this speech, but though that trait may explain the manner of her speech, it does not account for what, as Kent remarks, she "justly think'st, and hast most rightly said" (I.i.182). What she declares quite clearly in these lines is not only that she must have the freedom to love a husband, but also that it is in the nature of things for parents to be succeeded by children and for her to have a future that Lear cannot absorb or control. Her peculiar gravity in this scene, the austerity of her insistence on the word *bond* as well as her reiteration of the word *nothing*, reflects more than her temperament. It also suggests, even this early in the play, the particular sense of the nature of things that is evoked in Ecclesiastes—the sense of human vanity that comes with the awareness of the ultimate bond with death. At any rate, it is to the natural realities given expression in Cordelia's speech that Lear responds. His rage against her, like his cosmological rage throughout the play, is his refusal to "go gentle into that good night," his unavailing, as well as heroic, attempt to deny death and hold on to life.

Shakespeare's portrayal of this rage and denial is intelligible in Renaissance as well as modern terms. Montaigne's discussion of death and dying in "Of Judging of Others Death," for example, is remarkably apposite to Lear. In an argument that has analogies with Freud's, Montaigne remarks that a dying man "will hardly beleeve he is come to [the] point" of death and that "no wher doth hopes deceit ammuse us more...." "The reason," he says,

> is, that we make too much account of our selves. It seemeth, that the gen-
> erality of things doth in some sort suffer for our annullation, and takes com-
> passion of our state. Forsomuch as our sight being altered, represents unto it
> selfe things alike; and we imagine, that things faile it, as it doth to them: As they
> who travell by Sea, to whom mountaines, fields, townes, heaven and earth,
> seeme to goe the same motion, and keepe the same course, they doe.... We
> deeme our death to be some great matter, and which passeth not so easily,
> nor without a solemne consultation of the Starres; *Tot circa unum caput
> tumultuantes* Deos. *So many Gods keeping a stirre about one mans life....* No
> one of us thinkes it sufficient, to be but one.[26]

Shakespeare's depiction of Lear is clearly informed by such ideas. His portrait is more sympathetic than Montaigne's, but similarly ironic. Rage and cosmological pretension characterize Lear throughout the play. These feelings reach their apogee during the time when his denial of what Cordelia stands for is literalized by her absence from the play. Her return in Act IV heralds his significant recognition that he is "but one"—"They told me I was everything; 'tis a lie, I am not ague-proof" (IV.v.104–5)—and permits him to recover from his madness when he is physically reunited with her. But his inescapable attachment to her, his bond with her, always remains a prefiguration of his death. It is often difficult in our experience of *King Lear* to understand that Lear's denial of death is represented as much in his love for Cordelia as in his rage against her. It is even more difficult, but crucial, to understand that Cordelia's own love is itself a function of this denial, that the expression of her love at the end of the play is as much a signification of Lear's death as is the muteness of that love at the start. Granville-Barker hints at such a meaning as well as at Cordelia's general symbolic properties in his comments on her characterization. He observes that she does not change in the play, and that her cry of "No cause, no cause" to Lear at their reunion is essentially of a piece with her earlier declaration of "Nothing, my lord." He remarks that though "it is no effort to her to love her father better than herself, . . . this supremest virtue, as we count it, is no gain to him," and he asks, "Is there, then, an impotence in such goodness, lovely as we find it? And is this why Shakespeare lets her slip out of the play . . . to her death, as if, for all her beauty of spirit, she were not of so much account?"[27] The questions Granville-Barker asks and the paradox he discriminates are central to Cordelia's characterization and are at the center of most of the play's other paradoxes as well. They are best explained, I think, in terms (which Granville-Barker himself does not use) of the phenomenon of the denial of death, what Montaigne calls "hopes deceit."[28]

In all the myths of the choice among three sisters that Freud finds analogous to *Lear,* the woman representing the power of death is transformed into a woman representing the power of love. Contradictions and contraries of this kind are characteristic of the process of condensation in dreams, but Freud relates such contradictions in *King Lear* primarily to the human disposition to make use of the imagination "to satisfy wishes that reality does not satisfy" and to deny what cannot be tolerated. The profound human wish to deny "the immutable law of death" is represented both in the identification of the most beautiful sister with death and in the presence of choice itself:

> Choice stands in the place of necessity, of destiny. In this way man overcomes death, which he has recognized intellectually. No greater triumph of wish-fulfilment is conceivable. A choice is made where in reality there is obedience to a compulsion, and what is chosen is not a figure of terror, but the fairest and most desirable of women.[29]

In the old chronicle play of *King Leir,* the king has an explicit political motive that is associated with his testing of his daughters' love as well as with the division of the kingdom, and the two wicked daughters are forewarned of it while the good one is not. All three daughters, moreover, are unmarried, and the issue of their marriages is related to the love test and to politics. Shakespeare almost entirely shears away such surface motives and rationalizations for Lear's action in order to make its underlying motive of denial more stark and more compelling.[30] The whole of the scene echoes with negations and contradictions. Its sense of high order and ceremony is prefaced by Gloucester's casual talk of ungoverned instinct. The ceremony itself is a decoronation, deeply reminiscent of Richard II's undecking of "the pompous body of a king" as well as of Richard's ambivalence: "Ay, no; no, ays; for I must nothing be" (*Richard II*, IV.i.240, 191). The pun is not only on "Ay" for "I," but also "no" for "know." Richard knows no "I" and sees that he is to be no "I."[31] He thus seems to indicate and accept, more clearly than Lear ever does, that the loss of his crown also constitutes the loss of his life, that "nothing" is death. This meaning of the word becomes unmistakably plain in his final speech in prison when he says,

> Thus play I in one person many people,
> . . . .
>   But whate'er I be,
> Nor I, nor any man that but man is,
> With nothing shall be pleased till he be eased
> With being nothing.   (V.v.31, 38–41)

Lear himself does not acknowledge the ambivalence that Richard exhibits in resigning the throne, but he unquestionably acts it out. He invests Cornwall and Albany with his "power, / Pre-eminence, and all the large effects / That troop with majesty," but he wishes at the same time to "retain / The name and all th'addition to a king" (I.i.130–32, 135–36). Richard II also cleaves, unavailingly, to the "king's name," and in his case the implications of that wish are explicitly related to the Renaissance concept of the mystical union between the king's two bodies, between the body natural that is subject to time and death, and the body politic that is divine and immortal.[32] Richard's repeated invocations of his name ("Arm, arm, my name!" [III.ii.82]) signify the imminent severing of this union and his growing consciousness of death. Even though the universe of *King Lear* is not Christian, Lear's wish to "retain / The name and all th'addition to a king" would probably have been understood in the same context of ideas and have suggested the same implicit focus upon mortality. But in any case, his wish, even on its face, contradicts his ostensible desire to resign the "sway," "revenue," and "execution" of the king's power (I.i.136–37), and that contradiction governs his manner, his speech, and his actions throughout the opening scene.

The contradictions that govern Cordelia in the scene are less obvious, but more profound and more moving. What is compelling about her from the outset is that she continuously represents both sides of the process of denial: the heart's sorrow as well as its joy. She represents the vanity of denial but also its animating power, the love of life as well as the inescapability of death, the mother that nurtures us, as Freud suggests, as well as the Mother Earth that finally receives us.[33] She tells Lear the truth of his dying in the opening scene: "Nothing, my lord." She stands in mute rebuke to the folly of his attempt to deny it. And she eventually becomes that truth when she lies lifeless in his arms. But at the same time the very telling of that truth is replete with love—"What shall Cordelia speak? Love and be silent" (I.i.62)—which is what makes Lear's rejection of her seem unnatural on the literal as well as the symbolic level. As the play progresses she comes more and more to represent everything that binds Lear most notably to life and that makes his protest against death at once heartbreaking and heroic. Freud speaks of the resistance to death as essentially a reflex of the ego's wish to be immortal. But he undervalues human love, for another reason that we do not wish to die and see those close to us die, even the very old, is that we are capable of cherishing and loving others. Cordelia is an incarnation of this capacity.

Shakespeare endows Cordelia's representation of such love in *King Lear* with religious, and specifically Christian, overtones, and perhaps the greatest pain of her death, and of her tragic embodiment of the futility of the denial of death, is that the promise of these overtones also proves empty. Cordelia's counterpart in the chronicle play of *King Leir* is, like the whole of that play, explicitly homiletic and Christian. When she is rejected by her father, she turns to "him which doth protect the iust, / In him will poore *Cordella* put her trust," and later, as she acknowledges her sisters' "blame," she prays for God's forgiveness both of them and of her father:

> Yet God forgiue both him, and you and me,
> Euen as I doe in perfit charity.
> I will to Church, and pray vnto my Sauiour,
> That ere I dye, I may obtayne his fauour.   (ll. 331–32, 1090–93)[34]

Cordella's trust in God is fully vindicated at the end of the play when she and Leir are triumphantly reunited and he is restored to love and dignity.

Shakespeare intensifies, at the same time that he transmutes, the old play's association of Cordella with Christianity. There are unmistakable New Testament echoes in *King Lear*, and most of them cluster around Cordelia. They start in the opening scene, when France uses the language of miracle and faith to question Lear's judgment of Cordelia (I.i.220–22) and when he takes her as his wife:

> Fairest Cordelia, that art most rich, being poor;
> Most choice, forsaken; and most loved, despised:
> Thee and thy virtues here I seize upon.   (I.i.250–52)

The allusion to 2 Corinthians 6:10 is clear—"as poore, and *yet* [making] manie riche: as hauing nothing, and *yet* possessing all things"—and it resonates with the deepest preoccupations of the whole scene. The allusions and associations intensify at the end of the play. When Cordelia returns from France she says, "O dear father, / It is thy business that I go about" (IV.iii.23–24; cf. Luke 2:49); and shortly afterwards, the Gentleman who is sent to rescue Lear says,

> Thou hast a daughter,
> Who redeems nature from the general curse
> Which twain have brought her to.   (IV.v.201–3)

At the very end Cordelia's death is associated with the Last Judgment (V.iii.238–39), and Lear himself wishes for her revival in language that seems to echo the most profound of Christian beliefs:

> This feather stirs. She lives. If it be so,
> It is a chance which does redeem all sorrows
> That ever I have felt.   (V.iii.240–42)

But Cordelia does not live, and Lear, whether he dies thinking she does or not, is not redeemed by her. For in the pagan world of *King Lear* the New Testament's conception of death, and life, is the denial; the reality is that of Ecclesiastes, the pilgrimage of the heart in the Old Testament that insists above all else that death cannot be denied. Shakespeare, in all the plots of *King Lear*, at once summons up and denies the most profound energies of the comic and romantic impulses of the chronicle play of *Leir*, as well as of his other sources.[35] We expect and wish, for example, for Gloucester to recognize his good son Edgar, but he does so only at the very moment of his death and off-stage, and we wish, as Kent does, that Lear will recognize him as his faithful servant Caius, and he never does. The most painful of these denials of our romantic expectations, however, is the treatment of Cordelia. By associating her role with the Christian hope of redemption (an association that is strengthened by the play's simultaneous evocation and frustration of the generic expectations of the morality play as well as of romance[36]), Shakespeare deliberately violates, as Dr. Johnson perceived, not only "the faith of the chronicles" but also the profoundest "hope of the reader." We ourselves are thus compelled not just to view the process of denial, but to undergo it and endure it. There is no deeper generic transformation of a source in the canon, and it is the wellspring of the sense of grotesqueness as well as of desolation that is so peculiar to this tragedy.[37]

Such an understanding of the Christian evocations in the pagan world of *King Lear* can help clarify the religious issues that continue to vex criticism of the play, but it should not be interpreted to suggest that *King Lear* is thus either an argument against Providence or a homily on the inadequacy of pagan virtue.[38] Nor does it suggest that the play's conception of death is unique among Shakespeare's tragedies. The tragic sense that death informs as well as ends human life, and that after it, in Hamlet's last words, "The rest is silence" (V.ii.310), is as germane to *Hamlet*, *Othello*, and *Macbeth*, which have manifest Christian settings, as it is to *King Lear*. Christian belief does give a providential perspective to death in those plays, most strongly in *Hamlet*, where the intimations of another world of being become a part of the hero's consciousness; but such a perspective, even in the case of *Hamlet*, cannot absorb or fully explain the hero's actual suffering. Nor can it finally mitigate the effect of that suffering on us. We can spend much time gauging the level of irony in the endings of the tragedies, but when we see or read these great plays we do not construe the endings, we feel them, and what we feel is a paramount sense of suffering and loss. The distinction of *King Lear* is that the death of Cordelia compounds that feeling and focuses it. All of us are pagan in our immediate response to dying and death. The final scene of *King Lear* is a representation—among the most moving in all drama—of the universality of this experience and of its immeasurable pain.

NOTES

Portions of this argument appeared in abbreviated form in *William Shakespeare: His World, His Work, His Influence,* 3 vols., ed. John Andrews (New York: Charles Scribner's Sons, 1985), Vol. II, 524–31.

[1] See, e.g., William Elton, King Lear *and the Gods* (San Marino: Huntington Library Press, 1968), and Stephen Greenblatt, "Shakespeare and the Exorcists," *After Strange Texts,* eds. Gregory F. Jay and David L. Miller (Birmingham: Univ. of Alabama Press, 1985), pp. 101–23.

[2] Jonathan Dollimore, *Radical Tragedy: Religion, Ideology and Power in the Drama of Shakespeare and His Contemporaries* (Chicago: Univ. of Chicago Press, 1984), p. 157. His discussion of *Lear* is on pages 189–203. See also Walter Cohen, *Drama of a Nation* (Ithaca: Cornell Univ. Press, 1985).

[3] All references to *King Lear* are to the Folio text in *William Shakespeare: The Complete Works,* eds. Stanley Wells and Gary Taylor (Oxford: Clarendon Press, 1986).

[4] Significantly, Dollimore's attack on the humanist assumption that in tragedy men must suffer never really comes to terms with the suffering that is produced by death, the one event in human life, besides birth, that is ineluctable and universal.

[5] See especially John Holloway, *The Story of the Night* (Lincoln: Univ. of Nebraska Press, 1961), pp. 85–91. For a suggestive survey of biblical echoes in the play, which includes but does not give particular emphasis to Ecclesiastes, see Rosalie L. Colie, "The Energies of Endurance: Biblical Echo in *King Lear,*" in *Some Facets of* King Lear, eds. Rosalie Colie and F. T. Flahiff (Toronto: Univ. of Toronto Press, 1974), pp. 117–44.

[6] All quotations from the Bible are from *The Geneva Bible: A Facsimile of the 1560 Edition* (Madison, Milwaukee, and London: Univ. of Wisconsin Press, 1969).

[7] See Thomas McFarland, *Tragic Meanings in Shakespeare* (New York: Random House, 1966), pp. 149–71.

[8] See Holloway, pp. 75–80; and Joseph Wittreich, *"Image of That Horror": History, Prophecy, and Apocalypse in King Lear* (San Marino: Huntington Library Press, 1984).

[9] Allan Bloom comments on this speech in his fine essay on *Richard II* in *Shakespeare as Political Thinker,* eds. John Alvis and Thomas G. West (Durham, N.C.: Carolina Academic Press, 1981), pp. 55–56.

[10] *The Fool: His Social and Literary History* (London: Faber and Faber, 1935), p. 267.

[11] For thorough discussions of these commentaries, see Elton, King Lear *and the Gods,* pp. 270–72.

[12] Cited in the Arden *King Lear,* ed. Kenneth Muir (London: Methuen and Co. Ltd., 1952), p. 45. For a discussion of the ballad, see Hyder Rollins, "*King Lear* and the Ballad of 'John Careless,' " *Modern Language Review,* 15 (1920), 87–89.

[13] See J. V. Cunningham, *Tradition and Poetic Structure* (Denver: Alan Swallow, 1960), pp. 135–40.

[14] See Elton, pp. 249–53.

[15] For the argument that Lear's suffering and madness are purgatorial, see Paul A. Jorgenson, *Lear's Self-Discovery* (Berkeley and Los Angeles: Univ. of California Press, 1967).

[16] All references to *Pericles* are to the New Arden edition, ed. F. D. Hoeniger (London: Methuen and Co. Ltd., 1963).

[17] "*King Lear* and the Comedy of the Grotesque," *The Wheel of Fire* (London: Methuen and Co. Ltd., 1949), pp. 160–76.

[18] Barbara Everett, "The New King Lear," *Critical Quarterly,* 2 (1960), 325–39, esp. pp. 334–35.

[19] See especially "Of the Affection of Fathers to Their Children," *Montaigne's Essays,* trans. John Florio, 2 vols. (London: The Nonesuch Press, 1931), Vol. I, 437–59. Montaigne's assumption is that fathers not only often have to give up power to their children, but should do so.

[20] *The Yale Edition of the Works of Samuel Johnson: Johnson on Shakespeare*, 15 vols., Vol. VIII, ed. Arthur Sherbo (New Haven and London: Yale Univ. Press, 1968), 704.

[21] In the longer term, in the chronicles, Cordelia commits suicide after Lear's own death. Shakespeare's stress, of course, is on Lear's experience of Cordelia's death.

[22] *Fools of Time: Studies in Shakespearean Tragedy* (Toronto: Univ. of Toronto Press, 1967), p. 115.

[23] The ground-breaking study on this subject is Susan Snyder's "*King Lear* and the Psychology of Dying," *Shakespeare Quarterly*, 33 (1982), 449–60. My own analysis places more emphasis upon Freud's insight into the play, but I remain much indebted to her article.

[24] "The Theme of the Three Caskets," *Standard Edition of the Complete Psychological Works of Sigmund Freud*, ed. James Strachey, 24 vols. (London: Hogarth Press, 1953–74), Vol. 12, 301.

[25] *Works*, Vol. 12, 295.

[26] *Montaigne's Essays*, Vol. I, 694–95.

[27] *Prefaces to Shakespeare*, 2 vols. (Princeton: Princeton Univ. Press, 1952), Vol. I, 305.

[28] I think this is the phenomenon Stanley Cavell is really touching upon in "The Avoidance of Love," *Must We Mean What We Say?* (Cambridge: Cambridge Univ. Press, 1976), pp. 272–300, for in *King Lear* the avoidance of love (as well as the embrace of it) is fundamentally the avoidance of death.

[29] *Works*, Vol. 12, 299.

[30] For an interesting, if highly inferential, insistence on the political motives of the opening scene of *Lear*, see Harry V. Jaffa, "The Limits of Politics," in *Shakespeare's Politics*, eds. Allan Bloom and Harry Jaffa (New York: Basic Books, 1964), pp. 113–38.

[31] See Molly Mahood, *Shakespeare's Wordplay* (London: Methuen and Co. Ltd., 1957), p. 87.

[32] See Ernst Kantorowicz, *The King's Two Bodies* (Princeton: Princeton Univ. Press, 1957), pp. 24–91.

[32] *Works*, Vol. 12, 301.

[34] *The History of King Leir 1605*, gen. ed. W. W. Greg (Oxford: The Malone Society Reprints, 1907).

[35] For a discussion of the generic expectations of romance in *King Lear*, see Leo Salingar, "Romance in *King Lear*," *English*, 27 (1978), 5–22.

[36] See Edgar Schell, *Strangers and Pilgrims: From* The Castle of Perseverance *to* King Lear (Chicago: Univ. of Chicago Press, 1983).

[37] See G. Wilson Knight, "*King Lear* and the Grotesque"; and Susan Snyder, *The Comic Matrix of Shakespeare's Tragedies* (Princeton: Princeton Univ. Press, 1979), pp. 137–79.

[38] Cf. Thomas P. Roche, Jr., " 'Nothing Almost Sees Miracles': Tragic Knowledge in *King Lear*," in *On* King Lear, ed. Lawrence Danson (Princeton: Princeton Univ. Press, 1981), pp. 136–62.

David Farley-Hills

ANGER'S PRIVILEGE:
KING LEAR

Geoffrey Bullough includes among the possible sources of *King Lear* a contemporary account of a Kentish gentleman, Bryan Annesley, whose three daughters were in dispute about his state of mind. The third daughter, whose name was Cordell, defended her father from attempts by the eldest to have their father declared insane and his estate distrained. On Annesley's death in July 1604, Cordell erected a monument to her father 'against the ingratefull nature of oblivious time'.[1] There was a tenuous Shakespeare connection in that Sir William Harvey (the Countess of Southampton's third husband) was an executor of Annesley's will and later married Cordell Annesley.[2] Such a contemporary event might well have reminded Shakespeare of the old play of *Leir*, which dates from fifteen or so years earlier but was published in 1605, possibly (as Bullough conjectures)[3] as an attempt to profit by the current scandal.

Certainly if he was searching for material to explore the theme of ingratitude in high places, especially filial ingratitude, his mind must have gone back to those stories in Giraldi's *Hecatommithi* that had inspired *Othello* and *Measure for Measure*, and in particular to the third story of the eighth decade almost immediately preceding the story of Epitia (story 5) which he had used for *Measure for Measure*. Discussion of sources usually concentrates on narrative similarities, but thematic parallels are at least as important and perhaps more so in explaining how a writer manipulates his narrative material. The central theme of the eighth decade of *Hecatommithi* is ingratitude and each of the ten stories illustrates ingratitude in some form. As the stories continue, certain sub-themes develop which link the stories into smaller groups: we have already met the sub-theme of the corrupt magistrate in discussing *Measure for Measure*. The opening story of the eighth decade tells of the ingratitude of a boy who betrays his master and this leads the next story-teller, Don Lucio, to comment that his story will in turn illustrate a worse case of ingratitude because it involves the ingratitude of son to father: 'how much more binding is the tie of blood and Nature, and the obligation of son to father is

From *Shakespeare and the Rival Playwrights 1660–1606* (London: Routledge, 1990), pp. 182–205.

greater than any other that one can imagine'.[4] The theme of filial ingratitude is developed further when one of the ladies of the group, Fulvia, comments that Don Lucio's story shows how much greater a daughter's love (pietà) is than a son's. To this one of the men, Don Flaminio, replies that however much kinder women are than men by nature, there are worse examples of female ingratitude than the son's ingratitude of the previous tale.[5] This theme is then taken up by the teller of the next tale, Don Aulo, who introduces his narrative with the comment:

> It is true that women are very loving towards their fathers and mothers, not just because of the greater need they have for love than men, but also because they are soft and most kind by nature. But if it happens that any one of them should turn their minds to evil ways, they so improve on the evil of men that they may truly be called infernal furies in human shape and the story I am preparing to tell you will perhaps make that clearer than should be needed.[6]

Don Aulo's story introduces us into a world of intrigue and cruelty in high places that powerfully suggests the collapse of all order and decency and is centred, moreover, on the inhuman treatment of a king 'almost eighty years old' (presso a gli ottanta anni).[7]

The king of Scythia, Apesio, now nearing 80, has two daughters, Omosia and Agatia. Apesio is anxious that these should marry the sons of the previous king, Olbio, on whose death the low-born general Apesio had been elected king. He accordingly arranges that the wild (cruda) daughter, Omosia, should marry the mild Eumonio, while the proud Anemero, his brother, is to be mated with the 'pleas-antness' (piacevolezza) of Agatia, in the hope that such a union might calm him down. Agatia, we are told, is 'gentle and courteous, as women ought naturally to be'.[8] Apesio's intentions of settling the succession (compare Lear's 'that future strife/May be prevented now')[9] go suddenly awry, because Anemero has been smarting for forty years under the rule of the plebeian Apesio and proposes to his wife that the time has come to depose him. Agatia naturally refuses, more especially because the old King has been particularly generous to his son-in-law: 'having in particular given to him all his patrimony without keeping back the smallest part of it, as well as giving him considerable authority in the kingdom'.[10] The King's intention is that his sons-in-law should inherit the kingdom between them. The other daughter, Omosia, has similar thoughts to her brother-in-law, Anemero, plotting the death of her father so that she can become Queen. Seeing that her father is in robust health in spite of his age, she proposes to her mild husband that they should assassinate the old man. Eumonio refuses, reminding her of the ties of nature:

> that she held in such contempt reasons of consanguinity (le ragioni del sangue) and the laws of nature, which constrain even wild beasts to love the one who has begotten them.[11]

His wife considers he is mean-spirited (di animo vile) and humbler than a man should be (e humile più che ad huomo non si conviene), and turns to seek an alliance with Anemero:

knowing you to be a man of spirit and it seeming to me that you desire royal greatness not less than I myself desire it, I have decided to reveal to you these my masculine thoughts.[12]

Anemero agrees that they should kill their respective spouses, marry and take over the kingdom, but (like Goneril) she warns that they need to act 'i'th'heat': 'because thinking about great things is nothing if it leads to nothing'.[13] Like Goneril (and Lady Macbeth)[14] Omosia is a woman of awesome immorality. The kindly spouses are duly dispatched and the old King is confronted in the Senate by Anemero, who, failing to get support, drags his father-in-law (now described as old and weak) from his throne and hurls him down a flight of steps.[15] Omosia, not to be outdone, proclaims her husband king, reproving him, however, for not having killed the old man outright. At the end of the tale there is some sort of justice, for Omosia dies in childbirth, while Anemero's reign lasts scarcely a year before he is ousted, his sons killed in front of him and he himself sent into exile, where he dies after a long and painful illness: 'whence you see manifestly that the evil deed for good ends finally leads the evil-doers and the wicked to a miserable end'.[16]

I have presented Giraldi's tale in some detail because it seems to me that alone of Shakespeare's possible sources, this story gives the very atmosphere of aggressive evil that is so marked a feature of *King Lear*. As in *Lear* the central theme is the evil of filial ingratitude and this is specifically and powerfully associated with women. Nowhere else in Shakespeare are women presented as capable of generating so much violent and independent cruelty. Goneril not only instigates the evil, but stays in charge of the action, while her husband, Albany, like Giraldi's Eumonio, is presented as an essentially kindly man. Goneril's eventual 'marriage' to Edmund also resembles the transfer from good to bad husband in Giraldi's story. The destructive force of femininity becomes a central thematic concern as the world of the patriarchal Lear tumbles. This reveals itself tellingly in that strange, and apparently irrelevant nausea with feminine sexuality that Lear displays in his madness:

> down from the wast tha're centaures, though women all above, but to the girdle doe the gods inherit, beneath is all the fiends, ther's hell, ther's darknesse, ther's the sulphury pit, burning, scalding, stench, consumation, fie, fie, fie, pah, pah, Give mee an ounce of civet, good Apothocarie, to sweeten my imagination . . .   (IV, vi, 124–31)

Another aspect of Giraldi's story that seems to be reflected in *King Lear* is the regal authority of the protagonist, and it is just this insistence on regality that distinguishes *Lear* from the private catastrophe of Timon. Leir, in the old play, is of course a king, but he is a king enfeebled by age and presented as in his dotage. When his Gonorill comes to express her love for him in accordance with his request, she does so in the most absurdly flattering terms that would fool no one but a fool:

> I prize my love to you at such a rate,
> I thinke my life inferiour to my love.
> Should you injoyne me for to tye a milstone

> About my neck, and leape into the Sea,
> At your commaund I willingly would doe it:
> Yea, for to doe you good, I would ascend
> The highest Turret in all Brittany,
> And from the top leape headlong to the ground ...   (Leir, I, iii, 240–7)[17]

Shakespeare transforms this into a passage of courtly decorum which the Jacobean audience would recognize immediately (*pace* Bradley)[18] as appropriately deferential to a great king and to a father:

> Sir, I do love you more than words can weild the matter,
> Dearer then eye-sight, space or libertie,
> Beyond what can be valued rich or rare,
> No lesse then life; with grace, health, beautie, honour,
> As much as child ere loved, or father found ...   (Lear, I, i, 56–60)[19]

This is fulsome, of course, but certainly not more so than the language habitually served up for royalty in Jacobean England. A translation of Jean Bede's *Right and Prerogative of Kings* made by Robert Sherwood in 1612 makes the point:

> God will have us love [the King] more than our own blood, it sufficeth the King that we render unto him the service that children own to their most dear parents seeing that the honour due unto them is comprehended in the name of father and mother.[20]

Shakespeare has changed Gonorill's speech in the old text both to emphasize the deference owed to the great King and to exonerate him from failing to realize he is being hypocritically flattered. Conversely Shakespeare changes the deferential words of Cordella's refusal to express her love in the terms Leir demands in the old play to the startling rudeness of Cordelia's economically truthful reply 'Nothing my Lord'. Cordelia's blatant defiance of propriety serves to excuse the King's explosive reaction, whereas Cordella's gentle words turn away wrath and make Leir's response again unreasonable and foolish, a sign of his dotage. Shakespeare echoes the opening line of Cordella's response in Goneril's 'I do love you more then words can weild the matter':

> I cannot paynt my duty forth in words,
> I hope my deeds shall make report for me:
> But looke what love the child doth owe the father,
> The same to you I beare, my gracious Lord.   (Leir, I, iii, 277–80)

Cordella's reply is as carefully decorous in manner as it is firm in its refusal to flatter.

The sense of Lear's greatness, his extraordinary vigour in his old age (like Apesio he is around 80, yet we see him returning from hunting during the first Act), the impression given that he has been a king for many years and is in absolute control of his kingdom, that he is (as Kent tells him, I, iv, 32) the image of authority, his deep sense of political responsibility in arranging for the succession: 'that future strife/May be prevented now' (I, i, 44–5),[21] the generous willingness to relinquish power to ensure a satisfactory succession, he shares with Giraldi's Apesio. King Apesio has been on his throne for forty years, he is a warrior king approaching eighty and anxious to settle the succession, having, too, what James I calls (in *Basilikon Doron*)[22] the 'curse' of female heirs. Shakespeare's care in emphasizing Lear's regal stature has been oddly misunderstood in the democratic twentieth century, but it is crucial in understanding the transformation of the *Timon* theme of ingratitude. For by making Lear a king and emphasizing his outstanding kingly qualities, Shakespeare transforms a case of private (and not entirely undeserved) misfortune in *Timon* to a study of the breakdown of order in society, and by freeing Lear from the silliness that equally afflicts Timon and the old Leir he transforms stories of foolish weakness into a drama of classical proportions in which dark and destructive forces overwhelm a man who (to use Aristotelian terms) is 'better than average'.

Perhaps it is not so surprising in an age when kings have been either outlawed or emasculated and the authority of fathers questioned, that Shakespeare's presentation of his great King has been so misunderstood. His very act of wisdom and generosity in giving up power while he is still able to manage an orderly succession has been described (by those duly taking their pensions at 65) as political irresponsibility. His failure to detect flattery in the voice of decorum and love in the voice of rudeness has been condemned by an age as suspicious of politeness as it is approving of the kind of personal integrity that discounts the feelings of others. Lear's imperiousness, his aggressive authority, today associated with tyranny and selfishness, would to his early audiences appear as certain signs of greatness in a king. We can be certain of this because we have James I's opinion on the matter and Lear is every inch a Jamesean king.

One of the most obvious defects of *Timon* is that, uniquely in Shakespearean tragedy, the tragic protagonist lacks greatness, both in the sense that he has no clear status in his society and in the Aristotelian sense that he lacks 'magnanimity', greatness of soul. *Lear* sets out to remedy this lack, and what better way than by reflecting James's ideas of kingly greatness. It is the primary function of the opening scene to establish Lear's pre-eminence. This is done at the beginning of the scene by deliberate contrast. The disreputable Gloucester and his son Edmund, got 'tween unlawful sheets, are presented in a short dialogue with Kent (owing nothing to the *Leir* source material) whose purpose is to emphasize the illegitimate origins of Edmund and his father's sense of guilt and shame in begetting him: 'I have so often blusht to acknowledge him, that now I am braz'd to it' (I, i, 9–11). Gloucester's sin is truly being visited on the children as we learn that Edmund, away from court for nine years, is to be bustled away again to hide his father's shame. Bastardy, even in our own day, has carried a totally irrational stigma and was the subject of particular vituperation among the Elizabethans.[23] James explicitly warns his son of the evils consequent upon illegitimacy in a passage of *Basilikon Doron* that is relevant to the opening of *King Lear*:

> I trust I need not to insist here to disswade you from the filthy vice of adulterie: remember onely what solemne promise yee make to God at your Mariage: and since it is onely by the force of that promise that your children succeed to you, which otherwayes they could not doe; aequitie and reason would, ye should keepe your part thereof. God is ever a severe avenger of all periuries; and it is no oath made in iest, that giveth power to children to succeed to great kingdomes. Have the King my grand-fathers example before your eyes, who by his adulterie, bred the wracke of his lawfull daughter and heire; in begetting that bastard, who unnaturally rebelled, and procured the ruine of his owne Soverane and sister. . . . Keepe praecisely then your promise made at Mariage, as ye would wish to be partaker of the blessing therein.[24]

The morality of *King Lear* as a whole is not quite as straightforward as this, for while the consequences of Gloucester's adultery are duly spelt out in the action, Lear's licit fatherhood gets no reward. In *King Lear* we are in a pagan world without the comforts of Christian hope. Shakespeare has designed a neo-classical tragedy where is shown (in Fulke Greville's words) 'the disastrous miseries of man's life, where orders, laws, doctrine and authority are unable to protect innocency from the exhorbitant wickedness of power'.[25] The contrast between Gloucester and Lear in this, as in other ways, is to stress Lear's righteousness and the undeserved nature of his suffering.

Criticism has been taught by Bradley to see the morality of Gloucester's suffering as an exact parallel to Lear's.[26] In the quarto version of the play, however, Shakespeare spells out the contrast between them unequivocally in giving Edgar a short soliloquy at the end of Act III, scene vi whose dramatic purpose is to highlight Lear's undeserved suffering:

> How light and portable my paine seems now,
> When that which makes me bend, makes the King bow.
> He childed as I fathered . . .   (III, vi, 115–17)

The contrast is clear: the innocent child (Edgar) has been made to suffer for the sins of the guilty father (Gloucester): in contrast, the innocent father (Lear) suffers for the sins of his children. The two fathers are being contrasted, not compared.

It is a paradox of Shakespeare's handling of his material that the Christian play of *Leir* is given a pagan reading, while the pagan material taken from Sidney's *Arcadia* for the sub-plot is made to reflect a pattern of Christian morality. This is all the more notable because Sidney takes pains to reflect a pagan world in his romance. So Edgar asserts a confidence in divine justice as he contemplates his dying brother:

> The Gods are just, and of our pleasant vices[27]
> Make instruments to scourge us. The darke and vitious
> Place where thee he gotte, cost him his eies.   (V, iii, 171–3)

The Arden editor finds echoes of both the *Book of Wisdom* and the old play of *Leir* in these lines. Edgar's complaisant morality here, however, is challenged by the ending of the main plot where 'innocency' suffers equally with the guilty. Albany, like Edgar, finds a coherent pattern in the events that bring about the deaths of Goneril and Regan: 'This Iustice of the heavens that makes us tremble,/Touches us not with pity' (V, iii, 230–1). For Albany there is no Aristotelian pattern here. But the full irony of Albany's optimism appears at the end of the play when, having pronounced a somewhat facile intention of seeing wrongs righted: 'all friends shall tast the wages of their vertue, and al foes the cup of their deservings' (V, iii, 302–4), his attention is distracted by the dying King lamenting over the murdered corpse of Cordelia. Albany's shocked response is to renounce his right to the throne, so great in this play is the gap between hope and fulfilment. Kent's enigmatic question when he sees Cordelia dead in Lear's arms is the appropriate one for the play as a whole: 'Is this the promis'd end?' (V, iii, 263). Aristotelian pity is duly reasserted.

Just as James stresses the terrible consequences of breaking the marriage vows, so in both *Basilikon Doron* and *The Trew Law of Free Monarchies* (1598) he spells out the obligations and sacred bonds of parents to children and children to parents. He links this, especially in the latter tract, to the obligations of subjects to their king. The extended metaphors of king as father and father as king dominate *King Lear*. James also links this metaphor upwards to the king's filial relationship to God. This relationship is notably lacking in the world of *King Lear*, which shows, no doubt to the approval of King James, that secular government cannot hold, since (to quote the King), 'Monarchie is the trew paterne of Divinitie'.[28] Again *Basilikon Doron* can provide a commentary:

> Foster trew Humilitie, in bannishing pride, not onely towards God (considering yee differ not in stuffe, but in use, and that onely by his ordinance, from the basest of your people) but also towards your Parents. And if it fall out that my Wife shall out-live me, as ever ye thinke to purchase my blessing, honour your mother: set Beersheba in a throne on your right hand: offend her for nothing, much lesse wrong her: remember her
> *Quae longa decem tulerit fastidia menses;*
> and that your flesh and blood is made of hers: and beginne not, like the young lordes and lairdes, your first warres upon your Mother; but presse earnestly to deserve her blessing. Neither deceive your selfe with many that say, they care not for their Parents curse, so they deserve it not. O invert not the order of nature, by iudging your superiours, chiefly in your owne particular! But assure your selfe, the blessing or curse of the Parents, hath almost ever a Propheticke power ioyned with it: and if there were no more, honour your Parents, for the lengthning of your owne dayes, as God in his Law promiseth.[29]

How well James would have understood the import of Lear's great curse on Goneril at that performance in December 1606, how full of sympathy he must have felt at seeing the old king denied that deference to rank and paternity that was not just his due, but that God demands as a tribute to His orderliness. Equally acceptable would have been the illustration in the play of the vulnerability of kings. And notice that James specifically tells the young Prince Henry that after he has become king, his Mother must sit at his right hand as his 'superior'. How totally have modern commentators (like George Orwell and Freud) misunderstood the Jacobean mentality in suggesting that Lear should have known better than to expect deference once he had relinquished power. What impact those scenes must have had on the King as he watched first Goneril and then Regan defying God's ordinances in brutally denying their father the symbols of his rank and status as their father, inverting the order of nature:

> LEAR: When were you wont to be so full of songs sirra?
> FOOLE: I have us'd it nuncle, ever since thou mad'st thy daughters thy mother, for when thou gavest them the rod, and put'st downe thine own breeches, then they for sudden ioy did weep, and I for sorrow sung, that such a King should play bo-peepe, and goe the fooles among ...

(I, iv, 185–93)

The Fool, wise after the event, blames Lear for giving his daughters the opportunity for their wickedness, but this is to turn morality on its head and joins the paradoxes of daughters as mothers, of weeping for joy and singing for sorrow. Lear's blindness was not a moral blindness—indeed his motives for forgoing power are clearly entirely moral and honourable—but an error of judgement caused by a lack of knowledge (exactly that quality of *hamartia* Aristotle describes as the proper basis for tragedy in the *Poetics*).

Dramaturgically *King Lear* continues that exploration of neo-classical concepts of tragedy begun in *Othello* and culminating in *Coriolanus*. As in *Othello*, Shakespeare is more concerned with the aesthetic than with the moral effect of the action. The sub-plot (strictly breaking the 'rule' which prescribed unity of action) is primarily concerned not to assert a Christian morality, but to act as foil and contrast to the main. *Lear*, even more than *Othello*, fulfils Fulke Greville's description of pagan tragedy (already quoted) where Greville goes on to explain the effect of showing innocent suffering: 'so out of that melancholy vision, [to] stir up horror or murmur against Divine Providence'.[30] This is the Christian moralist's view of ancient tragedy. Shakespeare's more asethetic approach requires us to contemplate the 'horror' of a world before Christ's act of redemption. *Lear*, more than any other of Shakespeare's tragedies, achieves that catharsis of feeling through pity for the suffering of the powerless and fear for man's vulnerability. In doing so it manifests an attitude to character similar to that of *Othello*. There is a certain remoteness about Lear, as there is about Othello. This is partly a result of Lear's eminence, his status as king, and partly a result of the Lear rhetoric which, like Othello's, has a public, formal quality, and a quality of self-dramatization that befits a public figure, but also acts as a barrier to intimate acquaintance. We only begin to enter into Lear's mind when, in his madness, it becomes public. There are none of the self-revelatory soliloquies in *Lear* like those of *Hamlet* or Macbeth's soliloquy of self-doubt before the murder of Duncan. Instead, soliloquy is used (as it is with *Hamlet*'s rivals) to define Edmund's role as villain, or to inform the audience of Edgar's change of function. The audience are not encouraged in this play to adopt too close an identification with the hero; again the stress is on sympathy rather than empathy. As with *Othello*, however, sympathy requires a measure of identification and in *Lear* Shakespeare provides us with an extraordinarily convincing portrait of an old man, as much in his terrible vulnerability as in the obstinacy of ways entrenched over eighty years. Goethe's response is apt: 'Ein alter mann ist stets ein König Lear'.[31] Unlike *Othello*, however, *King Lear* also works equally powerfully on a mythic level. Commenting on the exceptional power of the play, Freud relates the pattern of the conflict between father and daughters to myths of the goddess of death.[32] Lear's struggle to remain himself as he is slowly torn to pieces by feminine forces against which he is doomed, re-enacts those ancient dionysiac rituals of the dismemberment of the king (or god) that Frazer recounts in *The Golden Bough*. If the play were merely about the redemption of King Lear (to use Bradley's famous phrase)[33] it could not have the universal power it so obviously has. To explain the power, Lear's suffering and death has to be understood as a sacrifice to unknown gods.

Lear, then, enters on to the stage in pointed contrast to Gloucester's shady privacy. The 1608 quarto stage direction marks a royal entry: 'Sound a sennet, Enter one bearing a Coronet, then Lear, then the Dukes of Albany, and Cornwell, next Goneril, Regan, Cordelia, which followers'; hierarchy is strictly preserved here, with the women taking second place as required by God (or the gods) and by Nature. Lear's first words are words of command and like the successful warrior king he is and has been over many years ('I have seene the day,/With my good biting Fauchon/I would have made them skippe', V, iii, 276–7), he immediately turns to the practical matter in hand, the arrangement of the succession: 'that future strife/May be prevented now'. James, in the audience, would have been uneasy at this point, for Lear's political settlement involves the division of the kingdom into three parts and James himself was emphatic and tireless in urging on his subjects the advantages of unity and in particular of union with Scotland. In *Basilikon Doron* he specifically warns his son to avoid the partitioning of his kingdom, quoting ancient British history on the danger:

> make your eldest sonne *Isaac*, leaving him all your kingdomes; and provide the rest with private possessions: Otherwayes by deviding your kingdomes, yee shall leave the seed of division and discord among your posteritie; as befell to this Ile, by the division and assignement thereof, to the three sonnes of *Brutus*, *Locrine*, *Albanact*, and *Camber*.[34]

Lear does, however, have the special circumstance of the 'curse' of female succession to contend with.[35] From Shakespeare's point of view this difference between the monarch on stage and the monarch in the audience must have been useful, for the last thing he would want is to incur the danger of having the audience identify the one king with the other. Shakespeare ignores the connections with Scotland he would have found in his sources.[36] Lear is no more James than Duke Vincentio is James, but (like the Duke) he is presented as a monarch acceptable to James's notion of what a king should be. It is noticeable that Shakespeare does not allow the play to dwell on the division of the kingdoms; it is not central to the play's agenda and the later trouble is caused not by the division itself—on the contrary the inheriting Dukes align themselves against the invading army of France—but by the malign nature of the inheritors. Tragedy would hardly have been averted if Goneril had been made the sole heiress.

If the division in itself, then, is not important, except in allowing Shakespeare welcome opportunity to distance Lear from James, Lear's handling of the division is crucial. Like the division itself, the request to each of the daughters in turn for expressions of their love, is a *donné* of the source material. Shakespeare retains it not only because it is convenient to the plot, but because it is essential to the characterization. Again modern commentators have often blamed Lear for asking such a silly question of his daughters, but James would hardly have seen it like that. Spenser, telling the same story in the *Faerie Queene,* writes of Lear's question as 'sage':

> and with speeches sage
> Inquyrd, which of them most did love her parentage?   (II, x, 27)

Milton, similarly, pauses in his *History of Britain* to comment that Lear's question was a 'trial [of love] that might have made him, had he known as wisely how to try, as he seem'd to know how much the trying behoov'd him'.[37] The question was eminently sensible, but not the reaction to the answers. James would almost certainly have approved the request, not only because it seems to echo Christ's request to his disciples when they complain of the woman anointing His feet with ointment: 'which of them, therefore, tell me, will love him most' (Luke 7:42)—and Shakespeare's wording is much closer to the Geneva wording than to the old play of *Leir*—but because James himself was obsessed with the need for declarations of love, as appears from his surviving correspondence.[38] It is surely one of the more bizarre products of public school reticence that sees anything perverse in a father asking his daughters how much they love him. Shakespeare's purpose throughout this first scene is clearly to stress the old King's need of love—the word itself appears insistently throughout this scene—and it is not only a mark of Lear's affectionate nature that he should think love so important, but psychologically it is exactly what we would expect of an old man, until now all-powerful, giving himself into the power of his daughters. Who would not want reassurance at such a moment?

There is nothing exceptional in either Goneril's or Regan's answer to their father's request: their answers are exercises in courtly hyperbole demanded by the occasion. Cordelia's reply, on the other hand, is shocking, and is intended to shock (the folio text actually tries to make it even more shocking—but fails—in having Cordelia repeat her 'Nothing'). James would, of course, be as outraged as Lear at such a breach of decorum, but would he have approved of Lear's response? The guidance James gives us on the subject of both anger and flattery is a great help in focusing on this problem, though it doesn't solve it.

That flattery was an occupational hazard of the powerful was a commonplace of Renaissance political commentary.[39] Marston makes it a central theme of his play *The Fawn*, which appeared about 1604. In it Duke Hercules of Ferrara adopts disguise only to hear truths about himself that flattery had kept from him—disguise was, as we have seen, one of the devices favoured by James to overcome flattery's hazards. Hercules, hearing for the first time what people really think of him, meditates on the perils of flattery:

> By Him by Whom we are, I think a prince
> Whose tender sufferance never felt a gust
> Of bolder breathings, but still liv'd gently fann'd
> With the soft gales of his own flatterers' lips,
> Shall never know his own complexion . . .
> Thou grateful poison, sleek mischief, flattery,
> Thou dreamful slumber (that doth fall on kings
> As soft and soon as their first holy oil),
> Be thou forever damn'd. I now repent
> Severe indictions to some sharp styles;
> Freeness, so't grow not to licentiousness,
> Is grateful to just states.   (I, ii, 306–10, 313–19)[40]

That James himself was much preoccupied with this problem we can see from a passage in *Basilikon Doron:*

> Choose then for all these Offices, men of knowen wisedome, honestie, and good conscience; well practised in the points of the craft, that yee ordaine them for, and free of all factions and partialities; but specially free of that filthie vice of Flatterie, the pest of all Princes, and wracke of Republicks: For since in the first part of this Treatise, I forewarned you to be at warre with your owne inward flatterer φιλαυτία, how much more should ye be at war with outward flatterers, who are nothing so sib to you, as your selfe is; by the selling of such counterfeit wares, onely preassing to ground their greatnesse upon your ruines.[41]

The difficulty, of course, is recognizing a flatterer when you see one, hence the need to move among your subjects incognito. Kings were in a notoriously difficult position, especially those who, like Lear, had been long in power, for it was in everybody's interest to tell them only what they wanted to hear. In spite of his acute awareness of the problem, James was himself highly susceptible to flattery.[42]

    In accepting his two daughters' assurances of their love, therefore, Lear is in no position to judge their truthfulness. His isolated position as ruler would inevitably preclude an intimate relationship with his daughters. The decorum with which they express themselves would make his task all the more difficult. Lear's error of judgement, therefore, is based on ignorance born of his isolation as king and the fault of the tragic kind Aristotle describes as most suitable for the hero of tragedy,

> whose fall into misery is not due to vice and depravity, but rather to some
> error, a man who enjoys prosperity and a high reputation, like Oedipus . . . [43]

Lear commits an error of judgement that, like Oedipus, he was in no position to
avoid. One of the earliest critical comments on the play to have survived, that of
Lewis Theobald, rightly sums up the play in Aristotelian (if somewhat moralized)
terms. The play calls both for pity for an overgenerous father and fear of the evil
consequences of human ingratitude:

> the first a caution against unwary bounty; the second against the base Returns
> and Ingratitude of children in an aged parent. The error of the first is to be
> painted in such colours as are adapted to Compassion; the baseness of the
> latter set out in such a light as is proper to Detestation. [44]

Theobald's emphasis on Lear's bountifulness reminds us again of Lear's Jamesean
affinities (we earlier heard James confessing to being overgenerous).

The problem of Lear's anger is more difficult to resolve, though it is very
different from what most commentators have assumed. His first response to
Cordelia's 'Nothing, my Lord' is one of shocked disbelief, as he asks her twice to
reconsider her reply. Her reformulations only make matters worse as she enters
into a somewhat cheeseparing view of love: 'I love your Maiestie according to my
bond, nor more nor lesse.' It is not just that 'bond' here is ambiguous (Shylock insists
on his bond in the judgement scene of *Merchant of Venice*), but that the language
of 'nor more nor lesse' seems to reinforce the commercial connotations of the
term. Antony's reply to Cleopatra's 'If it be love, indeed, tell me how much', puts
Cordelia's reply into uncomfortable perspective: 'There's beggary in the love that
can be reckon'd.'[45] This is not how most modern commentators have seen it,
because modern values place individual integrity higher than filial duty. To James,
however, in the audience, as to Lear on stage, Cordelia's language must have
sounded perverse in both manner and matter and Lear's explosion of anger would
have been felt to be appropriate enough. In a speech to Parliament on 21 March
1610 James declared: 'Kings are justly called Gods, for that they exercise a manner
or resemblance of Divine power upon earth.'[46] This absolute authority he later in
the same speech applies by analogy to fathers over their children, in a passage that
gives us more than a hint of how he might have responded to this opening scene
of *Lear*:

> Now a Father may dispose of his Inheritance to his children, at his pleasure:
> yea, even disinherite the eldest upon iust occasions, and preferre the youngest,
> according to his liking; make them beggars, or rich at his pleasure; restraine, or
> banish out of his presence, as hee findes them give cause of offence, or restore
> them in favour againe with the penitent sinner: So may the King deale with his
> Subjects. [47]

What appears to modern audiences as arbitrary self-indulgence in Lear, would to
James have been Lear's rightful exercise of his prerogative as king and father. It was,

moreover, as James himself pointed out to his son, the duty of a king to know when and how to get angry:

> And so, where ye finde a notable iniurie, spare not to give course to the torrents of your wrath. *The wrath of a King, is like to the roaring of a Lyon.* (Proverbs 20)[48]

This begs the question whether Cordelia's reply could be regarded legitimately as a 'notable injury' and King James's views on the virtue of anger in a king are hedged about with qualifications. In the *Trew Law of Free Monarchies* he again draws his favourite analogy between the king and subject on the one hand and father and child on the other, in insisting on the propriety of anger as a means of correction:

> As the kindly father ought to foresee all inconvenients and dangers that may arise towards his children, and though with the hazard of his owne person presse to prevent the same; so ought the King towards his people. As the fathers wrath and correction upon any of his children that offendeth, ought to be by a fatherly chastisement seasoned with pitie, as long as there is any hope of amendment in them; so ought the King towards any of his Lieges that offend in that measure.[49]

Clearly Lear seeks the 'amendment' of Cordelia before his anger is given full reign: 'Goe to, goe to, mend your speech a little.' Even when this warning if followed by another provocative insistence on packaging her love between father and husband, Lear's patience still holds: 'But goes this with thy heart?' Cordelia's insistence on the letter of his own moral law finally and inevitably leads to Lear's royal and paternal response to such open defiance:

> LEAR: But goes this with thy heart?
> CORDELIA: I good my Lord.
> LEAR: So yong and so untender.
> CORDELIA: So yong my Lord and true.
> LEAR: Well let it be so, thy truth then be thy dower ...   (I, i, 106–10)

There is nothing equivalent to this repeated attempt of the King to understand his daughter in the old play. In that, not only is Cordella careful to remain decorous and polite throughout, but she also makes clear that her stand is in opposition to her sisters' blatant and absurd flattery:

> I hope my deeds shall make report for me ...
> My toung was never usde to flattery.   (I, iii, 278, 302)

Cordelia and Lear engage in a dialogue of the deaf in which Lear's emphasis on rightful ceremony and social hierarchy fail to find a common language with Cordelia's insistence on personal integrity and truthfulness. Shakespeare is not asking us to apportion blame (since deafness is not blameworthy) but showing us how Lear's error of judgement stems from a clash of values.

James, writing about anger in *Basilikon Doron*, insists that care should be taken to weigh up the appropriateness of the response:

> But forget not to digest ever your passion, before ye determine upon any-thing, since *Ira furor brevis est:*[50] uttering onely your anger according to the Apostles rule, *Irascimini, sed ne peccetis* . . .[51]

It would be interesting to know whether in December 1606 James considered Lear had sufficiently digested his passion before his royal anger breaks out in the de-nunciation of Cordelia, and whether on this occasion anger truly (as Kent later puts it) 'has a priviledge' (II, ii, 76). Certainly the provocations are great; Cordelia's flouting of all decorum to king and father in full court and on such a formal occasion was no light misdemeanour. An assessment of Lear's conduct at this point requires the nice judgement that James liked to bring to bear on such matters. At least the King would have appreciated the King's difficulty—which is more than can be said of most modern commentators.

Far outweighing any consideration of the appropriateness or otherwise of Lear's judgement in this scene is the impression given of his authority. Even the fault (if fault it is) is the royal fault of peremptoriness. For Shakespeare is not primarily asking for moral judgement here, but asking us to experience the dramatic impact of the King's greatness in preparation for his fall and the collapse of his orderly world. Kent's intervention in attempting to persuade Lear to revoke his decision against Cordelia not only increases the dramatic intensity of the scene but rein-forces the impression of Lear's greatness. For at first Kent couches his intervention in the most deferential terms, witnessing at the same time to the affection as well as the awe that the great King has inspired:

KENT: Royall Lear,
        Whom I have ever honor'd as my King,
        Loved as my Father, as my maister followed,
        As my great patron thought on in my prayers.
LEAR: The bow is bent and drawen make from the shaft.   (I, i, 141–5)

That Lear has inspired love as well as required love has been often ignored. The moment on the heath when he notices the fool shivering with cold has been regarded as the awakening of a new humanity in the old man, the beginning of the redemption of King Lear. The description of Lear in Burbage's funeral elegy as 'kind Lear', however, is the right one, as even Goneril concedes. 'Hee alwaies loved our sister most' (I, i, 293), whatever else it implies, confirms Lear as someone to whom love matters. Indeed his angry reaction to Cordelia surely witnesses to this. The play is not about the redemption of King Lear, but about his damnation; damned not because of any sin he has committed, but, like the good pagans of Dante's *Inferno*, condemned because he lives before Merlin (and Christ).

Structurally *King Lear* is not patterned on the old morality plays (as *Macbeth* is), there is no pattern of spiritual development in the play. The pattern derives from its *de casibus* theme and is closely similar to that of *Timon of Athens*, a threefold pattern in which the hero begins in prosperity, then suffers rejection through the ingratitude of men (in Lear's case, women) and finally collapses into despair and death in a hostile world where supernatural aid is not forthcoming. While this essential structure remains intact, however, the proportions are radically altered. The period of prosperity in *Lear* is drastically reduced to the opening scene (in *Timon* it is the first two acts). This allows a much greater concentration on the tragic part of the action and is therefore more appropriate for tragedy, permitting a much more detailed and convincing presentation of the process of disintegration. Almost two acts (I, ii–II, iv) are devoted to the depiction of Lear's fall, brought about by his daughters' unkindness, in place of the single, sketchy third act of *Timon*. The change has immense advantages dramatically. By concentrating on the two figures of Goneril and Regan in sequence, in place of the scarcely differentiated creditors who refuse to help Timon, Shakespeare humanizes the action and so makes it more affecting and more terrible. Moreover the tormentors are next of kin, *unkind* in the Elizabethan sense as well as in our own. The repetition of Lear's humiliation, first with Goneril then with Regan, like the parallels established in the sub-plot, establish a pattern of brutality that prevents our comforting ourselves with the thought that Goneril is a rare aberration. Such repetition occurs in *Timon,* but without the same affective impact. *Lear* eschews all comic suggestion, except for the Fool's all too impotent asides, in engaging us emotionally in the events. One of the terrifying aspects of the scenes with the two daughters is the plausibility of the case that Goneril and Regan present—we remember Granville-Barker's opinion that Goneril's request that Lear should 'disquantity' his retinue is 'reasonable'.[52] The process in which the King is successively humiliated by his daughters is all too terrifyingly human. The thought of the hundred unruly knights ruining polite carpets no doubt inspired the lady in the Stratford audience to remark that Lear must have been a very tiresome old man to have about the house.

James, as he watched his December entertainment, would have had a different perspective. In an age when large retinues were regarded, not just as permitted, but required of people of high rank (the Earl of Pembroke in 1598 boasted he could produce 210 serving men in defence of his Queen)[53] Lear's wish to retain his hundred knights is modest. By abdicating he has not, of course, ceased to be of exalted rank. Gervase Markham, in a book published in 1598, is insistent on the obligation of the gentry to keep as large a retinue as their rank permits, both for the employment it affords and because an orderly society depends on a proper assertion of rank. A true gentleman, says Markham, should be:

> garded gallantly with a sort of seemly servants, always well appoynted as well as to shew his power, as to grace his person.[54]

Markham laments that the gentry nowadays neglect their duty and cut down on their retinues so that they can selfishly indulge themselves with the saving. G. B. Harrison notes the shock with which contemporaries received the news of the Earl of Essex's punishment, when the Queen ordered the dismissal of his retinue:

Tomorrow the Earl's household, being 160, are dispersed, and every man to seek a new fortune; some few are retained to attend him where it be her Majesty's will to send him. This is the greatest downfall we have seen in our days, making us to see the vanity of the world.[55]

Goneril explains precisely why she is engaged in this process: she seeks a confrontation with her father; in doing so she destroys the very fabric of the relationships on which her own authority rests:

And let his Knights have colder looks among you, what growes of it no matter, advise your fellows so. I would breed from hence occasions, and I shall, that I may speake, ile write straight to my sister to hould my very course, goe prepare for dinner.   (I, iii, 22–6)

The attack on Lear's retinue, as she admits here, has been planned in advance of any trouble they might cause. At the end of the first scene we hear Goneril and Regan planning their Father's humiliation almost as soon as he has handed power over to them:

pray lets hit together, if our Father cary authority with such dispositions as he beares, this last surrender of his, will but offend us.   (I, i, 307–10)

Goneril has just been describing the 'dispositions' to which she refers as a rashness and lack of self-knowledge that has always characterized him and is now exacerbated by old age. If this view of Lear is correct, that he 'hath ever but slenderly knowne himselfe', he clearly would be a difficult man to deal with. The view that the two daughters give of their Father, however, is clearly in contradiction to Kent's attitude to his sovereign and indeed hardly credible in a man who has successfully wielded power for so long. It is one of the ironies of much modern *Lear* criticism that this partial account of Lear has been treated as if it were incontrovertible testimony. Kenneth Muir tells us baldly: 'Goneril's diagnosis is near the truth.'[56]

When we are in any position to test the evidence, the attitude of Goneril and Regan is found to be false. In ordering Oswald to disobey the King, Goneril makes as her principal excuse the unruliness of the behaviour of both Lear and his retinue:

By day and night he wrongs me,
Every houre he flashes into one grosse crime or other
That sets us all at ods, ile not indure it,
His Knights grow ryotous, and himselfe obrayds us,
On every trifell when he returnes from hunting,
I will not speake with him ...   (I, iii, 3–8)

'Grosse crime', even reading crime as 'offence',[57] sounds improbable and the actual appearance of the 'unruly' knights, far from corroborating Goneril's accusation, show them (as we would expect of the retinue of so imperious a King) to be particularly concerned with ceremony and order:

> My Lord, I know not what the matter is, but to my iudgement, your highnes
> is not entertained with that ceremonious affection as you were wont, ther's a
> great abatement of kindness[58] apeers as well in the generall dependants, as in
> the Duke himselfe also, and your daughter.   (I, iv, 61–8)

The gentleman's words here not only bear evidence to that 'ceremonious affection'
in which Lear has been habitually held, but in his own language and attitude he
exhibits those qualities of courtly decorum that show a proper respect for rank and
order. This is certainly not the language of a riotous knight, indeed his complaint
centres on Goneril's flagrant impropriety. His respect for the King surely amply
reinforces Kent's admiration for and deference to his master. Similarly when one of
Lear's retinue reports to Kent the plight of the old King at the beginning of Act III
the tone is one of humane and respectful sympathy, not of disorderly roughness.
Lear's response to the servant's accusations of neglect is equally revealing:

> I have perceived a most faint neglect of late, which I have rather blamed as
> mine owne ielous curiositie, then as a very pretence and purport of unkind-
> nesse . . .   (I, iv, 72–6)

Far from showing arrogance or vanity, such extreme sensitivity and reticence as can
make an old man consider whether his impressions have been due to his own
vanity is surely remarkable here, and is on a level with his initial hesitations in
responding to Cordelia's rudeness. The absurdity of the accusations aimed at Lear
and his retinue is finally confirmed at the end of Act II, when Regan, as an excuse
for locking her Father out of her castle, informs us: 'He is attended with a desperate
traine' (II, iv, 308). When we next see him he is alone on the heath with the Fool.
Any close attention to the text, therefore, suggests we are to dismiss Goneril's
accusations that the knights indulge in 'epicurism and lust', turning the palace into a
'brothel' (I, iv, 267) as nonsense, and accept Lear's emphatic defence of them:

> Detested kite, thou liest.
> My train are men of choice and rarest parts,
> That all particulars of duty know,
> And in the most exact regard support
> The worships of their name.   (I, iv, 271–5)[59]

Once again it is worth noting the nature of Lear's defence, with its precise emphasis
on the courtly virtues of duty, honour and decorum.

With such evidence from the text, how then has the impression gained such
firm hold that the daughters' objections are 'reasonable', for few productions of
Lear fail to provide their quota of riotous knights? The combination of Lear's
imperiousness and his penchant for hunting, his peremptoriness as he commands
'Let me not stay a iot for dinner' (I, iv, 8) makes Goneril's view of him plausible to
a modern audience. This behaviour, however, is simply a reflection of his royal
nature and would remind a Jacobean audience yet again of his innate authority. It
is the kind of imperious behaviour they expected (and got) from their own mon-

arch. The hunting is stressed to show that the charge that her father is in his dotage (I, iii, 16–20) is as baseless as the other charges. Shakespeare needed to emphasize Lear's strength and robust health in order to make the fall tragic rather than merely pathetic, as it is in the old play of *Leir*. But the emphasis on hunting also has a special significance in relation to the play's royal audience, for James was inordinately fond of hunting. Indeed about the time he was coming in for considerable criticism for spending too much time on the hunting field and too little in the council chamber. Raymond Burns, in his recent edition of Day's *Isle of Gulls*, quotes from the Calendar of State papers for July 1603:

> the new king . . . seems to have almost forgotten that he is a King except in his kingly pursuit of the stags, to which he is quite foolishly devoted, and leaves them [his council] with such absolute authority that beyond a doubt they are far more powerful than ever they were before . . . [60]

Again Burns quotes a letter of the Archbishop of York to Lord Cecil, 23 December 1604, in the same strain: 'I wish less wasting of the Treasure of the Realm, and more Moderation of the lawfull Exercise of Hunting, both that the poor Mens Corn may be less spoiled, and other his Majestie's Subjects more spared.' Similarly Sir Francis Osborne's *Traditional Memoirs* are quoted:

> he dedicated . . . faire [weather] to his hounds . . . which was, through the whole series of his government, more acceptable, then any profit or conveniency might accrue to his people. [61]

These are hostile comments, but the reference in the first passage to the 'kingly pursuit' of hunting rightly acknowledges that this was regarded as the royal sport *par excellence*. Shakespeare is concerned with reinforcing the kingly image, and in a way peculiarly acceptable to James, not criticizing his hero, for Lear is not neglecting state business. In the drama of the period it is neglect of the hunt by rulers that often suggests unmanliness and unfitness to govern, as in the sudden cancellation of the hunt by Duke Alphonso in Chapman's *Gentleman Usher*.

The two great and terrible scenes in which first Goneril and then Regan attack the very basis of social order—that respect for forms and ceremonies which holds human wildness in check—expose man's feebleness and vulnerability in a demonstration that is all the more telling for being exemplified in such an imposing figure as Lear. His first response is, understandably, to call on divine aid (the goddess of Nature) to counter Goneril's impiety. When this fails to elicit a response and he is confronted by Regan in an identical situation, his doubts begin to grow that the universe may not guarantee the orderly world his reign has created:

> You heavens give me that patience, patience I need,
> You see me here (you Gods) a poore old man, [62]
> As full of greefe as age, wretched in both,
> If it be you that stirres these daughters hearts
> Against their Father, foole me not to much,
> To beare it lamely, touch me with noble anger . . .   (II, iv, 274–9)

Lear is still king enough to claim anger's privilege. The scene reaches its climax in the first sign of Lear's despair at the prospect of a disorderly universe, as the two sisters complete their auction of his status and dignity. In the equivalent scenes of *Timon* (in Act III) our primary response is that Timon's extravagance is meeting its sardonic rewards; here, on the other hand, the beleaguered King is a truly tragic figure of undeserved calamity. On both the human and the symbolic level the Timon situation is powerfully transformed, for as well as the pathos of an old man treated by his children with cruelty, Lear himself sees his plight as a comment on the fragility of man's claim to rational sovereignty:

> O reason not the need, our basest beggars,
> Are in the poorest thing superfluous,
> Allow not nature more then nature needes,
> Man's life's as cheape as beasts. Thou art a lady;
> If onely to goe warme were gorgeous,
> Why nature needes not, what thou gorgeous wearest
> Which scarcely keepes thee warme . . .   (II, iv, 267–73)[63]

This is an eloquent statement of that need for human ceremony and custom that modern anthropology and semiotics have been busy rediscovering. Without the complex signals of our interrelationships, human individuality has no meaning. In these lines the full power of the play's mythic force is revealed, for we see Lear as the defender of human meaningfulness in a world of disintegrating meaning. The patriarchal centre cannot hold. An abyss/abbesse of de(con)struction looms and weaves round him, the three sisters begin to reveal their identity as the harsh spinners, the Moirae. Not only Lear himself, but the whole of the society over which he has presided has been centred on a belief in an orderliness inherent in the world, which man can re-express in himself and in his society. The solidity is at the point of dissolution—the male certainties of fatherhood and kingship as a hierarchical model collapsing into a maelstrom of feeling uncontrolled and uncontrollable under the relentless force of his daughters' hostility. Behind the play (as Freud shrewdly hints)[64] lies the peculiarly male fear of undifferentiation, of loss of potency and, worse still, of being re-absorbed into the primal matter of mother earth. The father-daughter confrontation was perhaps suggested originally by Giraldi, whose Don Aulo, it is worth remembering, refers to evil women (and by implication his heroine) as 'infernal furies in human shape' (furie infernali in corpo humano). Male phallic rigidity in conflict with the fluidity and resilience of the feminine is the powerful psychological and mythic pattern underpinning the play. In *Lear* the long dialectical debate on the female/male dichotomy, which Shakespeare had conducted from *Hamlet* onwards, reaches its negative climax. The synthesis was to await *Antony and Cleopatra*.

Ostensibly Shakespeare leaves no doubt in the play about which side of the deconstruction debate he is on. The evil individualism of Goneril, Regan and Edmund and the benign individualism of Cordelia lead to the same sterile isolation, a world where dialogue is no longer possible, where men are islands. Of necessity this negative world collapses through its own incoherence. The deaths of Goneril and Regan and even of Cordelia are the logical outcome of this negativity. Lear's tragedy is that the forms and ceremonies of his civilized world are inadequate to reflect the divine will, for Lear inherits the just punishment of Adam's fall, not yet redeemed. Yet the power with which he endows the feminine and, even more, the brief glimpse we get of a world of love unstructured by authority in the scenes between Lear and Cordelia at the end, suggest an imaginative grasp of a different kind of order: what Holinshed describes (with different intention) as the 'gunarchie of Queen Cordeilla'. Again it is *Antony and Cleopatra* where this glimpse will become a vision.

The final vision of the play, developed over the last three acts, explores the full significance of a world without hope as, layer by layer, Lear is divested of his illusions. Patriarchy is unfrocked. In the last two acts of *Timon*, Timon's misfortunes convert him into the stereotype of the raging satirist as he sees the perversity of mankind in terms of other people. Lear's response is to look inward, to attempt to adjust to the vision of disorder his experience of suffering has presented:

> they flattered mee like a dogge, and tould me I had white haires in my beard, ere the black ones were there, to say I and no, to every thing I saide, I and no too, was no good divinitie, when the raine came to wet me once, and the winde to make mee chatter, when the thunder would not peace at my bidding, there I found them, there I smelt them out, goe to, they are not men of their words, they told mee I was every thing, tis a lye, I am not ague-proofe.   (IV, vi, 97–107)[65]

The attempt to understand the horror of this revelation that the world does not conform to the patterns men try to impose on it, at first proves too much for him. His mind loses its hold on reality and his mad fantasies take just those forms of blind condemnation of mankind that Timon asks us to accept as a vision of reality. Lear's incoherent and apparently irrelevant attacks on human justice and human sexuality are the mind of the humanist adjusting to a Calvinistic vision of the general depravity of human nature:

> thou rascall beadle hold thy bloudy hand, why dost thou lash that whore, strip thine owne backe, thy bloud hotly lusts to use her in that kind for which thou whipst her, the usurer hangs the cozener, through tattered raggs, smal vices do appeare, robes and furd-gownes hides all ...   (IV, vi, 164–9)[66]

What in Timon is mere railing out of personal pique, here becomes a desperate and moving attempt to establish new bearings in a world undergoing sea-change. Lear attempts to take refuge in a stoical patience that exchanges power for sanity, accepting impotence as a condition of holding on to meaning, but this too is a vanity, for the very ties of love are subject to the laws of destruction.

For a brief moment, in meeting again with his young daughter, love seems to triumph—as it did in *All's Well* and was again to do in the late plays. The demand for love which Cordelia failed to meet adequately in the first scene is now amply satisfied as she abandons the strict apportionment of feeling for an outpouring of affection that meets Lear's in generosity. It is ironic that modern commentators have frequently seen the fundamental change here as coming only from Lear, but it is equally Cordelia's puritanical rigidity that has given way in these late scenes, freeing her to accept her father's unbounded love. It is true that Lear himself sees Cordelia as 'a soul in bliss', while he is wracked in hell on a wheel of fire, but it is from his new sense of his own littleness in a hostile world that he derives this perception. The ending of the play destroys this vision of love triumphant. The Christian-like moment is shown to be illusory in a world before the birth of the God of love.

When Lear is fully restored to his sanity it is to meet yet again with defeat and he sees the possibility of happiness in an evil world only in terms of escape from it, 'like birds i'th'cage'. If it is to be happiness, then it will be a happiness in despite of the gods:

> have I caught thee?
> He that parts us shall bring a brand from heaven,
> And fire us hence like Foxes, wipe thine eyes,
> The good years[67] shall devoure em, flesh and fell,
> Ere they shall make us weepe, we'll see 'em starve first.   (V, iii, 21–5)

It is uncertain whether this is prophecy or defiance, but in either case it assumes the hostility of gods towards men. It is Lear and Cordelia that the gods will or must persecute by driving them out of the sanctuary of their love for one another. There is indeed no refuge for Lear and shortly we see him confirming the malice of the gods with Cordelia dead in his arms. One of his last acts, an act of extraordinary and tragic resilience, is to kill the man that hanged her. In the end we are left with a world without hope, with the three principal survivors, Albany, Edgar and Kent seemingly attempting to shuffle off responsibility for the future. This negativity is emphasized in the quarto text by having the final lines spoken by Albany just after he has attempted to hand over power to Kent and Edgar, to be met by Kent's refusal and Edgar's silence. The pessimism of the play reflects the orthodox Christian view of the pagan world.

In *King Lear* Shakespeare transcends the drama of his time in creating a play of classical intensity that yet retains his characteristic subtlety of detailed psychological realism. It is both a drama of personality, of the kind we see in *Othello,* and a masterly presentation of myth: a myth of man's attempt and failure to build a coherent structure of meaning from a hostile universe. Yet however much it transcends the theatre out of which it arose, it also has inescapable links with that theatre. As an exercise in the *de casibus* theme, on the fall of princes, it repeats the pattern of earlier plays like *Richard II,* but now explored, like *Timon,* in a pagan world. Like *Measure of Measure* before it, it uses James's view on kingship and kingliness to explore the nature of authority in a fallen world, here divorced from divine sanction, and so doomed—as Duke Vincentio's was not—to failure. As an exercise, like *Timon,* in the anatomy of anger as a response to a wicked world, it absorbs the role of the satirist into the tragic vision of man's helpless vulnerability.

It remains unique to its time and yet of its time. The great tragedies that were to follow show Shakespeare's power still at its height, yet none of them quite reproduces the overwhelming dramatic impact of *King Lear*.

NOTES

[1] G. Bullough (ed.), *Narrative and Dramatic Sources of Shakespeare*, London, Routledge & Kegan Paul, 1966, vol. 7, pp. 310–11.

[2] Ibid., vol. 7, pp. 270–1.

[3] Ibid., vol. 7, p. 270.

[4] *Hecatommithi*, p. 383: 'quanto piu e stretto il legame del sangue, e della Natura, e e maggior i'obligo del Figliuolo verso il Padre, che qualunque altro, che imaginar si possa.'

[5] Ibid., pp. 395–6: 'quanto sia piu benigna la natura delle donne, che quella de gli huomini ... fu egli nondimeno minore di quelli, che di alcune Donne si potrebbero raccontare.'

[6] Ibid., p. 396: 'Egli e vero ... che le donne sono verso i padri, e le madri loro amorevolissime, si per lo bisogno, che maggiore ne hanno, che i maschi, si anco perche sono di molle, e di benignissima natura. Ma se aviene, che alcune d'esse, alle male opere volgano la mente di tanto avanzano gli huomini scelerati, che si possono veramente dire furie infernali in corpo humano, e la novella, che io mi apparecchio di raccontarvi, cio vi fara forse piu, che non bisognerebbe palese.'

[7] None of the conjectured sources of *Lear* is as precise as this about the King's age—much more exceptional for the Elizabethans than for us.

[8] cf. *Lear* V, iii, 272–3: 'Her voice was ever soft/Gentle and low, an excellent thing in woman.'

[9] I, i, 44–5 these lines appear only in the folio text.

[10] *Hecatommithi*, p. 398: 'havendogli spetialmente egli dato tutto il patrimonio, senza ritenersene pure un picciolo, oltre che gli dava tanta auttorita nel Regno.'

[11] Ibid., p. 399: 'che s'ella havea cosi in dispregio le ragioni del sangue, e le leggi della natura, le quali constringevano anco le fiere ad amare, chi generate le havea.'

[12] Ibid., p. 400: 'conoscendo in te uno spirito grande, e parendomi per cio, che tu non debba meno desiderare la real grandezza, che la desideri io, mi son risoluta di communicar teco questo mio maschio pensiero.'

[13] Ibid., p. 401: 'perche il pensare alle cose magnifiche e nulla, s'elle ad effetto non si conducono.'

[14] Shakespeare often stores away hints and suggestions for later plays.

[15] *Hecatommithi*, p. 403: 'di gran nerbo, piglio a traverso Apesio vecchio, e debole, e a capo in giu lo gitto dalle scale, il quale diede cosi gran percossa, che quasi tutto si ruppe.'

[16] Ibid., p. 405: 'onde si vede manifestamente, che l'operar male, per havere bene, al fine conduce i malfattori, e gli scelerati, a misero fine.'

[17] Bullough, *NDSS*, vol. 7, p. 343.

[18] A. C. Bradley, *Shakespearean Tragedy*, London, Macmillan, 1904, 2nd edn reprinted 1926, p. 281; 'the hypocrisy is patent to us at a glance'.

[19] Line 60 is emended from the folio text.

[20] R. Sherwood, *The Right, and Prerogative of Kings*, London, N[icholas] O[kes] for William Bladon, 1612, pp. 20–1.

[21] The folio reading. There are no grounds for accusing Lear of political irresponsibility in abdicating (as asserted for instance by Bullough, *NDSS*, vol. 7, p. 288). The Emperor Charles V had abdicated to European applause to become a monk in 1555. Stage abdications are not uncommon and generally approved (as in Middleton's *Phoenix* and *Hengist, King of Kent*). See also R. Levin, *New Readings vs Old Plays*, Chicago and London, University of Chicago Press, 1979, pp. 149–51, who quotes James I as accepting the legitimacy of abdication.

[22] C. H. McIlwain (ed.), *The Political Works of James I*, Cambridge, Mass., Harvard University Press, 1918, reissued New York, Russell & Russell, 1965, p. 34.

[23] See for example, Lawrence Humfrey, *The Nobles: or, of Nobilitie*, London, T. Marshe, 1563, sig. S 3ʸ: 'But listen Bastards, with whom now each corner swarmeth, who also obtain the highest dignity, what Holy Scripture in the 3rd Chapter of the Book of Wisdom decreeth of them: the Imps shall be banished ... so shall this sport of Nobles be turned to sorrow, their mirth to mourning.'

[24] McIlwain, ed. cit., p. 36.

[25] Fulke Greville, *The Life of the Renowned Sir Philip Sidney*, London, Gibbings & Co., n.d., p. 163.

[26] Bradley, op. cit., pp. 262, 293–4.

[27] F; Q reads 'vertues'. Punctuation is modernized.

[28] *Trew Law of Free Monarchies*, in McIlwain, ed. cit., p. 54.

[29] *Basilikon Doron*, in McIlwain, ed. cit., p. 41.

[30] Greville, op. cit., p. 163.

[31] Quoted in Kenneth Muir (ed.), *King Lear* (Arden edition), London, Methuen, 1952, p. lii.

[32] S. Freud, 'The Theme of the Three Caskets', *Collected Papers*, translated under the supervision of Joan Riviere, London, Hogarth Press, 1925, vol. 4, p. 250.

[33] Bradley, op. cit., p. 285.

[34] McIlwain, ed. cit., p. 37.

[35] Ibid., p. 34.

[36] In *The Mirror for Magistrates*, Gonerell marries the Scottish King Albany; Bullough, *NDSS*, vol. 7, pp. 323–32.

[37] G. P. Krapp (ed.), 'History of Britain', *The Works of John Milton*, New York, Columbia University Press, 1932, vol. 10, p. 18.

[38] G. P. V. Akrigg (ed.), *The Letters of James VI and I*, Berkeley, Los Angeles, London, University of California Press, 1984. See especially the introduction, p. 19.

[39] Sir Thomas Elyot, *Book Named the Governor*, London, Dent (Everyman), 1962, II, p. 156, writes: 'But hard it is alway to eschew these flatterers, which, like to crows, do pick out men's eyes ere they be dead. And it is to noble men most difficult, whom all men covet to please.' Francis Bacon writes 'Of a King', *Essays Civil and Moral*, ed. E. T. Bettany, London, 1894, p. 93, 14: 'His greatest enemies are his flatterers; for though they ever speak on his side, yet their words still make against him.'

[40] G. A. Smith (ed.), *Marston, The Fawn*, London, Edward Arnold, 1964.

[41] McIlwain, ed. cit., p. 32.

[42] Akrigg, ed. cit., p. 17.

[43] Aristotle, 'On the Art of Poetry', *Classical Literary Criticism*, trans. by T. S. Dorsch, Harmondsworth, Penguin Books, 1965, p. 48.

[44] *The Censor*, 2 May 1715.

[45] M. R. Ridley (ed.), *Antony and Cleopatra* (Arden edition), London, Methuen, 1954, I, i, 14–16.

[46] C. H. McIlwain, 'A Speach to the Lords and Commons of the Parliament at White-Hall ... 1609', *The Political Works of James I*, Cambridge, Mass., Harvard University Press, 1918, reprinted New York, Russell & Russell, 1965, p. 307.

[47] Ibid., p. 308.

[48] McIlwain (ed.), *Basilikon Doron*, ed. cit., p. 41.

[49] McIlwain (ed.), *Trew Law*, ed. cit., pp. 55–6.

[50] This quotation from Horace (*Epistles*, I, ii, 62) is used in *Timon of Athens*, I, ii, 28.

[51] McIlwain, ed. cit., p. 52.

[52] H. Granville Barker, '*King Lear*', *Prefaces to Shakespeare*, London, Batsford, 1930, reprinted 1963, vol. 2, p. 28.

[53] L. Stone, *The Crisis of Aristocracy, 1558–1641*, Oxford, Clarendon Press, 1965, p. 212.

[54] I. M., *A Health to the Gentlemanly Profession of Serving Men*, (attributed to Gervase Markham), London, B.L., 1598, sig. D4ᵛ.

[55] G. B. Harrison, *A Last Elizabethan Journal*, London, Constable, 1933, reprinted Routledge & Kegan Paul, 1974, pp. 56–7 (under 1 December 1599).

[56] Muir, ed. cit., note to I, i, 297–8.

[57] Ibid., note to I, iii, 5.

[58] 'of kindness' is added from F.

[59] Text from Muir, ed. cit. QI is more than usually garbled at this point.

[60] R. S. Burns (ed.), *John Day's The Ile of Gulls*, New York and London, Garland Publishing, 1980, p. 21, n.34.

[61] Ibid., p. 24, n.39.

[62] F; Q reads 'fellow'.

[63] QI punctuation modernized.

[64] Freud, op. cit., vol. 4, p. 253–6.

[65] Some minor emendations; 'ague-proof' is the F reading.

[66] F reads 'great' for 'smal'.

[67] F.

CONTRIBUTORS

HAROLD BLOOM is Sterling Professor of the Humanities at Yale University and Henry W. and Albert A. Berg Professor of English at the New York University Graduate School. He is a 1985 MacArthur Foundation Award recipient, served as the Charles Eliot Norton Professor of Poetry at Harvard University (1987–88), and is the author of nineteen books, the most recent being *The Book of J* (1990). Currently he is editing the Chelsea House series Modern Critical Views and The Critical Cosmos, and other Chelsea House series in literary criticism.

A. C. BRADLEY held professorships of Modern Literature at the University of Liverpool, of English language and literature at the University of Glasgow, and of Poetry at Oxford. *Shakespearean Tragedy* (1904) established him as the preeminent Shakespeare scholar of the early twentieth century and remains a classic of modern Shakespeare criticism. His *Oxford Lectures on Poetry* were published in 1909, and *A Miscellany* in 1929.

HAROLD C. GODDARD was head of the English department at Swarthmore College from 1909 to 1946. In addition to *The Meaning of Shakespeare* (1951), he published *Studies in New England Transcendentalism* (1908) and edited a 1926 edition of the essays of Ralph Waldo Emerson.

BARBARA EVERETT is the author of *Auden* (1964), *Poets in Their Time: Essays on English Poetry from Donne to Larkin* (1986, *Young Hamlet: Essays on Shakespeare's Tragedies* (1989), and editions of *Antony and Cleopatra* (1964) and *All's Well That Ends Well* (1970). She is a Senior Research Fellow and Lecturer in English at Somerville College, Oxford.

WILLIAM ROSEN is Chairman of the Department of English at the University of Connecticut. He is the author of *Shakespeare and the Craft of Tragedy* (1960) and has coedited Shakespeare's *Julius Caesar* (1963; with Barbara Rosen).

RUSSELL A. FRASER is Professor of English at the University of Michigan. He has written *The War against Poetry* (1970), *The Dark Ages and the Age of Gold* (1973), *The Language of Adam: On the Limits and Systems of Discourse* (1977), *A Mingled Yarn: The Life of R. P. Blackmur* (1981), and *Young Shakespeare* (1988), and has edited *All's Well That Ends Well* (1985).

ROSALIE L. COLIE was, before her death in 1972, the Nancy Duke Lewis Professor at Brown University. She was the author of *Light and Enlightenment: A Study of the Cambridge Platonists and the Dutch Arminians* (1957), *Paradoxia Epidemica: The Renaissance Tradition of Paradox* (1966), *"My Echoing Song": Andrew Marvell's Poetry of Criticism* (1970), and other volumes. A collection of poems, *Atlantic Wall*, was published posthumously in 1974.

LESLIE SMITH has written *Modern British Farce: A Selective Study of British Farce from Pinero to the Present* (1989). He teaches in the Department of Literary/Media Studies at The Polytechnic of North London.

MICHAEL GOLDMAN is Professor of English at Princeton University. He has written *Shakespeare and the Energies of Drama* (1972), *The Actor's Freedom: Toward a Theory of Drama* (1975), and several collections of poetry.

ARTHUR KIRSCH, Professor of English at the University of Virginia, has written *Dryden's Heroic Drama* (1965), *Jacobean Dramatic Perspectives* (1972), *Shakespeare and the Experience of Love* (1981), and *The Passions of Shakespeare's Tragic Heroes* (1990), and has edited *Literary Criticism of John Dryden* (1967).

DAVID FARLEY-HILLS is Professor of English at the University College of Swansea (Swansea, England). He is the author of *The Benevolence of Laughter: Comic Poetry of the Commonwealth and Restoration* (1974), *Rochester's Poetry* (1978), *The Comic in Renaissance Comedy* (1981), and *Jacobean Drama: A Critical Study of the Professional Drama 1600–25* (1988), and the editor of *Rochester: The Critical Heritage* (1972).

BIBLIOGRAPHY

Anderson, Judith H. "The Conspiracy of Realism: Impasse and Vision in *King Lear.*" *Studies in Philology* 84 (1987): 1–23.

Asp, Carolyn. " 'The Clamor of Eros': Freud, Aging, and *King Lear.*" In *Memory and Desire: Aging—Literature—Psychoanalysis,* ed. Kathleen Woodward and Murray M. Schwartz. Bloomington: Indiana University Press, 1986, pp. 192–204.

Barber. C. L., and Richard P. Wheeler. "Inextricable Ruthlessness and Ruth: *King Lear.*" In *The Whole Journey: Shakespeare's Power of Development.* Berkeley: University of California Press, 1986, pp. 282–97.

Battenhouse, Roy W. "Moral Experience and Its Typology in *King Lear.*" In *Shakespearean Tragedy: Its Art and Its Christian Premises.* Bloomington: Indiana University Press, 1969, pp. 269–302.

Bayley, John. "The King's Ship." In *Shakespeare and Tragedy.* London: Routledge & Kegan Paul, 1981, pp. 7–48.

Bennett, Joseph Waters. "The Storm Within: The Madness of Lear." *Shakespeare Quarterly* 13 (1962): 137–55.

Berry, Ralph. "Lear's System." *Shakespeare Quarterly* 35 (1984): 421–29.

Bickersteth, Geoffrey L. "The Golden World of *King Lear.*" *Proceedings of the British Academy* 32 (1946): 147–71.

Birenbaum, Harvey. "The Art of Our Necessities: The Softness of *King Lear.*" *Yale Review* (1982–83): 581–99.

Block, Edward A. *"King Lear:* A Study in Balanced and Shifting Sympathies." *Shakespeare Quarterly* 10 (1959): 499–512.

Bloom, Harold, ed. *William Shakespeare's* King Lear. New York: Chelsea House, 1987.

Booth, Stephen. King Lear, Macbeth, *Indefinition, and Tragedy.* New Haven: Yale University Press, 1983.

Brockbank, Philip, " 'Upon Such Sacrifices.' " *Proceedings of the British Academy* 62 (1976): 109–34.

Brooke, Nicholas. "The Ending of *King Lear.*" In *Shakespeare 1564–1964,* ed. Edward A. Bloom. Providence: Brown University Press, 1964, pp. 71–87.

Bulman, James C. "The Persistence of the 'Old' Lear." In *The Heroic Idiom of Shakespearean Tragedy.* Newark: University of Delaware Press, 1985, pp. 147–68.

Burckhardt, Sigurd. *"King Lear:* The Quality of Nothing." In *Shakespearean Meanings.* Princeton: Princeton University Press, 1968, pp. 237–59.

Burke, Kenneth. *"King Lear:* Its Form and Psychosis." *Shenandoah* 21 (1969–70): 3–19.

Butler, F. G. "Lear's Crown of Weeds." *English Studies* 70 (1989): 395–406.

Calderwood, James L. "Creative Uncreation in *King Lear.*" *Shakespeare Quarterly* 37 (1986): 5–19.

Campbell, Lily B. *"King Lear:* A Tragedy of Wrath in Old Age." In *Shakespeare's Tragic Heroes: Slaves of Passion.* Cambridge: Cambridge University Press, 1930, pp. 175–207.

Campbell, Oscar James. "The Salvation of Lear." *ELH* 15 (1948): 93–109.

Cavell, Stanley. "The Avoidance of Love: A Reading of *King Lear.*" In *Must We Mean What We Say?* New York: Scribner's, 1969, pp. 267–353.

Chambers, R. W. *King Lear.* Glasgow: Jackson, Son & Co., 1940.

Champion, Larry S. "The Cosmic Dimensions of Tragedy: *King Lear, Macbeth.*" In *Shakespeare's Tragic Perspective.* Athens: University of Georgia Press, 1976, pp. 155–200.

Chaplin, William H. "Form and Psychology in *King Lear.*" *Literature and Psychology* 19, Nos. 3/4 (1969): 31–45.

Charlton, H. B. *"King Lear."* In *Shakespearian Tragedy.* Cambridge: Cambridge University Press, 1948, pp. 189–229.

Chaudhuri, Sukanta. *"King Lear."* In *Infirm Glory: Shakespeare and the Renaissance Image of Man.* Oxford: Clarendon Press, 1981, pp. 164–73.

Clemen, Wolfgang. *"King Lear."* In *The Development of Shakespeare's Imagery.* London: Methuen, 1951, pp. 133–53.

Cohen, Derek. "The History of *King Lear.*" In *Shakespearean Motives.* New York: St. Martin's Press, 1988, pp. 119–32.

Cohen, Walter. *"King Lear* and the Social Dimensions of Shakespearean Tragic Form, 1603–1608." In *Shakespeare: Contemporary Critical Approaches,* ed. Harry R. Garvin. Lewisburg, PA: Bucknell University Press, 1980, pp. 106–18.

Cohn, Ruby. "Lear Come Lately." In *Modern Shakespeare Offshoots.* Princeton: Princeton University Press, 1976, pp. 232–66.

Colie, Rosalie L., and F. T. Flahiff, ed. *Some Facets of* King Lear: *Essays in Prismatic Criticism.* Toronto: University of Toronto Press, 1974.

Coult, Tony. *The Plays of Edward Bond.* London: Eyre Methuen, 1977.

Creeth, Edmund. "The King of Life in *King Lear.*" In *Mankynde in Shakespeare.* Athens: University of Georgia Press, 1976, pp. 111–51.

Cunningham, John. "King Lear, the Storm, and the Liturgy." *Christianity and Literature* 34, No. 1 (Fall 1984): 9–30.

Danby, John F. *"King Lear* and Christian Patience: A Culmination." In *Poets on Fortune's Hill.* London: Faber & Faber, 1952, pp. 108–27.

———. *Shakespeare's Doctrine of Nature: A Study of* King Lear. London: Faber & Faber, 1949.

Danson, Lawrence. *"King Lear."* In *Tragic Alphabet: Shakespeare's Drama of Language.* New Haven: Yale University Press, 1974, pp. 163–97.

———, ed. *On* King Lear. Princeton: Princeton University Press, 1981.

Delany, Paul. *"King Lear* and the Decline of Feudalism." *PMLA* 92 (1977): 429–40.

Dollimore, Jonathan. *"King Lear* (c. 1605–6) and Essentialist Humanism." In *Radical Tragedy: Religion, Ideology and Power in the Drama of Shakespeare and His Contemporaries.* Chicago: University of Chicago Press, 1984, pp. 189–203.

Downes, William. "Discourse and Drama: King Lear's 'Question' to His Daughters." In *The Taming of the Text: Explorations in Language, Literature and Culture,* ed. Willie Van Peer. London: Routledge, 1988, pp. 225–57.

Dreher, Diane Elizabeth. "Lear: A Father in Turmoil." In *Domination and Defiance: Fathers and Daughters in Shakespeare.* Lexington: University Press of Kentucky, 1986, pp. 63–75.

Elliott, G. R. "The Initial Contrast in *Lear.*" In *Dramatic Providence in* Macbeth. Princeton: Princeton University Press, 1960, pp. 235–50.

Enright, D. J. *"King Lear* and the Just Gods." In *Shakespeare and the Students.* New York: Schocken Books, 1970, pp. 17–66.

Feder, Lillian. "Reason in Madness." In *Madness in Literature.* Princeton: Princeton University Press, 1980, pp. 98–146.

Fly, Richard. "Beyond Extremity: *King Lear* and the Limits of Poetic Drama." In *Shakespeare's Mediated World.* Amherst: University of Massachusetts Press, 1976, pp. 85–115.

Foreman, Walter C., Jr. *"King Lear."* In *The Music of the Close: The Final Scenes of Shakespeare's Tragedies.* Lexington: University Press of Kentucky, 1978, pp. 113–58.

French, A. L. *"King Lear."* In *Shakespeare and the Critics.* Cambridge: Cambridge University Press, 1972, pp. 144–205.

Frye, Dean. "The Context of Lear's Unbuttoning." *ELH* 32 (1965): 17–31.

Frye, Northrop. *Fools of Time: Studies in Shakespearean Tragedy.* Toronto: University of Toronto Press, 1967.

Goldberg, S. L. *An Essay on* King Lear. Cambridge: Cambridge University Press, 1974.

Goldman, Michael. "The Worst of *King Lear.*" In *Shakespeare and the Energies of Drama.* Princeton: Princeton University Press, 1972. pp. 94–108.

Gordon, George. "A Note on the World of *King Lear.*" In *Shakespearean Comedy and Other Studies.* London: Oxford University Press, 1944, pp. 116–28.

Greenblatt, Stephen. "The Cultivation of Anxiety: King Lear and His Heirs." *Raritan* 2, No. 1 (Summer 1982): 92–114.

———. "Shakespeare and the Exorcists." In *Shakespeare and the Question of Theory,* ed. Patricia Parker and Geoffrey Hartman. New York: Methuen, 1985, pp. 163–87.

Gregson, J. J. *"King Lear."* In *Public and Private Man in Shakespeare.* London: Croom Helm, 1983, pp. 177–88.

Harrison, G. B. *"King Lear."* In *Shakespeare's Tragedies.* London: Routledge & Kegan Paul, 1951, pp. 158–83.

Hathorn, Richmond Y. "Lear's Equations." In *Tragedy, Myth, and Mystery.* Bloomington: Indiana University Press, 1962, pp. 174–94.

Hay, Malcolm, and Philip Roberts. *"Lear."* In *Bond: A Study of His Plays.* London: Eyre Methuen, 1980, pp. 103–38.

Hays, Michael. "Reasons' Rhetoric: *King Lear* and the Social Uses of Irony." *boundary 2* 7, No. 2 (Winter 1979): 97–116.

Heilman, Robert B. *This Great Stage: Image and Structure in* King Lear. Baton Rouge: Louisiana State University Press, 1948.

———. "The Unity of *King Lear.*" *Sewanee Review* 56 (1958): 58–68.

Hennedy, Hugh L. King Lear: Recognizing the Ending." *Studies in Philology* 71 (1974): 371–94.

Hobson, Alan. "This Child-Changed Father." In *Full Circle: Shakespeare and Moral Development.* London: Chatto & Windus, 1972, pp. 11–32.

Hockey, Dorothy C. "The Trial Pattern in *King Lear.*" *Shakespeare Quarterly* 10 (1959): 389–95.

Hodges, Devon L. "Anatomy as Tragedy." In *Renaissance Fictions of Anatomy,* Amherst: University of Massachusetts Press, 1985, pp. 68–88.

Holbrook, David. "King Lear's Intemperate Outburst." In *Images of Woman in Literature.* New York: New York University Press, 1989, pp. 144–54.

Hole, Sandra. "The Background of Divine Action in *King Lear.*" *Studies in English Literature 1500–1900* 8 (1968): 217–33.

Holloway, John, *"King Lear."* In *The Story of the Night: Studies in Shakespeare's Major Tragedies.* London: Routledge & Kegan Paul, 1961, pp. 75–98.

Holly, Marcia. *"King Lear: The Disguised and Deceived."* *Shakespeare Quarterly* 24 (1973): 171–80.

Hoover, Claudette. " 'The Lusty Stealth of Nature': Sexuality and Antifeminism in *King Lear.*" *Atlantis* 11, No. 1 (Autumn 1985): 87–97.

Humphries, Jefferson. "Seeing Through Lear's Blindness: Blanchot, Freud, Saussure and Derrida." *Mosaic* 16, No. 3 (Summer 1983): 28–43.

Jayne, Sears. "Charity in *King Lear.*" In *Shakespeare 400,* ed. James G. McManaway. New York: Holt, Rinehart & Winston, 1964, pp. 277–88.

Jones, Emrys. *"King Lear."* In *Scenic Form in Shakespeare.* Oxford: Clarendon Press, 1971, pp. 152–94.

Jorgensen, Paul A. *Lear's Self-Discovery.* Berkeley: University of California Press, 1967.

Keefer, Michael H. "Accommodation and Synecdoche: Calvin's God in *King Lear."* Shakespeare Studies 20 (1988): 147–68.

Kermode, Frank. "Why *King Lear* Is the Cruellest Play." *Listener,* September 16, 1982, pp. 13–14.

Kettle, Arnold. "From Hamlet to Lear." In *Shakespeare in a Changing World,* ed. Arnold Kettle. New York: International Publishers, 1964, pp. 146–71.

Kirby, Jan J. "The Passing of King Lear." *Shakespeare Survey* 41 (1989): 145–57.

Kirsch, James. *"King Lear:* A Play of Redemption." In *Shakespeare's Royal Self.* New York: Putnam's, 1966, pp. 185–319.

Knights, L. C. *"King Lear."* In *Some Shakespearean Themes.* London: Chatto & Windus, 1959, pp. 84–119.

Kott, Jan. *"King Lear* or *Endgame."* In *Shakespeare Our Contemporary.* Translated by Bole-slaw Taborski. Garden City, NY: Doubleday, 1964, pp. 87–124.

Kozintsev, Grigori. *"King Lear."* In *Shakespeare: Time and Conscience.* Translated by Joyce Vining. New York: Hill & Wang, 1966, pp. 47–102.

Leggatt, Alexander. *King Lear.* Boston: Twayne, 1988.

Levin, Harry. "The Heights and the Depths: A Scene from *King Lear."* In *More Talking of Shakespeare,* ed. John Garrett. New York: Theatre Arts Books, 1959, pp. 87–103.

Löske, Olav. *Outrageous Fortune: Critical Studies in* Hamlet *and* King Lear. Oslo: Olso University Press, 1960.

Lothian, John M. King Lear: *A Tragic Reading of Life.* Toronto: Clarke, Irwin & Co., 1949.

Lynch, Stephen J. "Sin, Suffering, and Redemption in *Leir* and *Lear."* Shakespeare Studies 18 (1986): 161–74.

McCloskey, John C. "The Emotive Use of Animal Imagery in *King Lear."* Shakespeare Quarterly 13 (1962): 321–25.

McFarland, Thomas. "Reduction and Renewal in *King Lear."* In *Tragic Meanings in Shakespeare.* New York: Random House, 1966, pp. 127–71.

McIlroy, Bernard. *"King Lear:* The Tempest in the Mind." In *Shakespeare's Mature Tragedies.* Princeton: Princeton University Press, 1973, pp. 145–205.

Mack, Maynard. King Lear *in Our Time.* Berkeley: University of California Press, 1965.

Maclean, Norman. "Episode, Scene, Speech, and Word: The Madness of Lear." In *Critics and Criticism: Ancient and Modern,* ed. R. S. Crane. Chicago: University of Chicago Press, 1952, pp. 595–615.

Manlove, Colin N. *"King Lear."* In *The Gap in Shakespeare: The Motif of Division from* Richard II *to* The Tempest. London: Vision Press, 1981, pp. 101–31.

Mason, H. A. *"King Lear."* In *Shakespeare's Tragedies of Love.* London: Chatto & Windus, 1970, pp. 163–226.

Micheli, Linda Mcj. " 'The Thing Itself': Literal and Figurative Language in *King Lear."* Philological Quarterly 60 (1981): 343–56.

Montano, Rocco. "King Lear and the Case of Human Suffering." In *Shakespeare's Concept of Tragedy: The Bard as Anti-Elizabethan.* Chicago: Gateway Editions, 1985, pp. 242–63.

Mooney, Michael E. "Multiconsciousness in *King Lear."* In *Shakespeare's Dramatic Transactions.* Durham, NC: Duke University Press, 1990, pp. 129–49.

Morris, Harry. *"King Lear:* The Great Doom's Image, I." In *Last Things in Shakespeare.* Tallahassee: Florida State University Press, 1985, pp. 115–62.

Morris, Ivor. "Cordelia and Lear." *Shakespeare Quarterly* 8 (1957): 141–58.

——. "King Lear." In *Shakespeare's God: The Role of Religion in the Tragedies*. London: George Allen & Unwin, 1972, pp. 342–68.

Muir, Kenneth. *"King Lear."* In *Shakespeare's Tragic Sequence*. London: Hutchinson University Library, 1972, pp. 117–41.

Murphy, John L. *Darkness and Devils: Exorcism and* King Lear. Athens: Ohio University Press, 1984.

Myrick, Kenneth. "Christian Pessimism in *King Lear."* In *Shakespeare 1564–1964*, ed. Edward A. Bloom. Providence: Brown University Press, 1964, pp. 56–70.

Nevo, Ruth. *"King Lear."* In *Tragic Form in Shakespeare*. Princeton: Princeton University Press, 1972, pp. 258–305.

Nowottny, Winifred M. T. "Lear's Questions." *Shakespeare Survey* 10 (1957): 90–97.

Oates, Joyce Carol. " 'Is This the Promised End?' The Tragedy of *King Lear."* In *Contraries*. New York: Oxford University Press, 1981, pp. 51–81.

Olsson, Y. B. "Edmund and Lear (A Study in the Structure of *King Lear*)." *Durham University Journal* 78 (1985–86): 251–58.

Parker, M. D. H. "The Second Testing—Corruption and Salvation." In *The Slave of Life: A Study of Shakespeare and the Idea of Justice*. London: Chatto & Windus, 1955, pp. 125–48.

Partee, Morriss Henry. "The Divine Comedy of *King Lear."* *Genre* 4 (1971): 60–75.

Pauncz, Arpad, M. D. "The Lear Complex in World Literature." *American Imago* 11 (1954): 51–83.

——. "Psychopathology of Shakespeare's *King Lear."* *American Imago* 9 (1952): 57–77.

Perry, T. Anthony. "Withdrawal or Service: The Paradox of *King Lear."* In *Erotic Spirituality: The Integrative Tradition from Leone Ebreo to John Donne*. University: University of Alabama Press, 1980, pp. 99–115.

Pirie, David. "Lear as King." *Critical Quarterly* 22, No. 2 (Summer 1980): 5–20.

Presson, Robert K. "Boethius, King Lear, and 'Maystresse Philosophie.' " *Journal of English and Germanic Philology* 64 (1965): 406–24.

Rathkey, W. A. " 'Vex Not His Ghost.' " *English* 2 (1938–39): 355–61.

Reibetanz, John. *The Lear World: A Study of* King Lear *in Its Dramatic Context*. Toronto: University of Toronto Press, 1977.

Reiss, Timothy J. "The Lear of the Future." In *Tragedy and Truth: Studies in the Development of a Renaissance and Neoclassical Discourse*. New Haven: Yale University Press, 1980, pp. 183–203.

Ribner, Irving. "The Pattern of Regeneration: *King Lear."* In *Patterns in Shakespearean Tragedy*. London: Methuen, 1960, pp. 116–36.

Rosenberg, Marvin. *The Masks of* King Lear. Berkeley: University of California Press, 1972.

Rosinger, Lawrence. "Gloucester and Lear: Men Who Act Like Gods." *ELH* 35 (1968): 491–504.

Salingar, Leo. "Romance in *King Lear."* In *Dramatic Form in Shakespeare and the Jacobeans*. Cambridge: Cambridge University Press, 1986, pp. 91–106.

Scharine, Richard. *"Lear:* 'Suffer the Little Children.' " In *The Plays of Edward Bond*. Lewisburg, PA: Bucknell University Press, 1976, pp. 181–222.

Schoff, Francis G. "King Lear: Moral Example or Tragic Protagonist?" *Shakespeare Quarterly* 13 (1962): 157–72.

Selden, Raman. "King Lear and True Need." *Shakespeare Studies* 19 (1987): 143–69.

Sewell, Arthur. *Character and Society in Shakespeare*. Oxford: Clarendon Press, 1951.

Sewell, Richard B. *"King Lear."* In *The Vision of Tragedy.* New Haven: Yale University Press, 1959, pp. 68–79.

Shakespeare Survey 13 (1960). Special *King Lear* issue.

Shakespeare Survey 33 (1980). Special *King Lear* issue.

Siegel, Paul N. *"King Lear."* In *Shakespearean Tragedy and the Elizabethan Compromise.* New York: New York University Press, 1957, pp. 161–88.

Sisson C. J. "The Quandary: *King Lear."* In *Shakespeare's Tragic Justice.* London: Methuen, 1964, pp. 74–98.

Skulsky, Harold. *"King Lear* and the Meaning of Chaos." *Shakespeare Quarterly* 17 (1966): 3–17.

Smidt, Kristian. "The Divided Kingdom." In *Unconformities in Shakespeare's Tragedies.* New York: St. Martin's Press, 1990, pp. 129–49.

Snyder, Susan. "Between the Divine and the Absurd: *King Lear."* In *The Comic Matrix of Shakespeare's Tragedies.* Princeton: Princeton University Press, 1979, pp. 137–79.

Speaight, Robert. *"King Lear."* In *Nature in Shakespearean Tragedy.* London: Hollis & Carter, 1955, pp, 89–121.

Spencer, Benjamin T. *"King Lear:* A Prophetic Tragedy." *College English* 5 (1943–44): 302–8.

Spencer, Theodore. *"Othello* and *King Lear."* In *Shakespeare and the Nature of Man.* New York: Macmillan, 1942, pp. 122–52.

Stuart, Betty Kantor. "Truth and Tragedy in *King Lear."* *Shakespeare Quarterly* 18 (1967): 167–80.

Summers, Joseph H. " 'Look There, Look There!' The Ending of *King Lear."* In *English Renaissance Studies Presented to Dame Helen Gardner in Honour of Her Seventieth Birthday.* Oxford: Clarendon Press, 1980, pp. 74–93.

Taylor, Gary. "Revolutions of Perspective: *King Lear."* In *Moment by Moment in Shakespeare.* London: Macmillan, 1985, pp. 162–236.

Toliver, Harold. "Words of Command, Words of Suffering in *King Lear."* In *Transported Styles in Shakespeare and Milton.* University Park: Pennsylvania State University Press, 1989, pp. 123–52.

Tolmie, L. W. " 'No Seconds? All Myself?' An Essay on *King Lear."* *Southern Review* (Adelaide) 12 (1979): 38–62.

Traversi, D. A. *"King Lear."* In *An Approach to Shakespeare.* 2nd ed. London: Sands & Co., 1958, pp. 181–213.

———. *"King Lear."* *Scrutiny* 19 (1952–53): 43–64, 126–42, 205–30.

———. " 'Unaccommodated Man' in *King Lear."* In *The Literary Imagination.* Newark: University of Delaware Press, 1982, pp. 145–96.

Turner, Darwin T. *"King Lear* Re-examined." *CLA Journal* 3 (1959–60): 27–39.

Watkins, W. B. C. *"King Lear* in the Context of Shakespeare." In *Shakespeare and Spenser.* Princeton: Princeton University Press, 1950, pp. 75–110.

———. "The Two Techniques in *King Lear."* *Review of English Studies* 18 (1942): 1–26.

Weidhorn, Manfred. "Lear's Schoolmasters." *Shakespeare Quarterly* 13 (1962): 305–16.

Weis, René J. A. "Dissent and Moral Primitivism in *King Lear."* *English* 35 (1986): 197–218.

Whitaker, Virgil K. "The Rack of This Tough World: *Hamlet* and *King Lear."* In *The Mirror up to Nature: The Technique of Shakespeare's Tragedies.* San Marino, CA: Huntington Library, 1965, pp. 183–240.

Williams, George Walton. "Petitionary Prayer in *King Lear."* *South Atlantic Quarterly* 85 (1986): 360–73.

Winstanley, Lilian. Macbeth, King Lear, *and Contemporary History.* Cambridge: Cambridge University Press, 1922.

Wittreich, Joseph. *"Image of That Horror": History, Prophecy, and Apocalypse in* King Lear. San Marino, CA: Huntington Library, 1984.

Young, David. "The Maps of *King Lear."* In *The Action to the Word: Structure and Style in Shakespearean Tragedy.* New Haven: Yale University Press, 1990, pp. 77–98.

———. "The Natural Fool of Fortune: *King Lear."* In *The Heart's Forest: A Study of Shakespeare's Pastoral Plays.* New Haven: Yale University Press, 1972, pp. 73–103.

Zak, William F. *Sovereign Shame: A Study of* King Lear. Lewisburg, PA: Bucknell University Press, 1984.

ACKNOWLEDGMENTS

"The *Lear* Universe" by G. Wilson Knight from *The Wheel of Fire* by G. Wilson Knight, ©
1930, 1949 by G. Wilson Knight. Reprinted by permission of Routledge.

"The Patterns in Sacred and in Contemporary Literature" by Maud Bodkin from *Archetypal Patterns in Poetry: Psychological Studies of Imagination* by Maud Bodkin, © 1934 by Oxford University Press. Reprinted by permission of Oxford University Press.

"Lear, Tolstoy and the Fool" by George Orwell from *The Collected Essays, Journalism and Letters of George Orwell*, Volume 4, edited by Sonia Orwell and Ian Angus, © 1968 by Sonia Brownell Orwell. Reprinted by permission of Harcourt Brace Jovanovich, Inc.

"Poetic Experiment" by D. G. James from *A Dream of Learning: An Essay on* The Advancement of Learning, Hamlet *and* King Lear by D. G. James, © 1951 by Clarendon Press. Reprinted by permission of Oxford University Press.

"Pardon and Punishment" by Honor Matthews from *Character and Symbol in Shakespeare's Plays* by Honor Matthews, © 1962 by Cambridge University Press. Reprinted by permission of Cambridge University Press.

"Deus Absconditus: Lear" by William R. Elton from King Lear *and the Gods* by William R. Elton, © 1966 by The Henry E. Huntington Library and Art Gallery. Reprinted by permission.

"The Vision of *King Lear*" by James P. Driscoll from *Shakespeare Studies* 10 (1977), © 1977 by The Council for Research in the Renaissance. Reprinted by permission of *Shakespeare Studies*.

"Plays within Plays: *Othello, King Lear, Antony and Cleopatra*" by Howard Felperin from *Shakespearean Representation: Mimesis and Modernity in Elizabethan Tragedy* by Howard Felperin, © 1977 by Princeton University Press. Reprinted by permission of Princeton University Press.

"Lear" by Benedict Nightingale from *A Reader's Guide to Fifty Modern British Plays* by Benedict Nightingale, © 1982 by Benedict Nightingale. Reprinted by permission of Pan Books Ltd.

"The Skeptical Traveler: *King Lear* and the End of the Pilgrimage" by Edgar Schell from *Strangers and Pilgrims: From* The Castle of Perseverance *to* King Lear by Edgar Schell, © 1983 by The University of Chicago. Reprinted by permission of The University of Chicago Press.

"Maternal Images and Male Bonds in *Hamlet, Othello,* and *King Lear*" by Peter Erickson from *Patriarchal Structures in Shakespeare's Drama* by Peter Erickson, © 1985 by The Regents of the University of California. Reprinted by permission of The University of California Press.

"A World Within: Found Enclosure and Final Exposure in *King Lear*" by Barbara L. Estrin from *The Raven and the Lark: Lost Children in Literature of the English Renaissance* by Barbara L. Estrin, © 1985 by Associated University Presses, Inc. Reprinted by permission of Associated University Presses, Inc.

"Readiness, Ripeness: *Hamlet, Lear*" by Yves Bonnefoy, translated by John T. McNaughton, from *New Literary History* 17, No. 3 (Spring 1986), © 1986 by *New Literary History*. Reprinted by permission of The Johns Hopkins University Press.

"All Germains Spill at Once: Shakespeare's *King Lear*" by Bennett Simon, M.D., from *Tragic Drama and the Family: Psychoanalytic Studies from Aeschylus to Beckett* by Bennett Simon, M.D., © 1988 by Yale University. Reprinted by permission of Yale University Press.

"*King Lear*" by Harold C. Goddard from *The Meaning of Shakespeare* by Harold C. Goddard, © 1951 by The University of Chicago. Reprinted by permission of The University of Chicago Press.

"The New King Lear" by Barbara Everett from *Critical Quarterly* 2, No. 4 (Winter 1960), © 1960 by *Critical Quarterly*. Reprinted by permission of the author.

"*King Lear*" by William Rosen from *Shakespeare and the Craft of Tragedy* by William Rosen, © 1960 by the President and Fellows of Harvard College. Reprinted by permission of Harvard University Press.

"Redemption in *King Lear*" (originally titled "Redemption") by Russell A. Fraser from *Shakespeare's Poetics in Relation to* King Lear by Russell A. Fraser, © 1962 by Russell A. Fraser. Reprinted by permission of Routledge.

"Limits of the Pastoral Pattern in *King Lear*" (originally titled " 'Nature's Above Art in That Respect': Limits of the Pastoral Pattern") by Rosalie L. Colie from *Shakespeare's Living Art* by Rosalie L. Colie, © 1974 by Princeton University Press. Reprinted by permission of Princeton University Press.

"Edward Bond's *Lear*" by Leslie Smith from *Comparative Drama* 13, No. 1 (Spring 1979), © 1979 by the Editors of *Comparative Drama;* reprinted in *Drama in the Twentieth Century,* edited by Clifford Davidson et al., © 1984 by AMS Press, Inc. Reprinted by permission of AMS Press, Inc.

"Histrionic Imagery in *King Lear*" (originally titled "Acting and Feeling: Histrionic Imagery in *King Lear*") by Michael Goldman from *Acting and Action in Shakespearean Tragedy* by Michael Goldman, © 1985 by Princeton University Press. Reprinted by permission of Princeton University Press.

"The Emotional Landscape of *King Lear*" by Arthur Kirsch from *Shakespeare Quarterly* 39, No. 2 (Summer 1988), © 1988 by The Folger Shakespeare Library. Reprinted by permission of *Shakespeare Quarterly*.

"Anger's Privilege: *King Lear*" (originally titled "Anger's Privilege: *Timon of Athens* and *King Lear*") by David Farley-Hills from *Shakespeare and the Rival Playwrights 1600–1606* by David Farley-Hills, © 1990 by David Farley-Hills. Reprinted by permission of Routledge.

INDEX